The
Handbook of
Sailing

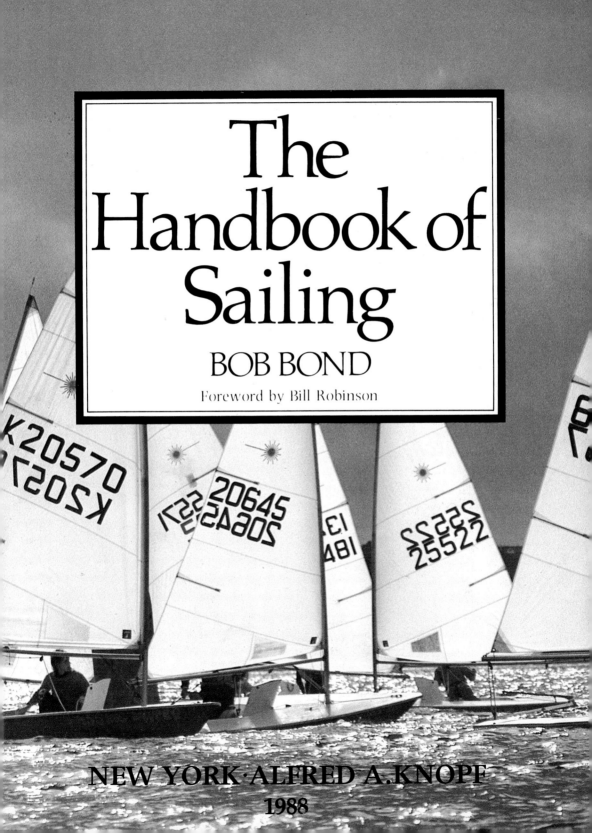

The Handbook of Sailing

BOB BOND

Foreword by Bill Robinson

NEW YORK · ALFRED A. KNOPF
1988

The Handbook of Sailing was conceived, edited and designed
by Dorling Kindersley Limited, 9 Henrietta Street, London, WC2E 8PS

Project Editor	Susan Berry
Designers	Sue Rawkins
	Steven Wooster
	Mark Richards
Editors	Cathy Meeus
	Julian Mannering
Contributing Editor	Stephen Sleight
Consultants for	Bill Robinson
American edition	E. Matthew Miller
	Jane Daniels
Managing Editor	Jackie Douglas
Art Director	Roger Bristow
Editorial Director	Christopher Davis

This is a Borzoi Book
published by Alfred A. Knopf, Inc.

Library of Congress Cataloging in Publication Data

Bond, Bob.
  The handbook of sailing.

  Includes index.
  1. Sailing I. Title.
  GV811.B58 1980   797.1'24   79–3496
  ISBN 0–394–50838–6

Printed in Italy by A. Mondadori, Verona
Published July 26, 1980
Reprinted six times
Eighth Printing April 1988

Contents

Basic sailing

Advanced sailing

Cruising

Navigation

Meteorology

Maintenance & safety

Appendix

Foreword

It is an axiom among experienced sailors that the more you sail, the more there is to learn. Like playing the piano, the basics are simple — learning the scale or learning how to tack, jibe and trim the sails — but the variations are infinite. Cornelius Shields, one of the top sailors in the history of the sport, once told me that he always learned something new every time he went sailing and that this was one of sailing's major fascinations.

It is an axiom too that you can only really learn by doing. But it is important to start by doing things right. Learning by trial and error can lead to some sad mistakes, but these can be avoided with the guidance of an experienced hand — or the kind of information contained in this book.

Obviously, in a complicated activity that deals with the forces of nature, there are pitfalls and dangers, and even the most experienced veterans of the sport can find themselves in a tight situation; witness the serious difficulties and casualties in the 1979 Fastnet Race in the Irish Sea. There might be a tendency to worry so much about the danger that the pleasure of sailing is lost, but such a pessimistic attitude is unproductive. Rather it is better to recognize the forces that are being dealt with and the possibilities of what can happen, and be prepared to face them. This is where book-learning can be a tremendous plus because there are so many aspects to sailing the great variety of boats in existence. Even the most active and experienced sailors, in the course of a long career, are not necessarily faced with every situation that can arise.

This book is not just for the novice. As I went through these pages as an editor and adviser, I found myself pausing here and there over an item and realizing that in my more than fifty years of sailing this was something I'd never actually done or experienced. While I admit that I still learn something new all the time when I am afloat, I thought I had learned everything that I could from books. For example, there is such extensive and practical information here on the operation of cruising boat equipment that rather than turning maintenance jobs over to professionals, one would just about be able to set up one's own boat yard.

Virtually everything you can learn about sailing from a book, you can learn from this book. The word "handbook" is apt. Everyone from a newcomer wanting to discover what the sport is all about to the veteran owner of a sophisticated cruising yacht can find helpful information here. I have never seen a more thorough or detailed rundown of all aspects of sailing so clearly and graphically presented.

Happy Sailing!

Bill Robinson

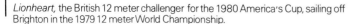

Lionheart, the British 12 meter challenger for the 1980 America's Cup, sailing off Brighton in the 1979 12 meter World Championship.

The development of sailing

Since World War Two, recreational sailing has spread to nearly every corner of the world. Throughout the Americas, Europe, Australia and, to a lesser extent, elsewhere, privately owned sailing boats are to be found partaking in every aspect of the sport. It is, perhaps, ironic that while the sport itself has mushroomed, the variety of sailing boats which can be found around the world has diminished sharply. The old working craft in which modern sailing craft have their origins have virtually disappeared from the ports of the developed nations.

Working boats

There was a time, within living memory, when ports around any coast could be identified easily by the type of working craft which set out to sea from them each day. Different fishing ports produced their own distinctive hull forms and particular rigs. The Chesapeake oyster boats, the fishing sloops of the Bahamas, and the Grand Banks schooners each had a specific task to perform, and the wide differences in their design were a reflection of this. Unlike the boats of today, nearly all of which are designed purely for pleasure boating, the older working craft developed out of specific needs and according to particular coastal conditions. Because these needs and conditions were so different, a wide variety of vessels was produced, for both coastal and ocean trading, for fishing in shallow waters as well as in deep seas, and for piloting as well as ferrying passengers.

The type of construction of boats also varied according to the availability of materials in the area in which it was built. Wood was the common material but in some areas it was not available and builders were forced to find an alternative. On Lake Titicaca in South America, for example, boats are built of reeds, since the lake is 4,000 ft above the tree line. In wooden boats, the number of joints needed for the hull made boat-building a progressively more expensive and labor-consuming task. When iron and steel became available, they largely replaced wood as the main construction material for larger vessels. Before the days of steam power, these different types of vessel were common sights around the ports and harbors of the world. Nowadays, power-driven working boats are more or less uniform throughout the world and only in the less-developed nations can original, locally designed sailing vessels still be seen in any number.

Modern derivatives

To understand the designs of modern sailing craft it is important to know something about the development of the older working boats, as many aspects of their hull form and rig have been assimilated into modern designs. Then, as now, one of the main concerns of the boat builders was the speed of their craft. Early boat builders realized that the efficiency of a sail — its capacity to power the boat — was directly proportional to its size. The larger the sails a boat could carry, the faster it would travel. However, large sails are heavy and difficult to manage without a large crew. In the parts of the world where labor was cheap, in Arabia for example, the boats were equipped with enormous lateen sails and a multitude of hands to work them and in some parts of the Middle East this is

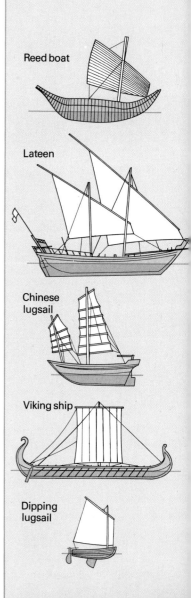

Rig development
With the exception of the Viking ship, with its large square sail, all the other rigs illustrated on this page are variations of the fore-and-aft rig and are to be seen in European and American waters today. Although both gaff racing cutters and J class yachts are themselves extinct, their rigs are carried on some smaller modern vessels.

Reed boat

Lateen

Chinese lugsail

Viking ship

Dipping lugsail

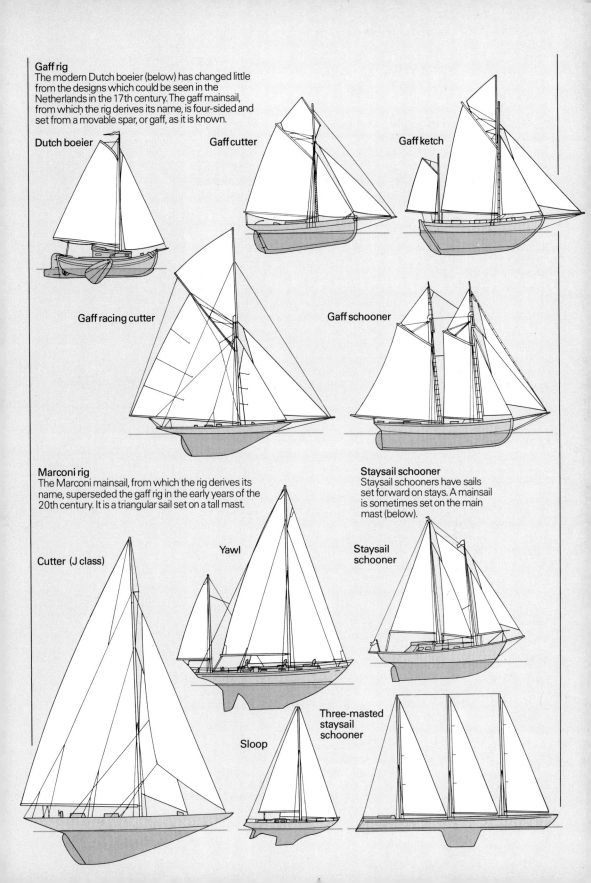

Gaff rig

The modern Dutch boeier (below) has changed little from the designs which could be seen in the Netherlands in the 17th century. The gaff mainsail, from which the rig derives its name, is four-sided and set from a movable spar, or gaff, as it is known.

Dutch boeier

Gaff cutter

Gaff ketch

Gaff racing cutter

Gaff schooner

Marconi rig

The Marconi mainsail, from which the rig derives its name, superseded the gaff rig in the early years of the 20th century. It is a triangular sail set on a tall mast.

Cutter (J class)

Yawl

Sloop

Staysail schooner

Staysail schooners have sails set forward on stays. A mainsail is sometimes set on the main mast (below).

Staysail schooner

Three-masted staysail schooner

still true today. The Arabian dhows, a typical example, were probably once the fastest small trading vessels in the world, and are still used.

In the West, different waters, cargoes and financial considerations necessitated different designs. Economic factors, for instance, demanded that crews were limited: the rig of a Thames barge, a boat which is bigger than most dhows, was designed to be handled by a crew of only two. Long journeys across oceans were most easily conducted in large vessels and the vast amount of canvas which was required to drive them had to be broken down into manageable units. Some of the enormous cargo vessels, which were built at the turn of the century, carried as many as seven masts. The variety of rigs which evolved in Europe and North America to meet all the different needs were numerous.

Rig variations

Square-rigged ships, particularly suited to sailing downwind, traversed the oceans by exploiting the steady trade winds. In European and other coastal waters, where winds are more variable, square sails were combined with fore-and-aft rigs. These latter rigs, which set the sails lengthways along the boat, were more suited to windward sailing. Barques and barquentines, brigs and brigantines, snows, schooners, ketches and yawls plied the coastlines. Each exploited its special advantages, whether of speed, ease of handling, cargo-carrying capacity, or of maneuverability in narrow channels.

In other parts of the world, different solutions were found. The Chinese lugsail, for example (popularly known in the West as the "junk" rig) is efficient both when sailing to windward and when sailing free, and can be easily reefed and managed by a small crew. Because the sail is made up in sections and stiffened by bamboos, it is also easily and cheaply repaired. Although this simple but efficient rig was never adopted on working boats in other parts of the world, designers have begun recently to recognize its advantages and the junk rig is being adapted for use on some modern boats.

In most parts of the world, the old work boats are no longer employed. The big square-riggers, as well as the smaller coastal vessels, were largely usurped by steam-powered craft in the early years of this century. Those which survived, the cutter, ketch, yawl and schooner, did so because their size and rig made them particularly suitable for recreational sailing. Many early cruising boats were old converted pilot cutters or fishing smacks and most present day yachts with their fore-and-aft rigs are adaptations of those types. All fore-and-aft rigs consist of a main mast with a headsail set in front of it and a mainsail set behind. Each rig varies a little from the others. The cutter, for example, has one mast with two or more headsails and a gaff or Marconi mainsail. The sloop rig (now probably the most popular in the Western world) has a single headsail and a mainsail. Ketches and yawls carry an additional mast, known as a mizzen mast, stepped in the after part of the boat. In a ketch, the mizzen is stepped forward of the rudder post and on a yawl it is stepped behind it.

Right, sloops making quick progress in a stiff breeze, their mainsails deeply reefed.
Inset, top, a gaff ketch, with all its sails set, reaches in a light breeze.

Inset, middle, a staysail schooner with a gaff mainsail, sets an array of staysails and headsails.
Inset, bottom, a modern cruising boat, rigged as a junk schooner.

The expansion of racing

The adaptation of working craft into recreational sailing craft is largely a phenomenon of the 20th century and only since World War Two has sailing become the popular activity it is today. Although the rapidity of growth is very recent, recreational sailing began in the Netherlands as long ago as the 17th century. At that time the Dutch were at the height of their seafaring powers, administering overseas colonies and, even more significantly, living in a country served by a network of estuaries and inland waterways. In addition to their naval craft, they employed boats for fishing and trading, and for public and private transport. These diverse needs resulted in the development of small, sophisticated boats, some of which were designed as yachts and used for purely pleasurable pursuits — in short, the Dutch became one of the first nations to regard sailing as a pastime.

Elsewhere in Europe, boating was still primarily functional. However, King Charles II of England had spent a long exile in Holland, and had become well acquainted with the many forms of boating. The Dutch presented the King with his first yacht on his return to England. Between 1671 and 1677 he had 14 more boats built, similar in style to the Dutch boat, which he sailed with his brother, the Duke of Clarence.

Early races

The first recorded yacht race took place in October, 1661, between the yachts of King Charles II and the Duke of York. It was from Greenwich to Gravesend and back on the River Thames, and was run for a wager of £100. The King lost on the first leg, but won on the return. The first recorded regatta of sailing boats organized by a club was conducted in south-west Ireland in 1720 by the Water Club of the Harbour of Cork. A little later, in 1749, a small fleet of racing yachts was established on the Thames and named the Cumberland Fleet after its patron, the Duke of Cumberland. The fleet consisted of small, open, gaff cutters, deep-keeled and bulky for their size. (This small club was absorbed by the Royal Thames Yacht Club in 1831, by which date yacht racing was firmly established in Britain.) In the 18th century, however, interest in the sport was limited to the very few and when Dr. Johnson suggested that "he who goes to sea for pleasure would go to hell for a pastime," the vast majority would have agreed with him. Not until the late 19th century did yacht racing become a popular sport, albeit that it remained exclusively a rich man's activity.

Yachting first gained the prestigious aura which now surrounds it in the sheltered waters of the Solent on the south coast of England. For those who could afford to build private yachts, it afforded a perfect setting for racing. As with horses, so with yachts, a means was found to gain excitement, prestige and money. In 1815 the Yacht Club was formed at Cowes. It was an aristocratic establishment and was later transformed into the now famous Royal Yacht Squadron in 1833. The club presided over the birth of

Right, *Candida,* an English 23 meter, racing in the Solent, in 1935.
Inset, left, *Barranquilla,* an old 12 meter, its racing life finished, has now been converted to a cruising yacht.

Inset, right, *Rainbow,* one of the fastest J class yachts of the 1930s, was almost 130ft long, and the successful defender of the America's Cup in 1934, though the challenger came close to winning.

yacht racing as we know it today and the Solent has retained its position as one of the most important yachting venues in the world.

Yacht racing developed almost simultaneously elsewhere in Europe and in North America. In 1835 the first yacht race in the US took place and was an informal competition around Cape Cod between the skippers of two schooners. The New York Yacht Club was founded in 1844 and held its first regatta in 1845. In France the *Société des Régates du Havre* was formed after a regatta off Le Havre in 1839.

The first racing yachts were all gaff-rigged. Most were gaff-cutters, though the Americans, in particular, tended to favor the gaff-schooner. At the beginning of the century, the yachts derived their hull shapes and sail plans from the commercial and naval craft then in commission, but as the requirements of racing were very different, it did not take long for designers to deviate from accepted criteria.

Early handicapping rules

In the early days of racing, it became quickly apparent that only those who were very rich could afford to build boats large enough to win races. As a general rule, the longer the waterline length of a boat, the faster it travels through the water. To minimize this inequality, a handicapping system was introduced in 1829 which divided yachts into six classes. Boats were classified according to the old commercial tonnage measurement. This rule measured a boat's potential speed according to its capacity for carrying cargo. As competition grew, designers sought ways of getting around the handicapping rules; yachts became longer to increase their potential speed and the beam (the width) was narrowed to reduce their bulk-carrying capacity so as not to incur too high a handicap.

This tendency towards long, thin boats raised a problem for designers. In commercial and naval craft, the ballast required to keep a boat upright when carrying a large amount of sail was carried inboard. With the reduction in beam, less space was available and to resolve the problem the Americans adopted a plan for carrying the ballast outside the boat. In the 1870s, the fashion was adopted in Europe. Large lumps of lead, hydrodynamically shaped, were attached to the keel of the boat and this, combined with the tonnage rule, resulted in the building of boats of quite freakish proportions. A well-known example was the British boat, *Oona*, built in 1866. It represented the last word in long, sleek, narrow boats and had a waterline length of 33ft 10in, a beam of only 5ft 6in and an enormous depth of 8ft. Its displacement was 12.5 tons of which 9.6 tons was lead keel. On top of all this was set some 2,000 sq ft of sail. The immensity of this sail area can, perhaps, be realized when it is compared with the 800 sq ft of sail carried by a modern racing yacht of the same length. It is perhaps not surprising that this strange craft was lost, with all hands, off the Irish coast the year it was launched.

Under these handicapping rules, boats were becoming increasingly unseaworthy. A new system was required. In 1886, a rule was conjured up by a yacht designer, Dixon-Kemp. It was intended

Right, the spinnaker is lowered as *Matchmaker,* a half-tonner, beats to windward after rounding a leeward mark during a race.

Inset, left, *Acadia,* a Class One boat, racing downwind during the Nassau Cup in 1978.
Inset, right, a friendly race off Antigua.

to halt the tendency towards what were known as "plank-on-edge" boats—thin narrow vessels like the *Oona*. Designers had to be encouraged to build boats with greater beam and this required a handicapping rule which did not tax the boat's width.

A boat's rating was then worked out by multiplying the waterline length by the sail area and dividing by 6,000. Thus a 15ft boat with a sail area of 200 sq ft would be a half-rater. The half-rater was the smallest of the rater classes, others including a two and a half, a five, a 23 and even a 40-rater, as well as others in between. But just as the tonnage rule had been exploited, so the Dixon-Kemp rule was interpreted by designers on both sides of the Atlantic in such a way as to enable them to build ever-faster boats.

The tonnage rule had resulted in deep narrow boats; the Dixon-Kemp rule resulted, towards the end of the 1890s, in boats that became known as "skimming dishes". As the breadth of the boat was not handicapped, so vessels became broader in order to carry their huge areas of sail. At the same time, ballast was dumped in order to reduce the displacement. Wide, light and shallow yachts became the common form.

The introduction of meter classes

The problem was not, in fact, resolved until 1907 when the rating classes were replaced by the meter classes. The rating of a boat was no longer governed by sail area and length alone. Other factors regarding the yacht's dimensions were taken into account, so as to ensure that more full-bodied craft were designed. The majority of boats were now to race at a rating which was named in meters. By the outbreak of World War One, the meter classes were prolific. Particularly popular were the 6, 8, 12 and 15 meter yachts, while the 5, 7, 9, 19 and 23 meter ones were also built. Not all the classes have withstood the test of time; after 1918, the 6, 8 and 12 meter boats were the only ones to survive in any significant numbers. The 6 meter emerged as a classic of design and was to survive for more than 40 years; a small number of them can still be seen sailing in various corners of the world. The only other meter class to survive is the 12 which is at present sailed exclusively for the America's Cup.

The 1890s, and the years leading up to World War One, became a golden era of yacht racing. The rating rules encouraged great steps in yacht design and boats of all sizes proliferated. Many of the boats of the 1890s were undoubtedly faster than present-day craft. Owing to their gaff rig, however, they failed to sail as well to windward as modern boats.

Local Regattas

In the era up to World War One, most yacht racing was in daytime events along the coast, as ocean racing was still in its infancy. In British areas such as Cowes, Harwich and Dover, there were big colorful regattas, and U.S. centers such as New York, Boston, Chicago and San Francisco were the scene of inshore racing. Until World War One, most of the New York racing was on the Lower New York Bay between Staten Island and Sandy Hook, but, with the increased commercial traffic in the port and industrial development along the shores of New York harbor, activity shifted to Long Island Sound after World War One, and these waters have been one of the major centers of Eastern racing ever since. Between

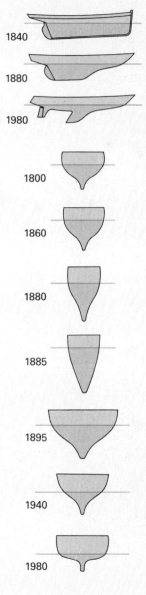

Hull development
The first three profiles show how hulls have changed in the attempt to make boats faster, by reducing wetted surface. The last seven profiles show hull sections which developed out of the handicapping rules introduced during the 19th and 20th centuries.

1840

1880

1980

1800

1860

1880

1885

1895

1940

1980

Right, *Independence* is one of the many American 12 meter yachts which have recently been built as contenders for the America's Cup.

the two World Wars, day regattas both in England and the U.S. continued to include large racing machines such as the lofty J-boats that competed for the America's Cup and in local racing in both countries until World War Two ended their era. NY 40s and 50s (designating waterline length), M boats and 12-Meters were among the other larger classes, but after the end of World War Two, only the 12-Meters and their smaller sisters survived and smaller classes took over in local events.

The America's Cup

Although some countries developed a program of national races, the event now known as the America's Cup achieved international prominence in the yachting calendar. The competition was first established in 1851 when the schooner, *America*, won the Royal Yacht Squadron Cup in a race around the Isle of Wight. This cup was taken back to the New York Yacht Club by the victorious Americans and the event later renamed the America's Cup. The cup has remained with the Americans ever since. Money and determination have seldom been in short supply, but challengers from France, England, Canada, Australia and Sweden have, as yet, been unable to wrest the cup away. The modern America's Cup boats are a reminder of the spectacular yachts which once raced in the coastal regattas of the 19th century. The 12 meter, the boat for which the cup is competed, remains the only example of the early large yachts to have been saved from obsolescence. Indeed, in the 1980s, the class appears to be growing in popularity, as more countries join the competition.

Sail plans

The gaff-rigged cutters of the early days of yacht racing carried huge topsails above their mainsails and, in light weather, they carried jackyard topsails which extended the sail out beyond the bounds of the gaff and the topmast. Booms were long and hung some feet over the stern while at the bow, great bowsprits enabled the yachts to carry a large number of headsails. These sail plans were long at the base and comparatively short in height in relation to the boat's length. At the turn of the century the tendency was for the sail plan to increase in height and shorten along the base. Topmasts were separate and were stepped on top of the mainmasts. In 1901, the 15 meter yacht, *Istria*, broke new ground by stepping a mainmast and topmast in one spar. The topsail was set on the upper part of the mast on a track and this represented the first step towards the development of what is now called the Marconi rig (because the rigging of the mast resembles a radio transmission mast) or Bermudan rig. It was developed so that a triangular mainsail could be carried and it appeared in the West for the first time in 1911, one of the first boats to adopt it being a six meter yacht. Its adoption through to the larger classes took a little longer and the first 23 meter boat to be seen with the new rig was the *Nyria* in 1921.

The Marconi rig is now used by some 90 per cent of modern boats, at least so far as recreational boats are concerned. However, the gaff rig is beginning to regain some of its lost popularity and a number of boat builders, recognizing the versatility of the old working boats, are beginning to reproduce the old hull shapes and rigs, although most use modern, synthetic materials.

Development of the Marconi rig
Right and below, the *Britannia* was built in 1893 for Edward VII of England, then Prince of Wales. In its lifetime it had seven different rigs (five are shown below), providing a clear picture of the development from the gaff rig to the Marconi rig.

1893

1910

1927

1928

1931

The origins of ocean racing

Regatta races were short events; at the most they took only a few hours to complete. The land was never out of sight and at the end of the day the comforts of shore life could be indulged in. In the 19th century, day racing was the only type which was conceived of. This attitude was linked to the idea that small boats were inherently unsafe in the open sea. By the beginning of the 20th century, this idea had been somewhat confounded. For many years, a small band of dedicated yachtsmen had cruised off the European coasts and further afield over the oceans. They had vindicated their belief that small vessels could be handled in the open sea and were quite safe in rough weather if sailed by a competent crew.

Early ocean races were confined to those ships which were large enough to guarantee comfort and whose destinations anyway compelled them to cross the Atlantic. In 1866, a race was organized for stakes which amounted to some $90,000. The race, between New York and Cowes, took place during the winter and the winning vessel made the passage in under 14 days, a time which compared favorably with those made by commercial steamships. Those who regarded this sort of activity with disfavor were able to cite the fact that six men were washed overboard during the race. There were four of these transatlantic races in the last decade of the 19th century and the boats which took part were cutters and schooners, all of them longer than 100ft. The races, isolated as they were, made little impact on the sailing fraternity or the public.

The growth of organized races

Though many sailing traditions had their roots in England, it was in America that the birth of ocean racing took place. Thomas Fleming Day, editor of the American magazine *Rudder*, set out to prove to the skeptics that small yachts could be raced safely at sea. The first race which he organized took place in 1904, and a course was set from Brooklyn to Marble Head, via Cape Cod. Its distance, 300 miles, was short by present‑day ocean racing standards. Nevertheless, those who set off were considered foolhardy, and there must have been some surprise when all the boats which crossed the starting line returned safely. Day himself took part in the race but had to be content with last place. Any disappointment he may have felt was most probably offset by the safe return of the other competitors. In 1906, Day organized the first Bermuda race — a 600-mile course from Newport, Rhode Island, to Bermuda. Only three boats entered and not all of them managed to finish. The same year witnessed the first transpacific race from Los Angeles to Honolulu. The Bermuda race continued to be held regularly until the outbreak of World War One. In 1922, the Cruising Club of America was formed and took on the organization of the Bermuda race when it was resumed in 1923.

In 1925, English yachtsmen instigated the first Fastnet race. This has subsequently become one of the most well-known events

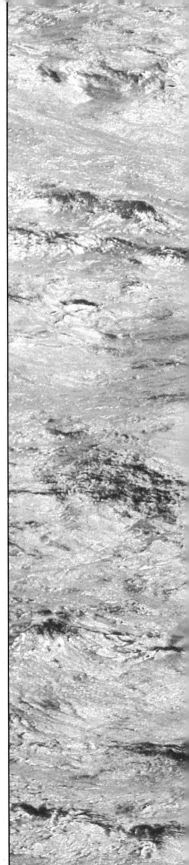

Right, a contender in a Southern Ocean Racing Conference event fast-reaching in the Atlantic. The SORC is a prestigious offshore racing series, similar to the Admiral's Cup. It is an annual event and was inaugurated in 1941.

Inset, top, *Charisma,* a Class One ocean racer, at speed in a big Atlantic swell. Inset, bottom left, racing yachts compete on a downwind leg off Houston, Texas. Inset, bottom right, boats in a Half Ton Cup class, racing to windward.

in the yachtsman's calendar. The Royal Cruising Club did not volunteer its support for ocean racing and, as a result, the Ocean Racing Club was founded. The first commodore of the club was George Martin, who won the first Fastnet race in his converted pilot cutter, *Jolie Brise*. The seven boats which took part in the race were all markedly different from the purpose-built vessels which now take part in the event; they were either converted pilot cutters or designs derived from other working craft. The concept of the specially built ocean racer did not then exist.

By the end of the 1930s, ocean racing had become firmly established. In Europe, in 1938 for instance, there were races from Dover to Kristiansand, Copenhagen to Warnemünde, Kingston to Clyde, an English Channel race and others. After the war, the Royal Ocean Racing Club took the lead in encouraging ocean racing and a rating rule and a system of time allowances encouraged boats of varied sizes and performance to compete in the many events which ranged from offshore regatta races to the Fastnet.

The vessels which participated in these races were mostly cruising boats or converted working craft for there was no thought at that stage of designing purpose-built craft. Americans alone had pursued this option, but sleek, well-canvassed boats which did so well in European races before World War Two were considered unseaworthy and were the subject of much criticism. In 1947, an English yacht appeared which was specifically designed to compete in offshore races. The *Myth of Malham*, designed by Laurent Giles, incorporated features which are now taken for granted in ocean racers. It had a high freeboard so that it retained a large internal depth while at the same time having a shallow draft. Its bow and stern were snubbed which allowed for a long waterline length in conjunction with a relatively short overall length. Its light build and small, but high-aspect, sail plan also heralded modern design.

Present-day racing yachts, though more sophisticated than the *Myth of Malham*, retain its characteristics. Interiors have become more spartan in order to reduce weight, the deck equipment more complex and expensive, and the decks themselves have become flush. Wood has become an outmoded material and has been replaced by fiberglass and metal alloys. As competition has grown, so expense has risen and a new "one-off design" can cost thousands of dollars.

Small offshore racers

While large and expensive boats have grown in numbers, so smaller ocean racers have proliferated. In 1950, both the Junior Offshore Group and the Midget Ocean Racing Club of America were founded.

The system of time allowances, though used for one of the great events, the Admiral's Cup, is not entirely satisfactory. The death of almost all the smaller meter classes left a gap in the world of pure yacht racing. In 1965, *Cercle de la Voile de Paris* offered the old Six Meter Cup for a new race between boats with a 22ft rating. This became known as the One Ton Cup. All the craft of a fixed rating race without any time allowances over both inshore and offshore courses; the first home is the winner. As the popularity of this form of racing has grown, the number of ratings has increased.

The American boat, *Yankee Girl,* beats out of the Solent at the beginning of the 1971 Fastnet race. The race is run from the Isle of Wight to the Fastnet Rock, off the coast of Southern Ireland, and back to Plymouth, on the south coast of England.

The pleasures of cruising

Competitive sailing constitutes only one facet of boating. Towards the end of the 19th century, a number of individuals discovered the delights of cruising. To make a passage from one port to another or simply to be afloat on the open sea were regarded by some to be more enjoyable than racing around a small, pre-determined course.

Those who now leave crowded marinas and head out to sea for a few days cruising must find it difficult to imagine the lonely course that Richard Tyrrell McMullen, one of the pioneers of cruising and now famous for his exploits, was then following. The professional skippers and crews who sailed the racing yachts, and others who made their living by the sea, regarded an amateur as nothing short of lunatic. But McMullen, an independent man with strong views, set out to prove that a small boat, properly handled, was as safe at sea as a larger boat. He realized that in heavy weather it was not the open sea which spelled danger to the sailor but the shoreline. McMullen sailed around the English coastline for over 40 years until he died, at the helm of his boat, in 1891.

The Royal Cruising Club

Though McMullen's activities were regarded with suspicion his ideas had been most certainly vindicated by the closing decades of the century. Other sailors followed his example, and by 1880 there were enough people who cruised around the estuaries and channels of Britain to justify the formation of the Cruising Club. In 1882, the club initiated a journal which recorded accounts of members' cruises. The club required member's logs to reflect good seamanship and navigation as well as the owner's ability to fit out a seaworthy yacht. In addition to this, members were encouraged to explore lesser known coastlines and record information for the use of other members. The club, which has now become the Royal Cruising Club, still publishes its journal and the same high standards still apply. In order to encourage these the club introduced cups, the first of which was the Challenge Cup, presented in 1896.

The spread of cruising

It could well be argued that by the turn of the century cruising had become an art in much the same way as racing had. The gulf which existed between the two activities, however, was considerable. Claude Worth's *Yacht Cruising*, which has become a classic book on the subject, was published in 1911. In it he wrote, "to make a sea cruise in a seaworthy little yacht, neither courting unnecessary risks nor being unduly anxious of the weather, and having confidence in one's knowledge and skill to overcome such difficulties as might arise, is, to one who loves the sea, the most perfectly satisfying of all forms of sport". Successful racing, in those days, on the other hand, depended upon expensive hybrid machines, a knowledge of tactics and a highly trained crew, each member skilled at some specialized task. In the sport of ocean racing today, the skills of both have been amalgamated. Both the tactics of inshore racing, employed by the skippers of such boats as *Britannia* in the summer regattas, and the skills of cruising are needed in equal proportions, if a boat is

A French yacht carrying extra sail in the form of a blooper and spinnaker enjoys the last of a sea breeze at the end of a summer's day.

to be sailed fast and safely across wide stretches of open water. After the early pioneering of McMullen, Worth and other English eccentrics, cruising grew rapidly throughout Europe. On the Clyde, in Scotland, where sheltered estuaries provided ideal cruising grounds, a club was established in 1909. Cruising also proliferated in Norway, where the fjords offered both a scenic environment as well as a sheltered one. One of their countrymen, Colin Archer, was the first qualified naval architect to devote himself to the designing of cruising yachts. A life spent designing working craft for Norwegian waters made him well-qualified to turn his attention to the needs of amateur yachtsmen. His heavy, double-ended craft were instantly recognizable and were regarded by many as the most seaworthy of deep-water vessels. Erskine Childers, who gave literary expression to the art of cruising in *The Riddle of the Sands*, commissioned Archer to design a successor to his boat, *Dulcibella*.

Ocean cruising

Cruising also extended beyond the bounds of local shorelines. Long voyages across oceans, as well as the exploration of foreign coasts and exotic ports attracted the imagination of a number of sailors. In 1866, two Americans, William Hudson and Frank E. Fitch, set sail across the Atlantic in a 26ft iron lifeboat named *Red, White and Blue*. They were the first two-man crew to cross the Atlantic and their feat set a precedent for long voyages in small boats. Other such journeys included the expedition undertaken by Captain John Voss in an American Indian canoe, *Tilikum*. He left Vancouver for England in 1901. Having sailed for 40,000 miles he finally arrived in Margate on the English coast. When asked where he had come from he astonished local inhabitants with his nonchalant reply, "Vancouver".

Perhaps the most famous of all 19th century circumnavigators is Joshua Slocum, a Canadian, who set sail alone from Boston in 1895 on a world trip which was to take three years. What made his achievement particularly spectacular was that he sailed around the world against the prevailing winds. Nobody attempted to circumnavigate the world for another 25 years and when they did so it was via the Panama canal which allowed them to avoid the rigors of the southern Atlantic, and Cape Horn.

Cruising today

Cruising, once regarded as an eccentric pastime, has become the foremost sailing activity and is looked upon as an ideal means of escaping from the duller routine of everyday shore life. Competing with the elements, discovering new coastlines and the fitting out and handling of a small boat at sea, offer to men a unique and varied round of activities. Moreover, the cruising man is not bound to sail boats that have been developed for specific racing purposes. He can buy, or have built, a boat which is ideally suited to his own needs. It can be a day sailor with neither competitive intentions or overnight cruising abilities. Its rig can conform to his own needs and tastes, and the accommodation can be designed with a special crew in mind. It is this flexibility which has made cruising one of the fastest growing sports since World War Two.

Right, a small cruising yacht explores some rugged coastline off the Isle of Skye in Scotland. Discovering new ports and shorelines, both in your own and foreign waters, is one of the most enjoyable features of cruising.

Cruising boats

The variety of cruising yachts ranges from converted lifeboats to specially designed and expensively built cruisers. The ones illustrated below represent a very small selection.

McMullen's yawl, *Perseus*

Claude Worth's cutter, *Foam*

A Folkboat – a popular small cruiser

A Westerly 33, a typical modern cruiser

The growth of sailing

Small open-boat sailing has proliferated over the last 30 years. Classes have multiplied and there is now such a variety that almost anyone planning to buy a sailboat will be able to find one that fulfils his particular needs. Small open boats have always existed even if the types to choose from were limited. In the 19th century, small sailing craft were to be found in every port. Like their larger counterparts, they derived their hull shapes and sail plans from work boats. Their immediate appeal was their relative cheapness and the comparative ease with which they could be handled. This remains the case today. But small boats of that period were very different from the modern designs. Small boats in those days, like the larger vessels, carried fixed ballast. On top of this was set an enormous spread of sail. Long bowsprits, overhanging booms and topsails were the norm. Today this outlook has been completely reversed. Sail areas have been shortened, while the ballast is provided by the crew members. Even centerboards, which were once made of heavy iron, are now made of wood or light alloys.

In the 19th century no national classes existed. Indeed, the concept of a one-design did not exist; boats were most usually one-offs. Only towards the end of the century did classes of small boats appear which could race on equal terms. The first one-design in Europe was introduced in 1887. Called Water Wags, these small dinghies were 14ft 3in and were sailed in Dublin Bay. This class, in fact, still exists today despite being nearly 100 years old.

The development of classes

The story of modern sailboat design begins between the two world wars. In Britain and the United States two classes were introduced which laid the foundations for modern small craft. In the 1920s, Frank Morgan Giles, a naval architect as well as a boat builder, built 14ft boats, rounded in section, which were undoubtedly the best small craft of their time.

In 1927 one particular 14ft dinghy was awarded international status and became known as the International 14. It was a restricted class, which means that design and shape could be altered as long as the boat conformed to a certain limited number of measurements. With this ruling, the International 14 quickly developed into a fast and sophisticated racing boat, owing in part to the design improvements introduced by Uffa Fox. Having had experience in the design of hydroplanes, he sought to introduce a "v" section which would allow the bow of the boat, when sailed fast off the wind, to lift out of the water, thus reducing the displacement and greatly increasing the speed. In 1928, he succeeded in achieving this with his own *Avenger*. Its impact was immediate, as it won 52 out of 57 races within the year.

The initial attraction of the International 14 was that different designs of this size could be successfully brought under the umbrella of one ruling. It thus opened the way for national racing. No longer was a sailor restricted to his local waters. In other words, the

Right, International 505 racing one-designs plane in ideal conditions. Inset, top, a Fireball, a popular racing one-design with a shallow draft skims across the water under spinnaker.

Inset, middle, a 505 races at Weymouth, England, in a championship event. Inset, bottom, a Mirror one-design, one of the most popular boats, is ideal for learning to sail.

International 14 brought about the rationalization of many designs. At the same time, because it was a restricted class and not a one-design, it encouraged development which has resulted in the numerous classes in existence today.

In the United States, by 1931, another form had evolved. Heavier than the International 14, with a chine hull (a hull which is not rounded but angular in section) it had a smaller sail area and was considerably slower. Nevertheless, the design, known as the Snipe, offered special charms of its own. The boats were much cheaper than others and, because of the chine hull, were ideally suited to construction by amateur boat-builders. Added to this, they were particularly seaworthy owing to their being half-decked. Not surprisingly, the class spread rapidly to Europe, and has maintained its popularity ever since.

Recent developments

Since the 1930s, sailing has advanced in the most spectacular fashion. The International 14 and the Snipe still represent the two poles. On the one hand, the restricted classes offer sailors the opportunity to test new ideas in the design of individual classes. At the same time, these designs have led, inevitably, to general advancements in all design. At the other end of the scale, mass-produced classes offer sailors the chance to compete on equal terms.

The number of classes is now almost too great to be counted. They vary from small single-handed sailing surfboards, like the Sunfish, to large open boats, like the Drascombe lugger, which can be used for cruising, and sailed by a whole family. The enormous variety now allows people, even on a small budget, to indulge in almost any form of sailing they choose.

Just as the types of sailing boat have proliferated, so has sailing itself spread, in many different forms, to countries all over the world. Since sailing was introduced into the Olympics, it has been developed by the communist countries such as East Germany and Russia which now produce world-class crews. The boats, unlike Western ones, are all state-owned and there is no recreational sailing, as such. New boats are allocated to the best crews and the quality of the boat you sail is determined by your ability.

In many European countries, particularly Norway, Sweden and Denmark, boats are often owned by clubs rather than individuals. Thus sailing has become, in those countries, an activity which is open to all. Sailing schools are another outlet for those who do not own their own boats, while those who wish to make extensive cruises can always charter boats.

Against this background of change, especially in the small boat world, there have been enormous developments in offshore racing as well as huge expansion in recreational cruising. Vast marinas which house the boats of enthusiastic millions are now familiar sights around most sailing coastlines. But the sea is far from over-crowded and many, many more people are destined to discover the exhilaration that sailing can bring.

A Tornado racing during the Olympic week at Weymouth. Catamarans are high-performance boats, their narrow hulls and light build enabling them to achieve very high speeds off the wind.

Overleaf, International Moths racing. A high-performance boat, the Moth is popular world wide for the exciting sailing it offers. It is strictly a boat for the very experienced sailor.

One-designs
The range of modern one-designs caters for nearly every need, from highly specialized racing through to cruising.

The Snipe, a pioneer design

The Enterprise, an early classic

The 470, an Olympic class racing boat

The Drascombe lugger, a traditional-type dayboat

Basic Sailing

The basic sailboat · Choosing a sailboat · Car topping and trailing
Equipment · Points of sailing · Tacking and jibing
Leaving from and returning to beaches, floats and moorings
Righting a capsized boat · Reefing · Anchoring
Stowing the boat · Rules of the road

Starting to sail

The first question most would-be sailors ask is: where do I begin? One of the best solutions is to attend a sailing course or go on a sailing holiday to learn the basic techniques and to establish whether sailing really appeals. Other possibilities are to join a sailing club as a crew member or to seek advice from an experienced sailor.

Most countries have a national sailing authority to look after the interests of sailors and to administer the rules drawn up by the International Yacht Racing Union. Most of these authorities will provide comprehensive lists of sailing schools and clubs and the classes of boats sailed.

While sailing is a sport which can be enjoyed by people of all ages and provides an excellent way of keeping fit and of getting out in the open air, it must be remembered that it can be dangerous if the basic techniques are not thoroughly learned and careful attention is not given to safety procedures. This basic sailing course aims to help beginners to learn about sailing in a methodical and safe way and also to provide useful hints on sailing techniques for more experienced sailors.

The basic boat

Once you have decided to take up sailing, the next thing you should consider is the boat. Sailing boats vary enormously according to the use for which they are designed, but it is possible to define the common elements.

Every sailing boat, irrespective of its size has four basic parts: a hull, a sail, a keel or a centerboard and a rudder. Each has a specific role to play in keeping the craft afloat, stable and moving in the required direction. The working of each has an effect on the other parts and the combination of different types of part determines the character of the boat.

The hull is designed to carry the crew and to provide a rigid structure to support the mast and sails. Its shape should enable the boat to move easily through the water when sailed upright, or even when heeled. Most hulls are pointed at the bow and blunt at the stern, but some are blunt at both ends and others are pointed at both ends.

Hulls are made from a wide variety of materials, principally wood, plastics or metal. Racing boats need to be as light as possible and their construction is a delicate balance between weight and strength. Family boats are more robust, the most important factor being durability.

The sails are the principal driving force of the boat, converting the airflow into forward thrust (see pages 324–7). The sails are constructed by joining curved panels of sailcloth to produce a triangular shape giving the greatest forward drive with the minimum of drag.

The size and shape of the sails will depend on the purpose for which the boat is designed. Racing boats have a relatively large sail area which produces a greater tendency to heel and this is balanced by the weight of the crew. Boats used for learning to sail often have only one sail, as do single-handed racing boats. Many one-designs have two sails rigged as on the boat shown opposite.

Sails can be divided into two principal groups, those used to drive the boat in a given direction (mainsail and jib), and those only used when the boat is sailing away from the wind to increase speed (spinnaker).

The sails are attached to the mast which is usually secured in a vertical position by wires. These are fixed to the side decks (shrouds) and to the bow (forestay). The foot of the mainsail is attached to the boom, which keeps it tensioned while enabling the mainsail to move easily across the boat when changing direction. It is controlled by a rope known as the mainsheet. Many boats have a boom vang which is attached to the boom and to the bottom of the mast to prevent the boom from rising. Where a boat has a jib, its front edge, the luff, is fixed to the forestay. The jib is controlled by the jib sheets. The sails are raised into position using ropes called halyards.

All sailing boats need to have a certain depth of hull under the water to counteract the sideways movement created by the force of the wind on the sails. Cruising boats have ballasted fixed keels, but one-designs always have adjustable centerboards which can be raised or lowered as required. The amount of centerboard used is closely related to the direction, in relation to the wind, in which the boat is sailing.

The rudder serves two purposes, to initiate major changes in direction and to provide increased resistance to sideways slip at the back of the boat. It usually comprises two parts: a rudder stock, which is fixed by special hinges to the transom, and a rudder blade, which can be raised if sailing in shallow water. The rudder is controlled by means of a wood or aluminium handle, the tiller. The rudder is only effective when the boat is moving forwards or backwards.

The boat

The boat, right, is a typical 4.2m (14ft) one-design with a Marconi rig. Not only is this a very popular type, but it has most of the features common to the majority of one-designs. It can be handled easily by two people, and does not require a high level of sailing expertise. The smaller pictures on the far right show a typical small racing boat (above) and a simple small catamaran (below).

Racing boat

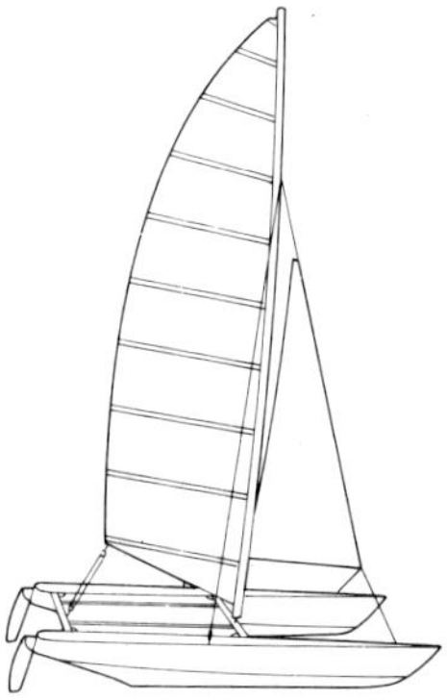

Catamaran

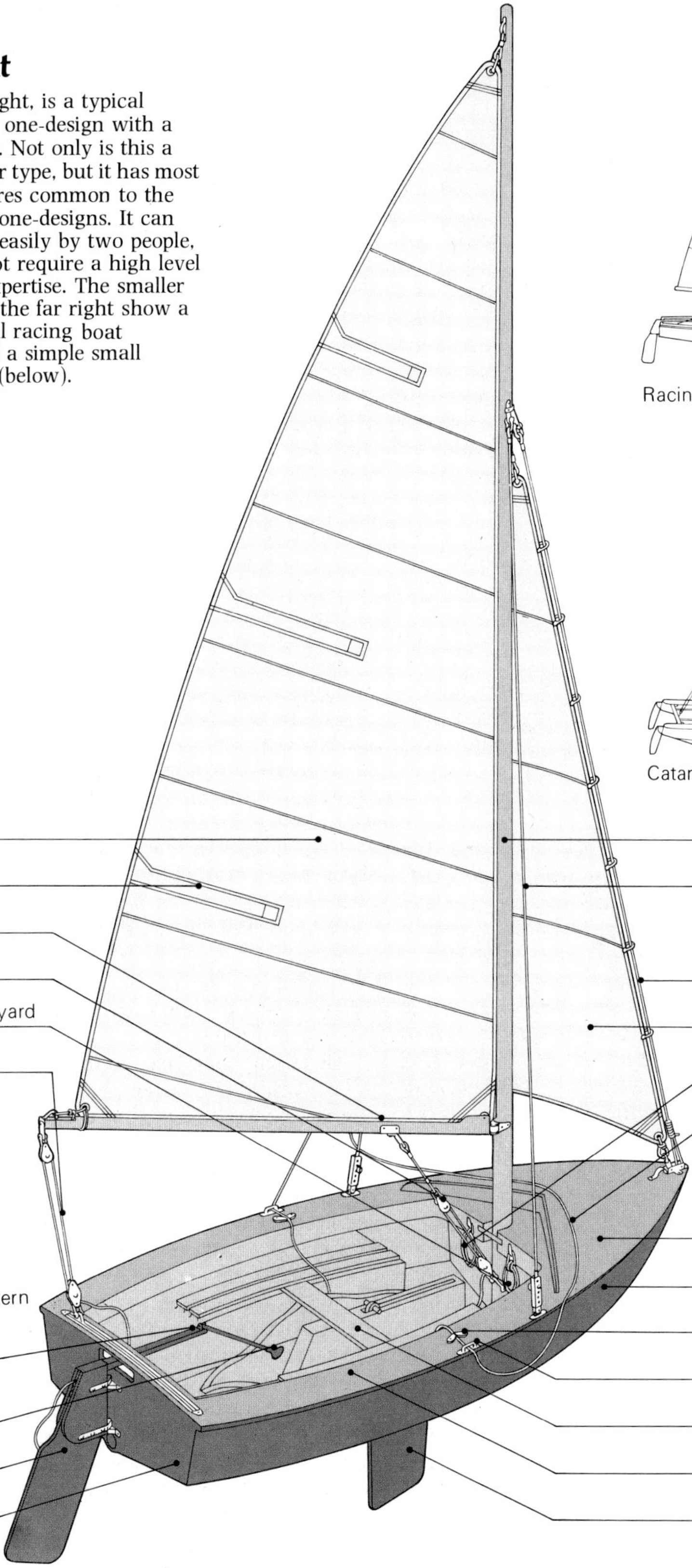

Mainsail

Batten

Boom

Boom vang

Mainsail halyard

Mainsheet

Stern

Tiller

Tiller extension

Rudder

Transom

Mast

Shroud

Forestay

Jib

Jib halyard

Jib sheet

Bow

Foredeck

Hull

Jamming cleat

Fairlead

Thwart

Side deck

Centerboard

Choosing a sailboat

Since the adoption of plywood and other lightweight materials for boat-building in the 1940s, the growth in sailing has been phenomenal. Widespread interest in the sport has now resulted in hundreds of designs becoming available worldwide, making it difficult to know which to choose when buying a boat.

Before setting out on the search for a boat, you should first decide what you intend to use the boat for: to learn to sail, to take on vacation, to use for family outings and occasional competitions or solely for racing. The size of your boat will be governed by a number of factors: how many people will be in it at any

one time, their combined weight, the carrying or towing capacity of your car and, of course, the amount of money you are prepared to spend. To find a suitable boat, look in the classified pages of sailing magazines and specialized publications to see what is available in the new and second-hand markets.

Generally speaking the different classes of one-designs can be divided into three types: those suitable for youth, family or racing use. If you are buying a boat exclusively for use by children, the most important consideration is their size and weight. All boats in the youth class below can be used for racing as well. For

General description	International Optimist		Topper		Wayfarer	
General description	Youth class	Youth class	Youth class	General purpose	General purpose	Racing
Length	2.31 m 7ft 7in	3.22 m 10ft 6¾in	3.34 m 11ft	3.30 m 10ft 10in	4.83 m 15ft 10in	4.20 m 13ft 9in
Crew	(1 child)	(2 children)	(1 child)	(2 adults)	(3 adults)	(3 adults) or (1 adult)
Ideal crew weight (10 per cent variation either side acceptable)	50 kg 110 lb	95 kg 210 lb	60 kg 132 lb	100 kg 220 lb	200 kg 440 lb	130 kg 286 lb
Level of skill required	Basic	Basic	Basic	Basic	Intermediate	Advanced
Suitable for car topping	✓	✓	✓	✓		✓
Other examples in general category	Scamp	Flipper	Sunfish	Heron	Kestrel Lazy E	Merlin Rocket Scorpion

Key

(child icon) Child

(adult icon) Adult

International Cadet    Mirror    International 420 children of up to 12 years a 3 m (10 ft) boat is suitable and from 13 to 16 years, a 4 m (13 ft) boat is needed.

The general and family category covers the widest range of boats. These can be used for a broad range of activities—training, camping, fishing or racing. A typical boat in this group is shown on page 35 and serves as the model for the basic sailing section as it is a good choice for the novice sailor. A growing number of people are interested in owning a family boat, purpose-built to a traditional design, with a simple rig and made from new materials.

In the racing category there is a wide variety of designs available, all characterized by a large sail area (often with the addition of a spinnaker and trapeze). They have lightweight hulls which need careful handling and storage ashore and the rigs are controlled by a complex system of lines and mechanical devices. If you are determined that your first boat is to be a racing one, choose a second-hand boat without a trapeze in the 3.6 m to 4.2 m (12 to 14 ft) range. Multi-hulls are gaining in popularity as general purpose designs are brought onto the market, but they are only suitable for experienced sailors. Two examples are shown.

The chart below gives several examples of boats in each category. There are, of course, many others and further information should be sought from an experienced sailor or from your local sailing club.

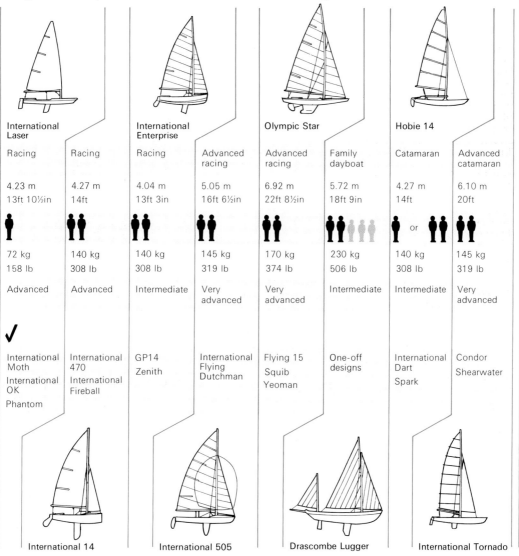

International Laser		International Enterprise		Olympic Star		Hobie 14	
Racing	Racing	Racing	Advanced racing	Advanced racing	Family dayboat	Catamaran	Advanced catamaran
4.23 m	4.27 m	4.04 m	5.05 m	6.92 m	5.72 m	4.27 m	6.10 m
13ft 10½in	14ft	13ft 3in	16ft 6½in	22ft 8½in	18ft 9in	14ft	20ft
72 kg	140 kg	140 kg	145 kg	170 kg	230 kg	140 kg	145 kg
158 lb	308 lb	308 lb	319 lb	374 lb	506 lb	308 lb	319 lb
Advanced	Advanced	Intermediate	Very advanced	Very advanced	Intermediate	Intermediate	Very advanced
✓							
International Moth	International 470	GP14 Zenith	International Flying Dutchman	Flying 15 Squib Yeoman	One-off designs	International Dart Spark	Condor Shearwater
International OK	International Fireball						
Phantom							

International 14   International 505   Drascombe Lugger   International Tornado

Car topping and trailing

Only a few sailors are able to keep their boats by the water's edge, enabling them to launch directly into the water. The vast majority store their boats on launching dollies in a boat park some distance from the water.

Those who keep their boats at home, or club sailors who travel regularly to distant race meetings, are faced with the problem of how to transport their boats and equipment.

The simplest way is to load the boat on the roof of a car, but the size and weight of boat which can be carried safely in this way is strictly limited. To carry the boat, two adjustable single bar roof racks, suitably padded, are attached to the roof guttering by clamps. The boat, together with the mast and boom, is placed on the roof racks and securely tied down. The sails and all other movable equipment are stowed inside the car.

Where a boat is too large for car topping, a specially constructed road trailer is attached to the tow-bar of the car by a ball and socket or drop pin. According to the type of trailer (see opposite), the boat is either placed directly onto the trailer, or it is loaded together with its launching dolly. The law on trailing varies from country to country. Details of regulations should be obtained from the local police before travelling.

Loading the boat

The boat is usually carried upside-down so that its sides rest firmly on the bars of the roof racks. If the boat has to be carried the right way up for any reason, the hull must be properly supported and it must either be covered or the plugs must be left out to prevent it filling with rainwater. The boat is carried with the bow facing forwards and should be secured to the roof racks by tie-down straps or ropes lashed across its width. It is also essential to tie the bow and the stern to the car bumpers to prevent the boat lifting off at speed. The mast and boom are tied to the roof racks separately. A special knot, the truck driver's hitch (see page 334) should be used to tighten the ropes. Padding should be taped to the bars and ropes to prevent damage.

Lifting the boat

If you are on your own, place the boat on the ground at an angle to the back of the car. Lift the bow so that it rests on the rear rack (1). Then lift the stern and push the boat forward over the front rack (2). With more than one person, use either of the following methods. Using the side method hold the boat at the bow and the stern and lift it from the side of the car so that the stern rests on the rear rack first. Then move the bow into position. Using the rear method hold the boat at each side and lift it from behind the car.

1

2

Side   Rear

Road trailers

There are two main types of road trailer to choose from, one has a T-frame and the other an A-frame. Each type supports the boat with specially shaped chocks or rubber rollers, and has a support for the mast. The T-frame type has a strong center strut. All parts of it can be adjusted to accommodate different sizes of boat and to ensure that the weight on the tow-bar does not exceed 23 kg (50 lbs). The A-frame type has the advantage that it can be used in combination with a self-stowing launching dolly. You must have a lighting board, conforming to national requirements, fixed to the trailer or transom of the boat (bottom right). Heavier one-design and cruising boats should be carried on trailers which are fitted with an over-run braking system.

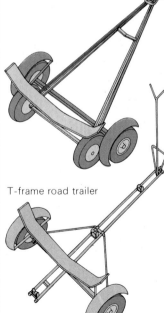

A-frame
combination trailer

T-frame road trailer

Loading the trailer

It is usually easier to load a trailer if it is already attached to the towing vehicle. If you are loading the boat directly onto a trailer, you will need two or more people to carry the boat onto the supporting chocks. Once loaded, tie the boat down carefully with straps or ropes to prevent it shifting. To load a boat on a combination trailer, line up the loaded dolly behind the trailer and pull it forward until it locates on the cross-beam-mounted loading rollers. Then pull it further forward until the dolly axle locates in the securing brackets. Bring down the dolly handles and lock the dolly onto the trailer.

Lining up the dolly
Pull the dolly forward behind the trailer in line with the loading rollers.

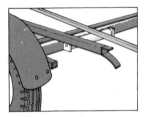

Securing brackets
Pull the dolly over the loading rollers to locate the axle in the brackets.

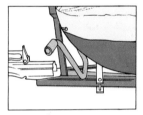

Dolly clamped to trailer
After lowering the dolly handles, clamp the dolly and trailer together.

Preparing for the road

Place the mast in the mast-support so that the heel rests on the aft decking or against the inside of the transom. Tape the shrouds and the halyards to the mast and pad the mast heel to prevent damage to the boat. Tie the mast to the support and to the central thwart. Remove or secure all loose equipment inside the boat. Fix the lighting board in place and connect it to the car socket. Check that the towing coupling is locked and the safety chain attached.

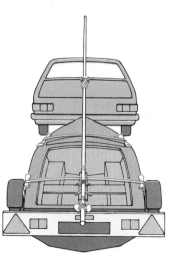

Clothing

Like many other sports, sailing makes special demands on your body, so it is important both for your comfort and your safety that you are properly equipped to go out in a boat. The equipment you need depends on the type of boat you are sailing, the weather and your resistance to cold. Unless you are fortunate enough to sail in tropical latitudes, you will often have to face bad weather and cold water. Open and partly open boats provide very little protection from wind and water. As weather conditions can deteriorate once you are afloat, and as the water temperature is often lower than the land temperature, your clothing must keep you as warm and as dry as possible.

You will need two basic layers of clothing, an insulating layer and water- and windproof clothing over it. The insulation can come from several layers of warm, loose clothing (such as vests and sweaters, jeans and socks) or specially made thermal underwear which traps and conserves the body heat in its fleecy, inner pile. Thermal underwear has the advantage of being very quick-drying.

The water- and windproof layer usually takes the form of a one-piece or two-piece suit. It must be specially designed for sailing, with proofed fabric and bonded seams. Small boat sailors usually wear the one-piece type while big boat sailors normally prefer the heavy duty two-piece.

Racing enthusiasts, whose boats generally afford the minimum of protection, also face being immersed during a capsize. This can result in a sudden, massive loss of heat from the body. The best form of clothing, therefore, is a close-fitting wet suit which has combined insulating and waterproofing properties. A one-piece waterproof suit can be worn over the top for extra protection.

As about 70 per cent of heat loss from the body is through the head, hands and feet, a scarf, wool hat, sailing gloves and non-slip sailing boots should be worn. In strong sunshine, you will need sunglasses and a hat with a brim.

The last, and most important, item is your safety gear. All sailors will need a lifejacket or buoyancy aid and, if you are cruising, a safety harness will also be necessary. Cruising does, however, require special preparation and this is discussed in greater detail in the cruising section which starts on page 150.

Basic sailing outfit
Your basic sailing gear should include light, warm underclothing, a waterproof layer, a buoyancy aid or lifejacket, hat, scarf, gloves and sailing boots or shoes. Both people in the picture above are wearing specially designed waterproof sailing suits; one is a two-piece (right), and the other a one-piece type (left).

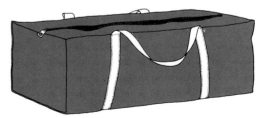

Sailing bag
Your sailing clothing should be kept in a soft waterproof bag. Some bags also have a waterproof compartment for wet clothing.

Heavy waterproof suit

A heavy duty two-piece waterproof suit gives the best protection for coastal cruising or ocean voyaging. You will be on the deck in all sorts of weather conditions and your clothes must be proof against wind, rain and breaking seas. The two-piece suit usually consists of a hooded jacket and chest-high trousers with a double-fold gusset and adjustable shoulder straps. It is designed and cut with the minimum number of seams. Insulating layers are worn underneath.

Wet suit

Most experienced sailors wear neoprene wet suits to combat loss of body heat in the water. The sleeveless "long John" type is the most popular as it does not restrict body movement. A hip-length jacket is usually worn over the top, and in cold weather, a hood, boots and gloves are worn.

Chest-high trousers

Hip-length jacket

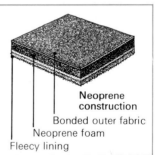

Jacket with hood

Double fold gusset

Neoprene
construction
Bonded outer fabric
Neoprene foam
Fleecy lining

Long John suit

Waterproofing

The wind- and waterproof properties of your clothing are very important. Most waterproof suits are made of heavy, plastic-impregnated or rubber-backed synthetic cloth doubled at the seat, knees and elbows to give extra protection. For the upper part of the suit, jackets are better than parkas as they can be worn open. The seams must be specially bonded.

Jacket fastening
Doubled storm flaps on jackets give extra protection, as do fixed or detachable hoods and collars.

Jacket cuff
Elasticated storm cuffs are used for preventing water from running up your jacket sleeve.

Trouser cuff
Trouser cuffs can be fastened with special studs or clips to make them more water-proof in heavy seas.

Safety equipment

It is very important to take proper safety precautions whenever you are sailing. All sailors must wear some form of additional buoyancy and there is a wide range of buoyancy garments to choose from. They divide into two groups: those which give the wearer some support in the water (known as buoyancy aids) and those which give total support and will turn an unconscious person face uppermost in the water (known as lifejackets). Most racing and inland sailors wear buoyancy aids (especially over wet suits) but many sea sailors choose lifejackets for added security. Buoyancy garments are worn over the top of all other clothing.

When working on the deck of a big boat, particularly on an ocean-going cruiser, you will need to wear a safety harness as well as your buoyancy aid or lifejacket. You will also need to make sure that your sailing boots or shoes have good non-slip soles (see Footwear, opposite) so that you have the maximum possible grip on a wet and sloping deck.

Buoyancy garments

There are many different designs of buoyancy aid and lifejacket, but all types should conform to standard safety requirements. The type of buoyancy aid shown right is made of closed cell foam and will give a minimum of 7.2 kg (16 lbs) flotation. It is front-fastened by a zipper and the side straps enable it to be adjusted for size. Lifejackets are either inflated automatically by pulling a cord attached to a gas cylinder or by mouth. Both types are pulled over the head and are secured by straps around the body. They are worn deflated. When fully inflated they should have 15.8 kg (35 lbs) of buoyancy.

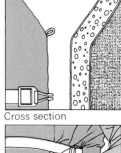
Cross section

Adjustable side straps

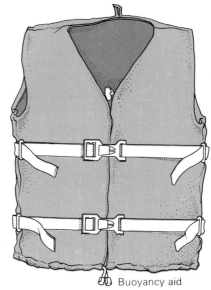
Buoyancy aid

Lifejackets
The lifejacket shown below has about 7.2 kg (16 lbs) of inherent buoyancy. The lifejacket shown right has none.

Floating position
Either of the two life-jackets illustrated (left) will, when inflated, automatically turn the wearer, whether conscious or unconscious, into a floating position, face uppermost.

Mouth-inflated lifejacket

Automatically inflatable lifejacket

Safety harnesses

Safety harnesses are designed to keep the wearer securely attached to the boat by means of a lifeline while working on deck. The lifeline must have a quick release clip onto the harness. The free end is attached to special deck eyes or to wire or rope lifelines rigged along each side deck. (see also Safety, page 308).

Adjustable loop harness

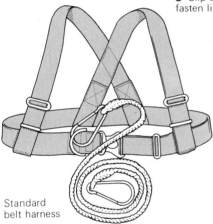

Standard belt harness

Fitting the harness
1 Step into the harness and position rings at sides.
2 Pull the strap of the harness over your head.
3 Clip both rings together and fasten lifeline.

Standard belt
This harness is held in position by adjustable shoulder straps. It has a quick release buckle fastening. As it can be difficult to put on, especially over thick waterproofs, each crew member should adjust and then mark his own harness.

Footwear

Whether you choose boots or shoes is a matter of personal preference, but your sailing footwear should have flat non-slip soles, which have maximum contact with the surface. Make sure that you choose a sole pattern which gives a secure grip.

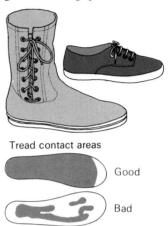

Tread contact areas

 Good

 Bad

Sole patterns
Sole patterns with deep wide troughs and many edges in contact with the surface give a far better grip than unbroken patterns with shallow troughs.

Good   Bad

Drown-proofing

If you are swept overboard when not wearing buoyancy equipment, you can conserve heat and energy by using the following technique. Relax into a crouching position. Your body will then float naturally below the surface of the water. Move your arms to bring your head up to the surface to breathe. Then relax into the crouched position again.
You can make a temporary buoyancy aid by removing clothing, tying the sleeves or legs and trapping air inside to make a floating bag.

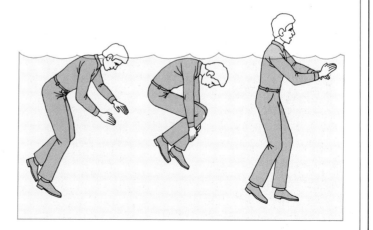

Rigging the boat

Before you can take your boat out on the water you will have to rig it. This means attaching all the equipment normally removed at the end of a day's sailing—principally the sails and rudder, but also any other loose equipment that might be lost or damaged if left in the boat. Whether the mast is removed or not will depend on the type of boat you are sailing and where it is kept. If you have to take your boat by road to the water, you will have to remove and re-place the mast each time you sail.

If you are buying a completely new boat, or if for some reason the boat has been totally dismantled, you will have the additional problem of fixing the wires (known as standing rigging) to the mast. If so, it is best to seek advice from an expert.

The mast itself is usually made of wood or aluminum, which can be in the form of a simple tube or a complicated spar with built-in tracks for sails and other fittings. On basic sailing boats it is sufficient that the mast supports the sails, but on sophisticated racing boats the mast is an important element in determining the overall performance of the boat and is designed to be tensioned to suit particular sailing conditions (see Advanced sailing, pages 134–7).

Mast rigging

On most boats the mast is supported by standing rigging attached to it at the hounds and to the boat at the chain plates. The spreaders prevent the mast bending and their inner ends are attached to a special mast fitting while the shrouds pass through the outer ends, secured with split rings and insulating tape.

Shroud tang
This fitting is riveted to the mast · at the hounds and the shroud itself is attached by means of a shackle. Care must be taken to ensure that the shackle pin is inserted from the outside to prevent mast damage.

Hounds

Mast

Spreaders

Shrouds

Forestay

Mast gate
Keel stepped masts are supported at the fore-deck by the mast gate, a strengthened slot in the aft end of the foredeck, closed by a simple latch.

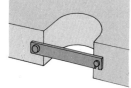

Bow fitting
The bow fitting is the attachment point for fore-stay, jib and bow painter, and must be securely bolted into the foredeck of the boat.

Adjustable rigging link
The shrouds can be attached directly to chain plates, but adjustable rigging links permit the mast to be set up at different angles and tensioned accordingly.

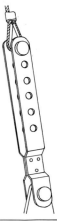

Heel fitting
The heel fitting holds the mast in place in keel stepped boats. The three pulley blocks are for the main, jib and spinnaker halyards. The mast heel can be positioned in the channel by moving the two retaining pins.

Stepping the mast

Most modern masts are light but unwieldy so it is often easier if two people cooperate to step the mast, although it is possible to do it without help. Depending on the boat design, the mast is stepped into the bottom of the boat (keel stepped, shown below) or onto the foredeck (deck stepped, shown far below). Make sure when you raise the mast that there are no overhead power cables – they will kill you if the mast touches them.

Keel stepping – two people
1 Lay the mast gently in the boat lengthwise. The other person then attaches the shrouds to the fittings on the side decks.

2 Insert the mast heel in the heel fitting. The other person pulls on the forestay while you lift the mast upright.

3 The other person then fastens the forestay to the bow fitting and you lock the mast gate.

Deck mounted fitting
Deck stepped masts are positioned in a recessed fitting in the foredeck. Some boats have a second fitting to enable you to adjust the mast.

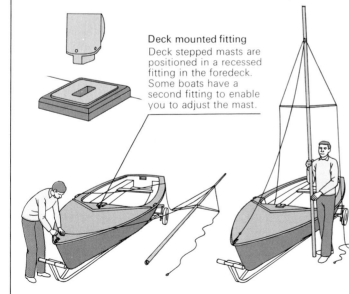

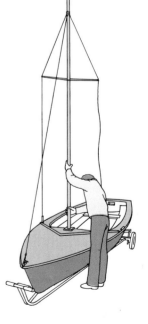

Deck stepping – one person
1 Lay the mast on the ground, with the leading edge uppermost, and attach the forestay and far shroud by shackling them.

2 Raise the mast to a vertical position adjacent to the mast step. Then check to see that none of the wires are fouling the mast.

3 Lean the mast towards the attached shroud and forestay and place it in the mast step. Then attach the other shroud.

45

Boat equipment

Apart from the standing rigging and the items of equipment which are fixed to the boat, you should have the following items of loose gear stowed in the boat before sailing: bucket, hand bailer, sponge, mooring line, anchor, two oars or a paddle, two spare plugs, maps and spare clothes kept dry in sealed plastic bags. The inside of your boat must be kept free of obstructions so everything should be stowed tidily and secured to prevent it being lost in the event of a capsize. Although some boats have quite large stowage areas under the fore, aft and side decking, much of this space will be taken up with extra buoyancy (see opposite).

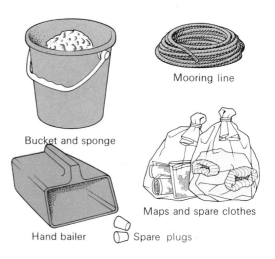

Mooring line

Bucket and sponge

Maps and spare clothes

Hand bailer   Spare plugs

Stowing plan
Always try and organize equipment so that it is easy to remove when needed. Most of it can be stored under the foredeck, as shown, with the more unwieldy items, such as oars and paddles, under the side decking.

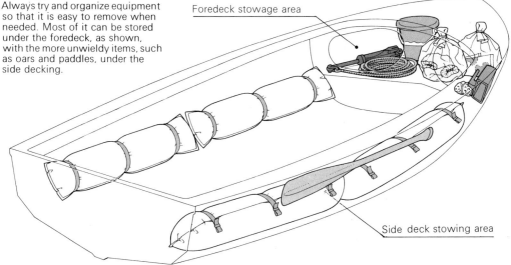

Foredeck stowage area

Side deck stowing area

Bailing

All open boats collect water. Any water in the bottom of the boat should be removed as the weight of water slopping to the side makes the boat hard to handle. Bailing can be done either by hand (using a plastic bucket and scooping the water over the side) or by using a patent bailing system. Some boats are fitted with automatic self-bailers which suck the water out as the boat gathers speed. Racing boats usually have hinged flaps in the transom to let the water out. They are large enough to rid the boat of excess water very quickly.

Methods of bailing
Hand bailing must always be done over the leeward side of the boat. Self-bailers (right) drain automatically but transom flaps (below right) must be opened by pulling the elastic cord attachment.

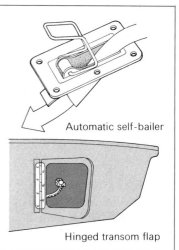

Automatic self-bailer

Hand bailing

Hinged transom flap

Buoyancy

All boats need some form of additional buoyancy. This can either be incorporated into the hull structure, as integral air tanks, or it can take the form of buoyant material, such as inflated plastic bags or polystyrene blocks, strapped to the hull. As important as the amount of buoyancy in the boat is its distribution.

Buoyancy at each end of the boat will float it in the event of a capsize, but ideally there should be sufficient additional side buoyancy to float the boat, when capsized, with the centerboard about 30 cm (1 ft) above the surface of the water. When righted, the boat should only contain about 30 cm (1 ft) of water.

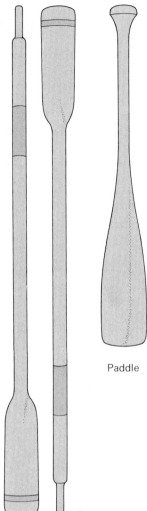

Paddle

Oars

Types of buoyancy

Buoyancy bags which are strapped into the boat should be checked from time to time to make sure that they are attached securely. In the case of inflatable buoyancy bags, there must be enough air in them to float the boat adequately. Integral buoyancy tanks are fitted with bungs, which should be taken out when the boat is ashore so that the air can circulate. Alternatively they are fitted with inspection hatches.

Polystyrene block buoyancy

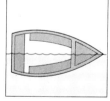

Inspection hatch
in buoyancy tank

Distribution of buoyancy

1 Bow and stern only. The boat floats level when capsized and is easy to right, but there is too much water when righted.

2 Bow, stern and side. The boat floats level in the water when capsized, is easy to right and can be bailed out without difficulty.

3 Full length integral side tanks. The boat is free of water when righted but floats very high when capsized and is difficult to right.

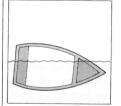

Too little buoyancy

Correct buoyancy

Too much buoyancy

Folding anchor

Folding anchors are useful as they take up less space, but a light Danforth anchor (see page 198) could be used if preferred.

Anchor
(extended)

Anchor
(folded)

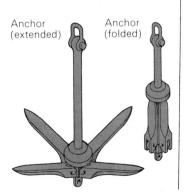

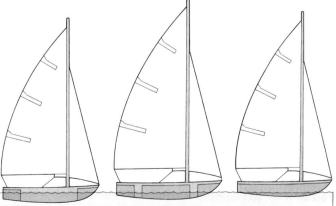
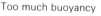

Rigging the mainsail

The sails are normally stored in the sailbag and must be rigged on the boat each time you go sailing. The way in which the mainsail is rigged will depend on the way the boat is designed but it is always first unrolled inside the boat, with the luff nearest the mast. If the sail has to be reefed (see pages 92–3), this should be done after the sail has been hoisted. The point at which the sail is fully hoisted depends on the launching conditions (see pages 74–85).

Order of rigging
The order of steps in rigging a mainsail is normally as shown left, but different classes of boat may have other requirements.

1 Sail onto boom
2 Battens into pockets
3 Head into track
4 Boom onto gooseneck
5 Hoist mainsail
6 Attach boom vang

Sail onto boom

The sail is fitted into a track on the upper side of the boom. It is important to make sure that the sail is fully stretched when fitting it onto the boom. There is normally a marker at the end of the boom to indicate how far the sail should be pulled out. The sail must be fastened securely in position at both ends.

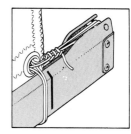

1 Slide clew of sail into mast end of boom, pulling it to marker at opposite end of boom.

2 Secure tack of sail to mast end of boom by inserting tack pin through sail and boom.

3 Pull foot of sail taut and fasten clew outhaul to boom and secure.

Battens

The battens act as sail stiffeners so that the shaped edge of the sail does not curl over. Most sails have three battens slotted or tied into stitched pockets.

Fiberglass tapered batten

Wooden batten with tie-ins

Plastic batten

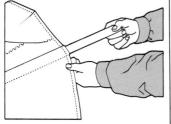

Fitting battens
Insert batten into pocket as far as possible and then push well down inside pocket to secure.

Sail onto mast

The mainsail is inserted into the mast track but normally only partially hoisted (right) while the boat is being rigged : a fully hoisted mainsail would flap out of control and should, therefore, only be hoisted at or after launching.

Headboard into track
Shackle the head of the sail to the main halyard (normally on the right hand side of the mast). Then thread the headboard into the mast track. Make sure that the main halyard is neither twisted nor fouling the rigging. Pull on the halyard at the base of the mast while feeding the luff of the sail into the mast track. Fasten halyard around cleat.

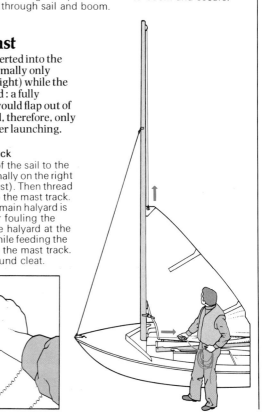

The gooseneck

The gooseneck is a fitting on the mast which allows the boom to move in any direction. It is attached to the mast below the mast track and is either fixed or sliding. The gooseneck fits into a shaped fitting on the boom which allows the boom to be rotated to make reefing easier (see page 93). It is locked with a square shank to prevent it unrolling.

Head

Luff

Batten

Leech

Tack

Boom

Clew

Fixed gooseneck

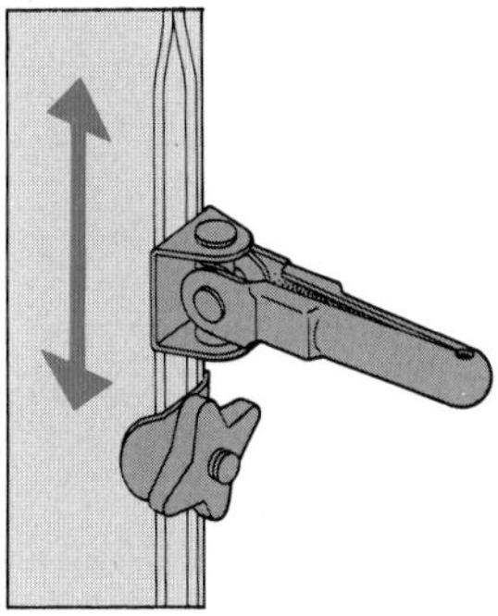

Sliding gooseneck

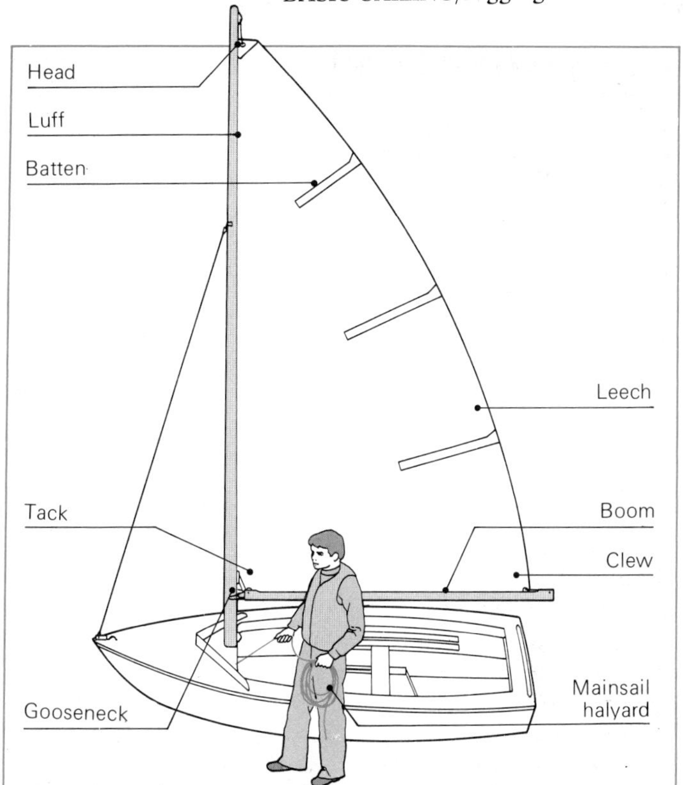

Gooseneck

Mainsail halyard

Hoisting the mainsail

When the sail is hoisted enough to lift the boom out of the boat, insert the prong of the gooseneck into the fitting on the boom. Hold the boom steady while pulling the sail to the fully hoisted position (above). Cleat the halyard and coil the spare line (see page 171 for instructions), stowing it neatly on the cleat as shown (right).

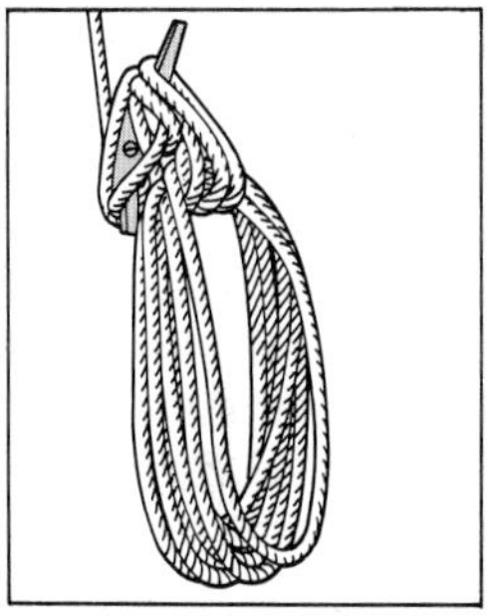

Boom vang

The boom vang is a device to prevent the boom rising when the mainsheet is let out, particularly when jibing (see pages 68–9). It is secured at one end to the base of the mast (or the kingpost on a deck-stepped mast), and to a keyhole fitting on the underside of the boom at the other.
The type of boom vang varies with the class of boat.
It can be tensioned as required. Two pulley blocks and a jammer provide a simple control.

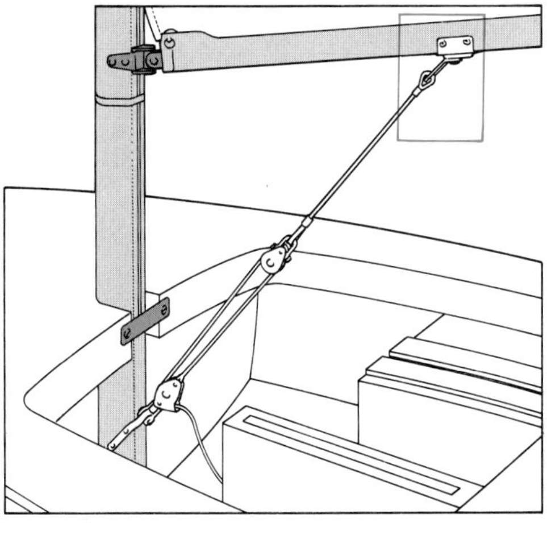

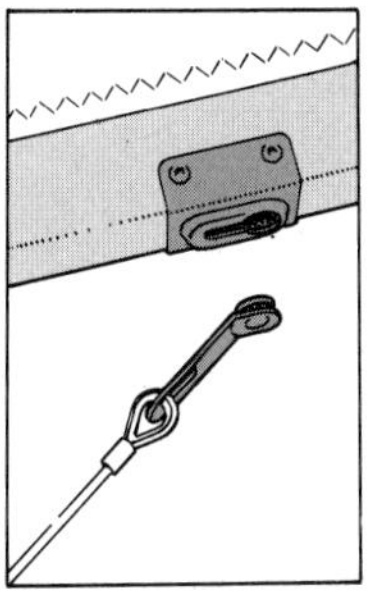

Fit the upper end into the keyhole opening on the boom (above) and the lower end to the base of the mast (left).

49

Mainsheet systems

The mainsheet is used by the helmsman to adjust and tension the sail correctly. There are two principal types of mainsheet system: aft or center, but center mainsheet systems are used mainly on racing boats. Both types of system usually have pulley blocks to give the helmsman more control over the mainsail and they often also include a traveller, a track across the boat along which the lower pulley block slides. The mainsheet system is normally left rigged on the boat.

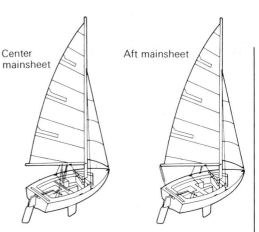

Center mainsheet

Aft mainsheet

Center mainsheet

There are several types of center mainsheet systems. Generally the lower pulley block is mounted on the centerboard casing and the upper blocks mounted individually onto the boom.

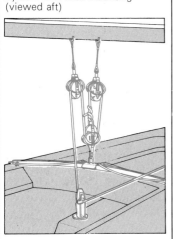

System with side mounting (viewed aft)

System with athwartships traveller (viewed forward)

Aft mainsheet

Aft mainsheet systems are found on most general purpose boats. They vary from very simple systems to much more sophisticated ones.

Basic system
This is the simplest form of aft mainsheet system and gives little control. It is usually found on very small boats.

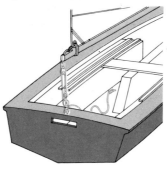

System with pulleys
This type helps the helmsman control the mainsheet but does not prevent the boom rising and the sail twisting.

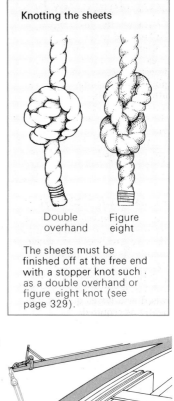

System with transom traveller
This type gives the greatest control as the double pulley blocks run on a transom traveller which helps prevent the boom rising and the sail twisting.

Knotting the sheets

Double overhand

Figure eight

The sheets must be finished off at the free end with a stopper knot such as a double overhand or figure eight knot (see page 329).

Rigging the jib

The jib is normally attached to the forestay with patent fastenings known as jib hanks. The jib itself is controlled by sheets attached to the clew of the sail. The sheets, which are controlled by the crew, lead around the mast, inside or outside the shrouds, to fairleads mounted on the side decks or tanks. The jib sheets are used to tension the jib correctly. Various modifications can be made to the position of the fairleads so that the angle of the jib can be altered to suit different requirements.

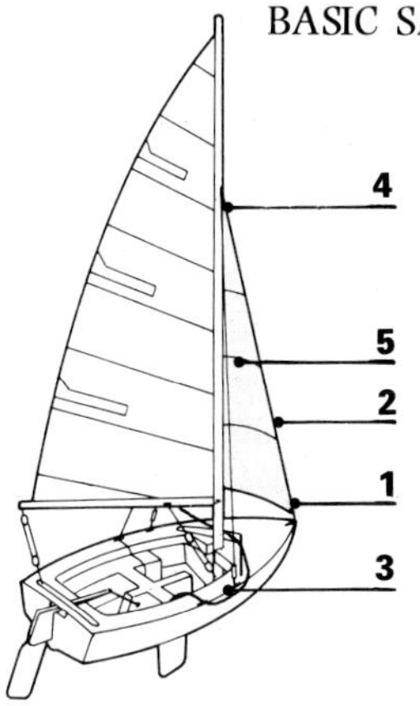

Order of rigging
The order of rigging the jib is usually as follows:

1 Shackle to bow
2 Fasten hanks
3 Fasten sheets
4 Shackle head to halyard
5 Hoist jib

Shackling to the bow

The tack of the jib should be fastened to the bow fitting. This has three eyes to which the forestay, the tack of the jib and the painter are attached. Normally the forestay is attached at (1), the tack of the jib at (2), and the painter at (3) but the position of each eye varies with the design of the boat.

Fastening the jib sheets

The jib sheets are fastened at the clew with a shackle or bowline knot (see page 331). They are led through fairleads and finished off with a stopping knot (see Knotting sheets, opposite). A jamming cleat holds the sheet in position, if required.

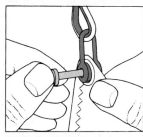

Fastening the hanks

Plastic or stainless steel hanks are used to fasten the jib to the forestay (shackles were formerly used). The hanks are fitted at right angles and then twisted to lock them onto the wire. The fastenings permit the jib to be raised or lowered quickly and neatly as required.

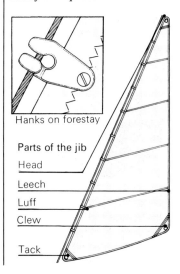

Hanks on forestay

Parts of the jib

Head

Leech

Luff

Clew

Tack

Hoisting the jib

Before hoisting the jib by pulling on the halyard, the head of the sail must be attached to the jib halyard. You should check first to make sure the jib halyard is not twisted. If the jib is not being hoisted straightaway, secure it to the forestay with a sheet. When the jib is hoisted, cleat the spare line.

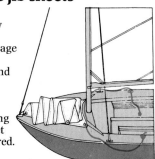

Shackling the halyard
If the head of the sail is attached to the halyard with a D shackle, make sure the shackle pin is tightened properly so it does not loosen when the jib flaps.

Moving a boat

All sailing boats are easily damaged when they are out of the water, especially when they are being moved about. The most vulnerable parts of the boat are: the bottom (mainly where the stern joins the transom), the bow (which is often damaged when turning corners) and the centerboard (which can slip down and drag along the ground if not properly secured in the retracted position).

Overhead obstructions, such as power cables, can be a source of danger as well as damage, and should always be borne in mind when stepping the mast or moving a rigged boat. If you are rigging a boat, particularly when close to a house or on the side of the road, you should always look above you as well as around you.

There are a number of different ways of moving the boat on land, from carrying it to wheeling it around on a specially constructed dolly. The method used depends on the weight of the boat, the distance it has to be carried, the type of ground and the number of people around to help.

All methods of moving a boat need more than one person, and most require several people. As with any operation involving a number of people, one of them should assume responsibility for coordinating the combined effort.

Carrying

At least four adults are needed to carry an average one-design. It is important to ensure that everyone is carrying an equal amount of weight. As a general rule, the front half of the boat is the heaviest (see below), so the lifting power should be concentrated there. Some boats are fitted with wooden carrying handles or bell ropes but most have nothing except the inner or outer edge of the side decking to grip onto. As soon as everyone has a comfortable hold, lift the boat and move it forward at walking pace. A long haul requires frequent stops and changes of side.

Gripping handle

Gripping bell rope

Gripping inner decking

Gripping outer decking

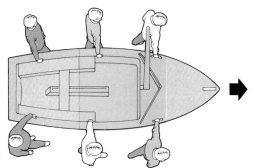

Rolling

When moving a heavy boat over sand, the use of three large rollers makes the task easy.

How to roll the boat
Place the first roller as far back under the bow as possible. Roll the boat forward until the first roller reaches the balance point. Insert a second roller under the bow. Roll the boat forward again and insert a third roller. Continue to move the boat forward until the first roller emerges at the stern. Then repeat the process.

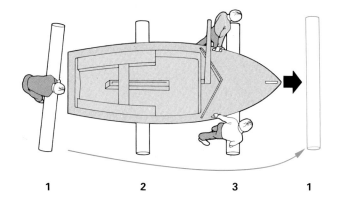

1   2   3   1

Wheeling

Wheeling a boat on a dolly is one of the most common methods of moving a boat. The boat must be correctly mounted onto and securely tied to the dolly (pages 38–9) and the wheels must be suitable for the surface. Small wheels are only suitable for hard ground, while very large wheels are better for soft sand and large inflatable wheels can be used on most surfaces.

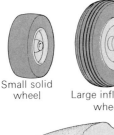

Small solid wheel   Large inflatable wheel

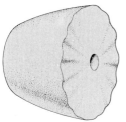

Very large plastic wheel

Launching

Before taking the dinghy onto a ramp, check to make sure it does not end abruptly and note the wind direction. If the incline is very steep and slippery, launch the boat with a line attached to it from the towing hitch of a car, for example, or held by someone on firm ground. Make sure the boat is fully prepared for launching (pages 44–55) before taking it down the ramp, and after launching return the dolly to the berth space – never leave it at the top of the ramp.

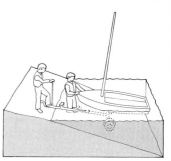

2 Float the boat off the dolly while the other person holds the dolly steady.

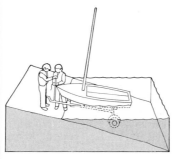

1 Untie the painter from the dolly. Hold the free end while the other person pushes the loaded dolly into the water.

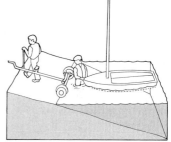

3 Move the boat to one side of the ramp to clear the gangway while the other person returns the dolly to the berth space.

Moving a catamaran

Because most catamarans are much wider than monohull boats they present handling problems. The newer designs are intended to be taken apart and stowed on specially designed trailers for towing. This type of trailer (right) comprises an 'A' frame supporting a box to accommodate the beams, trampoline, rudder and sails, and two cross beams to support the hulls. Some trailers have extending cross beams which allow the catamaran to be rigged and launched from the trailer. A catamaran launching dolly (far right) comprises a single axle passing through two large diameter wheels. The two shaped hull supports are made of fiberglass. The weight of the boat, once loaded, keeps it in position, if it is correctly mounted on the dolly.

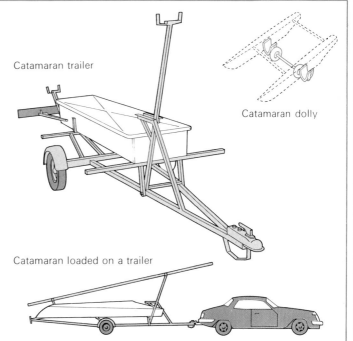

Catamaran trailer

Catamaran dolly

Catamaran loaded on a trailer

Rudder and tiller

The rudder is one of the principal boat controls and has to be adjusted constantly by means of the tiller when the boat is being sailed. The rudder is effective only when the boat is moving and can be used either for steering, or as an accelerator or brake. It also helps to prevent sideways slip in the water and has to be able to withstand pressure.

The majority of sailing boats are fitted with a rudder which has a pivoting retractable blade to enable the boat to be sailed into and away from shallow water. The blade normally extends some 60 cm (2 ft) below the stern of the boat. The depth of the rudder is important as at least part of the rudder blade must remain in the water when the boat heels. During sailing, the blade is held down by means of a shock cord (or lanyard) which is cleated to the side or underside of the tiller.

Parts of the rudder

The rudder and tiller are fitted together at the hood (1). The rudder stock (2) is fitted with a blade which can be raised (3) or lowered (4). A shock cord (5) keeps the rudder in position.

Tiller extension
Most boats have an extension fitted to the tiller so that the helmsman can steer the boat when sitting well out. The extension is attached to the tiller by a universal joint (right) which permits movement in any direction (below).

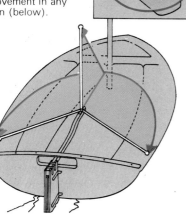

Fitting the rudder

The rudder is attached to the center line of the transom with two special hinges each comprising a metal rod (the pintle) which fits into an eye (the gudgeon). The rudder is best attached before the boat is afloat.

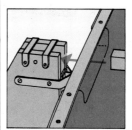

1 Align the pintles and gudgeons and drop the rudder into position.

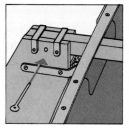

2 Push the tiller into the rudder hood through the slot in the transom.

3 Secure the tiller in place with the split pin.

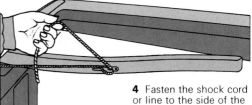

4 Fasten the shock cord or line to the side of the tiller to keep the blade in the down position.

Centerboards

Most one-designs are so light that their immersed areas offer little sideways resistance to wind and water. In the early days of sailing, oars or leeboards were used to prevent sideways drift but it was soon realized that a centrally placed board was most effective. In larger boats this takes the form of a fixed keel, but in sailing one-designs a retractable wood or metal board or plate in a watertight casing provides a better

solution. It can either be in the form of a simple, sliding board (known as a daggerboard) or a shaped centerboard which is pivoted at its forward end. In either case, the board can be adjusted to suit the course relative to the wind. For example, the closer to the wind the boat sails, the more depth of board is needed, whereas the further away from the wind, the less is needed (see Changing course, pages 64–5).

Adjusting the board

The depth of centerboard can be adjusted by pushing it backwards or forwards. The board pivots in a rigid, fixed casing (right). It can also be controlled by ropes attached to the side decking (below) which allows the crew to control the board without moving their position.

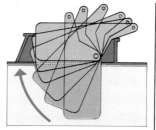

Daggerboard

The daggerboard is most common in very small boats as it takes up less room than a centerboard. It slides up and down in a watertight casing (below), held in position with a shock cord. Great care should be taken when the board is fully retracted or the boom may hit it.

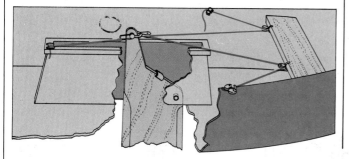

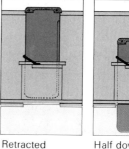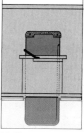

Retracted   Half down

Rowing and paddling

There will be a number of occasions when you may need to row or paddle your boat. Different methods of paddling are used according to the number of people and the position of the sails. With one person paddle over the stern with the sails down and the rudder stowed (right). (For paddling with two people, see page 77.)

Paddling stern first
Move the paddle from side to side, twisting it at the end of each sweep to draw the boat along.

How to row
1 Lean forward with arms extended.
2 Dip blades into water and straighten body, pulling on oars.
3 Complete stroke by leaning back and pulling arms into chest.
4 Push hands down to lift blades out of water and repeat from step 1.

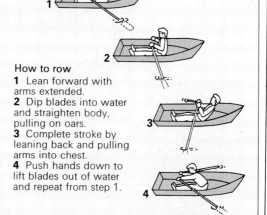

Primary controls

If you go back to the concept of the basic boat on pages 34–5 and ignore all the ancillary equipment in and around the hull, you can see that there are four major parts: the hull itself, the sails, the centerboard and the rudder. These four principal parts have been designed so that, if they are controlled correctly, the boat will respond by sailing an accurate course. But if, for any reason, the relationship between the controls is unbalanced, the performance of the boat will be affected and it will slow down, or turn towards or away from the wind.

A number of sailors never really grasp how these forces inter-react and, instead, they often use the rudder (the most obvious directional control) to correct their mistakes and, as a result, do not get the best out of their boat.

The following pages give a broad outline of the way various forces alter the boat's performance. It would be sensible to study them first before taking your boat onto the water. Any sailor who wishes to apply these concepts to his basic boat handling should practice sailing without the rudder to appreciate the turning forces the different controls exert.

The hull itself, while not strictly a control, helps determine the progress of the boat in the water. If its waterline shape (the immersed area of the hull) is changed for any reason, it will affect the performance of the boat, in the same way as the other controls do.

Position of the hull

Bow level
Correctly balanced, boat has right waterline shape. It travels at its fastest and sails a straight course

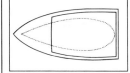

Bow down
With crew forward, boat has a short waterline shape. Bow dips and boat travels slower and turns towards wind.

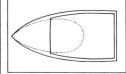

Bow up
With crew aft, boat has a short waterline shape. Stern drags and boat slows down. It turns away from wind.

Heeling forces

On an even keel, the waterline shape of the hull is symmetrical. But as soon as the boat heels to windward or leeward or when sailing in rough water the waterline shape changes and the immersed area alters. This creates an assymmetrical waterline shape, as the side of the hull which is closer to the water's surface presents a more curved waterline shape and the opposite side of the boat, a straighter waterline shape. The rudder and centerboard are no longer central: they are closer to the straighter edge and the boat will veer to this side.

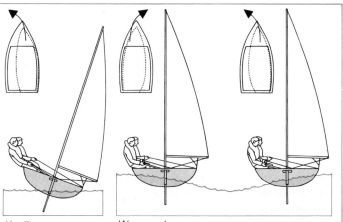

Heeling away
As the boat heels away from the wind the waterline shape turns the bow towards the wind.

Wave on beam
As the wave nears the beam of the boat, the windward side is immersed. Bow turns away from the wind.

As the wave passes, the leeward side is immersed. The boat then turns towards the wind.

Turning forces

To understand the way the boat's performance can be affected by the various controls, it helps to take an example of a boat on a particular course and see how the main controls, when altered in different ways, produce different turning forces. On a close reach (see Points of sailing, pages 62–3), the boat should be sailed with the centerboard three-quarters down, the tiller centered and the sails not fully pulled in. The hull of the boat should be on an even keel. A change in any one of these factors will prevent the boat from sailing an accurate course, turning it towards or away from the wind.

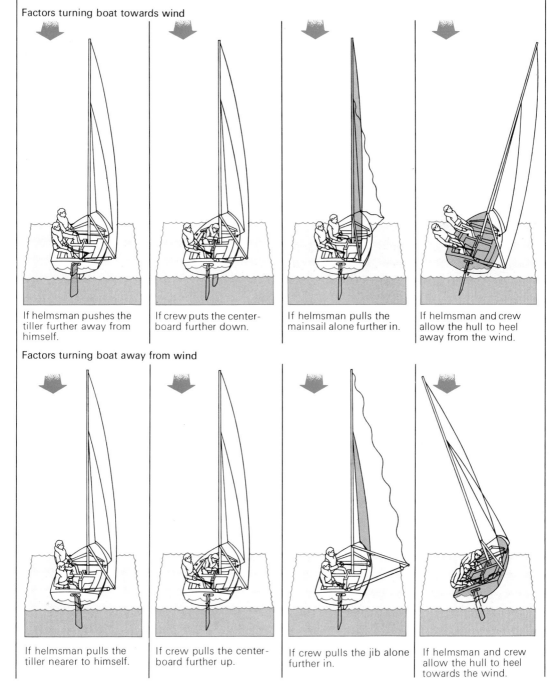

Factors turning boat towards wind

| If helmsman pushes the tiller further away from himself. | If crew puts the center-board further down. | If helmsman pulls the mainsail alone further in. | If helmsman and crew allow the hull to heel away from the wind. |

Factors turning boat away from wind

| If helmsman pulls the tiller nearer to himself. | If crew pulls the center-board further up. | If crew pulls the jib alone further in. | If helmsman and crew allow the hull to heel towards the wind. |

Function of the sails

Sails are the propulsion unit of
the boat. When set at the correct
angle to the wind, they convert
its energy into heeling and
forward driving forces. Most
boats have two sails, one fore,
and the other aft, of the mast,
and they must be properly
balanced. If set separately or if
out of balance, the sails exert a
strong turning influence on the
hull. This turning force can be
used to great advantage in some
situations but it is important to
make sure the sails work
correctly, and that the other
primary controls are also
coordinated with them, to
ensure that the boat sails an
accurate course.

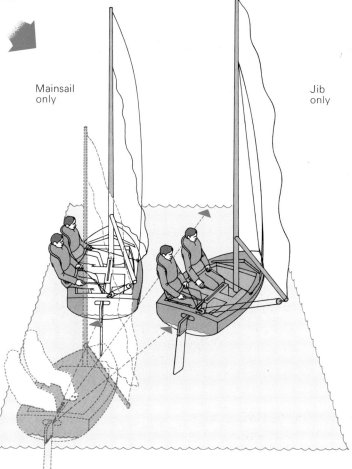

Mainsail
only

Jib
only

Mainsail only
The effect of using the mainsail
only can be seen by turning into
the basic hove-to position with
the tiller centered. Leave the jib
slack, but pull in the mainsail. The
boat moves forward and turns
towards the wind.

Jib only
The effect of using the jib alone
can be seen by putting the boat
into the basic hove-to position
with the tiller centered. Leave the
mainsail slack, but pull in the jib.
The boat moves forward and turns
away from the wind.

Setting sails

Your sails are setting
correctly when they are
pulled in to the point
where the luffs stop
fluttering. As an addi-
tional guide, tell-tales
can be sewn onto the
jib or the mainsail.
These are fine strands of
wool which fly free on
either side of the sail.
When the tell-tales are
parallel the sail is setting
correctly. The illustration
(right) shows how to set
tell-tales on a jib but the
method is the same for
both jib and mainsail.

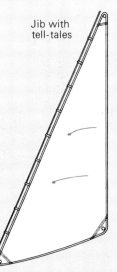

Jib with
tell-tales

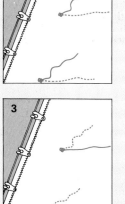

Checking sail setting
1 Tell-tales parallel.
Jib set correctly.

2 Tell-tales on wind-
ward side too high.
Pull in jib sheet.

3 Tell-tales on lee-
ward side too high.
Let out jib sheet.

Function of the centerboard

The centerboard has a significant effect on the ability of the boat to sail close to the wind. If you try to turn the boat towards the wind with the centerboard fully up the boat will move crabwise not forward, as the sails, particularly the jib, will pull the bow away from the wind. Lowering the centerboard makes the bow swing towards the wind. In the early stages of learning to sail, most people forget to lower the centerboard when getting away from the shore. If the boat does not respond and something feels wrong, check that the centerboard is down.

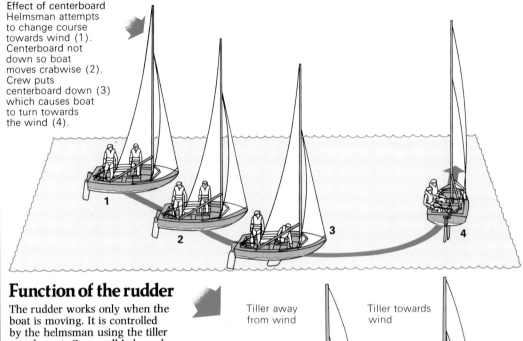

Effect of centerboard
Helmsman attempts to change course towards wind (1). Centerboard not down so boat moves crabwise (2). Crew puts centerboard down (3) which causes boat to turn towards the wind (4).

Function of the rudder

The rudder works only when the boat is moving. It is controlled by the helmsman using the tiller attachment. On a well-balanced boat it follows the natural movement of the boat as the combined changes of wind, speed and direction and the action of the waves turn it to windward and leeward. Major changes in direction and course are made by using the rudder in conjunction with other primary controls. Tiller movements should be smooth so that the rudder operates efficiently.

Tiller away from the wind
With the tiller pushed away from the wind (and the helmsman), the front of the boat moves towards the wind, the sails flap if not adjusted and the boat stops if it turns right into the wind.

Tiller towards the wind
If the tiller is pulled towards the wind (and the helmsman), the front of the boat moves away from the wind causing the boat to gain speed. The sails must be let out to keep them set correctly.

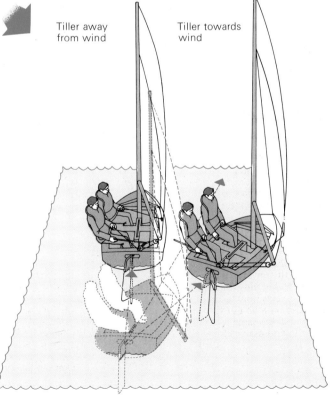

Tiller away from wind

Tiller towards wind

The role of helmsman and crew

To sail a two-man boat successfully both helmsman and crew have to coordinate their activities. To do so, they must first understand what their own function is in the boat. The helmsman is in charge of the boat and instructs the crew, informing him of any changes in course. He sits aft of the centerboard and controls the mainsheet and tiller. The crew sits further forward controlling the jib sheet and centerboard. He is responsible for changing and setting sails and usually controls any additional sails which may be used (such as a spinnaker, for example, see pages 112–9). Both helmsman and crew have to make sure that there are no obstacles in the path of the boat, and they are both responsible for balancing the boat so that the hull is in the correct attitude (see pages 56–7), if necessary by hiking out. In racing boats, which have larger sail areas and therefore heel more, the crew may have to transfer his weight out over the side of the boat by using a trapeze (see pages 107–9 for techniques).

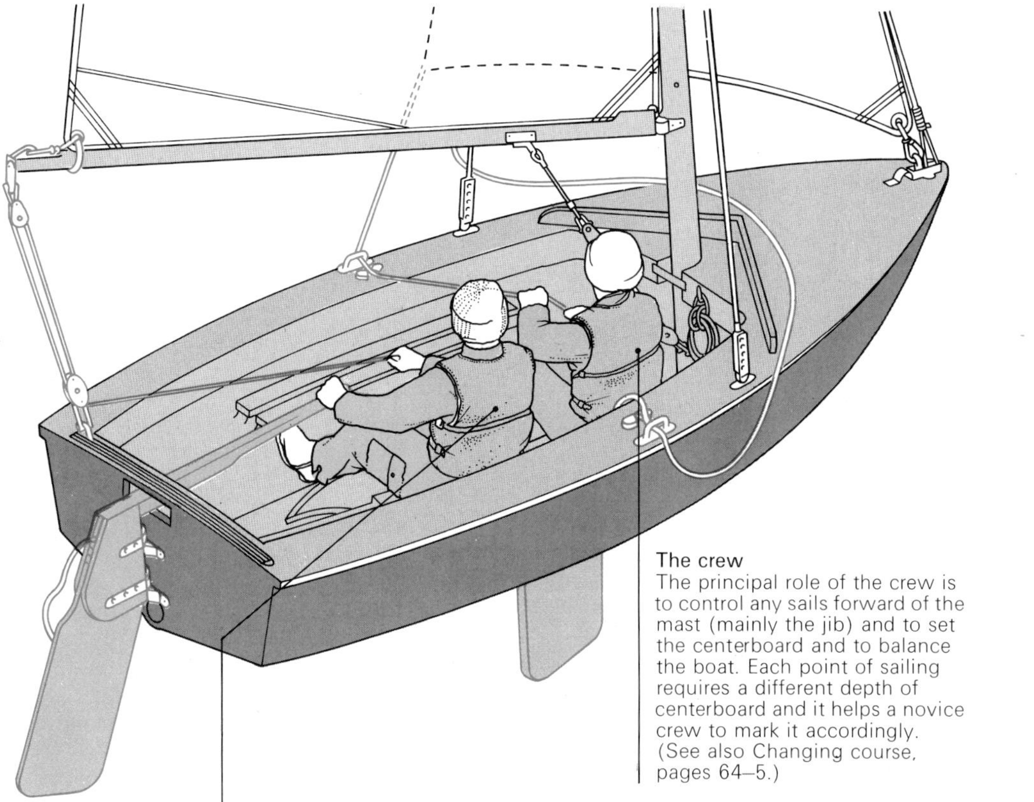

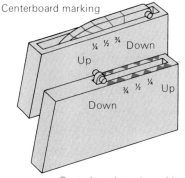

The crew
The principal role of the crew is to control any sails forward of the mast (mainly the jib) and to set the centerboard and to balance the boat. Each point of sailing requires a different depth of centerboard and it helps a novice crew to mark it accordingly. (See also Changing course, pages 64–5.)

Centerboard marking

¼ ½ ¾ Down
Up

¾ ½ ¼ Up
Down

Centerboard trunk marking

The helmsman
In a typical two-man boat, the helmsman sits at the transom end of the boat holding the tiller (or the tiller extension) in the hand nearest the stern, and the mainsheet in the hand nearest the bow. As well as steering the boat and setting the mainsail, he must make all decisions to do with sailing the boat. His instructions to the crew must be firm and clear, and given sufficiently early for the crew to respond in time.

Balancing the boat

One of the most important factors in correct sailing is the fore and aft trim and balance of the boat. It is the job of both helmsman and crew to keep the hull in the right attitude at all times, and they will have to be alert to any wind changes so that they can move themselves smoothly and rapidly around the boat. It is primarily the job of the crew to correct the trim and balance by moving fore and aft in the boat, and from one side to the other, sitting out if necessary using the toe straps (bottom) to secure himself. The further from the wind the boat sails, the less its tendency to heel, and curiously to the inexperienced sailor, the less stable it becomes so crew movements must be smooth and controlled.

Downwind positions
When the boat is on a run (with the wind astern) there is usually no heeling force. Helmsman and crew sit either on opposite sides or with the crew in the center to balance the boat.

Upwind positions
In moderate wind conditions, on a windward course, such as a reach or a close-haul, the heeling force will usually be great enough, in moderate wind conditions, to demand that both helmsman and crew hike out.

Sitting each side

Hiking out

Toe straps
To prevent the crew from falling overboard when they are hiking out, the boat is fitted with toe straps. These run along the bottom of the boat, on each side of the centerboard, and are secured at both ends as well as in the middle.

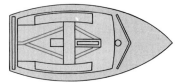

Wind indicators

It is essential for helmsman and crew to know exactly where the wind is coming from. This can easily be done either by natural observation or by using wind indicators. Many experienced sailors prefer to depend on observation of natural indicators. For example, moored boats (in non-tidal waters) point into the wind; smoke blows away from the wind, as does a flag, while waves on open water are at 90° to the wind. The sail positions of other boats also show wind direction.

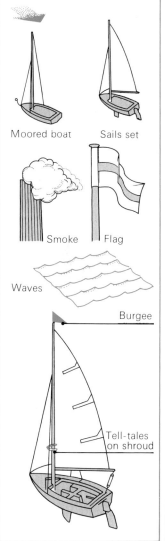

Moored boat   Sails set

Smoke   Flag

Waves

Burgee

Tell-tales on shroud

Basic sailing techniques

As soon as a sailing boat is launched, it comes under the influence of one dominating force, the wind. The wind governs everything that happens to the boat, and the direction and progress of the boat is dependent upon it. The wind is, however, both unpredictable and invisible so one of the first lessons a novice sailor has to learn is how to establish wind direction and strength.

An experienced sailor automatically uses all his senses to keep track of the wind but if you are a beginner you not only have to make a conscious effort to detect the wind but you need to learn to orientate yourself and your boat towards it. You can speed up the learning process by observation when not sailing (see wind indicators, page 61).

Once you have established the direction of the wind, the next step is to appreciate the constraints it will place on the course you sail. The position of the boat relative to the wind will determine the course it sails and these courses, known as points of sailing, require different settings for the sails and centerboard, and different distributions of crew weight to permit the boat to sail efficiently.

Once you have learned about wind direction, you can start sailing your boat on a specific course to develop an awareness of the proper set of the sails and the appropriate trim of the boat. As you progress, you will learn how to change direction towards and away from the wind and how to reorientate yourself in the process. You will also gradually learn how to steer a course to reach a particular objective as quickly as possible, and how to detect changes in wind direction and strength (see Advanced sailing, pages 100−48).

It is vital to remember that the boat cannot sail directly into the wind. In fact, most boats cannot sail at an angle of less than 45° to the wind so to achieve an objective lying within this area you must make a series of zigzag maneuvers towards the wind (known as tacking or beating) to bring you gradually to your chosen objective (see pages 66−7).

Points of sailing

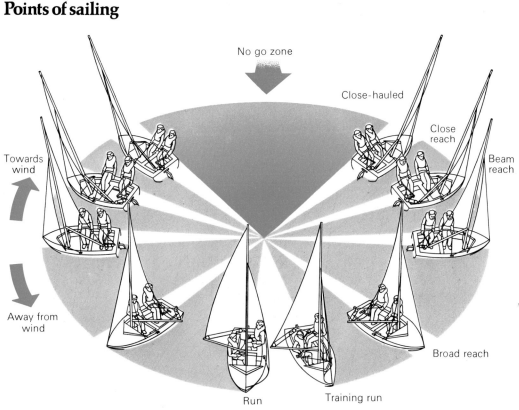

No go zone

Close-hauled

Close reach

Towards wind

Beam reach

Away from wind

Broad reach

Run

Training run

No go zone

The "no go zone" is the name given to the area about 45° on either side of the wind into which you cannot sail. If the boat sails too close to the no go zone, the luff of the jib will begin to flutter and the boat will begin to lose headway. At this point, the tiller must be pulled towards you to bring the bow away from the wind and to permit the sails to refill on a close-hauled course (right).

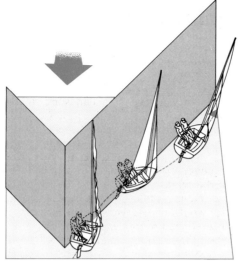

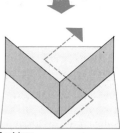

Tacking
Travelling in a series of zigzags towards the wind is known as tacking (see pages 66–7) and is the method used to reach an objective within the no go zone.

Starting and stopping

The normal starting point for all maneuvers is the basic hove-to position (see page 64). To start the boat moving, the helmsman pulls the tiller towards him to turn the boat away from the wind. The sails are trimmed and the boat sails off (below left). To start from a head-to-wind position is more difficult as it is necessary to pull the jib across the windward side, so that the bow blows away from the wind (below center).

Both sails can then be set and trimmed so that the boat moves forward. You can stop either by returning to the basic hove-to position, or by turning head-to-wind and allowing the sails to flap (below right).

Moving off from the basic hove-to position

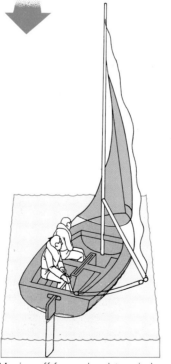

Moving off from a head-to-wind position by backing the jib.

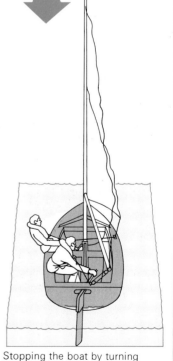

Stopping the boat by turning head-to-wind

Changing course

Having understood the various points of sailing, the next step is to learn how to set the sails and adjust the centerboard and crew weight every time a change of course is made. Taking the beam reach as a point of reference, courses which lie towards the wind are referred to as windward courses and those which lie in a direction away from the wind are known as leeward (or offwind) courses. It is sometimes necessary to stop briefly to rest, attend to something in the boat or to let a gust pass, and the simplest and quickest way of doing so is to put the boat into the basic hove-to position (bottom right).

Towards the wind

Turning the boat towards the wind is also known as going to windward or luffing up (see below). Starting from a basic hove-to position, the boat is steered onto a beam reach and the sails pulled in until they set (see page 58). To change course towards the wind the tiller is pushed gently away and the sails pulled in further as the boat turns. More centerboard is lowered to provide additional resistance and the tiller centered once the boat is on course.

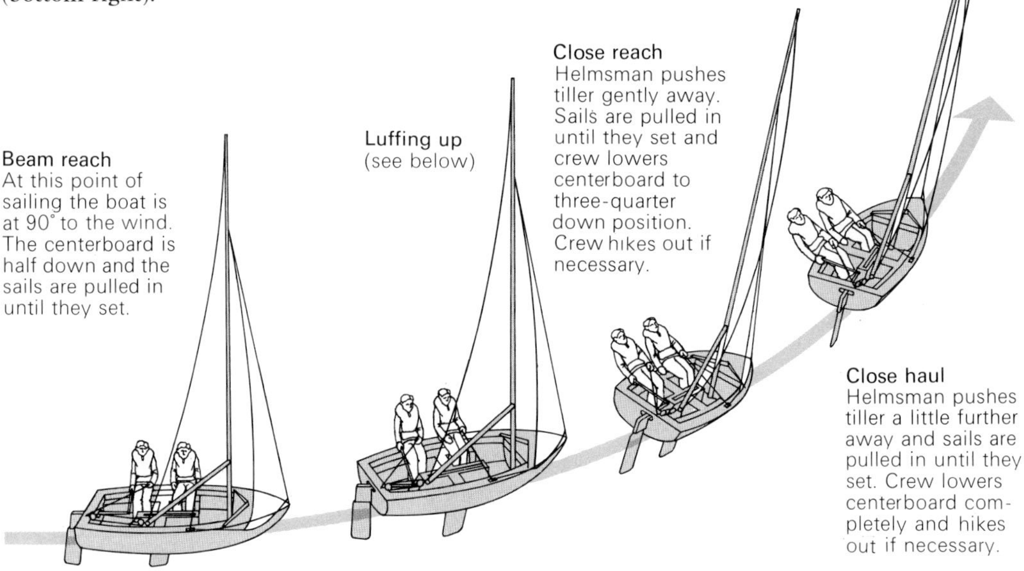

Beam reach
At this point of sailing the boat is at 90° to the wind. The centerboard is half down and the sails are pulled in until they set.

Luffing up
(see below)

Close reach
Helmsman pushes tiller gently away. Sails are pulled in until they set and crew lowers centerboard to three-quarter down position. Crew hikes out if necessary.

Close haul
Helmsman pushes tiller a little further away and sails are pulled in until they set. Crew lowers centerboard completely and hikes out if necessary.

How to luff up

In order to turn towards the wind (known as luffing up), the helmsman must push the tiller gently *away* from him. Both sails are gradually pulled in until they set on the chosen course and the crew lowers the centerboard by degrees to the correct position.

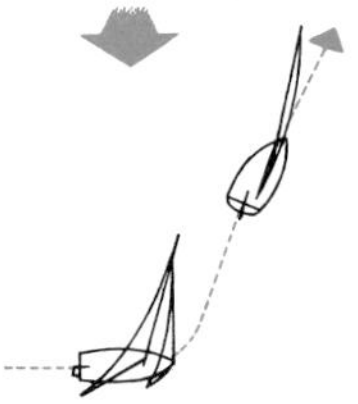

Basic hove-to

To heave-to, sail slightly to windward of a beam reach. The sails should be let out until the boom just clears the leeward shroud and the jib starts to flap. The boat will now only move very gently forward. An alternative method of heaving-to, more suitable for a longer stop, is shown in cruising, page 206.

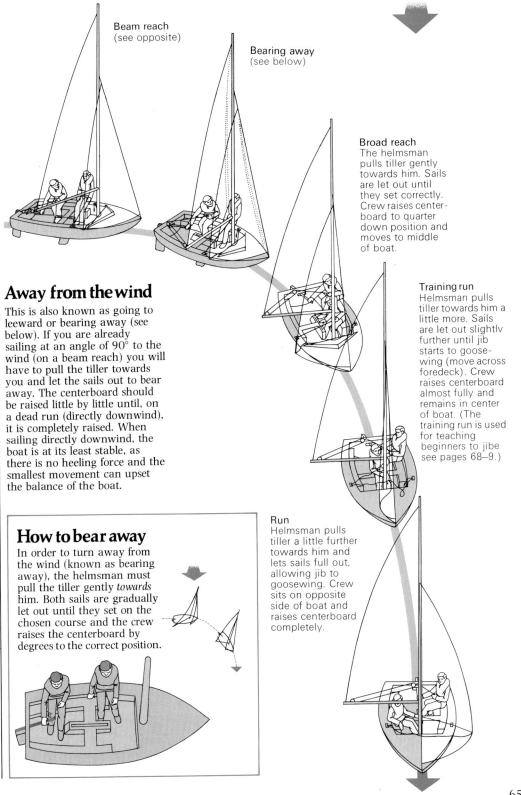

Beam reach
(see opposite)

Bearing away
(see below)

Broad reach
The helmsman
pulls tiller gently
towards him. Sails
are let out until
they set correctly.
Crew raises center-
board to quarter
down position and
moves to middle
of boat.

Training run
Helmsman pulls
tiller towards him a
little more. Sails
are let out slightly
further until jib
starts to goose-
wing (move across
foredeck). Crew
raises centerboard
almost fully and
remains in center
of boat. (The
training run is used
for teaching
beginners to jibe
see pages 68–9.)

Away from the wind

This is also known as going to
leeward or bearing away (see
below). If you are already
sailing at an angle of 90° to the
wind (on a beam reach) you will
have to pull the tiller towards
you and let the sails out to bear
away. The centerboard should
be raised little by little until, on
a dead run (directly downwind),
it is completely raised. When
sailing directly downwind, the
boat is at its least stable, as
there is no heeling force and the
smallest movement can upset
the balance of the boat.

How to bear away

In order to turn away from
the wind (known as bearing
away), the helmsman must
pull the tiller gently *towards*
him. Both sails are gradually
let out until they set on the
chosen course and the crew
raises the centerboard by
degrees to the correct position.

Run
Helmsman pulls
tiller a little further
towards him and
lets sails full out,
allowing jib to
goosewing. Crew
sits on opposite
side of boat and
raises centerboard
completely.

Tacking

Tacking is the term given to turning through the wind when sailing on a windward course. The actual process of tacking is simply a continuation of the luffing up maneuver (see pages 64–5) so that the boat turns sufficiently for the sails to fill on the opposite course (or tack).

The maneuver demands coordination on the part of helmsman and crew, who have to operate the boat controls smoothly and move their weight quickly across the boat. As in all maneuvers, the helmsman initiates and controls the activity while the crew carries out the instructions at the appropriate time. The helmsman, however, not only has to organize the activity within the boat, but is also responsible for taking other factors into account, such as the timing of the turn, whether the surrounding water is clear of obstacles and whether the wind direction has changed. Once the turn is completed he has to make sure that the sails are properly set for the new course, and the boat trimmed accordingly.

Occasionally the boat fails to make the turn, either because there was not sufficient headway, causing the boat to stop in the head to wind position (known as being "in irons"), or because the helmsman and crew failed to carry out their functions efficiently. The crew's job, which consists of releasing one jib sheet and grasping the other, and of moving across the boat, is relatively simple, but the helmsman has to control both the mainsheet and the tiller while moving across the boat. This can cause confusion for novice sailors and it is a good idea to practice the drill first (below).

The tacking sequence, shown opposite, is for a two-man boat with an aft-mounted mainsheet system, with the helmsman using the tiller without the extension (for methods using more complex controls, see pages 70 and 110 –1).

Land drill

To practice ashore, you need three stools, a broom handle and a length of rope, to represent the boat, as shown. The rope coil represents the boom end of the mainsheet. In the instructions "front" and "back" refer to the part nearest the bow and stern of the boat respectively.

1 Sit down on the side stool holding the tiller with your body well forward. Extend your front foot and tuck your back foot under.

2 Trap mainsheet in tiller hand as shown (far left) and push tiller away. Then move your body to the center of the boat.

Trapping mainsheet
To transfer the mainsheet to your tiller hand pass it over your tiller hand and trap it with the thumb.

3 Swivelling on the balls of your feet, change your hands on tiller as shown (left) and lift mainsheet away with free hand.

4 Sit down and centralize tiller. Allow free end of mainsheet to fall in area behind rear foot to keep it out of the way.

Changing hands
When you change hands put your free hand on the tiller under the mainsheet and lift the other away.

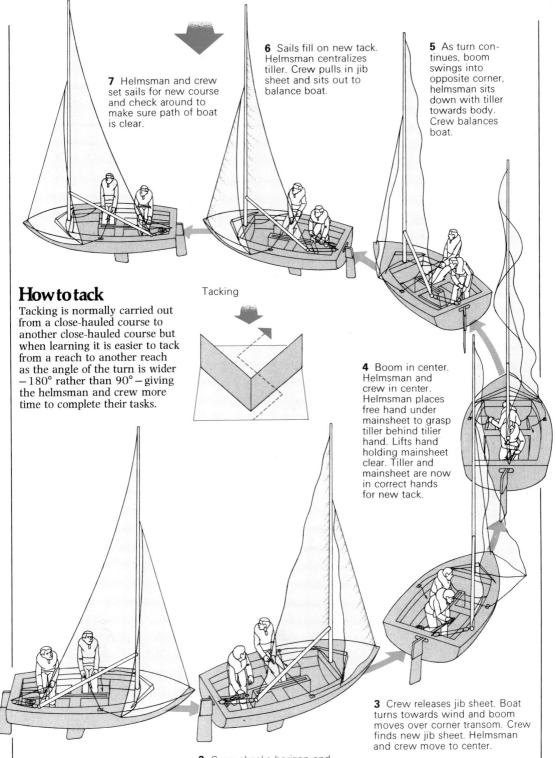

7 Helmsman and crew set sails for new course and check around to make sure path of boat is clear.

6 Sails fill on new tack. Helmsman centralizes tiller. Crew pulls in jib sheet and sits out to balance boat.

5 As turn continues, boom swings into opposite corner, helmsman sits down with tiller towards body. Crew balances boat.

How to tack

Tacking is normally carried out from a close-hauled course to another close-hauled course but when learning it is easier to tack from a reach to another reach as the angle of the turn is wider — 180° rather than 90° — giving the helmsman and crew more time to complete their tasks.

Tacking

4 Boom in center. Helmsman and crew in center. Helmsman places free hand under mainsheet to grasp tiller behind tiller hand. Lifts hand holding mainsheet clear. Tiller and mainsheet are now in correct hands for new tack.

3 Crew releases jib sheet. Boat turns towards wind and boom moves over corner transom. Crew finds new jib sheet. Helmsman and crew move to center.

1 Sailing on beam reach, sails set correctly. Helmsman checks new course is clear. Calls "Ready about".

2 Crew checks horizon and answers, "Yes". Helmsman transfers mainsheet to tiller hand, calls, "Hard-a-lee". Pushes tiller away.

Jibing

Jibing is the term given to making a major change of direction away from the wind (when sailing on a downwind course). The turn is made when the stern of the boat moves across the wind and the mainsail swings abruptly from one side of the boat to the other. Because of the speed of the maneuver, it is important that the boat is correctly balanced during jibing. The helmsman therefore needs to know the exact direction of the wind so that he can anticipate the point at which the boom will swing across the boat and coordinate his own actions and those of the crew.

Because jibing is a difficult maneuver to accomplish without unbalancing the boat in even quite moderate winds, it is better for beginners to learn the training jibe (opposite) in which the sails are sheeted in before the jibe making it less violent. There should be no delay between pulling in the mainsheet and starting the jibe or the boat will turn back into the wind. Experienced sailors often jibe without sheeting in the mainsail (pages 110–1).

As with tacking, the helmsman must make sure the surrounding water is clear before jibing. The helmsman and crew also need to be alert to other factors which might affect the success of the maneuver. For example, a common fault when jibing is to allow the boat to turn violently towards the wind as the boom swings across. By centralizing the tiller as the boom passes over the center of the boat, the helmsman can limit the turning movement of the boat and drive it forward in a straight line. Another point the helmsman should bear in mind is that the turn will be accelerated if the boat rolls to leeward and it will be more balanced if the boat heels to windward.

Land drill

To practice the land drill for jibing, you should set up the equipment in the same way as for tacking. The hand movements are similar to those for tacking (pages 66–7). Timing of movements in the actual boat will depend on the position of the boom. The instructions "front" and "back" refer to the part nearest the bow and stern of the boat respectively.

1 Sit on a side stool well clear of tiller. Grasp tiller in your back hand and mainsheet in your front hand. Tuck your back foot under and extend your front foot.

2 Pull in mainsheet to bring boom within 18in (46cm) of transom corner. Trap mainsheet under thumb and let free end fall by rear foot.

3 Pull tiller towards you and swivel your body to face stern. Slide your free hand under mainsheet and grasp tiller.

4 Lift hand holding mainsheet from tiller. When boom begins to swing across boat move to center of boat and centralize tiller.

5 Sit down on opposite side, let out mainsheet little by little to retain drive until sail is set on new course.

How to jibe

When learning to jibe, beginners usually find it easier to put the boat on a training run (at a slight angle to the wind) before the actual jibe takes place as there is then less risk of jibing accidentally. The boat (right) is travelling from a broad reach to another broad reach.

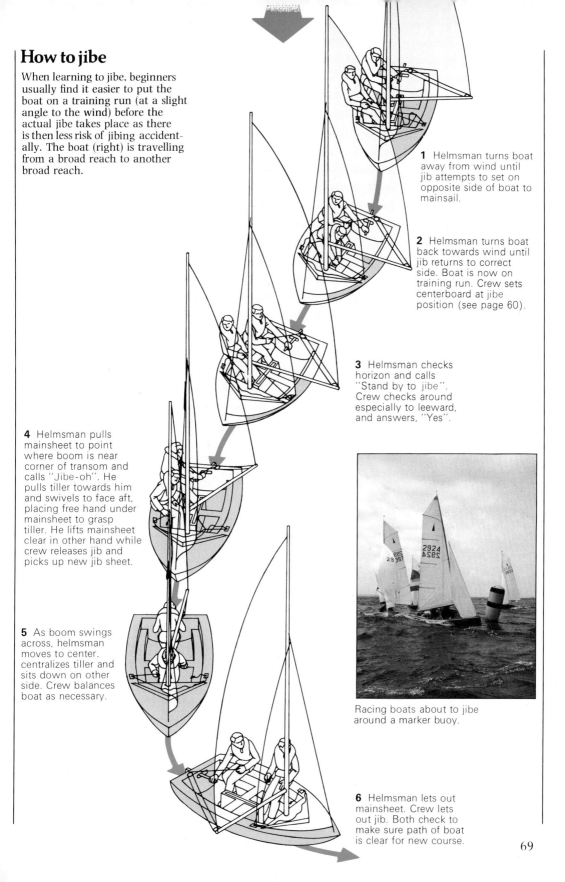

1 Helmsman turns boat away from wind until jib attempts to set on opposite side of boat to mainsail.

2 Helmsman turns boat back towards wind until jib returns to correct side. Boat is now on training run. Crew sets centerboard at jibe position (see page 60).

3 Helmsman checks horizon and calls "Stand by to jibe". Crew checks around especially to leeward, and answers, "Yes".

4 Helmsman pulls mainsheet to point where boom is near corner of transom and calls "Jibe-oh". He pulls tiller towards him and swivels to face aft, placing free hand under mainsheet to grasp tiller. He lifts mainsheet clear in other hand while crew releases jib and picks up new jib sheet.

5 As boom swings across, helmsman moves to center, centralizes tiller and sits down on other side. Crew balances boat as necessary.

Racing boats about to jibe around a marker buoy.

6 Helmsman lets out mainsheet. Crew lets out jib. Both check to make sure path of boat is clear for new course.

Tiller extension techniques

Most one-designs have a tiller extension to help the helmsman to steer while hiking out. If you are a novice sailor, you may find it easier to learn to sail in light winds, when sitting out will not be necessary, and when you will only need to use the tiller itself (see pages 66–9). But once out in normal strength winds, the tiller extension will have to be used and it is important you know how to do so. The diagram on page 54 explains how the tiller extension is fitted to the tiller with a universal joint which permits the extension to be revolved in any direction. Handling the extension is only difficult during tacking and jibing maneuvers when the extension has to be revolved over to the opposite side of the boat. (Boats with center mainsheet systems require a modified technique, see pages 110–1.) It is essential that the helmsman sits well forward of the end of the tiller to allow room for the extension to be swung over.

You may prefer to practice the drill at home first, using the tiller and extension from your boat, together with a coil of rope to represent the mainsheet and three stools to represent both sides of the boat and the transom.

Tacking

The basic maneuver is the same as that shown on pages 66–7. Only the movements with the tiller extension and mainsheet differ as shown.

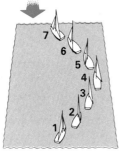

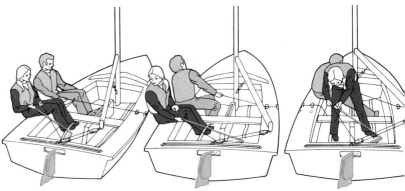

1 Helmsman sits well forward of tiller and holds mainsheet and tiller in separate hands with hand nearest tiller on extension with thumb on top. Checks area is clear.

2 Helmsman says, "Ready about". Crew checks. Replies, "Yes" Helmsman clips mainsheet under thumb, says, "Hard-a-lee", and pushes tiller away.

3 Helmsman waits until boom reaches quarter. Begins to move across boat. Crew releases jib sheet. Helmsman puts free hand on extension and lifts mainsheet.

Jibing

With a tiller extension, the mainsheet is only pulled in sufficiently to keep the boom off the shrouds. The movements with the extension and mainsheet differ as shown.

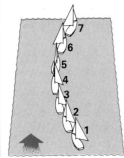

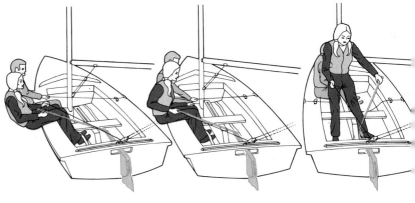

1 Helmsman puts boat on training run, checks area, especially to leeward and says, "Stand by to jibe". Crew checks and says, "Yes".

2 Helmsman checks boom is clear of shroud and clips mainsheet under thumb. Drops remainder of mainsheet behind her.

3 Helmsman puts free hand on extension, lifts mainsheet and says, "Jibe-oh". Moves to center taking extension around and forward to other side.

Good balance is essential prior to jibing. Here the helmsman and crew are correctly positioned prior to a jibe in light winds.

The jibe in this case has been rushed – the boat is not upright and is incorrectly balanced.

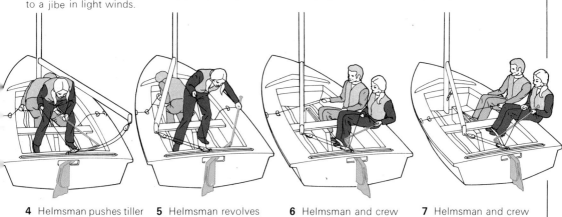

4 Helmsman pushes tiller away further and moves across boat facing aft. Crew picks up new jib sheet and balances boat.

5 Helmsman revolves tiller extension around and forward keeping tiller pushed away as boom starts to swing to new leeward side.

6 Helmsman and crew sit down on new windward side as boom crosses over leeward quarter. Helmsman centralizes tiller and crew sheets in jib.

7 Helmsman and crew then set sails and adjust centerboard to sail off on new course.

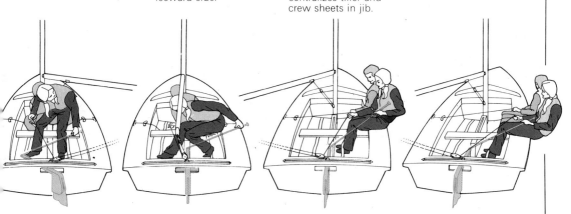

4 Helmsman pushes tiller extension away and waits for boom to start to swing across boat. Crew releases old jib sheet, picks up new one and moves to center.

5 As boom reaches center of boat, helmsman is also in center and centralizes tiller. Crew balances boat.

6 Helmsman sits down on new windward side, looks where she is going, and checks boom is clear of shrouds. Crew moves across boat to new windward side.

7 Helmsman and crew set sails for new course. Crew adjusts centerboard and helmsman and crew balance boat.

Going afloat

As a novice you need to be sure that your first few outings afloat are in light to medium strength winds. You should also check that the area you plan to sail in is suitable for a beginner. If in any doubt, ask the advice of an experienced sailor or, better still, arrange for one to accompany you on your first few trips. Before putting your boat into the water, make sure that you have all the gear you need (see pages 46–7) and that any loose equipment is securely tied in place.

If you have to launch the boat in a crowded harbor or narrow river, it may be wise to row or paddle to less congested waters before hoisting the sails. For your first sail, concentrate on sailing on a beam reach (preferably between two buoys so that you can practice tacking around them). If, for any reason, you find yourself in difficulties when sailing, simply let go of all the controls. This will have the effect of stopping the boat by turning it around automatically into the head-to-wind position. You will then have time to think about what to do next. If you wish to rest for a while, put the boat in the basic hove-to position (page 64).

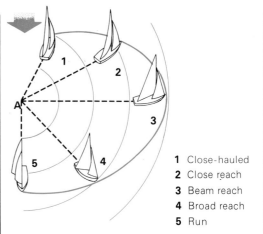

1 Close-hauled
2 Close reach
3 Beam reach
4 Broad reach
5 Run

Boat speed

Your boat speed will depend on several factors—the design of the boat, the strength of the wind and whether it is being sailed correctly on each point of sailing. The concentric arcs in the diagram above represent boat speed—the further the boat is from the center (A) the faster it is travelling. Average family boats are usually fastest on a beam reach and slowest to windward.

Steering a course

Once you have acquired the basic sailing skills, you can learn how to steer your boat on a predetermined course. You must remember when planning a course that the boat will not usually sail in the exact direction planned, particularly when close-hauled, as it will tend to drift sideways a little (see Leeway, opposite). If you are sailing in tidal waters the current will also affect the course being sailed, and you should ask expert advice about its direction and strength. The course, below, illustrates the different points of sailing you would use to sail around an island with the wind coming from the north. If the wind was from another direction the points of sailing would differ accordingly.

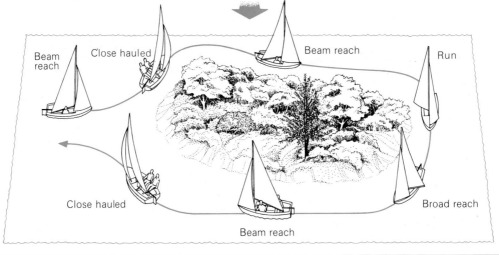

Practicing the techniques

While sailing on a beam reach practice using the basic controls. Lower the centerboard to the halfway position and set the sails correctly (page 58) and move your weight to balance the boat. Get used to the effect of moving the tiller towards and away from you, watching the effect this has by seeing how the boat moves in relation to the horizon. Practice pulling in and easing out the mainsheet until the movement is fluid and doesn't cause you to alter course. Keep a constant check to make sure that the sails are setting correctly.

Close reaching

Once you have the feel of the boat and have mastered reaching, turn the boat slightly closer to the wind onto a close reach. The sails will need to be pulled in a little more and the centerboard lowered to the three-quarter down position. You will need to sit out further to balance the increased heeling force from the sails. In light winds this is often the fastest point of sailing.

Close-hauled

When you are confident of your ability to handle the boat on a beam and a close reach, you can start sailing close-hauled. As shown on page 63, close-hauled is the nearest a boat can sail to the wind. Put the centerboard fully down and sheet in the sails until the mainsail stops fluttering on the luff and the jib is sheeted in tightly. You will need to sit further out to balance the boat and if the boat still heels over, let the mainsail out just enough to keep the boat upright. Don't make the mistake of thinking that when the boat is heeling over and throwing up a lot of spray that it is moving fast. The boat sails faster upright even if the mainsail has to be let out a little to do so. Steer the boat closer to the wind, watching the luff of the jib. As soon as it starts to flutter you are too close to the wind. Pull the tiller towards you until the fluttering stops. The boat is then on the correct close-hauled course. To sail well on a close-hauled course, you must keep trying to sail as close to the wind

as possible, without slowing the boat down. If you sail too close for too long (known as pinching) you will lose speed; if much too close to the wind, you will either stop or accidentally tack.

Broad reaching

To turn the boat onto a broad reach from a close-hauled course, pull the tiller towards you and let the sails out until the boat is travelling at about 130° to the wind. This means you are sailing offwind or downwind (the wind is coming more from behind the boat than from in front). In winds above 12–15 knots this is the fastest point of sailing for most boats. As you turn the boat away from the wind, ease the sails out, raise the centerboard to about a quarter down and move your weight inboard as the heeling force is reduced.

Running

If you continue to bear away you will move from a broad reach onto a run, with the wind astern. On your first outings it is better not to go more directly downwind than a training run (with the wind coming slightly over one quarter – the rear corner of the boat). The sails should be let out almost fully and the centerboard pulled nearly all the way up, leaving only just enough

board to enable you to steer the boat adequately. As there is no strong heeling force the helmsman and crew usually need to sit on opposite sides to balance the boat. If the boat moves further away from the wind until it is dead astern, you can set the jib on the opposite side to the mainsail. Although sailing away from the wind is pleasant in light winds, it requires much more skill in strong winds (see pages 131–3).

Tacking and jibing

The methods for tacking and jibing are shown on pages 66–9. If you need to use the tiller extension, see pages 70–1 as well. Practice both maneuvers on figure eight courses (see below) until you can carry them out smoothly and confidently.

Tacking on a figure eight course

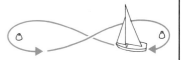

Gybing on a figure eight course

Leeway

Although the centerboard is designed to stop the boat moving sideways, it does not do so entirely. Thus when there are strong sideways forces on the boat (such as when you are sailing a close-hauled course) the boat will move sideways to some extent. This is known as

leeway and it has the effect of pushing you to leeward of your objective. Do not try steering closer to the wind in an effort to counteract leeway as this will simply cause the boat to slow down and the leeway to increase. The simple solution is to put in another tack instead.

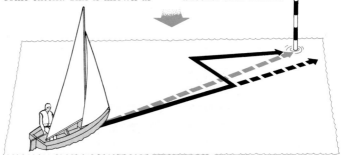

Leaving a beach

While most boats can be launched directly off a beach, launching in this way presents some difficulties. Apart from the possible problems of access from the road or parking lot (see Moving a boat, pages 52–3), the type of beach, flat or shelving, the direction of the wind (towards or away from the shore), and the state of the tide (high or low), can cause complications when leaving and returning.

Wherever possible, survey prospective launching sites at low tide so that you can see obstructions and the slope of the beach. If you cannot do this, as a guide, soft sandy beaches usually indicate a gentle slope and rougher, stony beaches are usually more steeply shelving with

large breaking waves at high tide. Before leaving any beach, always note the state of the tide and calculate your return accordingly (a set of tide tables will help). As a rule, try to leave and return in the period between two hours before and after high water, so that you do not have to pull the boat a long way.

The methods of leaving a beach shown below are for sailing away from the shore. However, in congested waters or where the bottom is very muddy it is often better to row or paddle away from the shore with the sails stowed and only to raise the sails when in deep water and clear of the shore. (For rowing, see page 55, for paddling, see pages 55 and 77.)

Weather and lee shores

A weather shore (right) has the wind blowing away from the shore (offshore wind), and it is easiest to learn how to leave a beach from one. A lee shore (far right) has the wind blowing onto it from the water (onshore wind), which makes leaving difficult, especially in strong winds which can create large breaking waves.

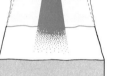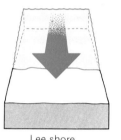

Weather shore   Lee shore

Leaving a weather shore

At the water's edge, the boat is faced into the wind, rigged and the sails are hoisted. The boat is pushed into the water and, once afloat, the helmsman gets in. There are two methods of leaving. The first, and most controlled, method (below left) should be used if there are

obstructions. The helmsman decides on a course and pushes the tiller away (1). The crew pushes the boat back and the bow away from the wind, and then jumps aboard (2). When the boat is pointing away from wind, the sails are set and the centerboard lowered, and the

boat sails off (3). Using the second method (below right), the helmsman and crew get aboard (1). The boat drifts back until it is at right angles to the wind (2). The helmsman steers the boat onto the chosen course, the crew lowers the centerboard, and the sails are set (3).

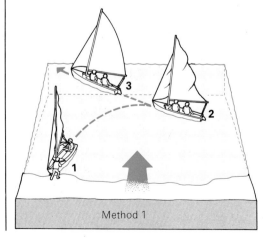

Method 1

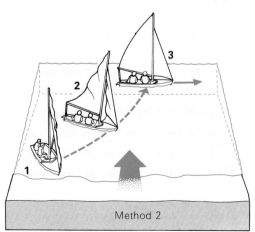

Method 2

Planning to leave a lee shore

Leaving a lee shore is especially difficult because the angle between the no go zone and the shoreline gives you little room to maneuver. If the wind is directly onshore, you have no option but to sail off using the narrow angle between a close reach and a close-hauled course. However, the wind is usually at an oblique angle to the beach, and once you have determined which edge of the no go zone is nearest the beach you can benefit from increased searoom by choosing to leave on the opposite tack. The curve of the beach can also be used to advantage on occasions to give a wider angle in relation to the wind in which to launch into. Always check that your course is not blocked by obstacles such as rocky outcrops or by other boats.

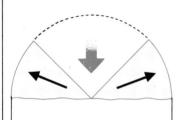

Wind directly onshore

Wind at an oblique angle

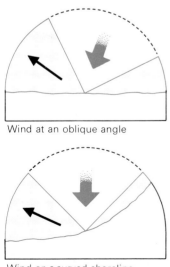

Wind on a curved shoreline

Deep water - lee shore

At the water's edge the rigged boat is faced into the wind (or removed from its dolly stern first and turned head-to-wind). The sails are hoisted and the rudder attached. Study the waves to allow the boat to be launched between them. The helmsman and crew stand on the side of the boat which will be to windward (1) and at the chosen moment, as a wave breaks on the shore, the boat is rushed into the water and helmsman and crew get aboard (2). The centerboard and rudder are lowered and the sails set to leave on a close reach to gain as much speed and searoom as possible before luffing up to meet the next wave (3). The course is kept nearly parallel to the shoreline until clear of the breaking waves. A lot of water will be shipped but this should not be bailed until well out to sea.

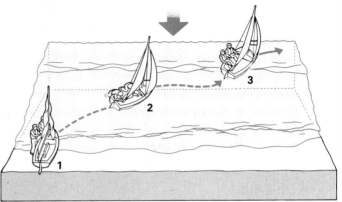

Shallow water - lee shore

At the water's edge the rigged boat is launched into the water, faced head-to-wind and the mainsail is hoisted (1). The crew walks the boat into the water to a depth of about 1 m (3 ft). The helmsman then gets in, hoists the jib and lowers the rudder and the centerboard as far as the depth of water will allow (2).

The crew pulls the boat forward at an angle to the wind and gets aboard while the helmsman pulls in the mainsheet to get the boat moving (3). As in deep water, a course almost parallel to the shoreline is followed (4) until the water is deep enough to lower the centerboard fully and to sail away close-hauled.

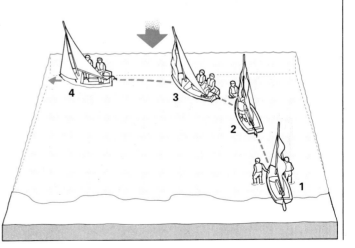

Returning to a beach

In general, returning to a beach poses fewer problems than leaving a beach because the boat is moving under control, enabling you to plan your course more exactly. Before returning to a beach it is vital to plan your approach, looking at the shape of the shoreline and noting any obstacles or potential dangers. Once you have determined the wind direction, you should plan a course towards your proposed landing site which provides escape routes so that you can abandon the approach if necessary without having to make a violent turn through the wind. As you approach the shore, check that the halyards are ready to be released and the sails lowered as soon as necessary. Watch the depth of the water as you will need to raise the rudder and the centerboard as the water gets shallower.

Returning to a lee shore
Single-handed racing boat returning to a lee shore in large waves. The approach is very fast on a run to avoid the waves breaking over the stern (see below).

Lee shores

As the wind is behind you, returning to a lee shore is easier than trying to leave one. However, it can be dangerous, particularly in deep water because of the likelihood of steep, breaking waves. Under these conditions, your approach should be as fast as possible to prevent the boat being over-whelmed by waves breaking over the stern. Other methods of returning to a lee shore are used if there are smaller waves, or if the water is shallow. When the boat touches the shore (whether in deep or shallow water) keep to the windward side of the boat when you jump out, otherwise a strong gust or a breaking wave could push the boat on top of you.

Deep water with large waves
Approach fast on a broad reach (1). When the boat hits the beach, helmsman and crew jump out and, keeping to the windward side, turn it head-to-wind and then lower the sails (2). Bring the boat out of the water.

Deep water with small waves
In smaller waves or if there are obstacles, turn into the wind off shore, lower the mainsail (1) and return under the jib alone on a broad reach. Near the landing site let the jib flap and allow the boat to drift in. Helmsman and crew jump out (2).

Shallow water
In the smaller waves associated with shallow water, sail the boat towards the beach until the water is about 1 m (3 ft) deep (1). Round up into the wind to stop (2). Crew jumps out to windward and holds the boat while the helmsman lowers the sails and gets out. Pull the boat up onto the shore (3).

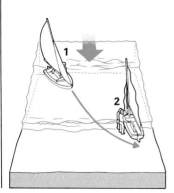
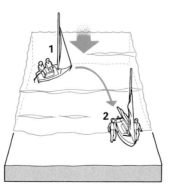
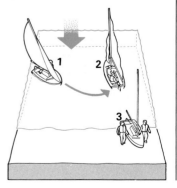

Weather shores

When you are approaching a weather shore you will have to tack up to your chosen landing site if the wind is blowing directly offshore. However, careful observation will show that in most cases, the wind is blowing at an angle to the shore, so

plan your course to enable you to land on the tack that gives the best approach. As the boat nears the shore the crew should be ready to jump out, holding the painter to prevent the boat drifting backwards, and away from the shore.

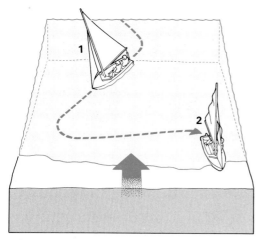

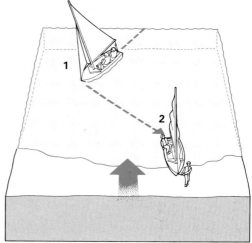

Deep water
Tack in close to the shore (1). Sail parallel to the shore with the sails eased until you reach your chosen landing point. Round up into the wind to land (2), raising the centerboard. The crew jumps out with the painter. The helmsman lowers the sails.

Shallow water
Tack towards the shore (1). As the water shallows the crew raises the centerboard. When near the shore on your final tack, turn head-to-wind (2). The crew jumps out with painter while the helmsman lowers the sails.

Paddling - two people

If the wind drops when you are returning to shore or if you are approaching a weather shore sheltered from the wind by trees, for example, you may find yourself becalmed (below). It will then be necessary to row or paddle. (For rowing, see page 55.) With two people you can paddle using the method described (right) with the sails hoisted. The same method can be used in normal sailing conditions provided the sails are lowered.

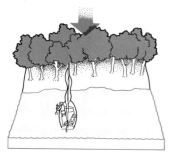
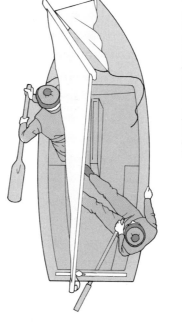

Two people paddling
The crew sits forward on one side of the boat, the helmsman sits on the other side aft (left). The crew leans over the side and paddles by plunging the paddle forward into the water and pulling it back and repeating the movement. As well as moving the boat forward, this will tend to turn the boat, so the helmsman uses the tiller to adjust the course (below).

Leaving a float

There are many occasions when it will be necessary to sail away from or return to a wooden float or dock. In some sailing areas the float will be the only possible means of access to the water and you will have to launch directly off the side (below) or down a ramp. Often there will be a separate ramp next to a network of floats or docks to launch the boat down (see Moving a boat, pages 52−3).

Using a float allows the boat to leave and return while remaining afloat and therefore maneuverable. Floats also provide a useful place to secure the boat while completing your preparations for going sailing and for leaving your boat for short periods. In tidal conditions, floats are normally used because

they move up and down with the rise and fall of the tide and therefore always provide facilities for launching directly into the water. However a float or dock jutting out into tidal stream can cause complications because the water flowing underneath it pulls boats against it on the uptide side and causes them to drift away on the downtide side.

Normally you launch and leave on the leeward side of the float, but under certain conditions it is necessary to leave from the windward side (see Leaving in tidal water, opposite). Before launching, it is important to make sure that all loose equipment is either removed from the boat or securely stowed inside it.

Launching

At least two people are needed. One person takes hold of the painter and one side of the boat, and the other person takes hold of the other side (1). Push the boat gently over the side into the water stern first (2), lead it to the end of the float and turn it head-to-wind. Secure the painter. The crew holds the boat while the helmsman get in and rigs it (3).

1   **2**   **3**

Lee shores

Once the boat has been launched, and faced into the wind (1), it is led to the end of the leeward side of the float. The helmsman hoists the sails, mainsail first and lowers the centerboard (2).When the boat is ready for sailing and the helmsman and crew have ascertained that their proposed course away from the float is free from obstructions, the crew unties the painter and pushes the bow away from the float and jumps aboard. The sails are then set and the boat sailed away close-hauled (3).

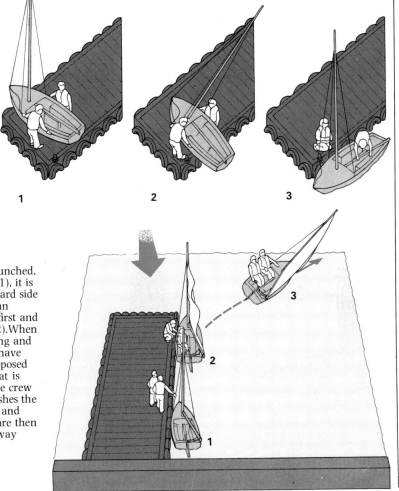

Weather shores

After launching, the boat is turned to face into the wind at the end of the float on the leeward side. The helmsman then gets in and rigs it. The mainsail is hoisted first and then the jib. The center-board is then lowered. When the boat is ready for sailing you should plan your course away from the float. If there is clear water astern, use the first method of leaving described (above right), but if there is an obstruction astern, use the second method (below right).

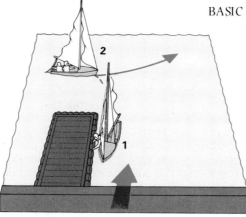

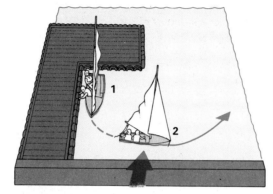

Clear water astern
With the helmsman already in the boat, the crew unties the painter and gets aboard, pushing the boat backwards (1). When clear of the float, the crew sets the jib on the windward side (backs the jib) to turn the bow away from the wind. The crew then releases the jib sheet (2). The helmsman sets the mainsail and the crew sets the jib on the leeward side to sail off.

Obstructions astern
The crew releases the painter and gets aboard pushing the bow for-wards and away from the float (1). The crew then backs the jib and the helmsman pulls the tiller towards him to turn the boat away from the wind (2). The sails are then set to sail away on a broad reach.

Leaving in tidal water

When leaving a pontoon in tidal water, in order to choose the most advantageous position you will need to study the strength of the wind in relation to that of the tide. If the effect of the tide is stronger, its direction will govern your choice of side for leaving. As a rule, leave from the side in the lee of the strongest element. Particular care should be taken when a strong wind is directly against the tide, as this will create waves on the downtide side of the float. Methods of leaving in three different wind-tide combinations are described below.

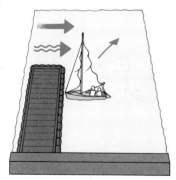

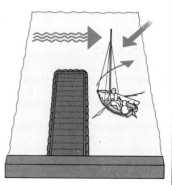

Wind and tide in same direction
Leave from leeward/downtide side with boat facing into wind and tide. Helmsman lowers center-board, hoists mainsail, then jib. Crew climbs aboard. Helmsman pulls tiller towards him. Crew then releases painter and backs jib. When turned sufficiently, boat can be sailed away.

Strong wind against weak tide
Leave from leeward/uptide side. Face boat out to sea. Helmsman rigs boat and hoists jib. Crew releases painter and gets aboard. Push boat forwards and away from float and sail away on jib only until clear. Lower center-board and turn head-to-wind to hoist mainsail, and sail off.

Strong tide against weak wind
Leave from windward/downtide side. Boat will face into tide. Helmsman rigs boat. Crew releases painter and gets aboard. Row or paddle away (see Rowing and paddling, page 55, and Paddling—two people, page 77). When clear, turn head-to-wind, hoist sails and sail off.

Returning to a float

As floats in popular sailing areas are normally crowded with moored craft and boats
leaving and returning, your approach should
be carefully planned to avoid collisions and to
ensure that you come in on the right course.
In tidal waters there may be the added compli-
cation of a current in opposition to the wind.
Ideally the boat should approach the float
to finish head-to-wind so that it slows down and
comes to a gentle stop. Your plan should allow
for escape routes in case of the failure of an
approach. Where the wind is at an angle to the
shore, it is preferable to return to the leeward
side of the float in non-tidal waters. When
you near the float, it is important that the
crew should be ready to catch hold of the edge of
the float, to prevent the boat drifting away.
As soon as the boat stops the crew should jump
out with the painter to secure the boat using the
knot appropriate to the mooring fitting (see
Knots, pages 328—35). If the boat is to be left
for a long period, the sails should be lowered and
the equipment stowed. It should also be tied at
the stern, using the end of the mainsheet if there
is no stern line, to keep the boat in position. If the
boat is to be removed from the water, the
launching procedure should be reversed (for
slipways, see page 53; for float launching
see page 78).

Coming alongside a float
The crew grasps the float and is ready to
jump out. The helmsman balances the boat.

Weather shore

A float on a weather shore
should be approached on a
course parallel to the shore. As
you near the float the sails
should be let out to slow down
and the boat turned head-to-
wind to come to a stop beside
the float. Once the boat is
alongside, the crew grasps
the edge of the float and gets
out to secure the boat. You
should plan an escape route to
take you away from the float
and the shore, ready to make a
new approach.

Approaching a weather shore
float
Sail towards the float on a
reach. Let out the sails to slow
down and turn into the wind to
stop beside the float. The escape
route is on a reach away from
the float. Two boats are shown
(right) approaching different
parts of the float.

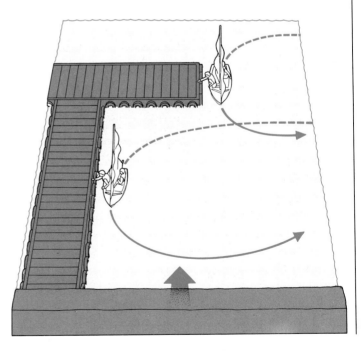

Lee shore

When approaching a float on a lee shore it is usually necessary to sail in close to the shore before luffing up to stop. Careful judgment is required to ensure that you turn in time to avoid hitting the shore, but not so soon as to overshoot the end of the float. If the float is parallel to the shore (below right) there may not be enough space for the boat to turn head-to-wind to stop. In that case the approach must be under the jib alone.

Approaches to three different floats on a lee shore are shown (below). Also indicated are possible escape routes.

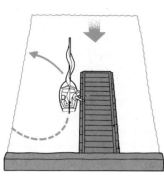

Float at right angles to shore
Sail in close to the shore on a broad reach. Round up into the wind and drift to a stop along-side the float.

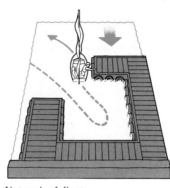

Network of floats
Approach on a broad reach and sail into the confined space, leeward of a float. Tack onto a close-hauled course and turn into the wind to stop at the end of the float.

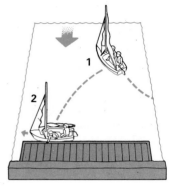

Float parallel to shore
Sail upwind of the float and turn head-to-wind and lower the mainsail (1). Sail in under the jib on a broad reach. When near the float allow the jib to flap and drift in sideways (2).

Returning in tidal water

In tidal waters you should plan your approach to finish facing into the strongest element. So before starting your return it is necessary to assess the relative strength of the wind and the tide.
For returning to a float the simplest wind-tide combination is when they are both in the same direction. It should be remembered, however, that the boat will continue to drift downtide even when the sails are lowered. The most difficult combination is when the wind and tide are in opposition. This creates waves on the windward side of the float, making an approach inadvisable from that side. When the wind and tide are at right angles, there is the widest choice of approach. You can either stop on the uptide side head-to-wind, or on the end of the float facing into the tide.

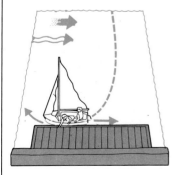

Wind and tide in same direction
Sail on a reach towards the float. When near the float, turn head-to-wind alongside to stop. Allow enough room to drift back with the tide.

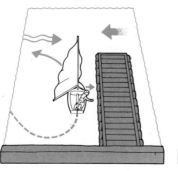

Wind against tide
Approach the leeward/uptide side of the float on a broad reach. Tack to bring the boat alongside the float. Let the sails flap and drift in sideways.

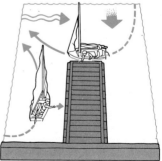

Wind and tide at right angles
To stop on the uptide side, approach on a reach. Turn head-to-wind near the float and drift in. To stop on the upwind side, turn head-to-wind, lower the mainsail and sail in under the jib.

Leaving a mooring

A mooring is a permanent anchorage for a boat. It consists of a heavy weight (usually of concrete) or a mushroom anchor, a length of chain and a buoy. A mooring is used to secure a boat in a estuary or lake where launching facilities are not available or when it is necessary to keep a keelboat afloat in all states of the tide. There are many different types of mooring (see below), but the boat is usually secured either by a rope strop attached to the chain under the buoy, or by a permanent mooring rope which is tied to a ring on top of the buoy.

As moorings are often laid close together, you need to take great care to avoid hitting other boats when leaving and returning. To reach a moored boat you will have to row out or get a lift in another boat. When you get out to the boat, the first thing you have to do is attach the rudder, then rig the mainsail and jib and prepare the boat for sailing. To make sure that it is released quickly, you should "single up" the mooring before leaving. This means threading the painter through the rope strop or the mooring ring (according to the type of mooring) and securing the end on board, to a cleat or round the mast. The rope strop or permanent mooring rope is then dropped and the painter can be easily released when you are ready to leave. After singling up, plan your course, taking into account both wind and tide.

Moorings

All moorings have three basic parts: a floating buoy, a length of chain and a weight or anchor. Three basic types are shown right. Sometimes several moorings are attached to an anchored ground chain and this is known as a trot of moorings (below).

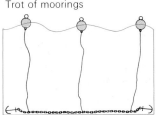

Trot of moorings

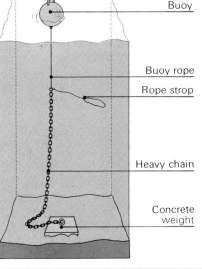

Buoy

Buoy rope

Rope strop

Heavy chain

Concrete weight

Types of mooring
A mooring with a light buoy attached by a rope to a heavy chain is shown left. A rope strop secures the boat. Above left is a mooring with a second small pick-up buoy. You moor to a ring on the chain. Above right is a mooring with a single buoy with a ring on top to which you tie the boat.

How to leave

To leave in non-tidal water, the crew first lowers the centerboard and singles up with the painter. The mainsail and jib are then hoisted. The crew frees the painter, grasps the mooring at the bow, pulls it along the windward side of the boat and releases it. The further aft the mooring is released the further away from the wind you will sail (see right). The helmsman then sets the mainsail and the crew sets the jib to sail off.

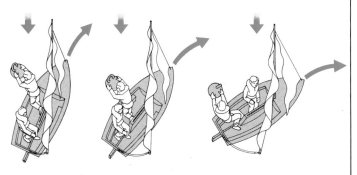

Released at bow
To sail away close-hauled the crew releases the mooring near the bow.

Released amidships
To sail away on a close reach the crew releases the mooring amidships.

Released astern
To sail away on a reach the helmsman releases the mooring astern.

Tidal water

In tidal waters the current will have a marked effect on the way you leave a mooring. A moored boat will face into the strongest element. If it is facing into the wind it is described as wind-rode (below left), but if it is facing into the tide it is tide-rode (below right). If the wind and tide are of equal strength and in opposition a boat will lie at right angles to the wind (below center).

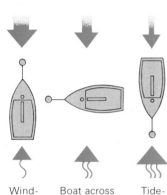

Wind-rode   Boat across wind   Tide-rode

Boat across wind

When the boat is lying across the wind and tide, the most controlled way to leave is under the jib alone as shown. However, to avoid obstructions you can turn the boat towards the wind by first hoisting the mainsail, or turn it towards the tide by first lowering the centerboard.

How to leave
The crew singles up and then hoists the jib (1). He drops the mooring to leeward and the helmsman lowers the centerboard. The boat drifts downtide and the crew sets the jib to sail clear of other moored boats (2). Then the helmsman steers into the wind to hoist the mainsail and sail off (3).

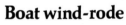

Boat tide-rode

If the boat is tide-rode and the wind is astern, it is important to remember that the mainsail should not be hoisted until the mooring has been dropped, otherwise it will fill immediately and the boat will sail off out of control. Sailing away under the jib alone allows you to leave slowly and safely.

How to leave
Prepare the sails for hoisting, single up the mooring and lower centerboard (1). You choose a course and the crew hoists the jib and drops the mooring to leeward and then sets the jib (2). Luff up and hoist mainsail (3). Sail off on your chosen course.

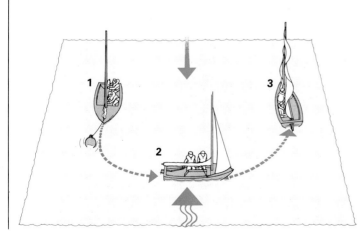

Boat wind-rode

If the boat is wind-rode in tidal water you should choose to leave on a downtide course, before turning towards your objective. As you are facing into the wind the mainsail can be hoisted immediately.

How to leave
The crew singles up and hoists the mainsail and then the jib. He lowers the centerboard and drops the mooring on the side which will be to windward to turn the boat. He backs the jib before setting it to sail off. When clear the helmsman sets the mainsail.

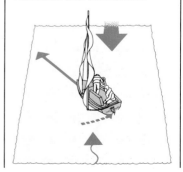

Returning to a mooring

Before sailing in towards your mooring, check the position of other moored boats and the way they are lying in relation to the wind and tide; your boat will end up facing the same direction. Plan your course to finish pointing into the element which is the strongest when the sails are lowered. Try to pass downtide of moored craft (or downwind in non-tidal water), to avoid the possibility of drifting into another boat, and never attempt to sail across a mooring line. Once the mooring has been picked up and the permanent mooring line secured (below), stow all the boat equipment and bail or pump out any water. If the boat is to be left for a long time, remove all loose gear when you leave. Sails, in particular, should be taken ashore as these may need to be dried (see Stowing after sailing, pages 96–7).

Securing a mooring

As the mooring comes within reach, the crew leans out over the windward bow, picks up the buoy and, if it is a small one, brings it onboard. He then cleats the buoy rope on the foredeck. Once the sails have been lowered, he secures the permanent mooring line, taking it through the bow fairlead to a cleat or around the mast (see Knots, pages 328–35. If the buoy is too large to be brought on board, the crew singles up with the painter (see page 82) before attaching the permanent rope after the sails have been lowered.

Picking up a mooring
The crew leans out to pick up the mooring to windward.

Non-tidal water

Your approach should be as slow as possible to give the crew the greatest chance of picking up the buoy. This is usually achieved by sailing in on a windward course (below left). However, in crowded waters a downwind approach may be necessary (below right). Always steer so that the mooring is on the windward bow when you stop so that it can be picked up without unbalancing the boat. When the mooring has been picked up, lower the sails and then raise the centerboard.

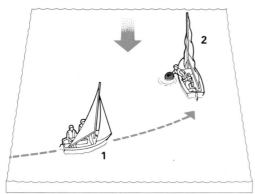

Upwind approach
Approach on a close reach (1). When near mooring, luff up to stop and the crew picks up mooring to windward (2).

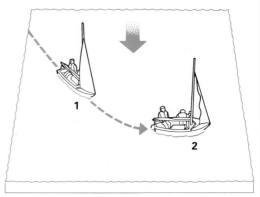

Downwind approach
Approach under jib alone on a broad reach (1). Steer onto a beam reach, release jib sheet to stop at mooring (2).

Tidal water

If you are returning to a mooring in tidal water, before starting your approach it is important to assess the strength and direction of the tide in relation to that of the wind and how it will affect your course. To judge the tide it will help you to look at the mooring buoys around you; a strong tidal current will produce a noticeable wake behind any object fixed in the water (below). You may also find it helpful to make a test approach before trying to pick up the mooring.

If the wind and the tide are in the same direction it is easiest to approach downwind. If the wind and tide are crossed, you can use this to advantage by positioning the boat so that you drift slowly towards the mooring before picking it up. If the wind is directly opposed to the tide, a downwind approach under the jib is preferable but, if the tide is very strong, it may be advisable to approach on a windward course.

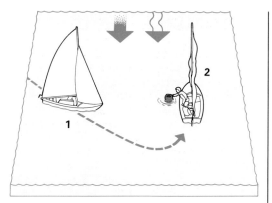

Wind and tide in same direction
Approach mooring on a beam reach (1). Luff up so that you stop with buoy amidships to windward (2).

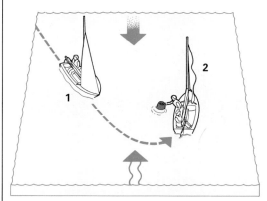

Buoy in tidal current
A strong tide produces a wake behind objects fixed in the water such as buoys, channel markers and mooring posts. Looking at these will help you to judge the strength and direction of the tide.

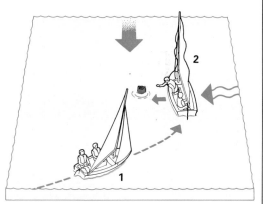

Wind and tide crossed
Approach on a close reach aiming uptide of mooring (1). As you near mooring, luff up and allow boat to drift downtide so that crew can pick up buoy to windward (2).

Wind against tide – downwind approach
Sail towards mooring under jib alone on a broad reach (1) and as you reach mooring, gently luff up and let jib fly to stop (2).

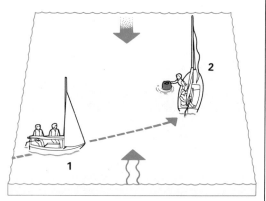

Wind against tide – upwind approach
Approach under jib alone on a beam reach (1). As crew picks up mooring to windward, luff up and then lower jib (2).

Capsizing

There are two main causes of capsizing. One of them is the result of the wind overpowering the boat and its crew so that the boat heels excessively until it fills with water and capsizes to leeward. The other is normally the result of a crewing error in strong winds, usually on a downwind course, so that the boat becomes unbalanced and capsizes, generally to windward. Although on the whole one-designs allow a fairly large margin for error on the part of the crew, racing one-designs don't, as they are more sensitive owing to their relatively larger sail area and lighter hulls.

Capsizing is an ever-present possibility in all unballasted boats, and it is important that you know how to deal with it. You need to be familiar with the correct righting techniques which should form part of your basic seamanship training. As a beginner you would be well advised to deliberately capsize your boat, but under supervision, to learn how to right it; your confidence will be improved if you have already capsized in a controlled situation.

All one-designs have some buoyancy so there is no danger that they will sink, provided that the buoyancy has been checked before launching. The amount of buoyancy is important (see pages 46–7): too much can cause the boat to blow away on its side or float so high in the water that the upturned centreboard is out of reach. If you buy a new boat, capsize it in shallow water to determine its behavior so that you can adapt your righting techniques accordingly. The method you use will depend to some extent on the circumstances of the capsize and the type of boat.

Before the development of the scoop method (shown right), a crew trying to right their boat had to swim it around head-to-wind so that it would not blow over again as soon as it was righted; alternatively, they sometimes found they had to lower the sails before attempting to bring the boat upright. The scoop method, however, has the advantage of permitting a boat to be righted irrespective of its position relative to the wind as the crew is already aboard to act as ballast. Some more complex capsizes will require modifications of the scoop method or even different techniques (see pages 88–9).

Whatever the circumstances of the capsize, the crew should stay with the boat. It is much more visible to a rescue launch than a lone swimmer and the shore may well be further away than it appears.

Righting a boat — scoop method

In this method, the crew is scooped up inside the boat as it is brought upright by the helmsman who stands on the centerboard and pulls on the jib sheet. Because the crew is already aboard when the boat comes upright, he acts as ballast and prevents the boat from capsizing again immediately after righting. When the boat capsizes to windward, the crew must wait for the sail to swing over to the other side of the boat before leaning over to help the helmsman aboard. Both helmsman and crew must understand their respective tasks and carry them out accordingly. The crew must also take care not to pull on the boat before the helmsman has climbed onto the centerboard or it may invert on top of him. Lightweight racing boats are particularly prone to inversion. The techniques for dealing with an inverted boat are described on page 89.

1 Crew checks that the centerboard is in the fully down position. He then sorts out the mainsheet while the helmsman swims to the transom and checks the rudder fitting is still in place.

4 The crew lies down in the boat, holding onto the toe straps or the thwarts, while the helmsman climbs onto the centerboard, using the jib sheet as a lever if necessary.

Position of the helmsman
The helmsman must take care to stand at the root of the centerboard, as close to the boat as possible, to prevent it breaking under his weight. He must be ready to let go of the jib sheet and grasp the side decking to lever himself aboard the boat as it comes upright. Throughout the righting sequence both helmsman and crew should talk to each other so that they know what is happening.

2 The crew holds the transom steady while the helmsman, taking the mainsheet over the rudder, swims to the centerboard, using the mainsheet as a lifeline until he gets there

3 When the helmsman has reached the centerboard and grasped it, the crew swims around to the inside of the boat, sorts out the upper jib sheet and throws it over to the helmsman.

5 The helmsman, after checking that the crew is ready, stands on the centerboard as close to the boat as possible and starts to pull on the jib sheet to begin the righting movement.

6 The helmsman continues to pull on the jib sheet until the boat is nearly upright and scrambles aboard over the side decking. Both crew members then prepare the boat to sail off immediately.

Righting a trapeze boat

In racing boats if the crew is not out on the trapeze you can use the normal righting method. However, for the occasions when the crew is trapezing, both helmsman and crew have to learn how to react very quickly in the event of capsize. They must perfect a righting technique which is rapid and efficient. The first priority is for the crew to unhook and climb out on the centerboard as rapidly as possible to prevent the boat from inverting. The helmsman performs the role normally carried out by the crew and is scooped up into the boat in the usual way.

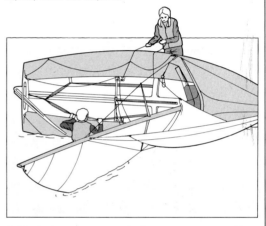

1 The trapezing crew moves her weight back onto the gunwale as the boat capsizes and unhooks rapidly from the trapeze.

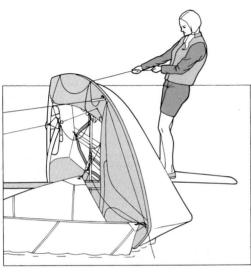

2 She grabs the jib sheet and scrambles out onto the centerboard, standing as close to the root of the board as possible.

3 The helmsman grasps the lower toe straps and is scooped aboard as the crew rights the boat by pulling on the jib sheet.

Righting single-handed

Single-handed boats can be difficult to right as the centerboard floats high in the water and the boat can blow away from you. If you sail single-handed you should develop a technique whereby you do not actually fall in the water, but start to scramble up over the gunwale as the sail hits the water, ready to right it by standing on the centerboard and pulling on the gunwale. If you do fall in the water, the boat can sometimes be righted by grasping the bow and sinking it so that the boat rotates to its normal floating position.

1 As the sail starts to hit the water, the helmsman should grasp the upper gunwale and begin to lever himself up, ready to climb over the side as quickly as possible.

2 He swings himself onto the centerboard, and rights the boat by pulling on the gunwale.

Righting when a spinnaker is set

If you have the misfortune to capsize your boat with the spinnaker set, the first task is to release one corner of the spinnaker so that it doesn't act as a sea anchor. The next job is to get the spinnaker down. If the boat inverts with the spinnaker set, bring it up to the normal capsized position before starting to right it in the usual way.

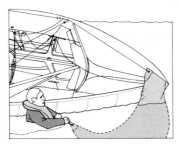

1 Crew finds one corner of the spinnaker and undoes the sheet from the clew.

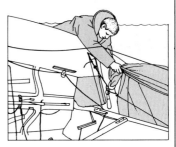

2 Crew then bundles spinnaker into pouch (or chute) before starting normal righting sequence.

Righting an inverted boat

If the crew are slow to react to a capsize, the boat can easily invert. The air is then trapped under the hull and the boat forms a seal with the water which can be difficult to break. The method you use to right an inverted boat will depend on the position of the centerboard. If you capsize with the centerboard fully retracted, or if it retracts during the capsize, recovery will be made harder because you do not have it to use as a lever to right the boat. Whatever the method, the boat should be righted so that the mast comes up towards the wind. This will then make recovery from the normal capsize position much easier, and will prevent the boat from capsizing again. It is best if one person pulls on the jib sheet, standing on the gunwale, while the other presses down hard on the stern to break the air seal. Once in the normal capsize position, the boat is righted in the usual way. If the centerboard has not retracted the job is made much simpler because one person can use it as a lever. It is important to make sure the jib sheet is brought over forward of the centerboard to prevent it slipping backwards.

1 Helmsman finds a jib sheet from inside boat. Helmsman and crew swim to other side of boat and crew climbs onto gunwale and grasps centerboard.

2 With helmsman and crew both kneeling on boat, crew starts to pull on centerboard while helmsman pulls on jib sheet.

3 Both helmsman and crew continue pulling until boat gradually turns over until it lies in normal capsized position.

4 Crew climbs onto centerboard aided by helmsman and righting sequence (see previous page) is followed in usual way.

Mast stuck

If you capsize in shallow water
your mast may dig into the mud
so that you have to be towed off.
Make sure that the righting line
from the towing boat is clipped
or tied to the shroud and taken
over the hull (below). Where
possible, arrange for the boat to
be pulled upright against the
wind (right).

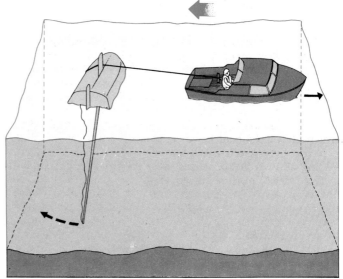

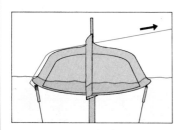

Towing

Every one-design should have a
painter attached at the mast and
led through a bow fitting. If a
single boat is towed in calm
conditions it can be fastened
alongside the towing boat (right)

or towed behind the rescue boat.
If more than one boat is
towed, each one can be attached
with a rolling hitch (see page
332) to a rope trailed from the
rescue boat.

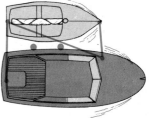

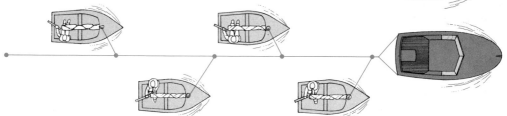

Crew trapped

Now and again, as the result of
a capsize, the crew gets trapped
either under the sail or in the
inverted hull. Neither situation
is dangerous although it can be
alarming if you do not know
the correct procedure to deal
with it.

Crew beneath sail
Push your hand up and make an
air pocket in the sail. Then,
keeping one hand above your
head to push the sail, work your
way, using a seamline to guide
you, to the outside edge.

Crew under sail

Crew under hull
There is plenty of air inside the
hull. Swim to an outer edge and
push yourself under the side
decking to get out.

Man overboard

Picking up a person who has fallen overboard requires quick, positive and well-rehearsed actions by whoever is left in the boat. The main point to bear in mind in organizing a man overboard drill is that in most cases there will only be one person left aboard to sail the boat. This means choosing a course of action which allows the boat to be controlled even if it is the helmsman who goes over the side, leaving only an inexperienced crew aboard.

The safest method is to put the boat immediately onto a beam reach, which is the easiest course to sail, release the jib so that you only have one sail to manage, and tack onto the reciprocal beam reach to return to the man overboard. Never attempt to jibe instead as this is likely to result in a capsize.

Having succeeded in reaching the person in the water and coming up alongside him, you have to get him into the boat. Wet clothing and

buoyancy garments restrict movement and he may be weak from cold or shock. If you are considerably smaller than the man overboard you are likely to find it difficult to help him aboard unassisted. If he is conscious and able to help himself, it is usually possible for him to gradually climb in if a gently rocking movement of the boat is encouraged to give him extra lift. In the event of the person being unconscious and the crew unable to lift him aboard, one answer is to tie a line around him, under his arms, heave him out of the water as far as possible and fasten him alongside the boat near the shrouds to tow him ashore. The alternative (for a more experienced crew) is to capsize the boat, tie the person into it and scoop him up using the normal righting method (see page 86). Make sure that you practice your man overboard drill until you are confident you can carry it out successfully.

Picking up a man overboard

When you rescue someone in the water you must make sure that he is positioned on the windward side of the boat when you stop. Otherwise there is a danger of sailing over him. Picking up the man to windward also helps to keep the boat well balanced.

1 Immediately the man goes overboard, take control of the helm (if you are the crew) and check his position in the water.

2 Let the jib flap and steer onto a beam reach straightaway to give yourself time to assess the situation. If it is not down already, lower the centerboard fully.

3 Tack onto a reciprocal beam reach, keeping sight of the person in the water.

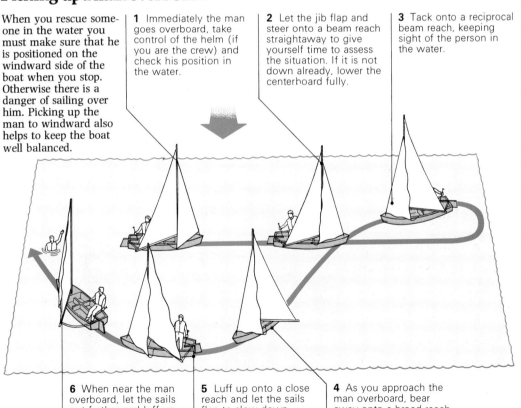

6 When near the man overboard, let the sails out further and luff up so that you stop with him to windward near the shrouds.

5 Luff up onto a close reach and let the sails flap to slow down.

4 As you approach the man overboard, bear away onto a broad reach to bring the boat slightly to leeward of him.

Reefing

Most small boats are designed with sails which can cope with wind strengths from near calm to 25 knots. Such sails are only really efficient in medium-strength wind conditions (from 10 to 15 knots), being either too small or too large for extremes. In light winds, the sail area can be increased by using additional, or larger, sails, and in strong winds the sail area can be reduced either by using smaller sails or by reducing the area of an existing sail (known as reefing).

There are three ways of reefing a boat: by using reef points on the sail; by rolling the sail around the boom: and by rolling the sail around the mast.

The method you use is governed by the type and design of your boat. The number of reefs you take in the sail will depend on the amount by which the sail area needs to be reduced to suit the wind conditions. Practice and experience will show you exactly when, and by how much, you will need to reef.

It is easier to reef a boat before launching it but if a change in wind conditions necessitates a reduction in sail area while afloat, you should put the boat into the full hove-to position first before starting to reef (page 206). Similarly, if you have to shake out a reef afloat, heave-to before reversing the process. Reefing is a seamanlike skill, practised by all cruiser sailors, and one which all novice sailors would do well to learn.

Although racing crews only very rarely ever consider reefing, even in the strongest wind conditions, there have been occasions when major international races have been won by judicious reefing.

Using reef points

The traditional way of reefing is by using reef points (thin lines stitched to the sail). This method is more likely to be found on traditionally built boats the principles having changed little since the days of the square-riggers. For each reefing position, the sail must be provided with a row of reefing points, attached to each side of the sail. The rows are curved slightly upwards to improve the reefed sail shape. At the end of each row the sail has two large eyes, one at the luff, and the other at the leech edge of the sail. These reefing eyes (or cringles) are used to fasten the sail to each end of the boom using thicker lines (known as reefing pennants).

Unreefed sail   Sail with one reef taken in

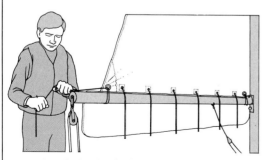

Fastening the leech cringle to the boom

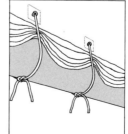

Tying the reef knots

How to reef

First loosen boom vang then release mainsail halyard and lower sail to point where luff cringle can be lashed to boom. Tighten halyard and cleat it. Lash leech cringle to boom (pulling it outwards at an angle of 45° to tension it). Gather up sail and tie it up using reef knots. Retension the boom vang.

Rolling the sail around the boom

This method can only be used on a boat which has a locking gooseneck. Because the rolled sail covers the boom vang fitting, you will need a makeshift attachment to the boom vang, such as a sail bag (see below) or a webbing strap. In preparation for reefing, the boom vang should be removed from the boom, the sail lowered to the correct position, the boom placed in the boat and the lower batten removed.

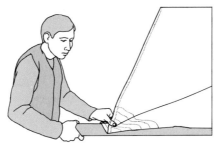

1 Before starting to roll the sail, tuck about 15 cm (6 in) of the leech under the boom to help it roll evenly.

2 Helmsman and crew rotate the boom and pull the sail out at both ends.

Sail

Sailbag

Sailbag inserted into rolled sail

3 Insert the foot of the sail bag, in the boom vang position, into the last three rolls of the sail. Leave the top of the bag and the drawcord hanging free, to attach it to the boom vang to tension the sail. Replace the boom and retension the boom vang.

Rolling the sail around the mast

Certain types of boat, in which the sail is fixed to the mast with a sleeve, can be reefed by rolling the sail around the mast. Differences in the design of some boats may alter the sequence of reefing, but the principles are the same. Boats with loose-footed sails usually have a tack downhaul and some boats have a locking mast. If so, they will need to be released and refastened at the points mentioned (right). Adjust the boom vang after the sail has been reefed.

1 Release the clew outhaul and remove the boom from the mast. Release the tack downhaul and unlock the mast (if necessary).

2 Rotate the mast until the required amount of sail has been reefed. Relock the mast in position (if necessary) and replace the boom.

3 Refasten the clew outhaul and the tack downhaul (if necessary).

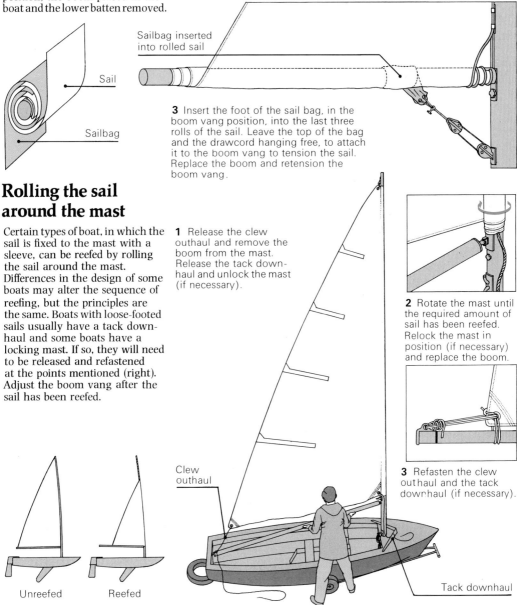

Clew outhaul

Tack downhaul

Unreefed   Reefed

Anchoring

Anchoring a dinghy is one of the least practiced skills in seamanship, and yet it is one of the most essential. There are occasions when knowing how to anchor, and having the equipment ready on board, could save you trouble – for example if you need to stop for a long period in tidal waters. Once a boat is afloat, and not actually sailing, the only way to prevent it drifting is to secure it to the seabed with an anchor and line. The type of anchor you need depends on the area where you are sailing, as some anchors are specially designed for certain types of seabed (right).

It is very important to make sure that the anchor is ready to use, with the line coiled neatly ready to be flaked (see opposite). The amount of line needed will depend on the depth of the seabed—you normally need about four times the depth you are anchoring in. The method below illustrates how to sail up to a chosen spot and drop anchor, while the two methods shown opposite demonstrate how to anchor off a beach, in tidal water. Sailing off an anchor is also shown opposite.

Types of anchor

There are several types of anchor, some of which are suitable only for specific types of seabed. Of those shown below, the plow or CQR will hold on most terrain, but of the other two, the folding grapnel and the mushroom, the former will hold only on rocky to firm ground and the latter only in soft ground.

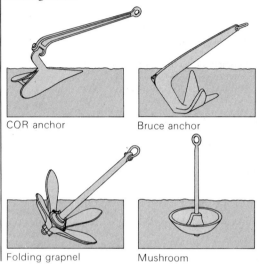

COR anchor   Bruce anchor

Folding grapnel   Mushroom

Anchoring

To anchor a small boat off-shore you will need an anchor weighing about 4 kg (8½ lbs) and a chain of about 2 m (6 ft), with a long line. Having selected your anchoring spot, you need to plan your approach so you can sail up to it on a beam reach, get the anchor ready and lower the jib. Don't forget to fasten one end of the line first, either to a cleat

or to the mast, or you will lose your anchor overboard. The key to successful anchoring lies in dropping the anchor at the right moment – just as the boat stops head-to-wind and begins to drift back from the anchoring point. When you have dropped the anchor, you must make sure the anchor is holding properly. This is best done by taking a range.

How to anchor
Luff up as you reach your anchoring point (1) until boat stops with wind blowing over side on which anchor is to be dropped. As boat drifts back, drop anchor (2), leading line through bow fairlead having first secured free end. Raise centerboard; lower mainsail (3). Test anchor and take range (4) (see page 105).

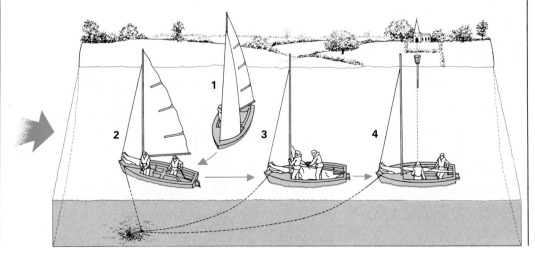

Anchoring off a beach in tidal water

There will be occasions when you wish to stop at a beach in tidal waters. Small, lightweight boats can, of course, be pulled up a beach but larger boats will be too heavy for a two-man crew to move and you will have to anchor. If you want to go ashore for some time you will probably need to retrieve your boat when the tide is higher or lower than when you arrived. The object of both the methods of anchoring shown is to make sure that the boat remains floating at all times and also that it is readily accessible when you want to leave. This is done by attaching an additional line (known as a tripping line) to the head of the anchor. As the method of anchoring you use will depend on the state of the tide, you will first need to find out whether the tide is rising (flood tide) or falling (ebb tide). Obviously where there is a considerable rise and fall of the tide, or where the shore slopes very gently you may not have enough tripping line (in the flood tide method) or be able to push the boat out far enough (in the ebb tide method) to retrieve it at the highest and lowest points of the tide. Experience will show you how long you can leave the boat. If in doubt, make a periodic check to make sure it is still afloat and can easily be retrieved.

Flood tide

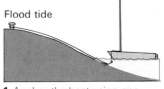

1 Anchor the boat using one line, having first attached a tripping line to the head of the anchor. Lead the tripping line up the beach and fasten it.

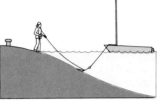

2 Recover the boat at high tide by pulling on the tripping line.

Ebb tide

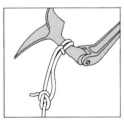

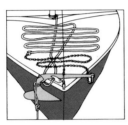

1 Fasten the tripping line to the anchor with a clove hitch and a bowline to secure it.

2 Place the anchor across the bow as shown, with the anchor line tied to the mast and flaked.

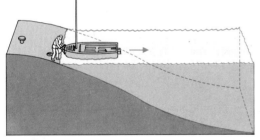

3 Push the boat out paying out the tripping line. Pull the anchor off the bow by tugging on the tripping line, which is then secured to the shore.

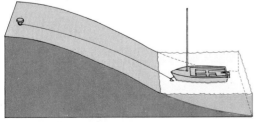

4 To retrieve the boat when the tide falls, unfasten the line and pull the boat in.

Retrieval and stowage of the anchor

To retrieve the anchor first hoist the mainsail. Then pull the boat forward on the anchor line, and begin to pull in the anchor over the windward side. Once it is on board, clean off any mud. Hoist the jib and put the boat into the hove-to position until the anchor and line are stowed, and then set the sails and move off.

As it is important to make sure that the anchor and the line are stowed ready for use, it is a good idea on larger boats to use a special container for them — for example, a milk crate with the divisions removed makes a good anchor box. Make sure one end of the line emerges through the side of the box so that you can tie it into the boat securely and flake the rest of the line into the box. Then lay the anchor over the top, and secure the box with a network of shock cord over the top.

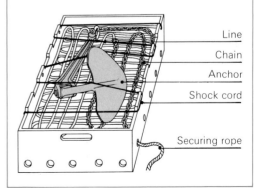

Line
Chain
Anchor
Shock cord
Securing rope

Stowing after sailing

As soon as the boat is removed from the water, the boat and the equipment should be hosed down with fresh water. The sails and sheets must be washed down thoroughly and then left to dry before being packed away. The equipment on the boat should be dismantled in the reverse order in which it was rigged (pages 44–55). The rudder and centerboard are stowed when the boat comes ashore. The mainsail and jib are let down and unshackled from their halyards which should be fastened to the shrouds at the side decking. Equipment left inside the boat should be properly stowed and inspection hatches and plugs removed to allow air to circulate and any water to drain away.

Rolling the jib

Most jibs have a wire luff and should, therefore, be rolled around the luff as shown below to prevent distortion. The jib sheets should be left attached, but rolled neatly.

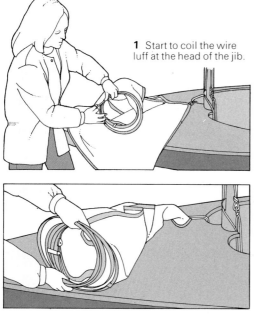

1 Start to coil the wire luff at the head of the jib.

2 Continue rolling until the jib forms a neat coil, smoothing any creases in the sail as you roll it.

3 Lay the coiled luff on the sail and fold the sail loosely before stowing it in the sail bag.

Folding the mainsail

Because the mainsail is large and unwieldy it is much easier to fold if it is laid flat on the ground first. Always make the folds towards the wind to prevent them blowing back. If two people work together, one either side of the sail, it makes the task much simpler. Remove the battens before you begin.

1 Starting at the foot of the sail, make the first fold about 1 m (3 ft) from the foot.

2 Make a similar sized fold nearer the head and lay the second fold on the first.

3 Continue folding until the whole sail is neatly in place.

4 Make sure the sail is smooth and free of creases.

5 Start to fold the sail across the folds previously made.

6 Fold the sail over and over until it is small enough to be stowed in the sail bag.

Storing the boat

Once you have removed all the equipment and stowed the sails you will have to store your boat until the next time it is sailed. The way the boat is stored depends on the size and type of boat and where it is kept. Small boats can easily be stored in simple racks which not only save space but afford good protection. Large boats are best stored on their launching dollies with their front ends supported (right) so that any water or condensation which collects in the boat drains out. The boat should be protected with a cover.

Covering the boat

Fix the cover firmly around the mast and make sure that the tie downs are secured. Ties to chocks on either side of the boat prevent it blowing over in a high wind. Most modern covers have a velcro strip fastening to make them quick and easy to put on (shown right), but laced covers (shown below) are also used.

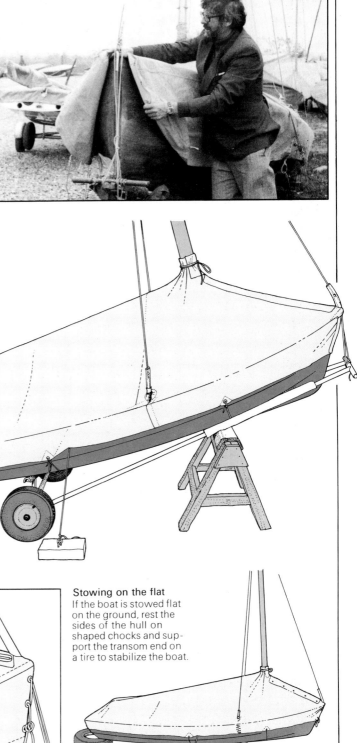

Laced cover

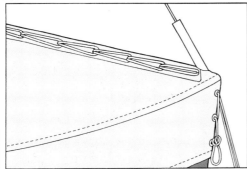

Stowing on the flat

If the boat is stowed flat on the ground, rest the sides of the hull on shaped chocks and support the transom end on a tire to stabilize the boat.

Rules of the road

As with any form of transport, there are rules governing the conduct of boats when they are afloat. The full name for these rules is the International Regulations for the Prevention of Collision at Sea, but for simplicity's sake they are often referred to as "the rules of the road".

There is a basic rule which states that power gives way to sail, but, in fact, it is often safer for a sailboat to ignore this rule and maneuver out of the way, particularly in crowded waters such as confined channels. Even in open water, you should still be prepared to get out of the way if there is any chance that you have not been noticed, or your course has been misunderstood by an approaching powered boat (it may easily be – the movement of sailing boats often appear unpredictable to non-sailors).

The principal rules to remember are to keep to the right in confined channels (see also pages 228–30, for further information) and, if you have to cross a busy channel, do so at right angles to the main flow of traffic.

The rules governing sailing craft alone and their relationship to each other are more numerous but for general purposes they can be grouped into three categories (see right). Anyone racing a boat will need to study the right-of-way rules used in racing (see pages 147–8).

Port and starboard

When the wind blows over your left bow (port side), the boat is on a port tack (see below) and when it blows over the right bow (starboard side) it is on a starboard tack (see below).

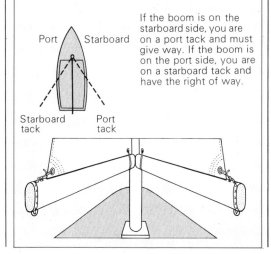

Port   Starboard

If the boom is on the starboard side, you are on a port tack and must give way. If the boom is on the port side, you are on a starboard tack and have the right of way.

Starboard tack   Port tack

Rights of way

There are three main rules to remember on a collision course; that, if in any doubt, you should pass behind another boat, not in front of it; that a boat on a port tack gives way to one on a starboard tack and that, when on the same tack, the windward boat should give way to the leeward one, and the overtaking boat to the slower one.

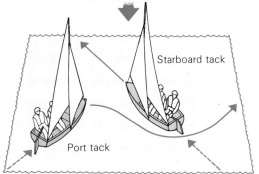

Starboard tack

Port tack

Opposite tack rule
When two boats are on opposite tacks, the port tack boat must keep clear of the starboard tack one.

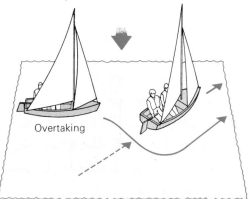

Overtaking

Overtaking rule
When both boats are on the same tack, the overtaking boat must keep clear of the slower boat.

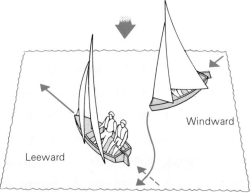

Windward

Leeward

Windward rule
When both boats are on the same tack the windward boat must keep clear of the leeward one.

Advanced Sailing

Advanced one-design handling · Trapezing techniques
Tacking and jibing a racing one-design · Spinnaker work
Single-handed sailing · Catamaran handling
Rough weather sailing · Tuning a boat · Racing

Improving your sailing

Once you have mastered the basic skills of sailing you will almost certainly want to learn how to make your boat go faster. Boat speed will depend on a number of factors: your skill as a sailor, the design of your boat and the way the sails and rigging are adjusted to suit different sailing conditions. The first essential is to improve your sailing skills by frequent practice and to understand exactly how the different controls affect the boat's performance on the various points of sailing. Once you have gained the necessary experience, you may choose to sail in a faster boat, like the modern racing boat, a 470, shown opposite.

Most modern racing boats are very finely tuned lightweight sailing machines with large sail areas. They require careful and highly skilled handling to do them justice, and they usually incorporate a number of fairly sophisticated controls to improve their performance. A number of racing boats have a trapeze system to enable the crew to move his or her weight further outboard to balance the relatively larger sail area and they also include a system for hoisting and lowering a spinnaker. The techniques for dealing with trapezing and spinnaker handling are dealt with on pages 107–9 and 112–19 respectively. The techniques for sailing catamarans, which are very fast indeed on some points of sailing, are dealt with separately on pages 122–9.

Learning how to tune your boat is an important part of making it sail faster and this is dealt with on pages 134–7.

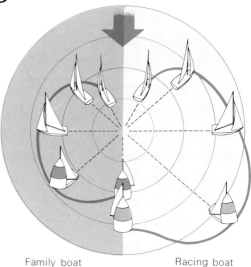

Family boat   Racing boat

Speed comparisons

A heavy family boat is slower on all points of sailing than a racing boat, given that both are sailed efficiently. The diagram, above, illustrates the difference in performance between the two types of boat. Both boats are faster on some points of sailing than others: for example, reaching courses are faster than running or close-hauled ones. Once you start to sail your boat competitively you will need to have a more exact understanding of how your boat performs on the different points of sailing to choose the most efficient course.

International 14s planing
All boats, without exception, sail faster once they begin to plane — in other words the bow lifts out of the water and the boat begins to travel on its own bow wave. Given the right wind and sea conditions boats will often plane automatically but they can also be induced to plane by using special techniques, see page 106.

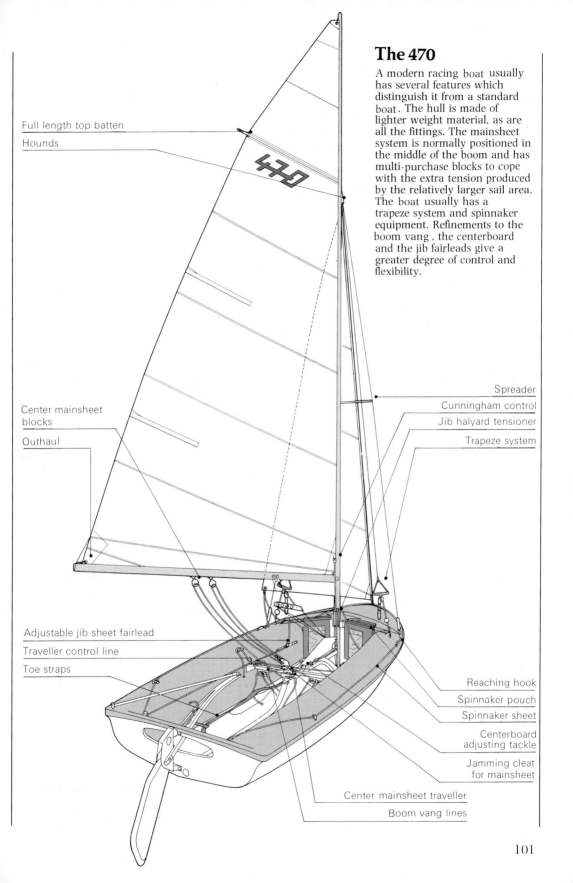

Full length top batten

Hounds

The 470

A modern racing boat usually has several features which distinguish it from a standard boat. The hull is made of lighter weight material, as are all the fittings. The mainsheet system is normally positioned in the middle of the boom and has multi-purchase blocks to cope with the extra tension produced by the relatively larger sail area. The boat usually has a trapeze system and spinnaker equipment. Refinements to the boom vang , the centerboard and the jib fairleads give a greater degree of control and flexibility.

Spreader

Cunningham control

Jib halyard tensioner

Trapeze system

Center mainsheet blocks

Outhaul

Adjustable jib sheet fairlead

Traveller control line

Toe straps

Reaching hook

Spinnaker pouch

Spinnaker sheet

Centerboard adjusting tackle

Jamming cleat for mainsheet

Center mainsheet traveller

Boom vang lines

Advanced techniques

Before starting to sail a high performance boat, such as a 470, you must be able to handle a basic one-design with a reasonable degree of competence. While the skills required for a high performance boat are no different, your sail setting and balance and trim must be more accurate to get the boat performing well. Your ability to steer a course to get the best out of the boat and your ability to read wind changes and to react to them are both equally important. It will help if you understand the basic theory of aerodynamics (pages 324–7) and are familiar with simple meteorology (pages 264–288).

Sail setting

High performance boats respond rapidly to changes in sail trim. There are no hard and fast rules to find the correct trim – it is usually a question of trial and error. However, one way of ascertaining more precisely if the sails are setting correctly is by using leech tell-tales on both sails. The use of tell-tales on the luff of the jib and mainsail has already been explained on page 58; additional tell-tales on the leech of both mainsail and jib give more precise information about leech tension. To get the tell-tale on the leech of the jib streaming horizontally aft, adjust the jib sheet tension and the position of the fairlead. The leech tell-tales on the mainsail can be made to fly out horizontally by adjusting the mainsheet tension and the position of the mainsheet traveller. If all three stream aft horizontally, the leech tension is correct.

Balance

It is essential for a one-design to be sailed upright at all times even if the mainsheet has to be eased to make it do so. Most people think that their boat is upright when in fact it is heeling at about 10°. However, if the boat is allowed to heel it will no longer travel in a straight line (see page 56). The only time it actually helps to heel a boat is when sailing in light winds. Then the boat should be heeled to leeward, which not only helps fill the sails, but also reduces wetted surface area and consequent drag. The simplest method of heeling the boat to leeward is to get the crew to sit on the leeward side. He should keep as low as possible in the boat so that he does not obstruct the flow of the wind between the jib and mainsail. Downwind, on a run, the weight of helmsman and crew should be spread as far apart as possible on opposite side decks to help prevent any rolling motion. On windward courses the crew must carry out minor adjustments of balance himself so as to leave the helmsman free to concentrate on steering a course.

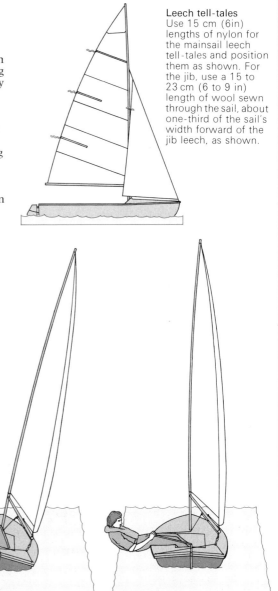

Leech tell-tales
Use 15 cm (6in) lengths of nylon for the mainsail leech tell-tales and position them as shown. For the jib, use a 15 to 23 cm (6 to 9 in) length of wool sewn through the sail, about one-third of the sail's width forward of the jib leech, as shown.

Incorrect balance
The boat is heeled, weather helm is created and drag increased.

Correct balance
The boat is upright, the helm is balanced and drag reduced.

Trim

A common mistake many beginners make is to sit too far aft in the boat which slows the boat and makes handling it more difficult. The helmsman and crew should sit close together to reduce the wind resistance produced by their bodies. In light winds, the weight should be shifted well forward so that the aft sections of the boat are raised out of the water and drag is reduced. This is true when sailing both upwind and downwind. One way of checking that the crew weight is correctly placed is by looking at the water leaving the transom; if it is very disturbed the transom is immersed too deeply. By moving the weight forward, the wake will smooth out. In stronger winds, and especially when sailing through waves the weight should be moved aft towards the middle of the boat, but with the helmsman and crew still close together. The bow and stern of the boat will then be able to rise easily over the waves and will avoid slamming down on them which slows the boat (see also pages 131–3 for rough weather sailing techniques).

Incorrect trim
The helmsman and crew are too far apart, making the bow and stern too heavy to lift over the waves easily.

Correct trim
Crew weight is concentrated together allowing the bow and stern to rise over the waves easily.

Weather and lee helm

Generally speaking, your aim should be to achieve a balanced helm on your boat. This means that the boat, in an upright position and with the sails set correctly, will sail a straight course even if the tiller is released. If you are constantly having to pull the tiller towards you to keep the boat on course the boat has "weather helm". The only immediate solution is to raise the centerboard until the helm becomes balanced. The opposite effect is known as "lee helm" and the remedy is to lower the centerboard.
To allow you to keep the centerboard fully down when beating, adjust the mast rake (see directions for tuning a boat, pages 134–7).

Boat with weather helm
To correct weather helm, check that the boat is upright and the sails are set correctly, then raise the centerboard until a balanced helm is achieved.

Boat with lee helm
To correct lee helm, check that the boat is sailing upright and the sails are set correctly, then lower the centerboard until a balanced helm is achieved.

Boat speed

Concentration on the course being sailed is vital for faster sailing. A moment's inattention can result in speed dropping considerably. Sailing close-hauled is the time when most beginners suffer from lack of concentration. It is essential that the boat is kept as close to the wind as possible without speed dropping. Constant attention should be paid by the helmsman to the jib tell-tales to keep them both streaming smoothly on both sides of the sail (see page 58). At times the windward tell-tale can be allowed to lift such as when pinching in strong winds (see pages 131–3), but on no account should the lee-ward tell-tales be allowed to do so. Different types of boat will sail closer to the wind than others and, in general, boats which plane to windward cannot be sailed as close to the wind as those which cannot plane on this point of sailing. Sailing to windward in strong winds or waves requires special techniques (see Rough weather sailing, pages 131–3). When sailing offwind, you must be careful to avoid violent changes of course and too much movement of the tiller – both can slow the boat down. If the boat can be induced to plane, considerable increase in speed can be achieved (see Planing, page 106).

Wind shifts

Although it may appear to be so, the direction and strength of the wind is never constant. Being aware of shifts in the wind and knowing how to use them to your advantage is an essential part of being able to get the best out of your boat. The time when you are most likely to be able to do so is when sailing as close to the wind as possible, on a close-hauled course to reach an objective on the edge of the no go zone. Any minor alteration in wind direction will be to your advantage or disadvantage depending on whether it is a "header" or a "lift" (below). A header is a wind shift in which the direction of the wind changes so that it points more from in front of you. On a close-hauled course, it will prevent you from reaching your objective on one tack. If ignored, the sails flutter, the boat comes more upright and slows down. To correct this, you have to pull the tiller towards you to get the sails to fill again. Your course then alters away from your destination and you will have to put in another tack. A lift is a wind shift which has the opposite effect to a header. As you sail along close-hauled, constantly luffing up and bearing away to find the edge of the no go zone, you will find that you will be able to sail closer to your objective than before the wind shift as the no go zone will have moved further away from you.

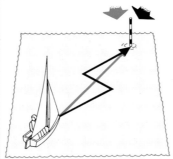

With a header on a close-hauled course the boat will fail to reach the objective in one tack.

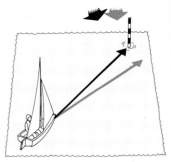

With a lift on a close-hauled course the boat will have no difficulty in reaching the objective.

Apparent wind

The sails always have to be set at a constant angle to the wind but you need to establish which wind. There are in fact two – the true wind and the "apparent" wind – a combination of the true wind and the wind which is caused by the movement of the boat (the created wind), which is always in the opposite direction to the boat's movement. When a boat is sailing with the wind forward of the beam, the apparent wind will be greater than the true wind. When the true wind is aft of the beam, it will be less. The diagrams, right, show how to establish the approximate direction of the apparent wind.

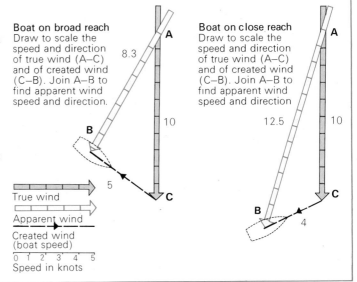

Boat on broad reach
Draw to scale the speed and direction of true wind (A–C) and of created wind (C–B). Join A–B to find apparent wind speed and direction.

Boat on close reach
Draw to scale the speed and direction of true wind (A–C) and of created wind (C–B). Join A–B to find apparent wind speed and direction

True wind

Apparent wind

Created wind (boat speed)

0 1 2 3 4 5
Speed in knots

Altering course

Many beginners find it hard to alter course from one point of sailing to another without slowing the boat down. It is important to use all the boat controls, not just the rudder, to achieve course changes (see page 56—7). Thus when bearing away, it is best to ease the main first, then allow the boat to heel to windward before moving the tiller. The jib should be kept sheeted in as this will also help the boat to bear away. This means that any excess movement of the tiller is avoided, to prevent slowing the boat down unnecessarily. To turn towards the wind the opposite procedure is needed. The boat should be allowed to heel to leeward, the mainsail is pulled in but not the jib and the centerboard is lowered. If you want to demonstrate to yourself just how much the boat will turn without the use of the rudder, practice sailing without one in an area free of other boats or obstructions. It is usually easiest if this is attempted in light winds with only one person in the boat. Being on your own means that you are responsible for all the adjustments and avoids any confusion between you and your crew. Keep the centerboard half-down and concentrate on balance and sail trim. Half-an-hour spent tacking and jibing around two buoys without a rudder will teach you more about balance and control than weeks of normal sailing, and although you will at first tend to sail around in circles you will quickly master the technique.

Boat control

Learning to sail slowly or to sail backwards requires considerable skill. To carry out either maneuver under control needs practice. You will often have to sail slowly coming into a float, for example. To do so, you either have to lower the jib or the mainsail depending on the circumstances (see pages 78—9). The boat handles very differently when sailed with either the jib or mainsail alone and you must practice to determine the characteristics of your boat. Some boats, for example will not sail well to windward under jib alone. To practice these skills, use a couple of buoys in a quiet sailing area and sail between them using first the mainsail and then the jib alone until you understand precisely how your boat handles under each sail.

Ranges

When sailing across a tidal stream or current it can be very difficult to judge if the course you are steering is going to take you to your objective. If you make no allowance for the current and point your boat directly at the objective you will end up some distance from it. Instead you must line up your objective with a fixed object behind it and steer to keep the two in line. You will then arrive at your objective although you won't have pointed directly at it.

The tidal gauge and the start line marker on the starting platform form a range.

The tidal gauge has moved to the left, so to bring it back in line you must steer to the left.

The tidal gauge has moved to the right, so to bring it back in line you must steer to the right.

Sailing backwards
1 Stop the boat head-to-wind. The crew pushes the boom well out. The sail will fill from ahead and the boat will move backwards.

2 Keep the crew weight forward. Steer by moving the tiller over towards the direction in which you wish the bow to move.

Planing

All boats will increase their speed if they can be induced to plane – lift up on their own bow wave and skim over the surface of the water. Most boats will only plane when there is at least 12 knots of breeze but the lighter the boat the more readily it planes. Generally they will plane readily on a reach, but some will also plane close-hauled or even on a run if the wind is strong enough. The secret of getting a boat to plane lies in anticipating when a gust is about to strike. Before it does, the helmsman should start to bear away and ease the sheets out to balance the crew weight and the heeling force

so that the boat is sailing exactly upright. When the bow begins to lift, the crew and helmsman should move aft while keeping the boat level. As the speed increases the sails should be sheeted in to allow for the shift in the apparent wind (it will move further ahead). When the gust passes, the boat can be held on the plane by luffing slightly to increase boat speed and to keep the apparent wind constant. If the boat begins to come off the plane, the crew weight should be moved further forward to keep the boat planing for a little while longer.

1 The boat is sailing below planing speed. The hull is making bow and stern waves and is trapped between them. Crew weight is in the middle.

2 The boat begins to plane by climbing onto its own bow wave. The crew moves aft to encourage the bow to lift.

3 The boat is planing; its stern wave has been left behind and the wake has flattened out. Crew weight is aft to keep the bow up.

Left, an Albacore planing fast on a reach, with the crew in the correct position. Above, a 470 planing on a broad reach with the spinnaker set correctly, the boat trimmed level and the bow well out of the water.

Trapezing

One of the key factors in keeping a boat upright, and therefore sailing faster, is the relationship of the crew weight to the centerline of the boat — the further away from the centerline the crew are positioned, the greater the ability of the boat to carry more sail because of the increased righting power. The usual way of placing the crew weight further away from the centerline is for the helmsman and crew to move further outboard, initially by hiking out with their feet supported by toe straps, and then by the crew moving completely outboard on a trapeze. First introduced in the 1930s, the trapeze only gained general acceptance in the 1960s as the most efficient way for the crew to gain more balancing power, especially in lightweight classes of boat. Most of the modern racing boats are now designed with such large sail areas that it is essential for the crew to go out on a trapeze in all but light winds when the boat is sailing to windward.

A standard trapeze system suspends the crew outside the boat by wires running from the hounds on the mast to a ring which is hooked onto a specially designed harness. Using a trapeze handle and the jib sheet to balance, a proficient crew can move quickly in and out of the boat, according to the changes in the wind and in the course. Fine adjustments to the balance and trim of the boat can be made by the crew bending his knees and moving along the gunwale (the outer edge of the side decking).

Many novice crews are frightened of using the trapeze because of stories of injuries and duckings. While it is true that trapezing is an advanced technique needing a lot of practice, once mastered, it is a skill that enables the crew to play an important and exciting role in helping the boat to perform better. Trapezing techniques are shown on the following pages.

The trapeze

The trapeze system on each side of the boat is supported by a thin wire fixed to the mast at the hounds. A handle is attached to the lower end of the wire, below which hangs a stainless steel ring, held in place by a cord. The systems on each side of the boat are joined by a length of shock cord.

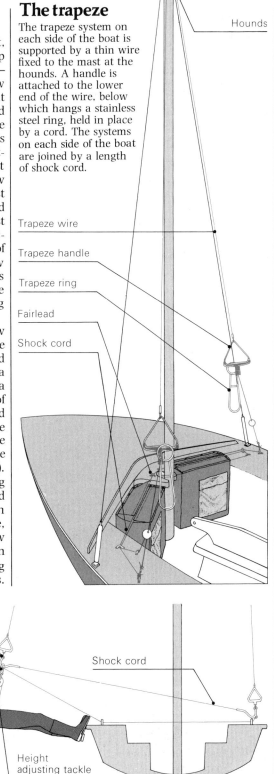

Hounds

Trapeze wire

Trapeze handle

Trapeze ring

Fairlead

Shock cord

Continuous system

Some boats are fitted with a continuous trapeze system which allows the crew to cross the boat quickly without having to unhook. The system (right) has a shock cord running between two hooks. A snap shackle, to which the crew is attached, using a height-adjusting tackle, runs on the shock cord.

Hook

Snap shackle

Shock cord

Height adjusting tackle

How to trapeze

It is best to start to learn to trapeze in medium winds and with an experienced helmsman who can sail the boat to compensate for any mistakes you may make. Once the boat starts to heel, the crew needs to be ready to move out quickly and smoothly to bring the boat back upright (see right). Novice crews should practice getting in and out on the trapeze (see below) and moving across the boat to trapeze on the opposite tack. Good communication between the helmsman and crew is vital as it is the helmsman's job to warn the crew of any changes in direction.

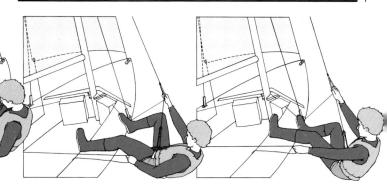

Getting out

1 Sitting well out, hook the trapeze ring onto the harness. With your front hand (nearest bow) grasp the handle and pull it outboard.

2 Slide out over the side decking and drop down until your weight is on the wire. Twist your body forward, and rest your front foot on the gunwale by the shroud.

3 Using the jib sheet to balance, push out with your front leg against the gunwale, keeping your body as near to right angles to the boat as possible.

Trapezing techniques

Normally, once out on the trapeze, you will tend to lean aft, but you must always be ready to brace yourself with your front leg if there is any sudden loss of speed. You will need to adjust your position constantly to keep the boat sailing upright. As the wind drops or the boat bears away you can come further inboard by bending your knees. By hooking onto the upper part of the trapeze ring you can lie out in a more upright position. To adjust the fore and aft trim of the boat, move along the gunwale. It is particularly important when planing on a beam reach to stand well aft (right). In addition to balancing the boat, you must watch the set of the sails and continue to trim the jib. You will soon learn to put yourself in the most streamlined position in relation to the helmsman.

The harness

For trapezing the crew wears a specially designed body harness (right) which has a hook (far right) on a metal plate to which the trapezing ring is attached. A broad back section gives the body full support. It is essential that the harness fits snugly, and is adjusted so that the hook is just below the waist. This will ensure that you are supported at the right angle, with your head up.

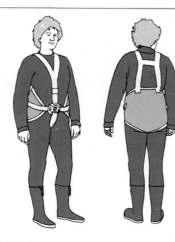

Trapeze hook
The trapeze hook is mounted on a metal plate with the opening facing downwards to make unhooking easier.

4 Bring your back leg (nearest stern) out to rest on the gunwale. Release the handle and continue to straighten your legs.

5 Lean back with your legs about a shoulder-width apart. More righting power can be gained by holding one arm out behind you.

Getting in
1 Swing your body back towards the stern of the boat, bend your knees and lean forward to grasp the handle. Bring your back leg over the gunwale, taking the strain on your front leg. Use the jib sheet to steady yourself as you come in.

2 Continue to move into the boat, bringing in your front leg last, making sure your foot doesn't slip forward of the shroud and keeping your body at right angles to the boat. Once seated on the side decking, unhook the trapeze ring.

Unhooking
To unhook after trapezing, pull firmly down on the trapeze ring and release it when it is clear of the hook.

Center mainsheet techniques

Many racing one-designs are fitted out with a center mainsheet system (see page 50), which gives the helmsman greater control over the shape of the rig than an aft mainsheet. However, because the system is fitted in the center of the boat, it impairs the helmsman's freedom of movement across the boat and different methods of tacking and jibing are needed from those described in Basic sailing. An alternative method for each maneuver, designed for boats with center mainsheets and long tiller extensions, is described below. These differ from the standard aft mainsheet methods in that the helmsman crosses from one side of the boat to the other near the transom facing forwards. When tacking he keeps hold of the tiller extension and the mainsheet throughout the maneuver giving him constant control. The helmsman moves across the boat without pausing to change hands on the tiller extension,

Tacking

It is important when tacking that the helmsman and trapezing crew coordinate their movements so that the boat is balanced. The crew must move in and out quickly on the trapeze.

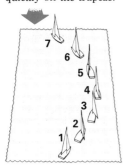

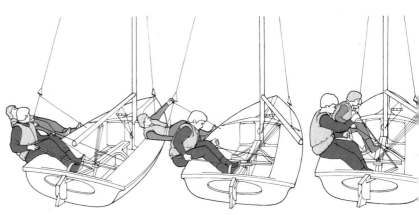

1 Helmsman checks to windward. If clear, instructs crew: "Ready about". He unjams mainsheet, and crew unjams jib sheet.

2 Crew replies, "Ready" Helmsman begins to move in and eases mainsheet as crew comes in and unhooks from trapeze ring.

3 Helmsman puts back foot across boat, pushes tiller firmly away. Crew also puts back foot across boat.

Jibing

When jibing, the helmsman takes hold of the mainsheet or falls (the part of the mainsheet running between the pulley blocks) to guide the boom across. This prevents it moving across too violently.

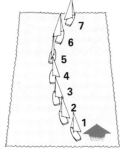

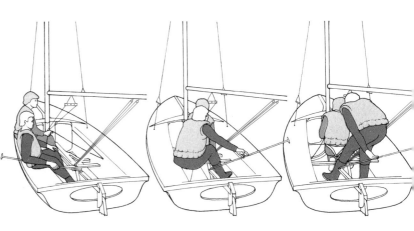

1 Helmsman balances boat as necessary, checks to leeward. If clear instructs crew: "Stand by to jibe". Cleats mainsheet.

2 Helmsman and crew each place back foot across boat. Helmsman revolves tiller extension over and aft to new windward side, leaving tiller central.

3 Helmsman changes hands on tiller extension behind back. Grasps mainsheet or falls. Crew moves into center of boat, keeping old jib sheet and grasping new one.

so less time is wasted in the middle of the tack. The extra speed gained using these methods of tacking and jibing has resulted in their adoption by many top racing crews. As you are most likely to encounter a center mainsheet on a high performance boat which is extremely sensitive to changes in the balance of the crew weight, it is important that your movements should be fluid and controlled at all times.

A multi-purchase mainsheet system on a high performance one-design.

4 Helmsman revolves tiller extension forward, moving across boat and holding mainsheet. Crew releases old jib sheet, grasps new one and crosses boat.

5 Helmsman sits down with tiller extension behind back. Grasps tiller extension with hand holding mainsheet. Crew takes new trapeze ring and hooks on.

6 Helmsman releases tiller from behind back and separates mainsheet, holding it in his front hand. Crew grasps trapeze handle, sheets in jib and moves out.

7 Helmsman centralizes tiller and sits out, and adjusts mainsail. Crew continues to move out and sets jib.

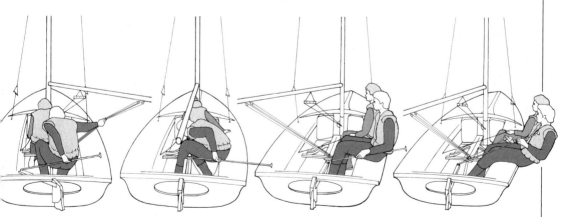

4 Helmsman pushes tiller away firmly. Crew balances boat while holding both jib sheets.

5 As boom centralizes, helmsman jerks tiller central and moves quickly to new windward side while crew drops old jib sheet and moves across.

6 Boom crosses to new leeward side. Helmsman grasps and uncleats mainsheet and sits on new windward side.

7 Helmsman trims mainsail and steers onto new course, while crew trims jib as necessary.

Spinnakers

A spinnaker is an additional, special sail used to provide extra driving power, mainly on courses away from the wind. It was developed from additional lightweight sails used on square-rigged ships when sailing during prolonged periods of light wind. It was originally designed for use only on downwind courses but the development of sailcloth construction and cutting techniques has resulted in sails designed to be used as far to windward as a close reach. Unlike other sails, the spinnaker is not attached along the length of the luff to a spar or stay and it relies on the force of the wind to keep it in position once hoisted. As the spinnaker is also loose-footed, it requires considerable skill to hoist it and keep it set properly.

There are many different spinnaker designs and types to choose from, according to your needs, and a number of different systems for stowing, hoisting and lowering the spinnaker. They range, depending on the type of boat, from an improvised system on an older boat to a sophisticated chute system on a high performance racing boat. These systems are designed to provide a means whereby the spinnaker can be hoisted and lowered quickly, with the minimum chance of a foul up, and stowed neatly without twists ready for hoisting again. Normally the type of system is dictated by the design of the boat. Most modern boats designed to be used with a spinnaker are fitted with a pouch stowage system or with a chute system (see pages 114–5). Either of these systems will enable a crew to handle a spinnaker with confidence and efficiency.

Handling a spinnaker demands skill on the part of both helmsman and crew and the key to successful spinnaker work lies in close cooperation between them. A standard routine for the major maneuvers (see pages 116–7) with a strict division of labor is essential. The division of tasks between the helmsman and the crew will vary according to the design of the boat and the systems fitted but, in general, the helmsman is responsible for looking after the equipment in the aft end of the boat and the crew for that in the forward end. Spinnaker work is best learned under the guidance of an experienced sailor, as mistakes can be costly in terms of equipment damaged or lost. Always remember that the sail, once set, exerts a strong pull and can easily become unmanageable.

Construction

Spinnakers are made from special lightweight nylon sailcloth which is reinforced to make it resistant to rips in the fabric. The stretch properties of spinnaker sailcloth are used to give a much more effective shape to the sail when set. The way the sail stretches is determined by the way the sail panels are cut and sewn together. Spinnakers designed for sailing downwind are cut with a fuller shape. Spinnakers designed for reaching or close reaching have a flatter shape.

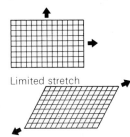

Limited stretch

Greater stretch

Spinnaker cloth
Spinnaker sailcloth is designed to resist rips and to have a limited stretch with the weave and a greater stretch diagonally across the weave. This gives a better sail shape.

Radial cut
Radial cut spinnakers are only rarely used because they tend to distort in the lower sections.

Horizontal cut
Horizontal cut spinnakers stretch mainly at the head. These are best for use on downwind courses.

Star cut
Star cut spinnakers remain flat under pressure and can be used on a close reach.

Tri-radial
This spinnaker combines the radial, horizontal and star cuts to produce an ideal all-purpose sail.

Radial head
A light weather sail for all around use, the radial head combines the radial and horizontal cuts.

Parts of the spinnaker

Apart from the spinnaker itself, you also need the appropriate ancillary equipment: a boom, known as a spinnaker pole, a halyard and hoisting system and a system of sheets led from each clew outside all the rigging to the side decking. The sheet on the windward side of the boat is known as the guy. Most crews adopt a continuous sheet system in which a single piece of rope is attached at each end to the clews. To use a spinnaker successfully you must make sure that the sheet leads or turning blocks are positioned so that the sheeting angle to the side decking is about 25°.

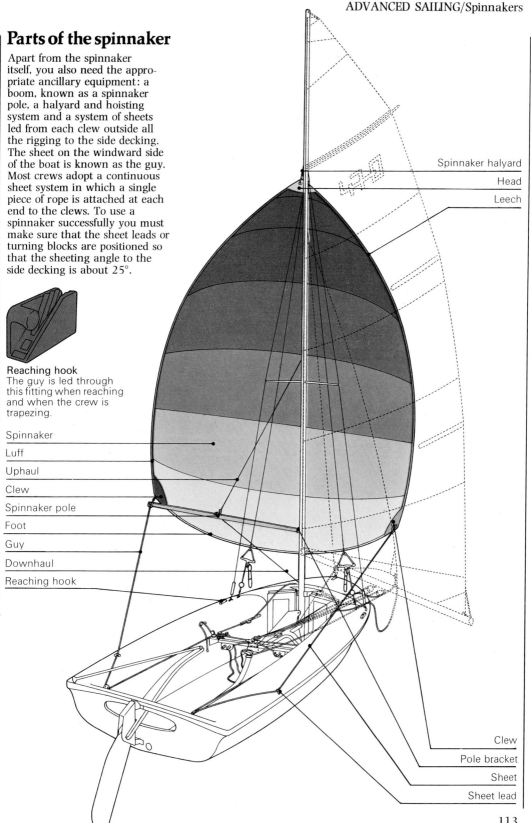

Reaching hook
The guy is led through this fitting when reaching and when the crew is trapezing.

Spinnaker

Luff

Uphaul

Clew

Spinnaker pole

Foot

Guy

Downhaul

Reaching hook

Spinnaker halyard

Head

Leech

Clew

Pole bracket

Sheet

Sheet lead

Pouch system

If your boat has a pouch stowage system for the spinnaker, there will be two fabric pouches, one on each side of the mast (right), which are closed by flaps secured with a shock cord. The spinnaker is hoisted directly from whichever pouch it happens to be stowed in. This means that it is vital that the spinnaker itself is free of twists and that the head and both clews are at the top of the pouch so they can be fastened quickly and easily.

Spinnaker pouches often have extra pockets, used to stow charts or sailing instructions.

Stowing the spinnaker

Before going afloat you must check that your spinnaker is properly packed in the pouch, without twists. If you are in any doubt, do a test hoist first before launching the boat. To do this, unpack the spinnaker from its pouch and remove any twists by working along each luff. Attach the halyard to the head and the sheets to the clews and then hoist and pack the sail.

Chute system

Many high performance boats have a chute stowage and hoisting system fitted. With this system, the spinnaker is stowed in a cloth sock or tube under the foredeck, which has a glass reinforced plastic opening either in front of or to the side of the forestay. As the spinnaker is hoisted it emerges from the fore-deck. The chute system has several advantages: the spinnaker cannot twist because it is pulled directly into the sock from the center of the spinnaker, and it is quick and easy to operate. However, the opening in the foredeck does allow water to get into the boat and can cause friction on the sail.

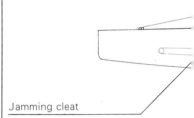

Jamming cleat

Spinnaker pole

The spinnaker is set from the spinnaker pole which is attached at one end to a bracket on the front of the mast. The other end of the pole is clipped to the guy. Special end fittings (below) allow the pole to be released quickly under pressure: When fitted, the openings should be uppermost. The pole hangs from a hook on the uphaul/downhaul, the position of which can be adjusted to alter the pole height if necessary (see right).

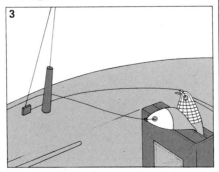

How to pack
Hoist the sail (1). One person then lowers the halyard while the other takes the windward clew and gathers the sail along the luff, packing it into the pouch (2). Holding the head, she gathers the remainder of the sail into the pouch, and packs the clews last. She then fastens the halyard under the reaching hook (3).

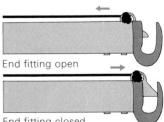

End fitting open

End fitting closed

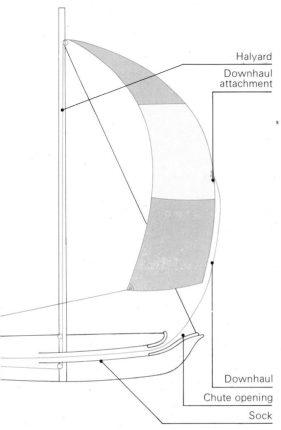

Halyard

Downhaul attachment

Downhaul

Chute opening

Sock

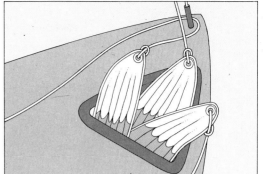

Spinnaker stowed in chute

Chute hoisting and stowage

The spinnaker is hoisted by the halyard which is attached to the head of the sail and led back from the mast to a jamming cleat near the helmsman. This halyard then continues running through the sock or tube and is fastened to the spinnaker in one of two positions (right), to form the downhaul. When the halyard attached to the head is released and the downhaul pulled, the spinnaker collapses and is pulled through the tube.

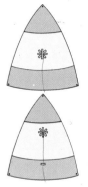

Downhaul attachment points

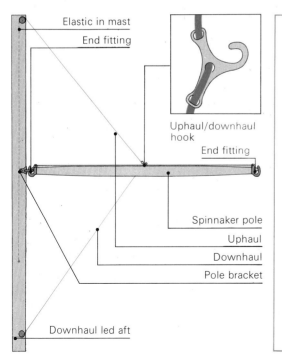

Elastic in mast

End fitting

Uphaul/downhaul hook

End fitting

Spinnaker pole

Uphaul

Downhaul

Pole bracket

Downhaul led aft

Pole height

The pole height must be adjusted so that when the sail is set the two clews are level. Normally the pole will be roughly at right angles to the mast (right), but if it is too high or too low (below), the sail will not set in the correct position.

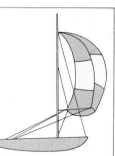

Pole set correctly

Pole too high

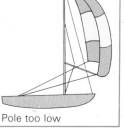

Pole too low

Hoisting and lowering

While hoisting and lowering the spinnaker the helmsman and crew must not forget to pay attention to their normal sailing duties. The helmsman must learn how to steer standing in the middle of the boat with the tiller between his knees, using his hands to help control the spinnaker. The method of hoisting and lowering you use will depend on the stowage system fitted. In all cases the best course on which to hoist or drop the spinnaker is a broad reach. The mainsheet and jib sheet are cleated prior to either maneuver. Before hoisting you must check that the halyard and sheets are attached and the sheets are correctly led outside the shrouds and forestay.

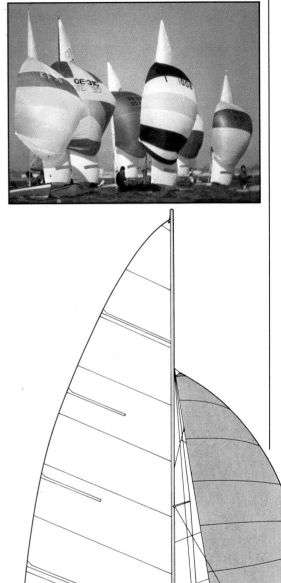

A well set spinnaker, like the ones on these Flying Dutchmen, will greatly increase your sailing speed.

Leeward pouch hoist

Hoisting to leeward from a pouch stowage system is much easier than hoisting to windward so, wherever possible, you should choose to hoist your spinnaker when the pouch in which it is stowed is to leeward. Before starting to hoist, the helmsman steers the boat onto a broad reach. The crew checks that the spinnaker is ready for hoisting and removes the halyard from its stowed position under the reaching hook.

How to hoist
Helmsman passes pole to crew who clips it to guy (left), attaches the uphaul/downhaul and fits pole to mast (below). Helmsman hoists spinnaker and, after cleating halyard, takes control of sheet and guy and sets sail. After fitting pole, crew sits to windward, puts guy under reaching hook and cleats it. She then takes control of sheet. Helmsman sits down to balance boat (right) and steers onto required course, while crew adjusts sheet and guy accordingly.

Windward pouch hoist

Before starting a windward hoist, the helmsman places the pole so that the crew can pick it up. The crew cleats the guy to the marked position (see Marking the sheets, page 119) and checks that the spinnaker is ready.

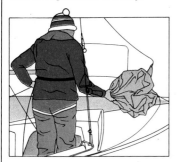

How to hoist
Crew removes spinnaker from pouch and holds it tightly bundled in her hands (above left). Helmsman takes up slack halyard and crew throws sail up and forwards to clear forestay, shouting, "hoist" (above right). Helmsman hoists rapidly and crew pulls on sheet to bring it to leeward. Helmsman takes sheet and guy, while crew fits pole to guy, uphaul/downhaul to pole and pole to mast. She then takes control of sheet and guy. Helmsman and crew sit down to balance boat.

Chute methods

Before hoisting from a chute, the crew cleats the sheet and guy to the marked positions (see Marking the sheets, page 119). The helmsman hoists the spinnaker, while the crew attaches the uphaul/downhaul to the pole and the pole to the mast and guy. To drop the spinnaker, the crew must keep the foot of the sail pressing against the jib luff as the helmsman pulls on the downhaul. When the sail enters the chute (below) the crew releases the guy and sheet and frees the pole.

Lowering - pouch stowage

With a pouch stowage system the spinnaker can be lowered to windward or to leeward. The windward drop is the safest because the crew weight is on the windward side throughout. The leeward drop should only be used if you need to have the spinnaker packed in the leeward pouch ready for a leeward hoist. The drop should be completed as fast as possible to prevent the sail tangling around the rigging.

Leeward drop
Helmsman steers onto a broad reach and prepares to lower sail. Crew uncleats guy and as helmsman releases halyard little by little, takes clew under boom and jib and packs sail. Once sail is in pouch, pole can be taken down.

Windward drop
Helmsman steers onto a broad reach, stands in middle of boat and uncleats halyard. Crew unclips pole from mast, removes uphaul/downhaul and unclips pole from guy. Crew then packs spinnaker into windward pouch, as described on page 114.

Playing the spinnaker

To keep the spinnaker setting correctly demands constant concentration. You must aim to keep the luff curling over and the sail on the point of collapse. To do this you have to adjust the sheet constantly and therefore should not cleat it. On a reach, when the boat is likely to sail at its fastest, the sheet will be under more strain and you will find the spinnaker harder to control. The closer to the wind you sail, the more crucial the sail trim becomes, and both the helmsman and the crew must be alert to the danger of the spinnaker collapsing. If this seems likely, the helmsman should bear away quickly to get the sail to fill again.

Spinnaker height
The spinnaker is setting well when the head of it extends horizontally from the mast. In strong winds, especially on a run, it will tend to set higher and it is often advisable to sheet the sail further forward by passing the sheet through the leeward reaching

hook rather than through the sheet lead. This holds the sail down and gives it a flatter shape, making it easier to control. In medium strength winds, the spinnaker halyard can be lowered 15–20 cm (6–8 in). This allows the sail to be set further forward, giving more drive. In light winds, when the spinnaker may not be filling properly, the pole should be lowered by adjusting the uphaul/downhaul to bring the clews level and to tension the luff.

Pole angle
You should aim to keep the pole as far aft as possible without allowing the spinnaker to collapse. Normally this means that the pole is kept roughly at right angles to the apparent wind and the guy is left cleated unless you alter course, but if you have difficulty in getting the spinnaker to fill, the pole can be allowed to point further forward. At no time should it touch the forestay as this may result in the pole being bent or broken.

A well trimmed spinnaker; the clews are level and the pole is not touching the forestay.

Whisker poles

When a spinnaker is not being used (or if the boat is not fitted with one) the jib can be goosewinged effectively by the use of a whisker pole. This is a short pole with a hook at each end. One end of the pole is hooked onto the clew of the jib and the other is hooked onto the spinnaker pole bracket on the mast (below). No uphaul/downhaul is needed.

Jibing

Jibing with a spinnaker set is a maneuver that needs to be completed smoothly and precisely in order to prevent the spinnaker becoming unmanageable. You will need to spend a lot of time practicing a set routine. While the crew concentrates mainly on manipulating the pole, the helmsman must be careful to keep the boat well balanced and the spinnaker set and under control throughout the jibe. To prepare for the jibe, the helmsman steers onto a run and checks that the area is clear. The crew adjusts the guy to bring the pole to an angle of about 45° to the center line of the boat to set the spinnaker square across the bow (see Marking the sheets, opposite). He then removes the guy from the reaching hook and cleats the sheet and guy. The boat is then ready for the mainsail and jib to be jibed first.

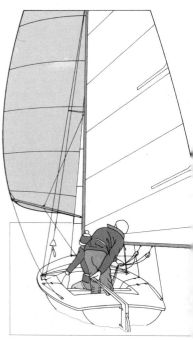

How to jibe
1 The helmsman and crew move to the center of the boat, and jibe the mainsail and jib by pulling them over to the new leeward side.

Marking the sheets

One way of making hoisting to windward, jibing and chute hoisting easier is to mark on the spinnaker sheets the points at which they are cleated for correct sail setting. For hoisting to windward, each sheet should be marked at the point at which it passes through the cleat when the clew has just cleared the forestay. This means that the guy can be cleated accurately before hoisting to windward. To find this point, before going afloat, take each clew in turn to a point about 1 m (3 ft) up the forestay. Cleat the sheet so that it is taut and mark the position on the sheet with paint or colored twine. To assist you to set the spinnaker square across the bow before jibing, hoist the spinnaker ashore and trim it so that it sets symmetrically in front of the boat. Cleat both sheets and mark them as before. When sailing, once you have set the sheets to their marked positions you will only have to make some minor adjustments.

When sailing with a spinnaker hoisted it is important that the crew sits to windward where he is able to see the luff of the sail clearly. This means that on a run or a broad reach, the helmsman usually must sit to leeward to balance the boat. On a beam reach or a close reach, the helmsman sits to leeward as long as the boat can be held upright. The crew should move out on the

trapeze as soon as the boat starts to heel, even before the helmsman moves to windward. The helmsman should aim to balance the boat to keep the crew out on the wire to give him a better view of the spinnaker luff.

When planing with the spinnaker, the helmsman and crew must use their righting power to the full to keep the boat balanced.

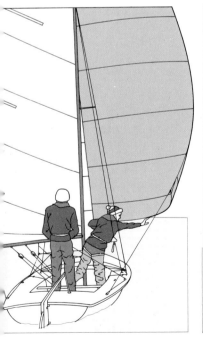

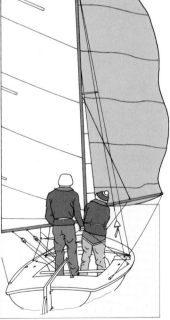

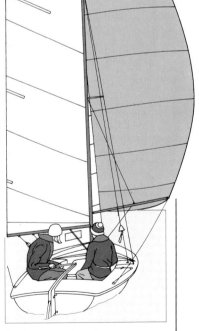

2 The crew removes the pole from the mast and clips it onto the new guy, while the helmsman steers with the tiller between his knees and controls the sheet and guy.

3 Pushing the pole out to the new side, the crew unclips it from the old guy and clips the free end of the pole to the mast. The helmsman keeps the spinnaker set.

4 The crew takes the new guy from the helmsman, cleats it and sits to windward. She then takes control of the new sheet. The helmsman balances the boat.

Single-handed sailing

Sailing single-handed has many attractions. Above all it provides an opportunity for you to test your sailing ability without a crew to help or hinder you. When you are in a boat by yourself, you take full responsibility for sailing it correctly and every success is your own. Many people choose to sail single-handed because one-man boats are often cheaper to buy and maintain than other boats as they are generally smaller and have simpler controls. They can usually be car-topped easily.

Single-handed boats vary from very small children's dinghies like the Optimist, to Olympic class boats such as the Finn. They normally only have one sail which is cat rigged, that is set from a mast positioned nearer to the bow than on boats with two sails. Some single-handers have an unstayed mast which, because it is allowed to bend, provides a highly effective sail shape.

It is as difficult to generalize about the handling characteristics of single-handers as it is about those of two-man boats. Each design has its own peculiarities and makes particular demands on its helmsman. Many one-man boats are very sensitive to changes in the balance of the crew weight and therefore you must always be alert to the effect on the boat of any movement you make. As there is only one

sail, it is particularly important that it should be tuned very accurately (see pages 134–7) and it is possible that you will have to continue to adjust the rig while sailing. On a Laser the clew outhaul adjustment is particularly important; as the wind gets stronger, the outhaul should be pulled out. Sailing upwind in a one-design with an unstayed mast requires a careful balance between the weight of the crew and the effect of mast bend to compensate for the heeling force. Single-handers usually compare most favorably with two-man boats when reaching in medium breezes, especially in waves, when they can plane almost continuously. As with other high performance boats, they are usually easiest to control on a reach. On downwind courses single-handed boats behave differently from two-man boats and can be difficult to handle. Because there is only one sail, there is a tendency for the boat to turn to windward which can be overcome if the boat is heeled to windward. In strong winds the mainsheet can be sheeted in to reverse the airflow over the sail and provide a heeling force.

As it is one of the most popular single-handed boats, the Laser has been used to illustrate this section. It is cat-rigged and has an unstayed mast and a loose-footed sail.

Tacking

As most single-handed boats are sensitive to shifts in the distribution of your weight in the boat, it is very important when tacking that you time your move across the boat carefully. When you do cross the boat it should be done smoothly and rapidly and you must sit out on the new side immediately. The boat must be kept upright throughout the turn.

1 The boat is sailing upright as the helmsman pushes the tiller away to start the tack.

2 As the boom nears the centre of the boat, the helmsman eases the mainsheet and starts to cross.

Jibing

In preparation for a jibe the boat should be moving as fast as possible. The centerboard (or daggerboard) should be a third to halfway down. Keep the boat upright or heeled to windward throughout the jibe. To prevent the mainsheet catching on the transom and to help the boom to cross smoothly, it is a good idea to pull in some mainsheet.

1 Sailing on a run, the helmsman changes the tiller extension to the new side

2 After cleating the mainsheet, the helmsman changes hands on the tiller extension.

Rigging the boat

On a Laser the sail is attached by inserting the mast into a sleeve in the luff. This means that the sail must be fitted before the mast can be stepped. The Cunningham control holds the mast in position. Although the parts of the boat are very light, it is easier to rig a Laser if you have help.

1 The sail is fitted onto the mast after joining the two mast sections.

2 The mast is held still, while the boom is fitted onto the gooseneck.

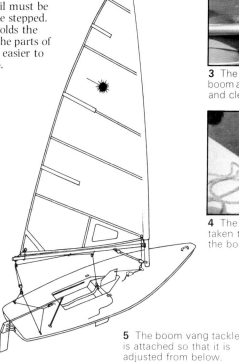

3 The clew is lashed to the boom and the outhaul tensioned and cleated on the boom.

4 The Cunningham control is taken through the hole, round the boom and cleated on deck.

5 The boom vang tackle is attached so that it is adjusted from below.

3 Keeping hold of the mainsheet, the helmsman rotates the extension and begins to center the tiller.

4 The helmsman sits down on the new side and changes hands on the tiller and mainsheet.

5 The helmsman balances the boat and trims the mainsail for the new tack.

3 The helmsman heels the boat to windward, moves the tiller and uncleats the mainsheet.

4 As the boom moves across, the helmsman moves to the new side and centers the tiller.

5 The helmsman sits on the new side with the tiller towards him to keep the boat upright.

Catamarans

Catamarans are lightweight craft which can carry a larger sail area and therefore can sail faster than monohulled boats, because of the greater stability given by the twin-hulled design. Apart from the design features made necessary by the twin hulls, such as the central bridge deck trampoline, twin rudders and a forestay bridle (see opposite), catamarans have several features not found on other high performance boats to help you cope with the higher speeds. The sails are particularly flat and the mainsail has full-length battens to keep it tensioned. Both the mainsail and jib are controlled by complex (multi-purchase) pulley systems for easier handling. A rotating mast is also fitted which allows a more effective air flow.

Sailing a catamaran requires a slightly different technique to sailing a monohulled dinghy. Because catamarans are generally more stable than monohulls, they are easier to jibe. However, they can and will capsize, sometimes even stern over bow (known as "pitchpoling"), if the bows dig into the water when the boat is travelling at high speed. An important point for someone new to catamaran handling to bear in mind is that because the fastest point of sailing is a beam reach, the boat must make maximum use of the speed gained on this course wherever possible. For example, it is most efficient to sail slightly off a close-hauled course or a dead run and to tack towards your objective, taking advantage of the boat's natural speed. Before going out in a catamaran, remember that it gives little protection to the crew. Because of the high speed at which it can travel, spray is thrown up with great force, so wearing efficient waterproof clothing is very important, especially in bad weather.

Catamaran types

Some different types of catamarans are: the Hobie, far right, which is a two-man catamaran, the Unicorn (center right) which is a single-hander, and the Dart, right, which is sailed single-handed without the jib and as a two-man boat with the jib. There are some variations in all the designs: the Hobie, for example, has a raised trampoline and the Spark has no boom (detail below).

Dart   Unicorn   Hobie

On the Spark, a small, lightweight catamaran, the mainsail has no boom.

On the Hobie, the trampoline is stretched on beams raised above the hulls.

The Tornado

The Tornado is an Olympic class two-man catamaran with a trapeze. Its slim fiberglass hulls are joined by two aluminum beams. Each has a centerboard. A trampoline, made of strong nylon mesh, is stretched between the beams and hulls. A special mast spanner from the mast to the boom allows the mast to rotate. The mainsail is held locked into position by the masthead halyard lock. The sails are controlled by multi-purchase sheeting systems. Foot loops and a restraining rope, which is hooked onto the trapeze harness, keep the crew in position when trapezing behind the helmsman.

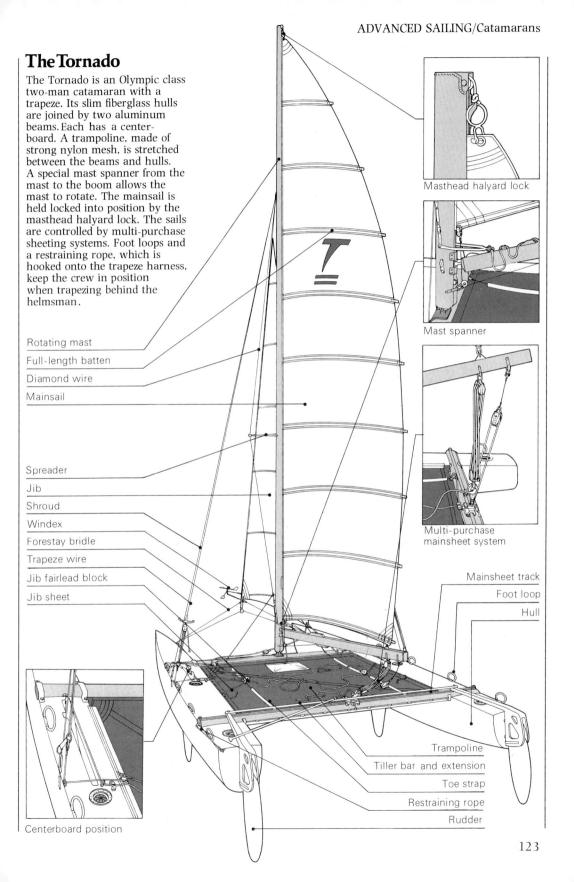

Masthead halyard lock

Mast spanner

Multi-purchase
mainsheet system

Rotating mast

Full-length batten

Diamond wire

Mainsail

Spreader

Jib

Shroud

Windex

Forestay bridle

Trapeze wire

Jib fairlead block

Jib sheet

Mainsheet track

Foot loop

Hull

Trampoline

Tiller bar and extension

Toe strap

Restraining rope

Rudder

Centerboard position

Catamaran handling

The techniques for catamaran handling vary to some extent from one design to another. Whether you choose to sail a two-man boat or a single-hander, you will need to be fit. Don't let the apparent lateral stability of the twin-hulled design lull you into a false sense of security — ability to concentrate and quick reactions are essential to cope with the higher speeds and most catamarans are unsuitable for beginners. You also need to be quite strong — although steering a catamaran normally only takes minor adjustments of the tiller, pushing or pulling the tiller over to tack or gybe the boat requires considerable effort.

To sail a catamaran well you need to have a very clear understanding of the difference between true and apparent wind (see Aerodynamics section) as the speed at which the catamaran sails exaggerates the difference between them, and the sails must be trimmed accordingly otherwise the boat will slow down or stall. Correct crew position is important in order to keep the boat level and to prevent it from nose-diving into waves.

The Tornado, above, is sailing fast on a reach. It is correctly balanced with the windward hull just clear of the water.

Windward sailing

The easiest point of sailing for catamarans is a beam reach. You will soon become accustomed to the fact that the apparent wind comes from much further ahead, so that the sails are set close to the centerline. The most important sail control is the mainsheet traveller which enables you to adjust the angle the sail makes to the wind without disturbing the sail shape. Many catamaran sailors sail their boats with the traveller alone, leaving the mainsheet to operate as a boom vang. The two centerboards should be adjusted as for monohulls, but because there are two, they can be moved independently to give better grip to either the leeward or windward hull. Their position is critical: too much centerboard and drag is created; too little and the boat drifts sideways. Crew weight should be adjusted to keep the hulls level fore and aft and the windward hull should be just clear of the water.

Upwind
On close reaches the mainsheet traveller is moved towards the centerline of the boat and the leeward board is lowered first. Even in medium winds, the crew should trapeze and the helmsman sit out. As the boat sails closer to the wind, both centerboards are fully lowered and the sails sheeted to the centerline. The helmsman steers the boat using the tell-tales or wind indicator (see opposite, above) to maintain speed rather than to sail closer to the wind. If speed drops, turn away onto a close reach and then luff up to a close-hauled course again. Crew and helmsman should be close together to present the least wind resistance and position themselves so that the tip of the leeward bow is just above the surface of the water.

Tacking
Tacking in a catamaran is a maneuver which often causes problems for those new to catamaran sailing. A mistake during the tack is likely to result in the boat stopping head-to-wind (see Getting out of irons, opposite). A set routine for tacking, as described right, should be developed and practiced.

How to tack

1 Helmsman and crew check around to see if area is clear to tack. Helmsman calls, "Ready about", and bears away a little.

5 When in the middle of boat, crew allows jib to back and helmsman swivels tiller extension to pass it behind mainsheet.

Wind indicator

Because of the high speed and rapid acceleration of catamarans, the apparent wind is liable to shift violently and increase or decrease in strength suddenly. It is crucial that the helmsman is aware of these changes so some form of wind indicator should be used. This is usually fitted on the forestay bridle, ahead of the luff of the jib, where it will register the smallest change in the direction of the apparent wind and will help you to adjust the sails to the optimum sheeting angle.

Wind indicator

Getting out of irons

When learning to handle a catamaran, you often fail to complete the tack. If you stop head-to-wind, the solution is to reverse the rudders and back the jib so that you can sail backwards until the bows turn towards your intended heading. Then sheet in the jib and pull the tiller towards you to sail off fast on the new close-hauled course.

2 Crew uncleats jib sheet, keeping it tensioned. (If he is trapezing, he prepares to come in.)

3 Helmsman calls, "Hard a-lee", and pushes tiller away and eases mainsheet. Crew eases jib sheet just a little.

4 Helmsman pushes tiller further over. Helmsman and crew start to move in and crew picks up new jib sheet.

6 Crew moves to new windward side, releases old jib sheet. Helmsman moves tiller extension over to new windward side.

7 Crew sheets jib to correct side as helmsman changes hands on mainsheet and tiller extension, and centralizes tiller.

8 Helmsman pulls in mainsheet to rotate mast on new tack and steers to gain speed on new close-hauled course.

Catamaran sailing downwind

One of the main principles to bear in mind when sailing a catamaran on a downwind course is that you should never sail directly away from the wind. Instead, you have to sail a zigzag course, known as "tacking downwind" (see below). Because a catamaran achieves very high speeds on a broad reach – far higher than on a run – it is worthwhile sailing from one broad reach to another and jibing across.

Although most monohulls also sail faster on a broad reach than on a run, it is not worth tacking a monohull downwind because the speed gained on the reach is not sufficient to compensate for the extra distance travelled. Provided you remember to keep the wind on the beam and adjust your course accordingly you will keep the boat sailing on the fastest course downwind.

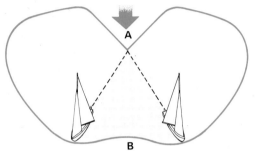

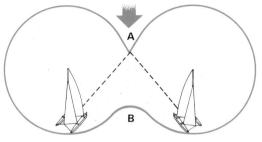

The blue line in each diagram represents distance travelled from A on different headings in a given time. Although the diagrams are not necessarily to scale, it can be seen that there is a greater speed difference between a broad reach and a run (A–B) with the catamaran than with the one-design.

Tacking downwind

The method for tacking downwind is very similar to tacking upwind, right. When learning the technique it helps to tack upwind first and then follow your tracks back on a downwind course. You must perfect a smooth jibing technique where the boom is handed across the boat by the helmsman while the crew concentrates on resetting the jib to get maximum drive out of the sails. Remember that if you are too slow at the jibe you will lose the extra momentum gained from the zigzag course.

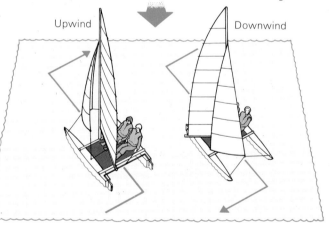

Upwind

Downwind

Setting sails

Because the downwind tacking course exploits the point of sailing with the greatest difference between true and apparent wind, it is important to make sure that the sails are setting properly all the time. Tell-tales are an essential aid to interpreting the flow of air over the sails. When you start sailing downwind, build up boat speed on a beam reach, and then turn the boat onto a broad reach. Use the mainsheet traveller to position the sail and allow the mast to rotate enough to bring the luff of the sail well forward. The crew should lie on the leeward hull and hold the jib sheet out and down (unless it is held by a device known as a barber-hauler which performs the same function).

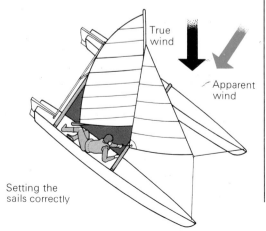

True wind

Apparent wind

Setting the sails correctly

Sailing in waves

As a general principle, waves move faster than sailing boats, which means that you have to get used to the idea that waves will overtake you from astern when you are sailing. Even if you are travelling obliquely across the waves, they will pass beneath the boat unless you attempt to prevent the situation occurring. It is vital to maintain boat speed and to do this you must stay on one wave for as long as possible. One of the ways of maintaining this position is to maneuver the boat so that

the sterns of the catamaran are picked up on a wave and the boat then travels with it down its face. If you lengthen the slope of the wave by sailing at an angle, you increase the length of time you are travelling with it. Maintaining this position is an advanced technique which takes quite a lot of practice to perfect but if you wish to race a catamaran, for example, you need to be able to exploit the waves as much as possible to gain whatever increase of speed you can.

By following a direct path over the waves, the catamaran will travel much slower and the bows will dig sharply into the back of the wave in front of the boat.

By travelling at an oblique angle across the waves, the catamaran will maintain its speed for much longer and reduce the likelihood of the bows digging into the wave in front of the boat.

The Tornado (above) is bearing away on a downwind course to improve boat speed.

Balance and trim

Apart from the actual angle of the boat approaching the waves, you must also think about the weight in the boat. By altering the position of the crew as the boat rides over the waves you can maintain boat speed for much longer. Even in quite small waves you can make an appreciable difference to boat speed by very simple alterations of fore and aft trim of the boat.

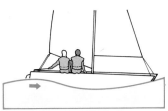

1 As the wave lifts the stern, concentrate on building up speed. Luff up slightly and then bear away when speed builds up.

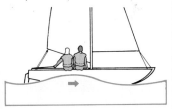

2 When the crest is under the rear beam, move your weight rapidly forward to prevent the bow rising and to build up more speed.

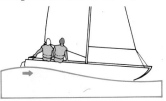

3 Ride the face of the wave for as long as possible until your boat speed drops and then luff up, adjust your sails and move your weight back.

4 Prepare for the next wave to catch up with you and then repeat the first step as it lifts the stern of the boat.

Catamaran sailing in rough weather

The sealed hulls of catamarans enable them to be sailed safely in very rough conditions. But as with other high performance craft, medium strength wind conditions are best for building up your experience as the catamaran is sailing at its optimum speed. Crews can learn how to handle the trapeze system when tacking and how to move quickly up and down the gunwale to the aftermost trapezing position.

However, only very experienced sailors should attempt to sail catamarans in strong winds and heavy seas. The two main points to bear in mind are to keep the boat moving as fast as possible when going to windward and to make sure the boat is balanced – keeping the hulls level by sheeting the sails well out and bearing away in gusts.

In rough weather, tacking should be kept to the minimum and should be carried out, if possible, in smaller waves wherever they appear. If you fail to get around on the tack, be prepared to reverse the rudders (see pages 124–5). Although you will often have to retract the centerboards on a reach to lessen the pressure on the sails, you must have the boards at least three-quarters down to tack. At all times, crew weight should be kept well aft except when urging the boat over the crest of a wave. Acceleration and deceleration will be very rapid so the crew must brace themselves securely using the foot loops or toe straps.

Spray or breaking waves can make visibility difficult, and some crews prefer to wear ski or swimming goggles to protect their eyes. Extra protective clothing will be necessary as the spray strikes hard enough to be painful.

The catamarans above and below are both sailing in rough weather on a reach – the helmsman and crew are well aft.

Righting catamarans

Catamaran capsizes are often spectacular because of the speed at which the boat is travelling when the capsize occurs. Ironically, however, a catamaran can capsize just as easily when it is moving slowly if the sails are over-sheeted. This results in the crew being unable to get the boat to respond quickly enough if a wind shift occurs and the boat then capsizes to leeward. By far the most spectacular, but rather less common, form of capsize happens when the bows dig into a wave and the boat somersaults forward, stern-over-bow. This normally only happens in rough conditions when the boat is travelling at very high speed. When it does happen, the first priority is to make sure the crew is released from the trapeze.

Catamarans invert easily and therefore your capsize drill needs to be rapid and well-rehearsed. The method for righting a small catamaran differs from that for a bigger one. The smaller types, like the Dart for example, can be righted by immersing the bows or sterns until the hulls are vertical in the water. It can then be easily pushed back to its normal sailing position. Larger catamarans will need to be righted by applying weight to the uppermost hull, using the jib sheet as a lever.

Should the boat prove impossible to right, you will need outside assistance to help you recover the boat.

Righting large catamarans

The helmsman and crew must react fast to prevent the boat from inverting. One of them grabs a jib sheet while the other sinks the bow or stern. As the boat comes upright the crew must jump aboard quickly to prevent the boat from sailing away on its own.

1 Helmsman and crew swim round to back of boat. Crew grabs jib sheet while helmsman steadies hull.

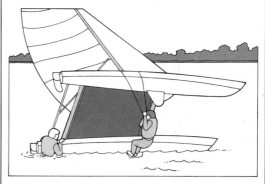

2 Crew uses lower centerboard and jib sheet to apply pressure to uppermost hull while helmsman applies pressure to lower hull.

Righting small catamarans

A number of smaller catamarans can usually be successfully righted by pushing the bows or sterns (it doesn't matter which) down into the water until they dip into the water sufficiently to allow the boat to become vertical. Once in that position, the boat can easily be pushed over into its normal attitude.

1 Helmsman and crew swim around to the bows or sterns of the boat and apply their weight to one end of the lower hull to immerse it.

2 As the uppermost hull drops, one person applies his weight to the end of the upper hull while the other continues pushing on the lower one.

3 When the boat is vertical, helmsman and crew swim to the front and push the boat over into its normal sailing position.

4 Once the boat is righted, they scramble aboard and prepare to sail off. Any delay may result in the boat sailing off on its own.

129

Catamaran assembly

Because of their great width, most catamarans have to be dismantled before they can be transported by road and have to be reassembled when you reach your sailing area. The procedure for assembling a Dart is shown here. It is one of the easiest catamarans to put together — with a little practice, two people can assemble it in a few minutes. You should choose a flat piece of ground on which to work. If you have to assemble the boat on concrete or another hard surface, put down some protective covering to prevent damage to the hulls.

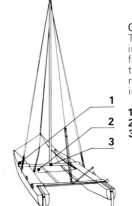

Order of assembly
The Dart can be divided into three basic sections for assembly: the hulls, the trampoline and the mast. It is put together in the following order:

1 Join hulls together
2 Fit trampoline
3 Step mast

Joining the hulls

Lay one hull on the ground with the inside edge uppermost. Insert the front and rear beams into their sockets on the hull. Stand the hull up on its keel and slot the beams into their sockets on the other hull. Each beam has self-locking devices which keep it in position in the sockets. The rear beam incorporates the track for the mainsheet traveller, sliding fittings for tensioning the trampoline and has permanently fixed toe straps.

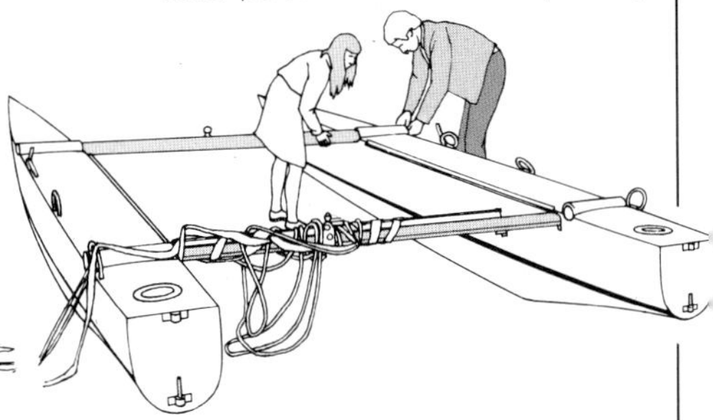

Slotting the beams into the hulls
One person slots the beams into the first hull (left). He then holds the second hull on its keel while the other person fits the beams (below).

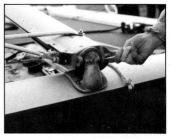

Attaching the trampoline

Attach the trampoline first to the front beam. Pass the edges through the tracks on the hulls to the rear beam. Insert the plastic tubing through the rear edge of the trampoline to stiffen it. Then lace the trampoline to the rear beam by passing the cord through the sliding fittings and behind the plastic tubing and tension it. Fasten the toe straps to the front beam.

Stepping the mast

Lay the mast along the trampoline so that the heel is resting on the mounting on the front beam. Insert the mast pin to stop the mast rotating while it is being stepped. Untie the rigging and attach the shrouds and the forestay bridle. Then raise the mast and connect the forestay to the bridle and the trapeze wires to the hulls. Assemble the sheeting systems. Just before sailing, attach the rudders and remove the mast pin.

Inserting the mast pin through the base plate and ball-and-socket mounting.

Lacing the trampoline to the rear beam by passing the cord behind the plastic tubing.

Stepping the mast by pulling on the trapeze wires and lifting it into the upright position.

Trapeze wire attached to its fitting by the shrouds, near the foot loop.

Rough weather sailing

There is no hard and fast rule about what constitutes rough weather. Conditions which might be safe enough for one type of boat sailed by an experienced crew could easily be too difficult for novice sailors on another type of boat. As a general guide, wind strengths above 20 knots can be considered as rough weather. A lot also depends on the state of the water and the area you are sailing in. When the wind and tide are opposed, the sea tends to build up making the conditions difficult to deal with. A wind strength of 15 knots coupled with a heavy sea could present more of a problem than a wind strength of 25 knots and calmer waters.

For reasons of safety, sailing clubs often cancel race meetings in strong wind conditions and discourage individuals from sailing. However, it is vital that you gain experience of rough weather conditions and the best solution is to go afloat with an experienced sailor and to have a rescue boat close by.

The rougher the conditions, the harder both you and your boat will have to work. You must check that all the fittings on your boat are securely mounted as they will have to take a great deal of strain. If you are in any doubt about the reliability of the rigging, for example, don't go out. You must remember to check your boat's buoyancy and the bailing equipment very carefully before going afloat in rough weather.

You can also make certain adjustments to the rig of your boat to make your task of sailing in rough weather easier. Detailed instructions on boat tuning are given on pages 134–7. The sails can be tuned to spill excess power automatically from the top by allowing the mast to bend and by flattening the mainsail using the clew outhaul, the boom vang and Cunningham controls. The sheeting angles should be adjusted to be as wide as possible by using the mainsheet traveller and adjustable jib fairleads. These adjustments are particularly important for upwind sailing.

Once you are afloat in rough weather, you will notice a great difference in the way the boat handles; every maneuver will seem more violent than under normal conditions. The heeling forces will be greatly increased and bearing away will not provide a restful solution as the boat will tend to plane; in strong winds, a high performance boat will plane almost constantly. The most stable course of sailing will be found to be a close-hauled one.

Crewing on a trapeze (below) in rough weather requires stamina and concentration to keep the boat moving upright in strong winds.

Close-hauled

In heavy weather, sailing close-hauled is usually the safest point of sailing. Power can be reduced by spilling wind from the sails, either by adjusting the rig, as described on the previous page, or by letting out the sheets. The technique for sailing upwind in strong winds and large waves varies according to the type of boat you are sailing, high performance or heavy family dinghy. However, one rule always applies: the boat must be kept absolutely upright. The helmsman and crew must use their righting power to the full by sitting out as far as possible.

High performance boats

When sailing a modern high performance boat that will plane to windward, sail slightly free of close-hauled until the boat begins to plane and then sail as close to the wind as possible while still planing. The jib should be eased slightly. The helmsman keeps the boat upright by constantly playing the mainsheet – it should never be cleated. Both the mainsail and the jib will usually have some twist in them which spills wind. Raising the centerboard slightly also helps to reduce the heeling force. The helmsman must give his full attention to steering through the waves approaching the bow of the boat. He adjusts the tiller

constantly, directing the boat over and around the waves to prevent them stopping the boat. If the boat is stopped, the driving force of the wind will become a heeling force and control will be reduced. The helmsman and crew need to position themselves close together in the middle of the boat to allow the bow and stern to lift freely in the waves. As a wave approaches the bow, luff up to sail over the face of the wave and bear away down the back of the wave. In very big waves the wind strength increases at the top of the waves and both members of the crew will need to sit out to balance the increased heeling force. This technique for sailing through waves is also used in heavy family boats.

Heavy family boats

Sailing close-hauled in a heavy family boat, which does not plane to windward in rough weather requires slightly different techniques from those used when sailing in a high performance boat. Because you do not have to keep the boat planing, you can use the no go zone to release the heeling force and keep the boat upright. You can sail a course very close to the wind if you use the following technique during the gusts. As the gust approaches, the helmsman luffs

Sailing a close-hauled course in strong winds can be made easier by allowing the sails to twist.

up a little and lets out the mainsheet as necessary to allow the boat to come upright. As the gust passes he bears away onto his original course. It is important not to slow down too much as you luff up or you lose some control. The crew must keep the jib sheeted in hard, unless an exceptionally strong gust blows.

Tacking and jibing

Changing course through the wind in rough weather demands much greater concentration than in normal conditions as the increased strength of the wind makes the movements much more violent. Maintaining the balance of the boat is crucial and you must not allow the boat to heel during a tack, or to roll during a jibe or you are likely to capsize.

Tacking

When tacking in rough weather the most important factor is maintaining the speed of the boat during the turn. It must be moving fast immediately prior to the tack. It is preferable to tack where the waves are smallest and the helmsman must watch carefully to pick the most advantageous moment. Start to tack when the bow has just passed the top of a wave. This reduces the possibility of the boat being stopped by a wave during the tack. The crew releases

the jib just as the boat starts to turn and sheets it in as soon as possible on the new side. The helmsman and crew must sit well out on the new windward side as quickly as they can to prevent the boat heeling. Do not sheet in the sails tightly until the boat has picked up speed again.

Jibing

Jibing in strong winds and large waves is a critical maneuver which must be tackled smoothly and precisely. The best moment to jibe is when the boat is moving at its fastest, either down a wave or after accelerating from a gust. At this point the apparent wind is at its weakest and therefore the pressure on the rig is least, so the boom moves across the boat more easily. It is very important when tacking downwind that the boom is not allowed to touch the shroud or it may break or snap the mast or the shroud during a jibe.

Reaching

In rough weather the beam reach, which in moderate or light wind conditions is considered an easy point of sailing, becomes a very fast and difficult course to control. Because of the power created by the strong winds, a high performance boat is likely to plane continuously. As with upwind sailing, you must be constantly on the look out for gusts — failure to anticipate and deal with them will result in the end of the boom hitting the water, so leading to a capsize. The sails must be adjusted constantly and the sheets must never be cleated. Just before a gust strikes the boat, the helmsman bears away and the sails are eased. As the gust hits, and the boat accelerates, the sails must be sheeted in again to keep the boat sailing efficiently as the apparent wind will have shifted ahead (see page 104). The helmsman and crew sit close together well aft to keep the bow lifted. The harder the gusts blow, the further away from the wind the helmsman will have to steer and the further aft he and the crew will have to sit. The centerboard should be just under halfway down to allow the boat to make leeway in large waves. When the gust passes, in order to maintain the apparent wind at a constant angle and strength, regain speed by luffing up.

Traversing waves

As the boat is sailing parallel to the waves, they do not restrict progress in the same way as when close-hauled but do not sail straight down the face of a wave or the bow will dig into the wave in front. Bear away down the face of the waves at a slight angle and as the boat accelerates, luff up a little to travel on the same wave for as long as possible. However, you must be careful not to stay on a wave so long that you end up to leeward of your objective. The crew weight should be forward as the bow moves down the waves and then moved aft as the boat accelerates.

Running

In rough weather, the run is the least attractive course to sail. It is difficult to balance the boat as there is no heeling force. On a dead run, the pressure of the wind in the mainsail can cause the top of it to twist forwards of the mast and this will tend to create a violent rocking movement. The best way to combat this is to tighten the boom vang and, if necessary, sheet in the mainsail slightly as well. Spreading the crew weight on opposite sides of the boat and lowering the centerboard to the halfway down position (or the fully down position in a single-hander), also helps to reduce rolling. In a two-man boat you can lessen the rolling movement by poling out the jib so that it wings out. In a single-handed boat the effective area of the mainsail and the turning movement can be reduced by sheeting in until the tell-tales fly out in the opposite direction, indicating that the airflow across the sail has been reversed. This provides a heeling force to leeward which makes the task of balancing the boat much easier.

Waves

On a run in rough weather you will find that the waves coming from behind will pick up the boat and it will start to surf. Unless you take action the boat will begin to overtake the wave in front and bury its bow in the back of it. If this is allowed to happen the boat will slow down dramatically and the pressure on the rig will increase. This makes the boat unstable and difficult to control. The problem can be avoided if you sail a faster course by luffing onto a broad reach. This enables the boat to traverse the waves as described in Reaching (above left) and it will sail faster. The apparent wind will shift ahead and this will also increase the boat speed.

Tacking downwind

An alternative to sailing on a run, which is often faster for high performance boats, is to tack downwind, sailing a zig-zag course across the wind by jibing. The optimum jibing angle will vary with the type of boat.

Any high performance boat, like the International 505 above, will plane easily on reaching courses in strong winds — the speeds achieved can be remarkably high.

Tuning a boat

If you want to get the best performance out of your boat you will have to consider ways of increasing the driving force of the sails and reducing the drag caused by the hull and standing rigging. For all boats, there is an optimum wind speed at which the heeling force of the sails is just balanced by the crew's maximum righting power, when sailing upwind. Because upwind sailing tests the efficiency of the rig, you tune your boat for best performance on that point of sailing. However, you have to make the decision before sailing about what strength of wind you are likely to encounter. You must then increase the driving force of the sails for winds below the optimum and reduce, in general, the heeling force for wind speeds above it.

Full sails provide more driving force than flat ones, but also create a greater heeling force and you will have to work out whether you have sufficient crew weight to balance it. In the old days, one boat would have several suits of sails for different conditions but modern technology has permitted one suit of sails to be adjusted for varying conditions by using different controls. Not all boats come equipped with all the controls mentioned in this section (nor, in some cases, do class rules permit all boats to have them). You must therefore make your own adjustments. Before you try to tune your boat, make sure you understand the basic principles of aerodynamics (see pages 324–7).

If the boat is a new one, or one you haven't sailed before, your first task is to test it out. Examine a similar boat you know to be fast and rig yours in the same way. You can then start to make any alterations necessary from that particular starting point. You will find that tuning can only be accurately carried out afloat, but there are a number of adjustments which can be made ashore first.

Put the boat on its dolly (in about 8–12 knots of breeze) and turn the boat until it is in the close-hauled position. Then set up the boat with moderate tension on the clew outhaul — enough to remove any small vertical creases in the sail along the boom. Don't add any tension

Masts

Masts are usually made of aluminium alloy which, unlike wood, is not affected by changes in humidity. The mast is one of the major controls affecting the shape of the mainsail although it cannot be adjusted directly except by changing it for a stiffer or more flexible one. Other controls, such as the spreaders and a mast ram (below right) are used to control the amount by which the mast bends and hence affects the sail shape. In normal conditions, when you should try to keep the mainsail as full as possible, the mast should be kept straight (right). To flatten the mainsail, the mast is allowed or made to bend fore and aft (far right). The mast can also be made to bend sideways and this will also affect sail shape. As the top of the mast bends to leeward, then the top of the sail will sag to leeward and hence become more twisted (see diagram right). This will cause it to spill wind, reducing the pressure on the sail and, consequently, the heeling force.

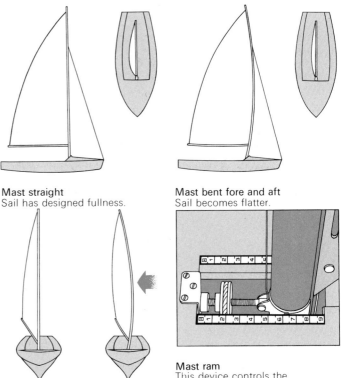

Mast straight
Sail has designed fullness.

Mast bent fore and aft
Sail becomes flatter.

Sideways bend
Mast straight (left) and bent to leeward (right).

Mast ram
This device controls the amount the mast can move forward at deck level, giving additional control over fore and aft mast bend.

to the Cunningham control unless there are horizontal creases up the luff. Sheet the mainsail in until the top batten is parallel with the centerline of the boat and then look up the sail and see where the point of maximum draft occurs (see page 324)—in most boats it should be about one third to half way along the chord from the luff (see page 324). The more your jib overlaps your mainsail, the further aft the point of maximum draft should be. Then look at the leech of the jib from the leeward side and adjust the sheet tension and fairlead position so that the slot between the jib leech and the mainsail luff is parallel all the way up. It is the slot shape and the leech tensions of both sails that are most critical in producing optimum performance of the boat. When you adjust the jib sheet angle or the tension, aim to have all the tell-tales on the jib luff streaming together and horizontally.

The remainder of the tuning can be done afloat. In very light winds and smooth water, you need to maintain the airflow without disturbance and this is done best with a flat sail shape. In some boats this can be achieved by

bending the mast by shroud tension alone (below) and by tightening the clew outhaul. In light winds and waves a fuller sail shape is needed to provide more power. As the wind strengthens, the sails are kept full, and the mast as straight as possible until the crew can no longer keep the boat upright. In higher wind strengths, fore and aft mast bend increases so that the sail flattens and by using mainsheet tension and traveller position, and by altering the jib fairlead position, the tops of both mainsail and jib can be induced to twist, spilling wind. Allowing the mast to bend as the wind increases not only flattens the mainsail and eases the leech tension, but it also widens the slot between the jib and mainsail and eases the jib leech which helps to reduce power. To be able to record all your adjustments, the various controls should be marked as appropriate. This means you can quickly adjust the controls to the right positions on subsequent occasions. Any tuning you do, however, should be tested out against other similar boats, and it will only be really effective if, in fact, you are also sailing the boat efficiently.

Spreaders

Spreaders are one of the main controls available to create or limit mast bend. They work by joining the mid-section of the mast to the shrouds. The amount that they distort the shrouds from their natural straight line determines the behavior of the mast under sail. It is important to realize that only the windward shroud and spreader are under strain and hence affect mast bend when sailing. Spreaders are not adjustable while sailing and must be altered before launching the boat.

Spreader angle
The angle of the spreaders to the centerline controls the fore and aft direction of the mast bend. If the spreaders are fixed in such a way that they do not distort the shrouds, they do not force the mast to bend. As the middle of the mast bends naturally, the spreader will move with it and try to force the shroud forward which will then resist the movement. Spreaders angled backwards pull the

shrouds aft of their natural straight line (right). When the shroud is under tension it tries to straighten, pulling the spreader and the middle of the mast forward. Spreaders angled forwards pull the shrouds forward of their natural straight line (far right) so that when the shrouds are under tension they pull the spreader and the middle of the mast aft, thus preventing the natural mast bend or even introducing reverse bend if the tension is great enough.

Spreader length
In the same way, the length of the spreaders can also be adjusted before stepping the mast to alter the degree of mast bend. When longer (under compression—near right) they stiffen the mast sideways or even induce reverse bend, but when adjusted so that the shrouds are not distorted (neutral—center right) they simply reduce any natural mast bend. When short (in tension—far right) they induce sideways. mast bend.

Spreader angle
The spreaders (above left) are angled backwards, pushing the center section of the mast forward. The spreaders (above right) are angled forwards pulling the center section of the mast aft.

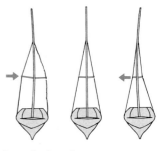

Spreader length
Spreaders in compression (above left), neutral (above center) and in tension (above right).

Center mainsheets

There are two types of center mainsheet systems – one with an athwartships traveller and another which is fixed to a raised bar in the center of the boat. With an athwartships traveller, the mainsheet is used, when sailing upwind, to tension the leech of the sail and control twist, while the traveller is used to control the angle of the sail to the center-line of the boat. Moving the position of the mainsheet blocks on the boom can help to control mast bend. When the pull on the mainsheet is straight down, the leech tension causes the top of the mast to bend back. If the blocks are moved aft, the boom is pushed forward at the mast which causes the mast to bend lower down. With the type of mainsheet system with the raised bar, the mainsheet is used to control the angle of the boom only; a powerful boom vang is needed to control leech tension and twist. The mainsheet cannot be used to bend the mast but the boom vang can.

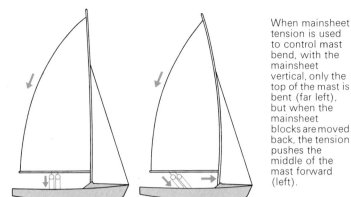

When mainsheet tension is used to control mast bend, with the mainsheet vertical, only the top of the mast is bent (far left), but when the mainsheet blocks are moved back, the tension pushes the middle of the mast forward (left).

A center mainsheet using an athwartships traveller to control the boom angle.

A center mainsheet with a raised bar: the mainsheet controls the boom angle.

Boom vang

This control is used to prevent the boom rising and therefore controls sail twist. It also imparts a similar force along the boom to that imparted by the center mainsheet shown top right. When using the mainsheet system with the raised bar it is vital to have a powerful boom vang. The lever type shown below is ideal. The boom vang needs to be easily adjustable at all times. Relatively minor adjustments of this control can greatly affect performance: easing the boom vang slightly when close reaching under spinnaker will let the main twist and allow the boat to be held upright more easily.

Battens

Many people do not think of battens as an aid to tuning. However, they can be very useful in achieving a correct sail shape. Battens can be made of a variety of materials but they must have a degree of flexibility – the amount depends on the sail in which they are used. A full, light weather sail needs more flexible battens than a flatter, heavy weather sail does. Battens which are not full length should be tapered in thickness so that they are more flexible at their inner ends; this will prevent a hard spot being formed in the sail. Full length battens, on the other hand, should be flexible, but not tapered, so that when they are bent between the hands they form a smooth curve. Full length battens can be used to adjust the camber in the sail by tying them into the sail either tightly or loosely. Every sail should have its own set of battens which are matched to the camber of the sail and each should be marked to show which pocket it belongs to and which way it is fitted.

Cunningham control

The Cunningham control allows tension to be applied to the luff of a sail. It consists of a line led through the Cunningham hole (or a block attached to it) and secured, usually around the gooseneck. The other end is controlled by a purchase system led back on either side of the boat to the helmsman. The purpose of this adjustment is to control the position of the point of maximum draft in the sail. As the wind strength increases, this point is pushed aft; tensioning the Cunningham will move it forward again. A side effect of tensioning the Cunningham is that the leech is flattened and the top of the sail twists slightly. The Cunningham control can be used on both mainsail and jib but is more commonly found on the former. As a rough guide, it should be tensioned just enough to remove any small horizontal creases in the luff of the sail.

Jib halyard

It is most important that all the weight of the mast is taken on the luff of the jib and not on the forestay. Halyards must be made of wire and halyard tension high enough to prevent the luff of the jib sagging off to leeward more than can be avoided. A sagging jib luff will cause the luff area to be too full and the leech to close up. The result will be that the boat will fail to point well and the heeling force will be increased. For boats that do not have shroud adjusters, the jib halyard is the only control which can be used to adjust shroud tension. It is essential that some form of powerful adjustment is fitted which can be readily controlled by the helmsman. Because the luff wire is built into the jib, increasing halyard tension will increase jib luff tension. This is not always desirable and the best arrangement is to attach only the cloth of the jib to the luff wire at the head and to control cloth tension by the use of a jib Cunningham control.

Jib fairleads

The jib fairlead position is critical for windward performance as this, and the sheet tension, control the jib leech tension and slot width. Ideally, it should be possible to adjust the fairleads both fore and aft, and athwartships. The latter allows a wider sheeting angle to be used in heavy weather to widen the slot and flatten the jib. Conversely, the sheeting angle can be moved inboard in lighter winds to give more fullness and a narrower slot.

Clew outhaul

This adjustment is used to apply tension to the foot of a mainsail. On many boats it will simply be a line attached to the end of the boom, passed through the clew cringle and tied at the required tension. It will not then normally be possible to adjust once afloat. High performance boats, on the other hand, often have an adjustable control with a purchase system inside the boom and a control line emerging by the mast and then led aft. Applying tension will result in the sail being made flatter in the bottom half so that the point of maximum draft will move aft. A general guide for setting the clew position is to pull it out just enough to eliminate any small vertical creases.

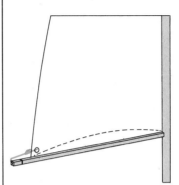

With the clew outhaul fairly slack the sail has quite a full shape (dotted line).

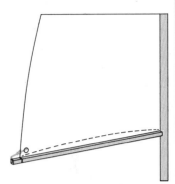

When the clew outhaul is pulled out tightly the sail is flattened (dotted line).

Combining controls

It is important to realize that all the controls should be adjusted together to achieve the required sail shape. The diagrams show the two extremes to which one particular sail can be adjusted. The diagrams on the right show a boat with a straight mast achieved by keeping the mainsheet and boom vang fairly slack, and the mast ram fully on. The clew outhaul is only just tensioned and the Cunningham is completely off. The top batten has been tied in very tightly. The result is a mainsail with maximum fullness. The diagrams on the right show the mast bent to the maximum amount allowed by the cut of the mainsail. The bend is achieved by having the mast completely off, with a lot of tension on the mainsheet and boom vang. The bend of the mast, helped by the other mainsail controls flattens the mainsail. The clew outhaul is pulled out to as far as possible, the Cunningham is pulled fully down and the top batten tied in loosely: a very flat sail results.

Keeping the mast straight with little tension on any control gives a full sail.

Allowing the mast to bend and tensioning the controls results in the sail becoming very flat.

Introduction to racing

Once you have become proficient in the basic sailing methods and have acquired an understanding of faster sailing techniques, you may wish to test your sailing ability in competition with others. Racing your boat in properly organized events not only provides an exciting hobby which can rapidly become a way of life, but is also one of the most effective incentives for improving your sailing.

Most races are normally organized through sailing clubs, at a local level, and by class associations, on a wider level, so the first thing anyone interested in taking up racing should do is to join a club. If you already own a boat that you wish to race, you must find a club which will accept your boat and which provides racing for boats in that class. If you do not have a boat, you should be careful to join a club which provides the type of sailing that you wish to participate in, and accepts the type of boat that you may eventually wish to buy. When considering joining a club, it is always sensible to contact the secretary first, who can give you all the information you need and who can also help you find a proposer and seconder.

Racing at both the club and national levels is usually organized according to the design or class of boat or according to a handicap system. Courses are laid out by the racing officials and are designed to test the sailors' skill on the various points of sailing. Some different types of courses are shown on pages 140–1.

Having decided to start to race your boat, you need to consider how you can give yourself the best chance of winning by making sure that you and your boat are prepared properly. Success at racing, as with many of the other sports, is largely the result of careful attention to detail. Your performance will benefit if you spend time practicing all the faster sailing techniques. You must also make sure that you are getting the best out of your boat by experimenting with adjustments to the rig and seeing that it is in peak condition before a race.

An understanding of the racing rules, which to a newcomer to sailing competitions often seem totally bewildering, is essential. To master them completely takes a great deal of experience but every beginner should make himself familiar with a few basic principles as a foundation for building a more complete knowledge. An introduction to some of the more important rules is given on pages 147–8.

Fireballs competing for position on the reaching leg of a championship race.

Boats for racing

While most people interested in competitive sailing choose a high performance boat, there are no strict rules governing what boats are suitable for racing; you can find competitions for almost any type of boat. However, most races, other than handicap events, are limited to boats within certain design specifications or classes. This ensures that only boats of similar performance potential are competing. If you already own a boat that you want to race, in order to make sure that it fully conforms to the class regulations, it is necessary to get it measured and given a class certificate by your club or class association. If you are going to buy a new boat, you will have to decide what sort of class you wish to sail in.

Many children enjoy racing and clubs often organize events for small boats like the Optimist.

The 505 is a high performance boat which is widely raced at all levels.

Design classes

The rules laid down by class associations vary. Some only accept strict one-design classes, while others accept restricted development ones. In the former, only boats built to an identical design are accepted whereas in the latter they only have to conform to broad rules on hull length and rig. With a one-design class, of course, if you win, you will have the satisfaction of knowing that it was due to your superior sailing ability. However, very few boats are strictly one-design, the majority allow maximum and minimum measurements, known as tolerances, and variations in fittings. Restricted development classes provide the greatest scope for a racing enthusiast, who is also interested in boat-building and design, to improve his boat. Many design innovations have originated from these classes.

The International Moth is an example of a restricted development class. These European-built Moths both have fiberglass hulls.

The Shearwater is an example of a one-design boat. It is built to strict specifications, allowing only small variations in the hull, rig and fittings, between boats in the same class. This and other one-design catamarans have become very popular as racing boats.

This US-built Moth differs from the boats shown above. Its "wings" are of another design and its hull is made of wood.

Racing courses

There are many different types of racing, ranging from a small club event involving only about ten boats, to a national championship regatta in which hundreds of boats may be racing. The courses also vary enormously. Races are conducted over a predetermined course laid out by the race organizers, the object being to finish the distance in a faster time than the other competitors in your class. Some championships assess a competitor's performance over a series of races.

The most common form of course is a simple triangular one in which three marks are rounded (usually to port) over a number of laps. However, many clubs are situated in areas which are not suited to such a layout and, when club racing, you must expect to find courses of all shapes and sizes (see below). Most race organizers try to arrange their marks so that the first and last legs are to windward. This means that the starting line often has to be moved at the last minute to account for changes in wind direction. Starting lines and starting procedures are possibly the most important and complex single aspect of racing and these are discussed in greater detail on pages 143–4.

Club racing

Courses for club racing vary enormously from club to club and are normally limited by the type of waters at the club. Many clubs use a race box onshore whenever possible, but the start line usually can be altered to cope with changes in the wind direction. Although committees normally try to set a windward start, this is not always possible and you need to be prepared for the possibility of a downwind start. Some clubs lay their own marks for each race, while others use permanent ones.

On tidal waters clubs often use navigation marks. Club courses can be any shape and buoys are rounded either to port or starboard. The course is usually indicated on a course board just before the start. You must then check it carefully and note down on a chart how each buoy should be rounded.

Starting line
A typical club starting line is shown right. The range markers on shore determine the position.

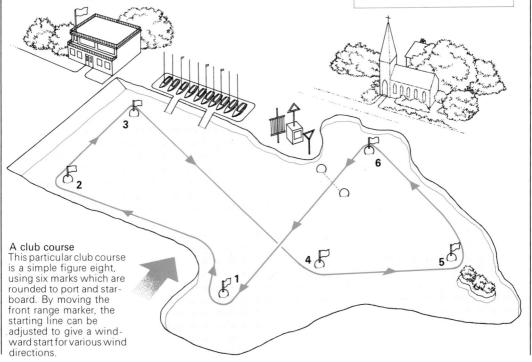

A club course
This particular club course is a simple figure eight, using six marks which are rounded to port and starboard. By moving the front range marker, the starting line can be adjusted to give a windward start for various wind directions.

Open regattas

Clubs which hold open regattas will normally try to arrange for the course to be a simple triangular one with a starting line laid square to the wind, usually from a committee boat. The standard triangular course (right) is an equilateral triangle with windward, wing and leeward marks (A, B and C respectively), giving windward and reaching legs. To incorporate a run a further lap is added around the windward and leeward marks, known as a "sausage". On most such courses, the buoys are always left to port, the start is at the leeward mark and the finish is at the windward mark.

Key

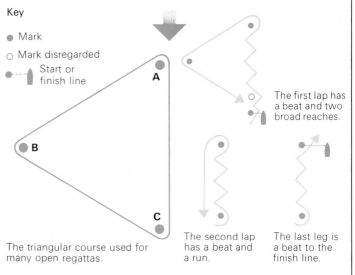

● Mark
○ Mark disregarded
●---◣ Start or finish line

The triangular course used for many open regattas.

The first lap has a beat and two broad reaches.

The second lap has a beat and a run.

The last leg is a beat to the finish line.

Championship courses

The courses used for championship events are based on the Olympic course which is a further refinement of the standard triangular course. The start and finish lines are placed outside the triangle giving a longer first and last beat. Usually two triangles, "a sausage" and a finishing beat are sailed. The championships for the majority of classes are held on open water and often courses are laid well away from land to try to ensure a steadier breeze.

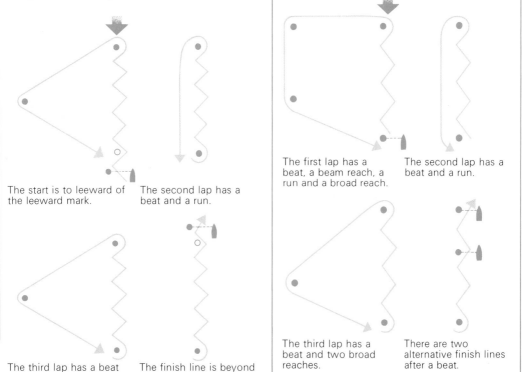

The start is to leeward of the leeward mark.

The second lap has a beat and a run.

The third lap has a beat and two broad reaches.

The finish line is beyond the windward mark.

Alternative course

The principal shortcoming of the Olympic course is that it places a premium on beating, broad reaching and running, and does not incorporate a beam reach. An alternative course, as shown below, designed to test crews on more points of sailing, is under consideration by the racing authorities.

The first lap has a beat, a beam reach, a run and a broad reach.

The second lap has a beat and a run.

The third lap has a beat and two broad reaches.

There are two alternative finish lines after a beat.

Alternative forms of racing

Boat-for-boat racing in one-design and restricted development classes provides exciting racing, but there are other forms of racing which are equally popular and in some cases more common. Colleges, universities and many clubs often organize team racing, where the object is for the team rather than the individual competitor to win. This provides a quite different type of racing, involving an increased use of tactics and placing less emphasis on faster sailing. Many club races are organized on a handicap system so that several different types of boat may race together. This is popular with regatta committees who want to see as many boats competing as possible. The most individual form of racing is match racing, which is conducted between two boats. The America's Cup is probably the best known match racing event.

Team racing

Team racing, shown right, is usually organized between two teams of three or four boats in the same class. A match usually consists of two races, with the teams exchanging boats in between the races. The object is for the team, rather than the individuals, to win. Because of the scoring system, it is not necessary for a team to have first place to win the race. Thus the emphasis is less on individual prowess and boat speed and more on tactical ability. A good knowledge of the rules is vital and it is essential to be able to evaluate the overall position of your team at any time, as this will determine your tactics. For instance, if you are in second place with your team mates in fourth and fifth places, you will know that this is a losing combination and you will have to attack the opposition. The easiest way to improve your position is to try to slow down the boat in third place so that your team mates can pass him. This will give you second, third and fourth places – a winning combination. Team racing is, without doubt the best way to improve both your boat handling and knowledge of the rules.

Team racing in Enterprises. E19402 is helping a team mate to pass E19538 by allowing its jib to flap, thus disturbing the airflow reaching E19538.

Handicap racing

Handicap racing is common in clubs where no one class has enough boats to make single class racing worthwhile. But it is more usual for clubs to organize separate starts for their single class fleets and then to have a start for a handicap fleet to cater for those members who own boats other than those regularly raced. The most widely used handicapping system is based on "yardstick" numbers which are given to each class of boat. In races for mixed fleets, the time each boat takes to complete the course is recorded and, by using a set of tables, a corrected time in relation to the yardstick numbers is worked out, giving the finishing positions. The yardstick numbers are corrected as evidence is built up from the information supplied by clubs to try to make the handicap system more accurate. In addition to handicapping classes of boat, some clubs handicap individual helmsmen. At the start of each season a helmsman with a proven consistent record is given the "scratch" rating. The other helmsmen are awarded handicaps around this level on the basis of their known ability. After each race the handicaps are adjusted.

Match racing

Match racing is a classic form of racing between two boats of the same class. It is often conducted in the form of a series of races between pairs of competitors making up a tournament. Each competitor must race against every other competitor and the overall winner is the one with the most wins. The match race really starts five or ten minutes before the actual start of the race as the two boats come together and attempt to get the best position for the start proper. The boat winning the start has a decided advantage and can control the other boat from ahead. However, as match racing is often very close, one bad tack can lose the race for the leading boat.

Starting lines

The simplest form of starting line, from an organizing committee's point of view, uses an onshore range. More equipment and organization is needed for a start line using a committee boat (see page 146). Nearly all starts use a defined line, the exception being the gate start, which is often used for large fleets of dinghies (see page 144). The length of the start line is a very important factor — a line at least one and a quarter times the total length of the fleet is usually recommended.

A windward start for a fleet of Fireballs using a simple committee boat start line (see bottom left).

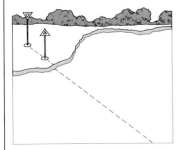

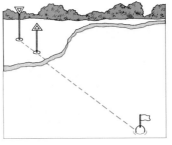

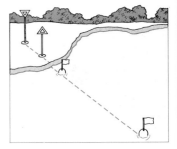

Onshore range with no outer or inner limit mark
This is the simplest form of start line, using a range onshore to define a line. However, the amount that the range can be moved to take account of changes in wind direction to provide a windward start is often limited. Because there are no inner or outer limit marks, competitors may start anywhere on the line.

Onshore range with outer limit mark
This line is similar to the first, but uses an outer limit mark beyond which competitors may not start. The mark does not have to be on the line which is defined solely by the range, but it helps the competitor if it is.

Onshore range with inner and outer limit marks
This type of line has marks at each end to define the area in which boats must start. The marks need not be on the range line, but organizing committees should try to ensure that they are.

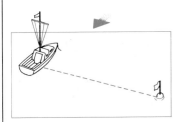

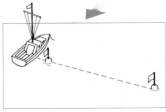

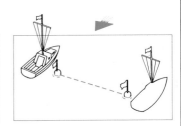

Simple committee boat start line
With a committee boat start line, it is easier to ensure that the start is to windward. It does, however, require a suitable committee boat and race organizers with the knowledge to lay good starting lines. The line itself is usually defined as being between the mast of the committee boat and an outer mark.

Committee boat start line with inner and outer limit marks
This is the same arrangement as for a simple committee boat start, with the addition of an inner limit mark to keep the competitors away from the committee boat. The inner mark does not have to be on the line, but it is an advantage if it is.

Start line between two buoys
Some race organizers lay two buoys to define the start line. The committee boat can position itself at either end of the start line and does not have to anchor, which is an advantage in rough weather. Also it is easy to alter the angle of the line if necessary, in case of a shift in the wind direction.

Gate start

A gate start is often used when a large fleet of dinghies is racing in a championship as it is supposed to give a fairer start to the majority of the fleet. The starting line is defined by the path of a boat sailing away from a committee boat. One of the competing boats is chosen to act as "pathfinder". About 30 seconds before the start the pathfinder sails away from the anchored committee boat close-hauled on port tack, closely followed by a launch, the gate launch. To prevent the pathfinder being fouled by other boats, a guard boat is positioned to leeward of it. Approximately ten seconds before the start, the gate launch drops a free floating mark to indicate the inner limit of the line. As soon as the start is signalled, the competitors are free to cross the line between the mark and the stern of the gate launch. The pathfinder continues on port tack until signalled to join the race by the gate launch which either stops or drops another mark to form the outer limit mark. A gate start can be quite successful in moderate non-shifting winds, but is less effective when the wind is light and changeable because it relies on a consistent close-hauled course. Critics of the gate start

A gate start for 505s. K6551 is the pathfinder and the fleet is starting behind the gate launch to the left of the picture.

claim that it takes the skill out of starting and thus penalizes the experts, and the congestion of a normal starting line is simply transferred to the windward mark. When participating in a gate start, you must be careful to keep to leeward of the course that the pathfinder will follow otherwise you may get caught on the wrong side of the line and may not be able to return. You should approach the stern of the launch close-hauled on starboard tack, not on a reach, to avoid becoming trapped between a close-hauled boat and the launch. If you were to find yourself in such a position you would be disqualified in the event of a collision.

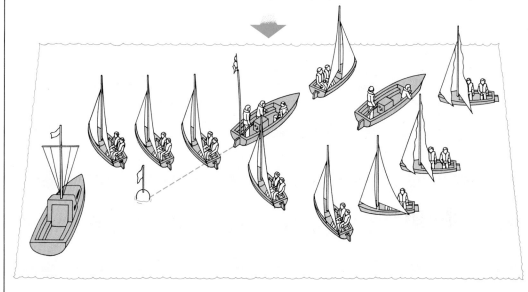

After dropping the inner limit mark, the gate launch closely follows the pathfinder with the guard boat to leeward. The boats which have crossed the path made by the gate launch have started, while the others are still waiting.

Preparing for a race

Before you go afloat for the race there are certain preparations and checks that you should make. It is very annoying to reach the start line and discover that in the rush to get afloat you have left behind your spinnaker or some vital piece of equipment. The time you will need to spend on preparing your boat depends on the type; a Flying Dutchman, which is complicated to rig and tune, may take you two or three hours to prepare, while a Laser, which has much simpler controls, will probably only take a few minutes. You must make sure that the hull is smooth, clean and free from grease or oil. All the equipment and rigging should be checked very carefully for signs of wear and any doubtful item should be replaced before it fails. Many people forget to do this and then blame a lost race on a piece of equipment that broke. This is really no excuse, as it could have been avoided with a little extra attention to the boat. You must always make sure that you have rigged the boat correctly for the conditions (see Tuning a boat, pages 134–7). Any items of boat equipment stipulated in the class rules or sailing instructions should be securely stowed aboard. These might include an anchor and warp, for example, and a paddle or two. You must have the right sort of clothing for the expected weather conditions, as it can affect your performance if you are suffering from cold or heat. Whatever type of clothing you wear should not restrict your movement and it should present as little wind resistance as possible.

You may also want to take a supply of food and drink with you if you are expecting to be on the water for some time. While it is not always possible to eat during a race, you may well be able to have something to drink: if it is high in glucose it will help to replace lost energy.

You should read the sailing instructions thoroughly and familiarize yourself with the scoring system well before the race, so that you can clarify any unclear points with the race committee. It is always a good idea to take the instructions with you, because, under stress in the middle of the race, you may find it difficult to remember some vital point. The instructions can be carried in a polythene folder to keep them dry. Sometimes the rules stipulate that all competitors must take a safety disc or tally with them. The purpose of this is to enable the race committee to find out easily if any competitors have failed to return from the race. To make sure that competitors remember to carry these discs, the race organizers generally penalize the failure to do so with disqualification. This also applies if the competitor fails to return his disc within a certain time limit after the race ends. To help you to remember yours, it is a good idea to write a note on the side-decking of your boat.

Catamaran sailors preparing for a race. The boats are being thoroughly checked before going afloat.

Scoring systems

Many racing events are organized as series of races in which the winner is the boat which achieves the best score overall. There are various scoring systems and it is very important to familiarize yourself with whichever system is being used before you start, so that you can assess your position relative to that of your rivals as the series progresses. The usual system used for championship and other major events, is the Olympic system. Under this system there are, ideally, seven races to make up the series, but never less than five. The points are allocated as follows: first place 0, second 3, third 5.7, fourth 8, fifth 10, sixth 11.7, seventh and lower, the place plus 6 points. Boats which did not start, or which retired or were disqualified score points equal to the number of entrants in the series plus 1. Each competitor may discard one result, and the one with the lowest points at the end of the series is the winner. Other systems are weighted differently.

Signals and flags

At race meetings, instructions and information regarding the events are conveyed by means of flags and pennants and sound signals. There is an internationally agreed system of code flags used at most race meetings with which you should familiarize yourself. However, in case your club operates another system, you should always check your sailing instructions carefully beforehand. The signals relate to rules applying to the meeting as a whole, starting procedures and instructions during the race, for example, indicating a change in the course. Some of the most commonly used flags are illustrated below. They are usually displayed from the starting box or start (committee) boat. Normally a number of flags are displayed simultaneously, (see right). You must listen for the sound signals which draw your attention to the changes in the flags and be ready to move towards the starting line when you see your class indicated. When your class flag is lowered, the race has begun.

Above is a committee boat at the start line. There is less than five minutes before the race begins, as the preparatory flag shows.

Flags

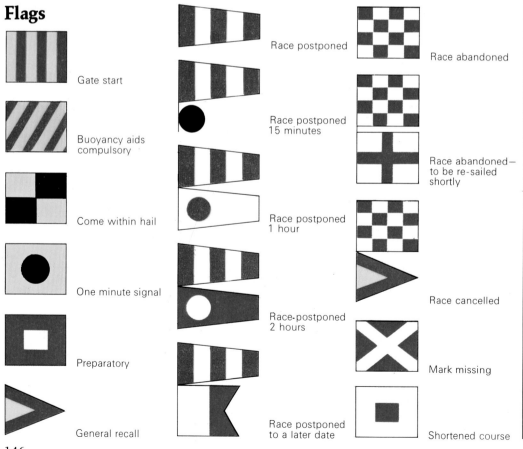

Gate start

Buoyancy aids compulsory

Come within hail

One minute signal

Preparatory

General recall

Race postponed

Race postponed 15 minutes

Race postponed 1 hour

Race postponed 2 hours

Race postponed to a later date

Race abandoned

Race abandoned— to be re-sailed shortly

Race cancelled

Mark missing

Shortened course

Rules

When you are racing you will often find yourself in close proximity to other boats. It is for these occasions that a knowledge of the racing rules is vital if you are to avoid incidents which could result in your disqualification. To start with, a familiarity with a few basic rules will be sufficient. But as your racing skills and experience develop, you should make an effort to extend your knowledge by reference to the official rule book of the International Yacht Racing Union, available through your national sailing authority. Some basic rules are described on this and the following page. The explanations are simplified to give a clearer understanding: for the official wording, consult the rule book. As an inexperienced racing sailor, however, it is best to keep clear, if in doubt.

Clear astern—definition
A boat is clear astern of another when it is behind an imaginary line drawn at right angles from the aftermost part of the hull of the other—red is clear astern of green (above) and overlaps yellow.

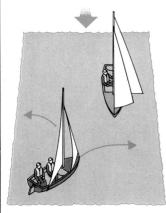

Opposite tack
A boat on a port tack (red) must keep clear of a boat on a starboard tack (green). (Rule 36)

Same tack—overlapped
When overlapped, a windward boat (red) must keep clear of a leeward boat (green). (Rule 37)

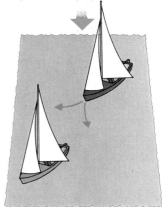

Same tack—clear astern
A boat clear astern (red) must keep clear of a boat clear ahead (green). (Rule 37)

Protests

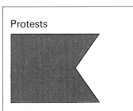

If an incident involving an infringement of the rules occurs and you know that you are in the wrong, you should comply with the penalty set out in the sailing instructions. However, if you believe that you are in the right, you must protest to the other competitor and display the protest flag shown above.

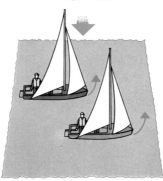

Same tack—luffing
After the start, a boat clear ahead or to leeward may luff at will. Thus the green boat may luff and the red boat must keep clear. A restriction is described right. (Rule 38)

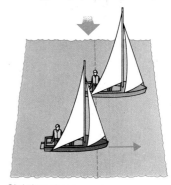

Sighting abeam
If the helmsman of the windward (green) boat, when looking across his boat can see that he is ahead of the mast of the leeward (red) boat, the latter may not luff.

Obstructions and marks

One of the most critical parts of any race is rounding a mark. This is the time when many boats converge and are jostling for an advantage, and you need to be particularly aware of your rights in order to gain the best position, while avoiding collisions. There are a number of rules which apply specifically to the rounding of marks and the avoidance of obstructions. When approaching a mark or an obstruction, you must watch the other boats around you and decide who has right of way. You must also be prepared to respond quickly if a boat with rights over you in that situation hails for more room.

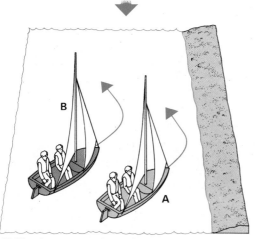

Hailing for room at obstructions
This rule applies when two close-hailed boats are approaching an obstruction on the same tack. If the boat which is to leeward or ahead (A) has to tack, it may hail the other boat (B) for room. (Rule 43)

Stars in trouble rounding a windward mark: the boat in the foreground is in irons, blocking the way for the boats approaching from behind. Several boats are on port tack and have no right of way over boats approaching on starboard tack.

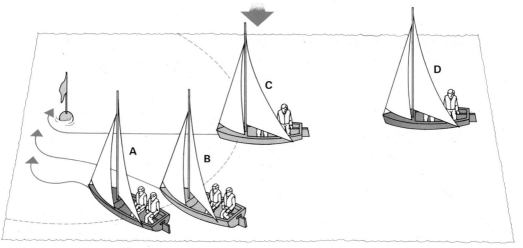

Rounding marks
When two or more boats are about to round or pass a mark or obstruction on the same side, an outside boat must give room to any boat overlapping it on the inside: A gives way to B and C, but B gives way only to C. Boats clear astern may only establish an inside overlap when the boat ahead is more than two boat lengths from the mark or obstruction. Therefore D may not ask A, B or C for room. (Rule 42)

Cruising

Choosing a cruising boat · The basic cruising boat · Interior layout
Deck equipment and how to handle it · Using an engine
Leaving from and returning to floats, marinas and moorings
Rafting up · Drying out Basic handling under sail · Reefing
Anchoring · Spinnaker work · Night sailing
Sailing in storms and fog · Passage planning

Starting to cruise

Most people start their sailing in one-designs and move on to cruising boats when the rigors of small boat sailing no longer appeal, although this is not always the case and some people do learn to sail on big boats. However, they can only safely do so by accompanying an already experienced sailor, learning under his instruction. Cruising boats differ in that they are mostly much larger, and include sleeping accommodation (ranging from a couple of berths on the smallest to up to about 12 on the very largest) and they usually have a fixed keel (or keels). Needless to say, they are usually far more expensive than one-designs, and it would be foolhardy for a novice sailor to attempt to skipper a cruising boat – he could cause considerable and costly damage both to his own and other people's boats.

Cruising boats are rarely designed to be sailed single-handed and one of the major differences between cruising and one-design sailing is that cruising relies much more heavily on team effort: many cruising boats will need at least three people to handle the boat – a skipper and a crew of two. In cruising, with the emphasis on sailing longer distances, a high proportion of time is spent in company with other people. Because the living accommodation on board most cruising boats is fairly cramped it is important to be carefully organized in terms both of crew skill and personality.

Anyone who cruises is usually going to travel some distance and the chances are that they will be sailing in crowded waters, often in major shipping lanes. Although most countries do not require sailors to hold certificates of competence, it should be a prerequisite for any cruising skipper to be thoroughly familiar with the rules and regulations governing shipping, and to have a clear idea of how to navigate in all conditions – including bad weather or at night. Most countries have formal courses in cruiser handling and navigation which any sailor, novice or experienced, would be well advised to attend.

One of the major pleasures of cruising is being able to visit new ports and new sailing areas. If you are planning to sail long passages, offshore for several days, you need to be well prepared and your trip carefully planned (see pages 156–157).

Cruising offers a great deal more scope than one-design sailing in many respects: it is particularly suitable for a family as vacations can be spent on board. The range of boats on the market is enormous, both new and second-hand, but some careful planning is needed before buying one. The pages on choosing a cruising boat (152–3) offer suggestions as to types of boat available. More specific advice on how to go about buying a boat is included in the appendix (see pages 336–9).

Many sailors will go cruising by crewing on other people's boats. The crew has particular responsibilities aboard and a good crew will be much in demand, provided he follows the guidelines on pages 156–7 and can handle his part of the work confidently.

Many people will want to start racing their boat once they have acquired some cruising experience. If so, they should join a good yacht club and offer their services as a crew.

Although ocean cruising and racing are beyond the scope of this book, many family cruising boats are seaworthy enough to cross oceans and fast enough to race, once the skipper and crew have adequate sailing experience.

One of the most important skills to learn in handling a cruising boat is how to dock it or moor up (above). Full instructions are given on pages 176–203.

One of the great pleasures of sailing is arriving in a new port (left) at the end of a good day's sail. Here, two newly arrived boats are rafting up (see pages 186–7) to a float.

There are many facets to cruising. The modern Swedish half-ton racing boat, above, and the vintage gaff sloop (left) while appealing to very different types of sailor, give equal pleasure to both.

The basic cruiser

Most medium-sized cruising boats have broadly similar layouts, both internally and externally. The cruiser, right, is a Contessa 32, a Marconi sloop, which provides comfortable accommodation without sacrificing sailing performance. It can be used for both cruising and racing, and serves as the model to illustrate cruiser handling techniques on the following pages. Other modern cruisers may differ a little in design and layout but the basic seamanship skills remain the same.

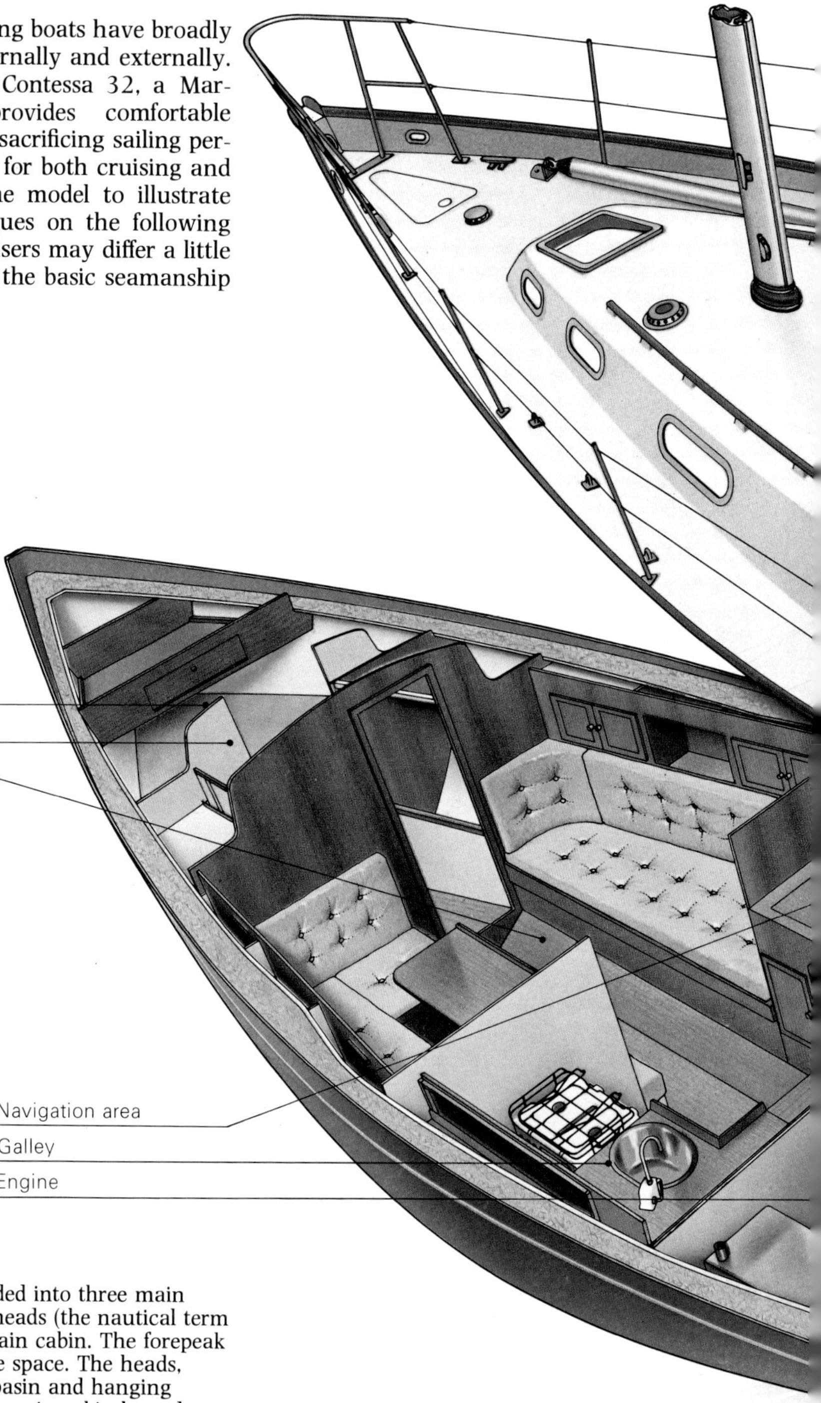

Forepeak

Heads

Main cabin

Navigation area

Galley

Engine

Internal layout

The accommodation is divided into three main sections: the forepeak, the heads (the nautical term for the lavatory) and the main cabin. The forepeak has two berths and stowage space. The heads, which also include a washbasin and hanging locker, are divided from the main cabin by a door. The main cabin contains one double and two single berths, the galley, the navigation area and stowage space. The engine is under the companionway.

External layout

The external layout of the deck area is organized so that the major controls are all within easy reach of the cockpit. The deck is made of fiberglass with a non-slip surface, surrounded by a guardrail. It also provides ample, uncluttered working space. More detailed explanation of all the deck equipment and how to handle it is given on pages 162–171.

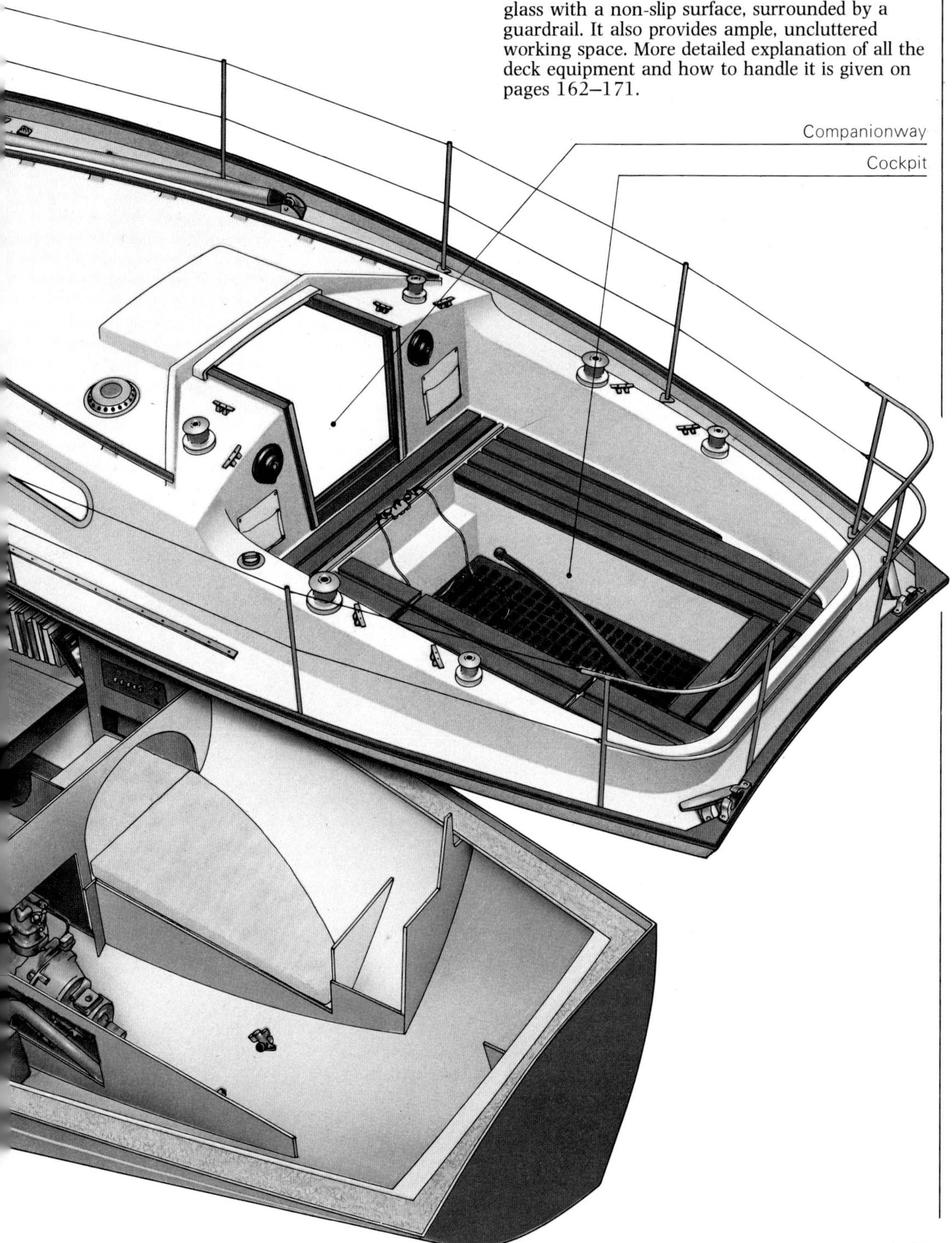

Companionway

Cockpit

Planning a cruise

For those who enjoy cruising, there are few activities more pleasurable and satisfying than setting off under sail, making a successful passage and a safe arrival in port. Success, however, comes with careful planning. In your first sailing season, if you are a novice boat owner, you will probably begin by making day trips, but as you gain experience and confidence, you will probably wish to go further afield.

The number of people you carry on board depends on the size of the boat, and the number of berths, although this does not apply to a day sail where you can carry a few extra "passengers". However, when planning any cruise, particularly if it is to be a long one, the composition of your crew is a vital consideration. Make sure that an adequate number of crew are experienced enough for the passage you are undertaking, particularly if night-sailing.

Ensure that the crew are all properly briefed before they come on board, and know what clothing to bring with them, packed in a lightweight, foldaway bag. Tell them if they need to bring foul weather gear, and if so, the type.

Obviously, you will have to plan out the prospective journey in advance (see Navigation, pages 258–9). From this you should be able to calculate the number of hours you will be sailing, and whether the crew you have is adequate for the passage you are planning. Once the cruise is fixed up and the crew notified, you need to start thinking of the boat itself. It must be checked to make sure it is seaworthy and that all the equipment works. Your food, fuel and water must be organized and your provisioning must take into account where and when you may be stopping. You must have some spare food and water aboard.

Your boat must be adequately insured and your papers in order before setting sail, particularly if you are going abroad.

Leave nothing to chance. Make alternative passage plans, so that if for any reason the weather forecast for your prospective route is bad, you could make an alternative passage. Consider the possibility that your crew, particularly if children are included, may not be as enthusiastic about sailing as you are, and so allow some time for entertainment ashore.

Once you have gathered the crew together, show them over the boat and explain how all the equipment, inside and out, works. Allocate them bunks and locker space, and encourage them to stow their personal belongings away in a ship-shape fashion. If you have any particular idiosyncracies make them known at the outset, and make sure that they all understand all the safety precautions that may be necessary.

Once the crew and boat are ready, it is the skipper's job to assess the best method of leaving the slip (above).

Coast Guard services

The United States Coast Guard (USCG) aids and protects the boating public principally in the areas of enforcement of boating regulations and safety. It makes patrols to check for reckless boat handling and hazards to navigation; it operates many aids to navigation (from unlighted buoys and daybeacons to lighthouses) as well as radiobeacons and many of the stations of the worldwide Loran-A and Loran-C systems; it aids boatmen in any kind of trouble and conducts rescue operations at sea. In many of its safety functions it is assisted by its civilian support organization, the Coast Guard Auxiliary (USCG Aux), which also offers courses for the boating public and promotes education and efficiency in boat operations. The US Power Squadrons (a non-governmental private organization) also promote boating safety through education in navigation, seamanship, and boat handling.

Provisioning the boat

Provisioning your boat, whether from the start of the season, or for a particular cruise, is not a difficult task but it does require time and thought and should be one person's responsibility alone; on most boats, the skipper takes charge or appoints someone else to buy the goods. Food is not the only consideration when provisioning a boat. Other mundane requirements, from lavatory paper to a medical kit, must also be on board. Quantities depend on the number of people on board, the type of the cruise, and the habits of the crew. Make a menu plan before shopping and, when catering for the crew, buy what you think you will need and allow 25 per cent more for unforeseen circumstances. You can keep dry, canned and bottled goods on board throughout the season. Make sure when stowing your food you can reach the items you need regularly. Perishables

should be stored in airtight containers and meat and dairy food in the coldest locker. If you are day cruising, only bring aboard the extra items you need during the sail but you will find it pays to cook any food at home first and reheat it aboard, to leave more sailing time. If a weekend outing is planned, take a couple of pre-prepared meals with you, and any additional food to make extra light meals or snacks. If you are going cruising for longer than a weekend, you need to consider other aspects when stocking up. Firstly, what sort of stove is there on board? With two burners, a grill and an oven you can indulge in gourmet cooking but with one burner only, you are limited to providing simple but nourishing meals. Complete meals in a can are useful for times when normal preparation would be difficult. Aim to start the day with a good breakfast, making sure that your

crew all eat something hot. Keep flasks of hot soup handy in cold weather, at night or in heavy weather and arrange to eat main meals, if possible, when you are at anchor or in port. It is useful to keep high protein energy-giving food in a plastic container – dried fruit, cake and chocolate are ideal. Whenever possible, arrange for cooking to be shared by all crew members and try to give those who are easily seasick the opportunity to do their share when in port or at anchor. When cooking, keep liquids stowed securely. Make sure anyone cooking knows how to use the stove and that they take care not to let clothes, pans and so on catch fire. When cooking in heavy seas, the cooks should wear oilskins, seaboots and rubber gloves, as protection from scalds or burns, as well as strapping themselves in, if they think it is necessary.

Watch-keeping

Passage making is tiring both physically and mentally and more so in rough weather. If every member of the crew is to be alert, it will be necessary for them to have sufficient sleep and rest, skipper included. When sailing at night or in heavy weather, it is necessary to divide the crew into two groups (known as watches) and establish a watch-keeping system. This allows the boat to be adequately manned by the "duty watch" while the off-duty watch recharges its energies, asleep or resting. A crew member on duty watch who has not had sufficient sleep is a risk. It is, therefore, important to create an atmosphere below which is conducive to sleep. It helps to keep light and noise to a minimum.

The traditional 24-hour watch-keeping system is one of four hours on duty and four hours off duty, with two short dog watches when everyone is normally awake (right). Another established system, sometimes known as the Swedish system, is one where the length of the watches changes between day and night (far right). For some people, the longer watch periods can prove too long. Some experienced skippers develop their own system based on one or the other and operate them successfully. It is important, of course, to space meal times sensibly and to use the times when all hands are awake to carry out sail changes, for example. Seamanship experience has to be distributed between the watches, the most experienced members working with the least experienced. The changeover must be carried out on time; if you are tired you tend to become fractious if not relieved of your post on time! Those taking over should be awoken in plenty of time to get ready for their watch.

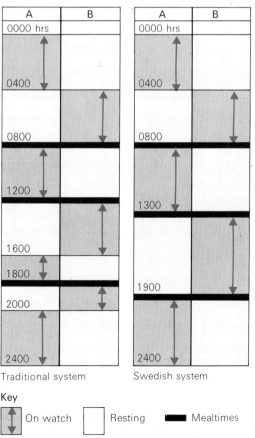

Traditional system   Swedish system

Key

On watch   Resting   Mealtimes

Accommodation

The type of accommodation in a cruising boat is limited by the size and shape of the boat. In those smaller than 9 m (30 ft), you can expect only the most basic fittings and comforts, with little privacy. In larger boats, the amount of space below decks allows for more elaborate fittings, as well as for an increased number of berths.

Every sailor has a different idea about the function of the interior of the boat. This largely depends on how the boat is to be used, whether for short weekend sailing trips, with much of the time spent in marinas or on moorings, or for longer distance cruises. If you plan only short trips you may find that a boat with elaborate fittings, and an interior primarily designed for comfort in port, is suited to your needs. However, if you think that you are likely to spend even a

moderate amount of time under way, it is worth making sure that the accommodation on your boat is designed with an emphasis on convenience when sailing. The layout on the following pages is suitable for a boat which is above all a sailing craft, but also has a moderate degree of comfort.

An important point to consider when looking at the accommodation inside the boat is the number of berths that can be used when the boat is under way. Bunks with no means of keeping a sleeping person from falling out when the boat heels are not practical. Other points to look for include lockers with strong catches, flat surfaces which have raised edges, known as fiddles, to prevent objects sliding off and plenty of grabrails around the cabin.

Internal layout

The internal layout of a typical aft cockpit cruiser is shown right and below. The galley and navigation areas are near the companionway for ventilation and ease of access to the cockpit, and the main cabin is in the widest part of the boat to give the maximum living space.

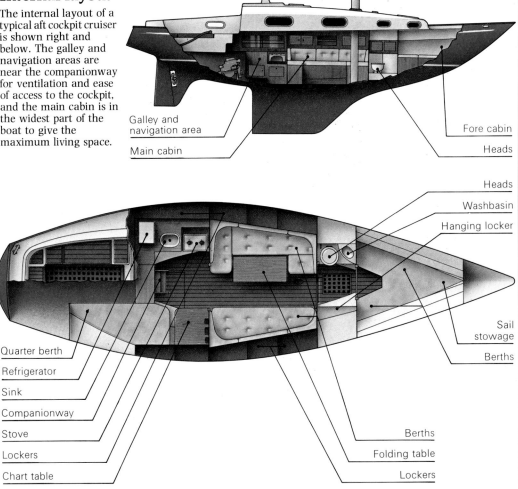

Galley and navigation area

Fore cabin

Main cabin

Heads

Heads

Washbasin

Hanging locker

Quarter berth

Refrigerator

Sink

Companionway

Stove

Lockers

Chart table

Sail stowage

Berths

Berths

Folding table

Lockers

Galley

The galley should be equipped with a small stove, mounted on gimbals and fuelled by bottled gas, kerosene or alcohol, a small stainless steel sink, refrigerator, a work surface and cupboards, with special fittings to keep dishes from moving about. It is useful to have a strap which can be fitted across the galley area to keep the cook in position when the boat is heeling. Always have a fire extinguisher and a fire blanket in the galley area.

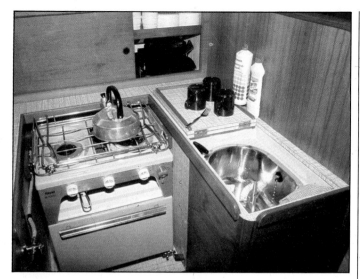

Because the galley is compact it must be carefully laid out to allow access to all the fittings.

Cooking on board
It is useful to have an insulated box fitted into the galley (right) to keep food fresh on board. A stove with gimbals and brackets to keep sauce-pans in place will enable you to cook even when the boat is heeling. If it is a gas stove, as a safety measure always be careful when using the cooker to turn the gas supply off at the cylinder before switching off at the stove.

Navigation area

The navigation area should be sited close to the companionway so that the navigator can communicate easily with the helmsman in the cockpit. There must be a table, preferably facing forwards and large enough for an open chart, and bookshelves for the navigator's reference material. The radio, depth sounder and other equipment should be mounted around the navigation area. The quarter berth, behind the navigation area, is suitable for use when sailing. The batteries are stowed under the berth.

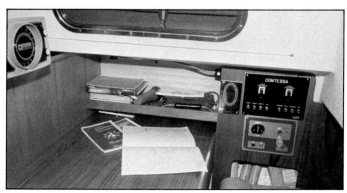

Left, the navigation area must be out of the way of the main living and working areas, with all the instruments near to hand. Above, the panel over the navigation desk has the main switches for the electrics and the engine.

Main cabin

The main cabin occupies the center of the boat and is the living area. Traditionally the cabin is lined with wood or wood veneer, but any smooth finish, not easily damaged by water, would do as well. Some people fit carpets in the main cabin area but these deteriorate quickly as they inevitably get wet when sailing. Most modern boats are lit inside by electric lights operating from the engine battery. The light fittings should be designed to be as flush as possible. The cabin, shown right, has seats along each side which convert into one double and one single berth. The latter is fitted with leecloths (see below).

Right, the best way to provide a secure berth for use at sea is to fit leeboards or leecloths.

Far right, the main cabin must be large and comfortable enough to allow the crew to relax when not sailing.

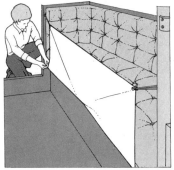

Stowage areas

Stowage on cruisers is always limited and every available corner is used. Lockers are generally built into the sides of the cabin for food and personal possessions. The lockers should have strong catches so that they don't fall open when the boat heels. You can have fittings built into the lockers to prevent breakables moving about inside. Additional stowage space is found underneath the seating. Every skipper will have his own system for stowing provisions and gear and you should make sure you know where everything is kept so that, if something is needed in a hurry, it can be easily found. Always stow your own possessions neatly.

Folding table

Tables are space consuming items and it is helpful if they can fold away neatly when not in use. The type shown below opens out into a full-sized table. The leg is telescopic and when the table is lowered it forms the base of the double berth.

If you have glasses or bottles aboard, they should be stowed in special lockers which prevent them sliding around.

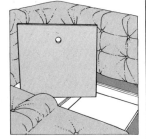

Larger items can be stowed under the seating. These areas must be kept clean.

To extend the table to its full size lift the top open and rest it on the sliding arm.

Heads

The heads are in a small compartment between the main cabin and the forepeak, separated by sliding doors. There are many different types of marine lavatory but, in general, they are pump operated. Check the marine regulations before use. It is normally possible to fit a small hand basin into the compartment and in larger boats hot and cold showers can also be added, but these are a luxury on a boat and most cruisers have only cold water washing facilities. The floor of the compartment is slatted so that water does not collect. A hanging locker for wet oilskins, in which you can also stow some of the sails, is useful.

A hanging locker, closed by a zip-fastened flap, is the best place to stow wet oilskins.

Seacocks underneath the bowl normally control the inlet and outlet pipes of a marine lavatory.

There is rarely much space in the heads and all fittings must be small and carefully arranged.

Care of the interior

Keeping your boat clean and in order down below is more than simply a matter of good looks, although pride in the appearance of your boat is also important. In the damp and poorly ventilated conditions below decks, any dirt that is allowed to accumulate will soon start to form mould and create an unpleasant smell. Before and after each trip you should empty and clean out the whole boat, leaving the lockers and stowage areas open so that air can circulate. It is also essential to keep the bilges and water pipes clean. The bilges should be pumped out and a patent bilge cleaner poured in. Check all the equipment regularly, including the stove and gas pipes, water pumps, seacocks and the heads.

Forepeak

The forepeak lies under the foredeck and has two berths. However, these are usually not suitable for use when sailing because, in addition to being in the part of the boat where the motion is greatest, the forepeak is also the main area for stowing sails and when a sail change is necessary there is bound to be disturbance. A locker above the berths provides useful additional stowage space. Items which are not needed often, such as emergency water supplies, can be stored under the bunks.

The forepeak has room for two berths (left), but is normally filled with sailbags (above).

Deck equipment

The pressure of the wind on the large sails of a cruiser means that the deck equipment for handling them must be robust and securely fixed. The forces are so great that the crew cannot control the larger items of equipment without the assistance of winches and blocks, which are fitted at convenient points around the deck. Most cruising boats have broadly similar layouts and once you are familiar with one boat, you won't find it hard to get to know another. The standing rigging and the main fittings are shown below. The layout of each area of the deck is described on the following pages.

The Contessa 32

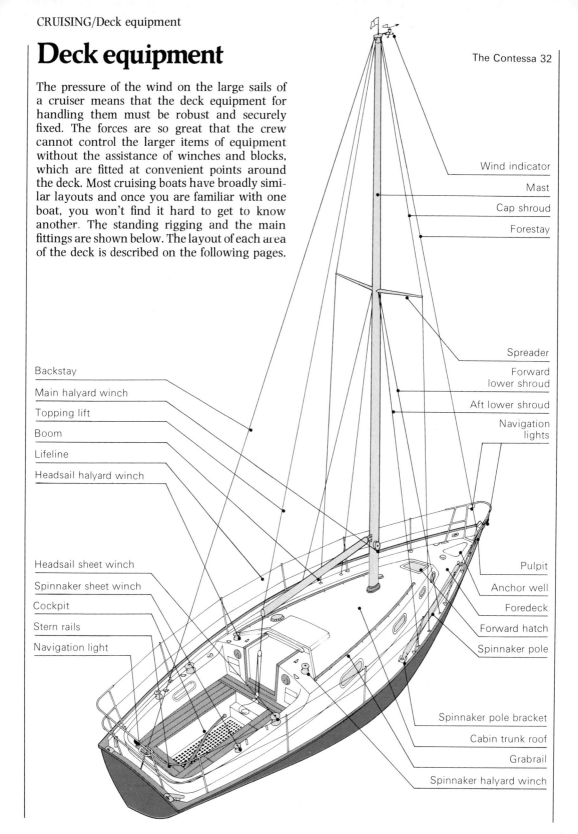

Wind indicator

Mast

Cap shroud

Forestay

Spreader

Forward lower shroud

Aft lower shroud

Navigation lights

Backstay

Main halyard winch

Topping lift

Boom

Lifeline

Headsail halyard winch

Headsail sheet winch

Spinnaker sheet winch

Cockpit

Stern rails

Navigation light

Pulpit

Anchor well

Foredeck

Forward hatch

Spinnaker pole

Spinnaker pole bracket

Cabin trunk roof

Grabrail

Spinnaker halyard winch

Foredeck

Because the foredeck is the most exposed part of the boat, it must be organized to provide as much protection for the crew as possible. Most foredecks, therefore, have a strong tubular steel framework at the bow, called the pulpit, which is firmly bolted into the deck. The crew can brace himself against this while working on the foredeck. Guardrails or lifelines, supported by stanchions, run from the pulpit to the back of cockpit to provide security for the crew on deck. All headsail rigging and changing takes place on the foredeck so the area can become very cluttered if all equipment is not properly stowed as soon as you have finished using it. It also helps to keep the area clear if the anchor is stowed in an anchor well instead of on the bow fitting, which acts as a fairlead for the anchor chain (see above and pages 202–3). The two cleats and bow fairleads, one on each side, are used when mooring up. Any lines not in use should be coiled and stowed away – if left on deck they could fall overboard or trip someone. The forestay is fixed to the foredeck at the bow fitting to which the headsail tack fitting is also attached. Although a single forestay is more common, some boats have twin forestays and others have solid grooved foils fitted so that sail changes can be carried out rapidly (pages 204–5). The jackstays, to which the crew attach their own lifelines from their harnesses, run from the cockpit to a securely mounted fitting behind the anchor well.

Parts of the foredeck

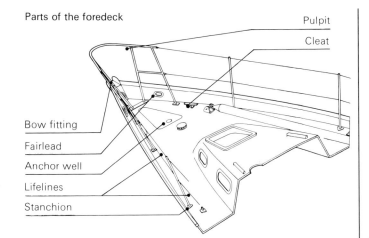

Pulpit
Cleat
Bow fitting
Fairlead
Anchor well
Lifelines
Stanchion

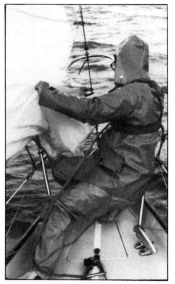

When changing headsails, the crew can brace himself safely against the pulpit. For additional security in rough conditions it is advisable to wear a harness and attach the lifeline to the jackstays, as shown above.

Lacing

To prevent the sails being blown or washed off the foredeck, most people interlace the lifelines near the bow of the boat with a thin braided cord. This not only helps protect your equipment, but provides additional security for the crew working on the foredeck.

The jackstays, which run the length of the deck, are made of steel wire covered with plastic tubing. They are shackled at the bow to an eye bolt securely mounted through the deck (right). The bow fitting (far right) comprises a metal plate and D ring to which the forestay and headsail tack shackle are fitted. The anchor chain lead is also shown.

Cabin trunk

The center section of the deck is raised to form the cabin trunk, giving standing room in the cabin below. The deck in this area must be particularly strong and is reinforced to support the mast, standing rigging and sail handling equipment. The roof also has to be strong enough to withstand the pressure of large breaking waves. The small cabin windows (or lights) must be watertight. Ventilators, set into the roof allow air into the cabin. Grabrails are fitted along each side of the roof to provide a hold for the crew when working on deck.

Parts of the cabin trunk

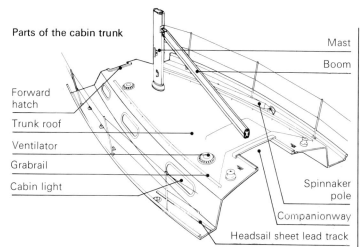

Mast
Boom
Forward hatch
Trunk roof
Ventilator
Grabrail
Cabin light
Spinnaker pole
Companionway
Headsail sheet lead track

Forward hatch
The forward hatch is normally fitted into the front end of the cabin trunk. Made from toughened plexiglass with a watertight seal, it is primarily for light and ventilation in the forepeak when moored, but it can also be used for easy access to the sail stowage area below. However, it should always be kept firmly closed when under way or water may enter the cabin.

Spinnaker pole stowage
The spinnaker pole is normally stowed on the forward area of one of the side decks. The most secure arrangement is to clip it onto two specially designed brackets bolted onto the deck.

Side decks
On each side of the raised trunk roof run the narrow side decks. The deck edge is finished off with a raised section to prevent anyone slipping under the lifelines. The stanchions are bolted through the side decks and often incorporate eyes at the base for clipping on your harness lifeline. The headsail sheet lead tracks are set on each side deck just forward of the cockpit. These allow the sheeting angle to be adjusted.

Companionway
The main access to the cabin is through the companionway. This is usually sited at the aft end of the cabin trunk and is closed by a sliding hatch and washboards (wooden partitions). The hatch should be kept closed while sailing to prevent water entering the cabin. Grab handles, fitted inside the companionway, provide a secure hold when going below or coming on deck, even when the boat is heeling.

Stowing on deck

The cabin trunk roof can be used as a place to stow larger items of equipment which cannot be accommodated below, or which must always be readily accessible on deck, like the life raft. If you decide to keep equipment on deck, you must make sure that it is stowed so that it will not get in the way of the crew working on deck and is securely tied down. The life raft is normally stowed either forward of the mast or, if the forward hatch makes this inconvenient, between the mast and the companionway. It should be tied onto specially shaped chocks on the cabin trunk using quick release knots. The deflated tender can also be lashed to the grabrails behind the life raft, as shown right.

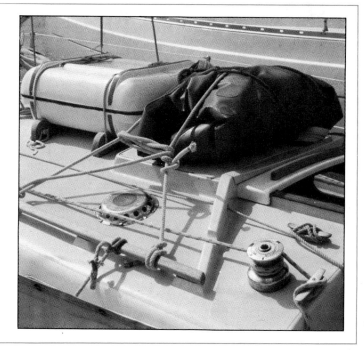

Mast

The majority of cruising boats are fitted with aluminum masts which are strong and light. As on a one-design, the mast can be deck stepped or keel stepped. A keel stepped mast is shown below. It has a rubber seal where the mast passes through the deck to prevent water running down inside the cabin. It is supported by a single spreader rig (right) with three pairs of shrouds. The cap shrouds run from the masthead to the deck and the four lower shrouds are fixed on either side near the spreader roots and to the decks. The forestay and backstay are attached to the masthead and to reinforced plates at the bow and stern. The backstay can usually be adjusted (see page 167). A wind indicator and the radio aerial may be attached to the masthead, which is also an alternative position for the navigation lights. Many of the sail controls are mounted at the bottom of the mast. These usually include the main halyard winch, the topping lift, the bracket for attaching the boom vang and the headsail and spinnaker halyard turning blocks. The spinnaker pole bracket is mounted on the front of the mast.

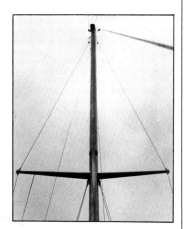

The base of a keel stepped mast showing the rubber deck seal and the headsail and spinnaker halyards.

A side view of the bottom of the mast showing the main halyard winch and cleat. The blocks fitted under the boom are part of the reefing equipment.

Boom vang

The boom vang tackle is securely shackled to an eye on the underside of the boom and to a bracket at the bottom of the mast. The lower block is fitted with a jamming cleat to allow it to be adjusted.

Boom

The boom, like the mast, is normally made of aluminum. It is fitted to the mast by a gooseneck and is not removed unless repairs are needed. When the mainsail is not hoisted, the boom is held up by the topping lift. This is a length of rope shackled to the aft end of the boom, led via the masthead to the base where it is cleated.

Along the top of the boom there is a groove which holds the foot of the mainsail. The aft end is finished with a metal cap fitting which incorporates eyes for the clew outhaul lashing, the topping lift shackle and the mainsheet attachment. The boom vang and fittings for the reefing lines are fixed on the underside of the boom (see pages 215–7).

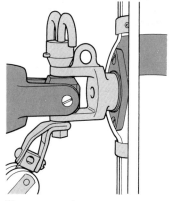

The gooseneck
The boom is bolted to the gooseneck on which the ram's horn reefing fitting and tack downhaul eye are also mounted.

Aft end of the boom
The topping lift and mainsheet are shackled on top and underneath the boom respectively. The halyard is shown stowed on the clew outhaul eye.

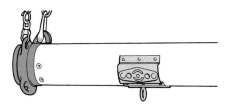

Cockpit

The cockpit is usually sited at the aft end of the boat. It comprises a self-draining footwell with seating on each side. At the stern, there is a rigid framework known as the stern rail which serves a similar function to the pulpit at the bow. Unless there are specific tasks to perform forward on deck, it is safest for the crew to remain in the cockpit while sailing (see right). As many controls as possible are led back to the cockpit for ease of access. All the controls and instruments used by the helmsman must be easily visible from his position at the tiller.

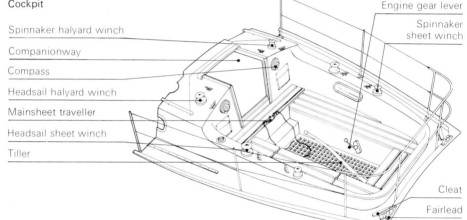

Cockpit

Spinnaker halyard winch

Companionway

Compass

Headsail halyard winch

Mainsheet traveller

Headsail sheet winch

Tiller

Engine gear lever

Spinnaker sheet winch

Cleat

Fairlead

Spray hood

A spray hood or dodger fitted over the companionway effectively reduces the amount of spray that can enter the cockpit and permits you to keep the companionway hatch open in all but rough weather conditions.

Tiller and wheel

On boats up to about 11 m (36 ft), the choice of a tiller or wheel is a matter of personal preference, but on larger boats a wheel is easier to handle. Many tillers are designed to lift up out of the footwell when stowed.

Instruments

Many boats have a large number of instruments and indicators in the cockpit. However, unless you are experienced, these can often confuse rather than help you and most sailors would be better off relying only on the basic instruments. The compass is the principal instrument in the cockpit and the best arrangement is to have twin compasses mounted on each side of the companionway (bulkhead) so that the helmsman can see them easily from either side. Other basic instruments are the distance log, knotmeter, and fuel gauge.

Weather cloths

Weather cloths, made of plastic or sailcloth, are fixed to lifelines along the cockpit. They give a measure of protection to the crew from wind and waves and are a convenient place to display the boat's name or number.

Stowage

Most boats are fitted with cockpit lockers under the seating in which most large items of boat equipment can be stowed, including fenders and warps. As the lockers are usually deep, it is essential to organize all the equipment inside them so that the items you use often are kept near the top. A separate self-draining locker houses the gas cylinder. Small open stowage spaces in the side of the cockpit are useful for keeping the winch handles in.

Horseshoe life ring

Horseshoe buoys always must be kept where they can be reached quickly, preferably in specially designed holders attached to the stern rail (below left). In addition to providing buoyancy for a man overboard, a horseshoe buoy acts as a marker to help the boat return to the right place. For use at night, each buoy must be fitted with a light which will switch on automatically when thrown into the water (below right).

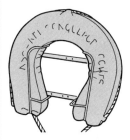

Backstay tensioner

Many boats are fitted with an adjustable backstay which allows you to control the tension of the forestay. A common way of adjusting the backstay is by a wheel controlling a bottle screw at the base. When you are not sailing, the backstay tension should be slackened.

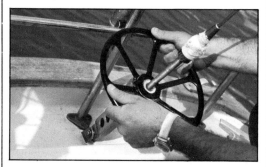

Man overboard pole

The man overboard pole or dan buoy is a floating marker which can be seen in large waves. The pole is weighted underneath, with a central float and a flag on top. It is used to mark the position of a man overboard, for example. The dan buoy is normally stowed in a holder on the backstay where the crew can easily find it and release it quickly in an emergency.

Washboards

The access to the companionway on most boats is closed by washboards. These can be used to close the opening completely, or partially if only one or two are used. In very rough conditions one-piece reinforced boards are more suitable, as washboards can become dislodged.

Rigging the headsail

Most cruising boats carry several headsails which
are suitable for different conditions. They are all
rigged in precisely the same way, very much like
one-design headsails. Bending on sails is the job of
the crew and it is the skipper's job to tell the crew
which sail to use. They are normally bagged up
with the number and name of the sail on the
outside of the bag. Most people bag their sails
with the tack of the sail protruding from the top
of the bag so that it is impossible to attach the
sail upside down. If in doubt, check the sail first to
make sure it is the right way up. The tack is
usually marked with the sailmaker's label.
If the boat has twin headfoils, sail changing can
be achieved more quickly because you do not have
to hank the sail to the forestay. Once the tack
and halyard are attached the luff is fed into
the groove and the sail hoisted (see page 204).

Order
The headsail should be
bent on in the following
order:
1 Attach tack of sail to
bow fitting
2 Attach hanks to
forestay
3 Fasten sheets to clew
4 Lead sheets back
through fairleads
5 Secure end of each
sheet with stopper knot

How to rig

Remove the tack from the bag
and fasten it to the bow fitting.
Hank on the headsail working
from the tack up the luff to the
head. Attach the two sheets to the
clew of the sail and lead the sheets
back aft (normally outside the
shrouds and back through the
fairleads into the cockpit). Finish
the ends with a stopper knot.

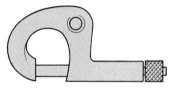

The headsail is fixed to the
forestay by piston hanks (above).
When attaching them, make sure
that they are all put on in the same
direction (right) otherwise the luff
will be twisted and the sail will
not run freely up the forestay.

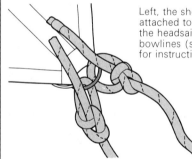

Left, the sheets may be
attached to the clew of
the headsail using
bowlines (see page 331
for instructions).

Above, the sheet is led through the fairlead which
slides on a track and is used to adjust the sheeting
angle when sailing (see page 213).

Stowing

Once the sail has been
bent on it may be left on
deck for some time until
ready to be hoisted. It
can be stowed in the sail
bag or along the lifelines.

Right, the sail stowed in
the bag with the head
and tack protruding.
Far right, the sail stowed
along the lifelines, neatly
rolled and secured.

Rigging the mainsail

The mainsail of a cruising boat is not usually unrigged unless the boat is to be left for a long period of time. So you will not need to bend it on each time you sail. Although one person can bend on the mainsail alone, it helps to have two people doing the job because it requires some strength to pull the foot of the sail out to its full length along the boom. Before you bend it on, take the sail out of its bag and insert the battens in the same way that you do for a one-design mainsail (see pages 48–9). It helps to mark the battens for the right pockets. Unless the mainsheet has been removed for other reasons, you will not have to rig it each time you bend on the mainsail. It remains shackled onto the end of the boom and to the mainsheet traveller. Instructions for hoisting the mainsail are given on page 205.

Order

The mainsail is bent on in the following order:
1 Insert clew end of foot into boom track
2 Pull clew out to end of boom
3 Fasten tack at goose-neck. Fasten clew to end of boom.
4 Insert slugs into mast track
5 Close mast gate
6 Secure sail on boom

How to rig

Insert the clew end of the foot of the sail into the boom track and pull it along to the end of the boom. Then secure the tack at the gooseneck and fasten the clew out-haul lashing to the boom. There is usually a mast gate at the bottom of the mast track which must be removed before you insert the head of the sail into the track. When all the slugs (or sliders) along the luff have been fitted into the track, lock the mast gate.

Above, the foot must be pulled along the boom to its full length.
Left, when it is fully stretched out, the clew outhaul (if it is not the adjustable type) is led through the eye on the boom end and back through the sail and secured as shown.
Right, the slugs in the luff of the sail are inserted into the mast track and the gate fitted into place to keep them in position.

Stowing

Once the sail has been bent on it must be stowed along the boom. The techniques for folding it are shown on page 205. Once folded and neatly bundled, it should be secured with shock cord or sail ties until ready to be hoisted (right).

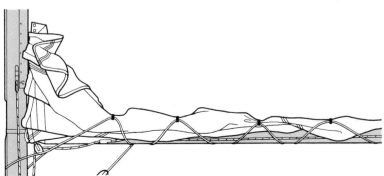

Winches

Winches are a sophisticated, but essential part of the boat's equipment. They are positioned on the boat where appropriate to provide extra purchasing power to haul on halyards and sheets—they often have two or even three speeds. Normally one person puts the sheet or halyard around the winch and pulls on the end (known as tailing, below) while the other person winds the winch, using a winch handle to do so. The latest development in winch design includes a self-tailing winch which can be operated by one person alone.

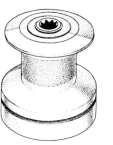

Standard winch   Self-tailing winch

Loading a winch

It is important to be able to load a winch correctly. On a cruising boat, there is a lot of pressure on the sails and if you trap your fingers in a winch you could be badly injured. Always use two hands to wind the sheet onto the drum and keep the heel of your hand nearest the drum. Before loading the winch, spin the drum to check which way it turns— you will find that most winches, in fact, turn clockwise.

Once the sheet is fully winched in, it should be fastened around a cleat to prevent it from slipping on the drum (see Cleating a rope).

Releasing a sheet

Never unwind a sheet from a winch. Instead give a sharp tug upwards on the sheet and only release it when all the turns have unwound from the winch. If you have accidentally locked the turns on the winch (known as riding turns) you will have to release them first (see page 207).

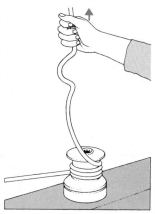

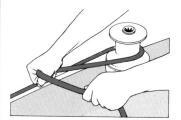

1 Using both hands, loop the sheet around the winch in the same direction in which the drum itself rotates.

2 Keeping the heel of your hand nearest the drum, take three or four turns on the winch before pulling on the sheet.

Using a winch handle

The majority of winches are operated by a top-mounted handle which engages in the central socket. Make sure the winch handle is always stowed safely—it can easily be lost overboard and is expensive to replace. With a two-speed winch, the handle is turned in a clockwise direction for one speed, and counter-clockwise for the other.

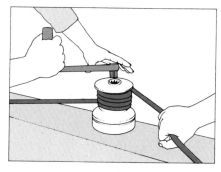

1 While one person tails on the winch, the other grasps the handle of the winch and slots it into the central socket.

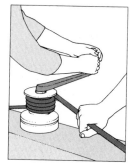

2 The person tailing must neither let the sheet tail foul the handle nor pull down so much that riding turns are formed.

Handling lines

Learning how to handle lines properly is one of the essential skills of seamanship. It is vital both for safety and smooth boat handling to make sure that all lines are stowed neatly and tidily. Never leave mooring lines lying around on deck. They should always be coiled and stowed away after use in one of the cockpit lockers. All lines should be washed in a mild detergent at least once a season to remove any grease and oil. If a line becomes badly kinked, trail it in the water behind the boat to straighten it out.

Heaving a line

You will often have to heave a line to someone in another boat or on a float. Never rely on a previously coiled line and make sure that you have checked that it is long enough to reach your objective before throwing it. Coil it up as shown (below left) and then divide the coil so that about one third is in your throwing hand. If throwing right-handed, put your left shoulder towards your objective, swing your arm and heave the line.

1 Divide the coil and keep one third in your throwing hand.

2 Aiming slightly higher than the objective, swing the coil forward, allowing the remainder to uncoil.

Coiling a line

All lines should be coiled and secured so that they are ready for use. There are several methods of coiling a line – the one below is commonly used. When coiling the line, take about an arm's width for each coil, and make sure a twist is put into the line in order to flatten it.

1 Coil line looping it clockwise. Make a clockwise twist in line.

2 When almost all of line is coiled, bind most of remainder around coil.

3 Pass looped end of line up between bound part and top of coil.

4 Take loop right over top of coil and pull free end tight to fasten.

Cleating a line

If you fail to cleat a line properly it may slip or jam immovably. The line should always be led to the back of the cleat first which prevents it from jamming. You should also take one full turn around the cleat before making the figure eight turns. There are several ways of securing a line on a cleat – two methods are shown below.

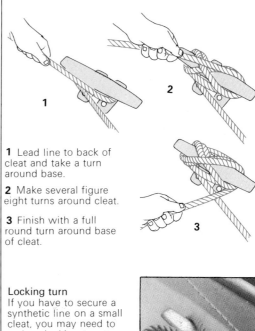

1 Lead line to back of cleat and take a turn around base.

2 Make several figure eight turns around cleat.

3 Finish with a full round turn around base of cleat.

Locking turn

If you have to secure a synthetic line on a small cleat, you may need to make a locking turn to secure the line. It is very important, though, that the locking turn can be released under tension. The simplest method is to slip a loop of the line under an additional turn on the cleat (right).

171

Tenders

For times when you are stopped at moorings you will need to carry a tender with you on the boat to get to and from the shore. Tenders can be either rigid or inflatable. Most cruising sailors prefer the inflatable type as these have the advantage of being easy to stow on deck where space is limited. Normally they are rowed or paddled, but some sailors fit outboard engines to their tenders. Most tenders are designed to carry a maximum of four people, fewer if you are also carrying stores to and from the boat. The distribution of weight in tenders is crucial and they must never be overloaded. Everyone must wear a buoyancy aid or lifejacket, even if they can swim. It is important for all cruising sailors to learn how to handle a tender competently, as boats are often moored in tidal waters which are difficult to row in.

A tender can be either towed or stowed on deck depending on the size of your boat. On larger boats, a rigid tender can be stowed upside down on the coach roof or in davits at the stern but usually it is towed when weather and sea conditions permit. When towing a rigid tender you must make sure that the rope is long enough, otherwise it will collide with the stern of your boat in waves. It is a good idea to fix a second rope with plenty of slack, in case the first breaks or comes undone. The oars and all loose gear must be removed from the tender before towing. An inflatable can also be towed, but you must make sure that the bow is pulled out of the water and tied close to the transom of your boat. However, when deflated an inflatable can conveniently be stowed by lashing it behind the liferaft on the cabin trunk.

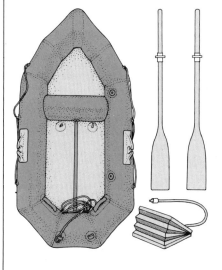

Types of tender
There are various types of tender. These fall into two groups, inflatables (left) and those of rigid construction – usually wooden or fiberglass (right). Whichever type you choose, it must be small and light enough to be easily stowed, but large enough to carry four people safely. An inflatable tender is inflated using a foot pump. It is usually stowed deflated on deck. A fiberglass tender must be towed, unless you have a cruiser with enough room on deck to stow it there.

Getting in and out

Getting in and out of a tender requires some care to avoid upsetting it. After launching the tender into the water, secure the painter near the shrouds to a stanchion or deck cleat. The oarsman gets in first, stepping into the middle of the tender, and sits down on the central thwart. The oars are passed to him, followed by any stores that are being transported. The remaining crew members then get in one by one, sitting down immediately and keeping the boat trimmed. Those already in the tender steady it against the side of the boat. The oarsman fits an oar into the outboard rowlock and one of the crew casts off and pushes the tender clear before the oarsman fits the second oar into the other rowlock. For getting out reverse the procedure.

Crew weight

Tenders, whether inflatable or rigid, are fairly unstable and you must, therefore, pay special attention to the distribution of crew weight in them. Try to place an equal weight of crew or stores on each side and make sure that it is trimmed level. It is very important that no one remains standing in the tender any longer than absolutely necessary in order to keep the weight as low as possible. Never overload your tender—it is better to make two journeys, than to risk sinking.

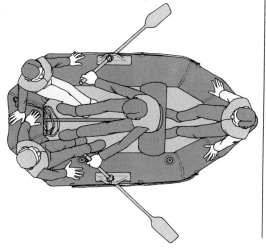

Rowing in tides

When rowing a dinghy in tidal waters you must take great care to avoid being swept downstream, especially in an inflatable dinghy which is more difficult to control than a rigid one. You must plan your course carefully to allow for the tidal drift. When rowing against the tide, it is best to keep to the shallow water where the current is weakest for as long as possible before finally heading towards your objective.

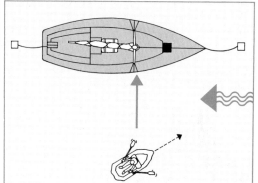

Checklist

Before going afloat you must always check that you have certain items of equipment aboard, in addition to your clothes, personal possessions and sleeping gear, and water and fuel. Even if you only plan to be sailing for a few hours, you should not take the risk of being stranded out at sea without provisions and equipment, in case of an unexpected delay or failure of any part of the boat. The most basic items of equipment are given below, but every skipper will develop his own ideas on what to add to the list. It is always helpful to keep a list of these essential items and check it before each cruise. Safety should always be your first consideration, so you must check that you have sufficient lifejackets, safety harnesses and a big enough life raft for all members of the crew. Flares, fire extinguishers and a first aid kit are also essential. Other items that you should

always keep aboard include navigation instruments and reference books, tools for carrying out emergency repairs and spare items of essential boat equipment.

- Safety harnesses
- Lifejackets or buoyancy aids
- Life raft
- 12 assorted flares
- Fog horn
- Lifebuoys with lights and sea anchors
- Man overboard pole
- 3 fire extinguishers and 1 fire blanket
- First aid kit
- Waterproof flashlights with spare batteries and bulbs
- Radio
- Binoculars

- Spare gas cylinder
- Spare winch handle
- Spare bilge pump handle
- Spare navigation light bulbs
- Navigation instruments
- Tide tables and other reference books
- Charts
- Log book
- Plastic bucket and lanyard
- Spare dock lines and sheets
- Emergency supply of canned and dried food
- Water in a separate container
- Tool kit, whipping twine, and marline spike, sailmaker's needles and palm

Boat handling under power

Most cruising boats are fitted with an engine which is used if the wind drops, if a foul tide has to be crossed or if the boat has to be maneuvered in a crowded marina – or indeed in any other situation where speed and distance have to be carefully judged. There will, of course, be occasions when the boat will have to be handled under sail in confined and congested waters, but it would be better not to take the risk with larger boats unless you are forced to. However, you must always be ready to deal with sudden engine failure and your sails and anchor should be prepared for just such an emergency. Under engine, or even drifting, the boat will have certain handling characteristics which need to be clearly understood if your progress in a marina, for example, is not to be both embarrassing and, possibly, expensive!

Types of engine

Many small cruisers have an outboard engine instead of an inboard one, as outboards save space and weight. In the old days, outboard engines tended to be unreliable but modern types are less prone to suffer from the effects of exposure to salt water. The outboard is usually operated by a gear lever and throttle on the engine itself and, depending on the type of engine, the boat is steered either with the rudder or by turning the engine around, as if it were a tiller. The inboard has an ignition key in the cabin and a gear lever and throttle in the cockpit. The tiller or wheel is used to steer.

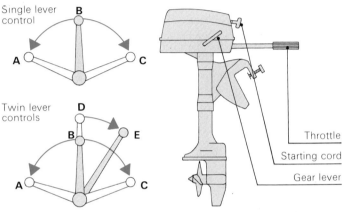

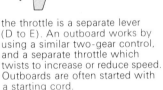

Single lever control

Twin lever controls

Throttle

Starting cord

Gear lever

An inboard engine with a single throttle and gear control is operated by pushing the lever from neutral (B) towards (C) for forward gear (the further you push, the more acceleration) and towards (A) for reverse. With the twin lever type, the throttle is a separate lever (D to E). An outboard works by using a similar two-gear control, and a separate throttle which twists to increase or reduce speed. Outboards are often started with a starting cord.

Propeller effects

One of the most notable characteristics of a boat being handled under engine power is the propeller side effect, or prop walk as it is called. This occurs because water density increases with depth which means that the lower blade is working in denser water than the upper blade. A side paddle effect is created which in turn forces the stern of the boat to move in the same direction that the propeller rotates. A right-handed or clockwise-rotating propeller causes the stern to swing to starboard when the boat is moving forwards. When going astern, the propeller will rotate in the opposite direction (counter-clockwise) and the stern will move to port. This effect is most apparent at slow speeds and is usually more pronounced when going astern.

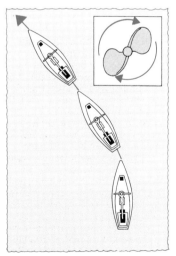

If the boat has an engine with a clockwise-rotating propeller, in forward gear the stern of the boat will swing to starboard and the bow to port.

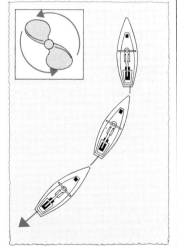

In reverse gear, it rotates counter-clockwise, and the stern swings to port and the bow to starboard.

Using an engine

The effect of prop walk can be used to advantage when handling a boat under engine power. It turns a much tighter circle in the opposite direction to the rotation of the propeller – therefore a boat fitted with a clockwise-rotating propeller turns a tighter circle to port than it does to starboard – both in forward gear and reverse gear. The effect is even more pronounced in reverse gear and in some boats you will find it difficult when reversing to get the boat to turn in the same direction as the propeller rotates, unless you are going quite fast. This, of course, would be dangerous in a crowded marina and the solution is to alternate short hard bursts on the throttle in forward gear with short hard bursts in reverse, keeping the tiller or wheel hard over in the same direction throughout. Obviously, when you don't have a lot of space for turning the boat around, you should turn in the direction the boat adapts to most easily. Don't forget that even when under power, the boat will still have a tendency to drift as well (see below) and you must take this into account when planning your movements in a harbor. If you are handling an unfamiliar boat, make sure you have established which way the propeller rotates before you start maneuvering under power.

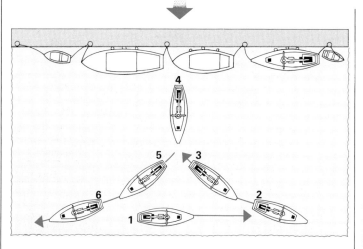

A boat with a clockwise-rotating propeller turns using prop walk and downwind drift. Having reversed directly upwind (2–4), the boat goes ahead with the tiller hard over (4–6) to complete the turn.

Off-center installations

In some boats, the propeller shaft is positioned to one side or the other of the centerline, more commonly so on older boats which have had auxiliary engines fitted after construction. There is a pronounced tendency with these types of installation for the bows of the boat to turn away when in forward gear from the side on which the propeller is mounted (with the opposite effect in reverse gear). You must make sure that the propeller itself rotates in the direction which counters the problem rather than exacerbates it – with a starboard-mounted propeller shaft, do not have a clockwise-rotating propeller.

Drifting characteristics

When the boat is not actually under way (either sail or power) it will start to drift. The way it moves will be determined by the wind or tidal conditions and also by the shape of the boat itself. Although the effect of the tide will not vary, regardless of the design of the boat, the effect of the wind will differ according to the design of the boat. A boat with a shallow draft (one which draws very little water), such as a multihull or small modern cruiser, will tend to be strongly affected by the wind and will drift quickly. This is because there is relatively little of the boat underwater compared with the amount above water. A boat with a long deep hull will have more grip on the water and will drift less quickly. When drifting with the wind, most sailing yachts do not move sideways – the bow points downwind, largely because there is a deeper underwater shape aft, and the bows and mast catch the wind (known as windage). You need to establish exactly how your boat drifts – some boats will not lie steadily but will veer around. In some boats you might even manage to steer the boat downwind under bare poles, while retaining good steering control. To find out, experiment in plenty of open water in different wind and sea conditions. In some cases, if the boat does not lie steadily when drifting, lashing the tiller down will produce a consistent drifting motion (although this is used only when hove-to).

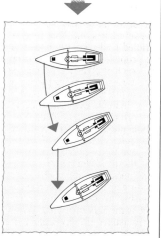

Small cruiser with a tendency to drift so that the bow points downwind.

Equipment for docking

When docking your boat at a slip or pier, or rafting up alongside another boat, you must first consider how to attach the docklines to keep the boat from moving around and possibly damaging itself and other craft. Each line to the shore affects the boat in a particular way, so in order to moor alongside safely you must understand the function of each line.

As most cruising boats spend a good deal of time berthed alongside, it is also important to pay special attention to the equipment used for tying up. While you will always try to avoid stopping in a berth exposed to the full force of the wind and waves, sometimes you have no choice, and your gear must be reliable under such conditions. All cleats and fairleads must be securely bolted into the deck and designed to keep wear on the lines to a minimum. The lines themselves must be of good quality rope and you must check them regularly for signs of wear – it is too late to discover that a line is worn when it gives way in a gale in the middle of the night. Fenders must be of a suitable size and shape for your boat and must be strong enough to withstand chafing against rough walls, sometimes under considerable pressure.

Dock lines

Each line used for docking a boat has a different function. The bow and stern lines position the boat and can be used by the crew, when coming alongside, to check its speed. They must be strong enough to carry the main load of the boat and long enough to allow for the rise and fall of the tide, unless you are berthed at a floating dock. As a general rule, their length should be three times the tidal range. If your bow and stern lines are long enough and are adjusted at half tide, they may not need to be adjusted at high and low water. Springs prevent the boat from moving backwards and forwards. These need not be as long as your bow and stern lines; one and a half times the tidal range should be sufficient. However, you will need to adjust your springs periodically with the rise and fall of the tide. If you are going to leave the boat for some time, you must allow sufficient length for the full tidal range. When lying alongside a dock wall, do not lead springs through or under the rails, but take them through the fairleads and then outside all the rigging. Fore and aft breast ropes keep the bow and stern close alongside, particularly when loading. They are not essential when bow and stern lines and springs are also used, but, when lying alongside a floating dock, can be used to replace the bow and stern lines. Slip lines, which are sometimes rigged when leaving an alongside berth, should never be used instead of permanent lines. This can result in your lines becoming worn in the middle rather than at the ends and you may waste a whole line instead of only a short length at the end.

Names of lines
All lines used for mooring are called docklines until they are rigged in position for use, when they are given particular names as shown below.

1 Bow line   **4** Aft breast rope

2 Stern line   **5** Fore spring

3 Fore breast rope   **6** Aft spring

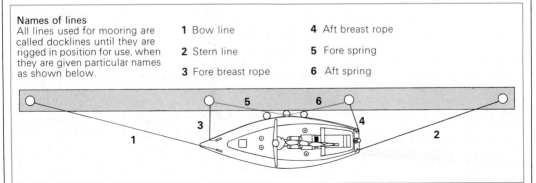

Fenders

Fenders are usually made of either plastic or occasionally rope and are hung from the grabrails or lifelines over the side of the boat to prevent it making contact with the bulkhead, dock or another boat alongside. They are made in a variety of shapes to suit different situations. You should use at least three fenders when berthed alongside. They need not be spaced along the whole length of the boat but only in the middle section where the beam is greatest. You will, however, need more than three fenders on board as there may be times when a boat rafts up alongside you and has insufficient fenders to protect both craft. When docking alongside an uneven bulkhead or dock it is often necessary to hang a plank called a fender board outside the fenders to protect the boat. Different types of fender are shown right, including a bow fender (bottom right).

Alongside a dock at least three fenders are needed.

A fender board protects the boat from damage by uneven surfaces.

Chafe

All ropes are liable to chafe, but dock lines are very susceptible. Chafe most often occurs where the line enters the fairlead and where it is rubbing on the edge of a pier. Wear on the rope can be reduced by threading plastic tubing onto the line in any place where chafing is likely. Usually the friction on the line will keep it in position.

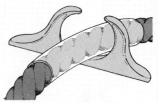

Protection in fairlead

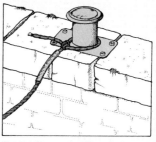

Protection on bulkhead

Cleats and fairleads

Cleats can be bought in a variety of shapes and sizes. In general the larger a cleat, the less the wear on lines and the easier it will be to make up a line on it. There should be no sharp edges anywhere on the cleat. Every boat should be equipped with at least four deck cleats for mooring and larger boats should have more. A Samson post or central bollard, which provides a stronger point at which to secure lines and the anchor chain, is often fitted on the foredeck and sometimes at the stern as well. Fairleads located at the bow and stern of a boat are used to guide lines onto the boat and prevent them from becoming entangled in the lifelines and rigging. Fairleads can be open at the top or closed. The latter are generally preferable as the line cannot slip out. Sometimes they are set into the raised edge around the foredeck. Like cleats, fairleads should have no sharp edges which could cause excessive chafe on your lines. A method of protecting against chafe is described, above right.

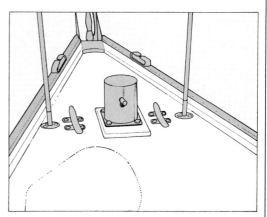

The layout of a foredeck with a central bollard, showing the cleats and fairleads.

Preparation for docking

When coming in and out of congested harbors and marinas, if you have an engine, you should always use it. This does not mean, however, that you should not bother to learn how to handle your boat under sail in such situations. Inevitably, there will come a time when, owing to engine failure, you will have to maneuver under sail and you must be prepared for such an eventuality. This means that you should practice regularly, preferably at times when you have room to make a mistake. Because of the risk of engine failure when motoring, you should always have at least one sail ready for hoisting and an anchor ready to be dropped in case of need. It is bad practice to leave from or return to a berth under power with the mainsail cover on, the headsails bagged in the fore cabin and the anchor stowed. Should the engine fail, it would take some time for the sails to be hoisted or the anchor dropped – by which time you could have drifted into another boat, causing considerable damage.

Choosing a slip

The choice of slip is an important consideration when preparing to dock the boat. Wherever possible, try to choose a slip sheltered from the wind, bearing in mind any changes that have been forecast. A leeward slip places much less strain on the boat and is more comfortable for you than a windward one. If this is not possible, lying head-to-wind prevents wind blowing through the cabin.

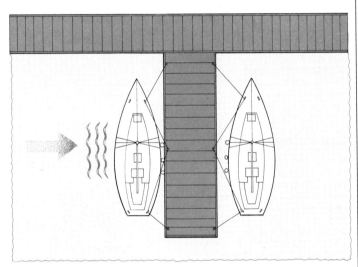

The boat on the windward side of the float is subjected to waves and is blown against it. The boat to leeward is protected.

Effects of wind and tide

Probably the most important consideration when docking is the effect of wind and tide. The effect they have varies from boat to boat and it is important therefore that you are familiar with the drifting characteristics of your craft (see page 175). The effect of prop walk also has to be considered (see pages 174–5) and it should be used to help you wherever possible. When approaching a slip, the main requirement is to stop the boat in the right position. In the absence of a tidal stream, this usually means approaching head-to-wind, using the boat's natural wind resistance to stop. Where a tidal stream is also present, this will often have more of an effect on the boat than the wind and, therefore, a final approach heading into the tide is better (see right). Similarly, when leaving a berth, the effect of the wind and tide on your boat will determine the correct direction in which to leave.

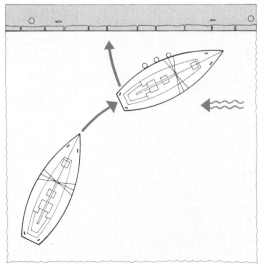

Making an approach to a leeward berth, the boat turns head-to-tide to stop and prop walk is used to bring the stern alongside the pier.

Crew preparation

A good skipper will always make sure that the crew know what is expected of them well before leaving or approaching a berth. The crew should be briefed on their responsibilities and given time to prepare the necessary lines and fenders. Once this has been done, a good crew will often go through a whole berthing maneuver without a word being spoken — a skipper shouting orders and a crew rushing about in a panic is a sure sign of bad preparation. When leaving, the crew must know in what order the lines are to be released and be sure to check that no lines are left trailing in the water where they may foul the propeller. When making an approach, one way of preparing the crew is to make a dummy run. This will also help the skipper to judge the effect of the wind and tide and allow him to see the type of mooring fittings ashore. Once the berth has been inspected, the skipper should be able to tell the crew on which side to tie the fenders and which lines to prepare. Usually to begin with only a bow and a stern line will be used. The best way to rig these is to decide on the approximate length of line that will be needed to reach the fittings on shore and pass the line through the fairlead and pull through

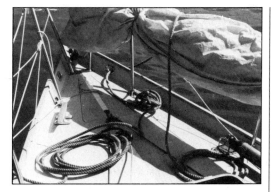

The correct length of bow line is neatly cleated and coiled on the foredeck ready for docking.

that amount. Then cleat off the line and coil up the part that is going ashore. If there are bollards or cleats on shore, a bowline can be tied in the shore end. Fenders should be tied onto the lifelines or grabrails with a round turn and two half hitches. If you intend to tie up alongside another boat always ask permission beforehand.

Crew routine

The routine for leaving a slip varies with each situation but when making an approach the standard procedure described here can usually be followed. Having prepared the lines as above, one person takes the bow line and another the stern line and leading them outside all the rigging, bring the coiled lines and themselves to a position near the shrouds. If there are enough crew members, one stands by the bow cleat and another by stern cleat. As the boat is brought near the slip, the fenders are dropped over the side and the members of the crew with the lines stand outside the lifelines, holding onto the shrouds. As soon as the pier is near enough, they step ashore and the one holding the stern line immediately makes it fast aft of the boat by dropping a bowline over a cleat or bollard or taking a turn around whatever fitting is available. A crew member on board quickly takes up the slack and, keeping a turn around the stern cleat, gradually lets out the line, slowing the boat down until it stops. Meanwhile, the other crew member onshore makes the bow line fast, well forward of the boat. The lines are then adjusted to position the boat correctly in the berth. Always keep the excess

Two members of the crew stand near the shrouds, ready to step ashore with the bow and stern lines.

After the boat has stopped, you must adjust the lines to position the boat correctly in its berth alongside the pontoon.

line onboard to avoid cluttering up the pier or, if you are stopping alongside another boat, someone else's deck. This also enables you to adjust the lines from your own boat. Once the bow and stern lines have been secured the springs and breast ropes can be rigged.

If you have misjudged the amount of line needed, the excess length should not be left ashore, but taken on board.

Docking

When considering leaving from and arriving at a berth, you must remember that every situation is different and is made up of a combination of factors: the relative strength of the wind and tide, their direction in relation to the boat, the handling characteristics of your boat and the presence of obstructions in the vicinity. As the skipper, it is your responsibility to make an accurate assessment of the conditions and decide on an appropriate method of leaving or approaching. There are no rigid rules to help you decide which method of leaving and returning to use in any situation. You must learn to apply your knowledge of your boat and the experience you have gradually built up to work out the best solution. The methods and examples given on the following pages are intended to show how to approach some common situations and to indicate how you can apply the solutions to other sets of circumstances. Methods for leaving from and arriving at a berth, both under engine and under sail are given. In the majority of cases you will use your engine, if you have one, as this gives greater control. Always remember to start the engine and allow it to tick over in neutral for a few minutes before you need it.

When you are leaving a berth much use is made of springs rigged as slip lines to pivot the boat so that either the bow or the stern points away from the pier or float. This prevents the boat rubbing alongside as you try to leave. If, as is often the case, you are moored with other craft ahead and astern, this method of "springing off" your boat from a berth helps you to steer clear. When there are other boats nearby you must take particular care to avoid fouling them if a strong tide is running. In order to be in a better position for leaving in relation to the wind and tide, it is possible to turn the boat in the berth without power by using lines. This is most commonly done when leaving under sail (see page 183), but it can also be a useful maneuver if you want to reposition the boat after you have arrived alongside.

The boat below is leaving a berth using a fore spring to pivot the bow out.

Slip lines

A slip line is one which is led ashore through a ring, or around a bollard or cleat, with both its ends made fast on board. Its main use is for leaving a berth when you want to be able to release a line without having to go ashore to do so. This is particularly useful when leaving from alongside a high pier wall as it is difficult for the crew to get aboard at the last minute. The way a slip line is led ashore is important if it is to be released easily when it is time to leave. When there is a ring on shore, the end which is to be released should be led up through the ring if it is lying on top of a pier, or down through the ring if it is hanging on the face of the pier. This is so that the ring lifts away from the pier when the other end is pulled to retrieve the line. There must be no knots or splices in the end of the line which runs through the ring or around the bollard or cleat, or it may jam. When retrieving the line, you should pull it through steadily, without jerking, otherwise the line may tangle. As soon as the line is free of the shore fitting, it must be pulled in quickly to avoid the possibility of it fouling the propeller.

The boat, right, is about to leave, with the crew aboard ready to release the slip line.

Turning under lines

It is often easier to leave in one direction rather than the other from an alongside berth (see Leaving under sail, page 183). If the direction in which you are pointing makes it difficult to leave, the best solution is to turn the boat by the use of lines, as shown. When turning the boat, it is easier to move the end of the boat facing the strongest element out first. In the diagrams, the boat is shown bow into tide, so the lines are rigged to move the bow away from the pier. If the strongest element were coming from astern, it would be better to bring the stern out first by leading the line from the stern and using an aft spring from the bow. Always place fenders on the far side of the boat before turning, and use one to protect the corner nearest the pier.

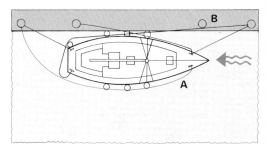

1 Rig a new line (A) from the bow, outside all the rigging on the side of the boat away from the pier, to the shore astern of the boat. Lead the existing fore spring (B) from the shore around the stern and cleat it on the outside corner.

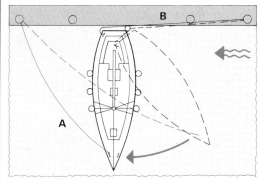

2 Release the other lines. Then pull on the fore spring (B) from on the boat or on the shore to start the boat turning. Take up the slack, or if necessary haul, on the bow line (A).

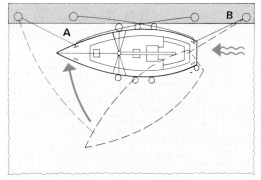

3 Once the boat has turned and is lying against the pier facing in the new direction, make fast the new bow and stern lines (A and B) and, if you are not leaving immediately, rig new springs.

Springing off under power

If when leaving from a berth, you were simply to cast off all your lines, engage forward gear and attempt to steer away from the pier, the stern would probably crash into the pier. The way to avoid this is to turn one end of the boat away from the pier before motoring away. In small boats this can be achieved by one of the crew pushing off from the pier with a boat hook, but in larger craft you have to make use of springs as shown right. Nearly all methods of leaving under engine are based on two alternatives: either springing the bow or the stern off first. The end which is turned first will depend on the position of your boat in relation to the wind and tide (see below). Before attempting to spring off you must use a spare fender to protect the corner of the boat nearest the pier. Once you have rigged the spring as a slip line, the last line your release will be that one under the most strain — normally the bow line if you are leaving bow first and the stern line if you are leaving stern first.

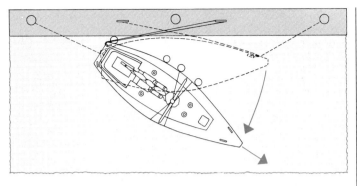

Leaving bow first
Rig the fore spring as a slip line, and cast off the other lines. Motor gently astern and turn the stern towards the wall as the boat starts to pivot. Once clear of obstructions, release the spring and motor out.

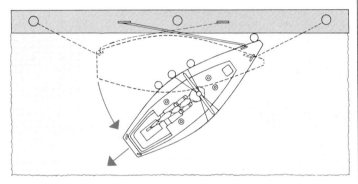

Leaving stern first
Rig the aft spring as a slip line, and cast off the other lines. Motor gently forward and turn the stern away from the wall. When turned sufficiently, release the spring and motor out astern.

How to leave

Whether you leave bow or stern first depends primarily on the position of the boat in relation to the direction of the element, wind or tide, which has the strongest effect. The tidal current normally runs parallel to a wall or pier, but the wind could be coming from any direction. The methods you choose when the tide is the determining factor are shown right. The diagrams below right indicate how to leave when the wind is stronger and is coming from a direction within the sectors shown. These sectors cannot be rigidly defined and the area not covered may allow departure by either method. When a strong offshore wind is blowing, you can leave by releasing the lines and drifting away, but this is less controlled than springing off.

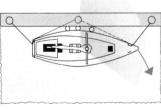

Bow into tide
Leave bow first.

Stern into tide
Leave stern first.

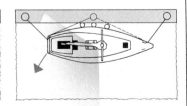

Wind forward of the beam
Leave bow first.

Wind aft of the beam
Leave stern first.

Leaving under sail

It is possible under most conditions to leave a berth under sail alone, but if the wind is much weaker than the tide your control will be reduced and it is safer to leave under engine. It is normally best to leave with the bow facing into the tide, as this gives more control over the steering and allows you to stop if necessary. If you are not already head-to-tide, the solution is to turn the boat by using lines (see page 181). Once you are facing into the tide, the way you leave will be governed by whether the wind is onshore or offshore or in the sectors fore or aft of the beam. If the wind is onshore you may have difficulty leaving under sail (see below right). If the wind is offshore and far enough forward of the beam to prevent the mainsail filling, you can hoist it first and delay hoisting the headsail until the lines have been cast off, leaving the foredeck clear. If the wind is on or aft of the beam, you must leave under the headsail alone (pictured right). In the same way as when leaving under engine, release the lines under most strain last and use fenders to protect the boat.

The wind conditions have dictated that the boat,right should leave its berth under the headsail.

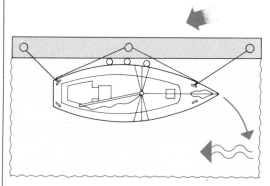

Offshore wind ahead of beam
Hoist mainsail. Release shore lines. Once boat has drifted clear, trim mainsail, hoist and trim headsail.

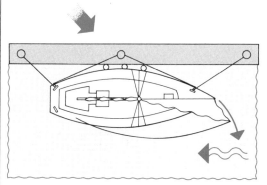

Offshore wind aft of beam
Hoist headsail. Cast off lines and trim headsail. Once clear, turn head-to-wind to hoist mainsail.

Onshore wind

If there is an onshore wind blowing, even at a slight angle, it can make leaving under sail difficult or even impossible unless you use some rather complicated methods. You may be able to get a tow from a boat with an engine to take you clear of the slip where you can hoist your sails head-to-wind and sail off. Alternatively, it may be possible to take a long line and attach it to a fixed point, such as a buoy or jetty, and pull the boat away to a position where you can hoist a sail and leave. A further solution is to take the anchor out in the tender and drop it at a point at right angles to the bow and pull the boat away on the anchor (see Laying an anchor from a dinghy, page 200). If you arrive at a berth with an onshore wind and expect to leave soon after, it is a good idea to lay your anchor before docking as long as there is no danger of fouling other boats.

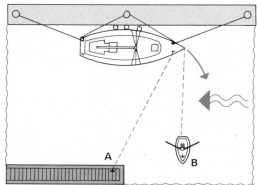

Onshore wind
The boat can either be pulled away by attaching a line to the jetty (A) or by laying an anchor (B).

Arriving under power

When planning your approach to
a berth, brief the crew thoroughly
and, where possible, make a dummy
approach first to examine the securing
points and to assess the relative strength
of wind and tide. In most cases when
arriving under power you will already
have motored into the harbor, but if you
come in under sail, make sure your
engine is switched on in plenty of time.
Don't forget that you can use prop walk
to help you dock the boat (see page 174).

When docking a large boat, such as the
one with a lot of windage, right, planning
and teamwork are vital.

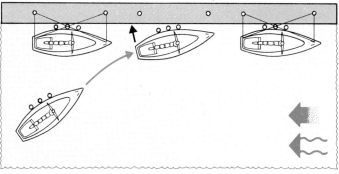

Wind and tide together or opposed

If wind and tide are parallel to the
shore, whether from the same
direction or opposed, a similar
approach is used. Come in to the
berth with the bow towards the
strongest element. The lines are
prepared as usual (see page 179),
and the engine put into neutral
when you wish to slow the boat
down. However, when the wind
and tide are opposed, you may
need to use the reverse gear on
the engine in the final stages to
stop you.

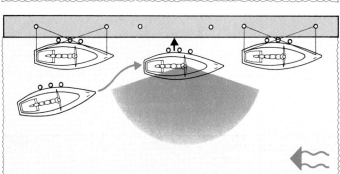

Onshore wind

When the wind is blowing onto the
pier , the bow and stern lines are
prepared in the usual way. Bring
the boat parallel with the pier and
put the engine into neutral as you
do so. The wind will then blow
you gently onto the pier .

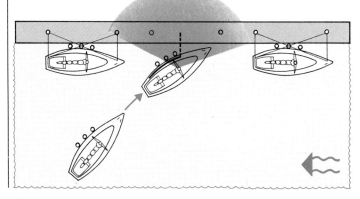

Offshore wind

When the wind blows off the berth,
you need to take the windage on
the bow into account, as your bow
will blow away from the pier if
you do not. Get the crew to lead
the stern line well forward and
motor into the berth at a sharper
angle than you would normally.
They must get the bow and stern
lines ashore quickly, and pull the
boat into position with the lines.

Arriving under sail

Docking under sail alone is no easy matter and your movements will have to be very carefully judged. If you are practicing, pick a day with medium strength winds and keep the engine running in case you get into difficulty. The success of the operation depends on your ability to handle the boat under sail at slow speeds, as well as having an efficient crew who can respond quickly to instructions. The wind shadow effect from harbor walls, buildings and other boats will affect wind speed and direction. This might easily wreck an otherwise perfectly planned approach and any good skipper would have planned an escape route in advance to cope with this kind of problem. Broadly speaking, much the same rules apply to docking under sail as under power. If the tide and wind are parallel to the pier, approach bow-on to the strongest element. If you are travelling too fast in the final stages you can reduce speed quickly by getting your crew to back the mainsail (by pushing it out to the shrouds and holding it there) or by partly lowering the headsail and holding out the leech to keep it filled, or by lowering it altogether. Bear in mind it is usually easier to speed up than it is to slow down.

The boat above has been sailed into a berth under mainsail only. Bow and stern lines are sent ashore before the mainsail is lowered.

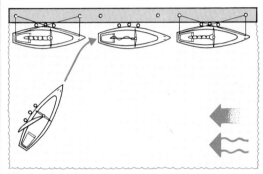

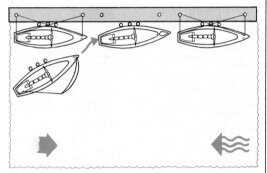

Wind and tide together or strong wind opposed
With wind and tide together, or with them opposed but with a stronger wind, approach the berth under mainsail alone on a close reach, letting out the mainsheet as necessary to control boat speed. As you reach the berth, turn the boat into the wind, and back the mainsail if necessary to slow down in the final stages. Once alongside, fasten bow and stern lines ashore and drop and furl the mainsail quickly.

Strong tide opposing weak wind
With the tide stronger than, and opposed to, the wind, approach downwind under headsail alone. Keep the sail sheeted in lightly, and if the approach is too fast, lower the headsail a little and get a crew member to hold the leech out, or take the sail down altogether and make the final approach under bare poles. Get the stern line and an aft spring ashore first and secure them to act as a brake.

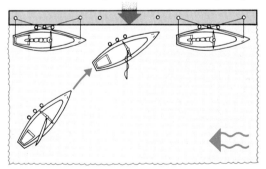

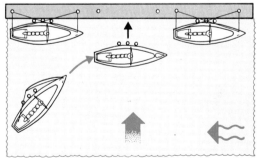

Offshore wind
With the wind blowing offshore, come in against the tide. If the wind is forward of the beam, come in under the mainsail, and if it is aft of the beam, come in under the headsail. Sail into the berth, and adjust the speed by letting out the sheet. Get the bow and stern lines ashore quickly but don't pull on the stern line until the mainsail is lowered. (The diagram above shows the approach under mainsail.)

Onshore wind
When the wind is blowing onto the berth, make the approach under headsail alone. Lower the mainsail to windward of the berth and sail downwind under the headsail. About a boat's length to windward of the berth, turn the boat almost parallel with the pier, with the bow pointing slightly upwind. Lower the sail (or allow it to flap) and let the boat drift sideways into the berth. Fasten the bow and stern lines.

Rafting up

Rafting up is the term given to berthing alongside another boat (or boats), whether next to piles, a pier, a float or a mooring. It is not an ideal way of berthing because if a boat on the inside of a raft wishes to leave first it causes considerable inconvenience. Another disadvantage to rafting up is that the crews of the boats in the raft will have to cross other boats to get to and from the shore. In a crowded harbor, however, there is often no choice. There are certain precautions you should take before rafting up. Try and find out if the harbor limits the number of boats in a raft. If there is someone on board the boat you are rafting up to, ask permission first. You need to make sure that your lines are long enough to secure your bow and stern to the permanent fixing – float, pier, or whatever – if you find yourself either in tidal waters or on the outside of a raft of several boats. Try and avoid a raft where only the inside boat is secured to the pier or piles – such a raft will swing backwards and forwards making your stay uncomfortable. It also helps to minimize swaying motion if you raft up alongside a boat larger than your own. You always need to make sure that the masts are staggered; if adjacent, and the boats roll, the rigging may be fouled.

As a matter of common courtesy, always walk forward of the mast when crossing over other boats – it helps to preserve privacy.

Joining a raft

When rafting up to another boat, you need not worry about facing in the same direction. If the wind or tide demand you approach from the opposite direction, it may be a help – the masts will then be staggered naturally. It is your responsibility to make sure that your boat is secured with bow and stern lines to a permanent fixing, as well as being attached by springs and breast ropes to the next boat. In tidal waters, it is best not to leave the boat unattended.

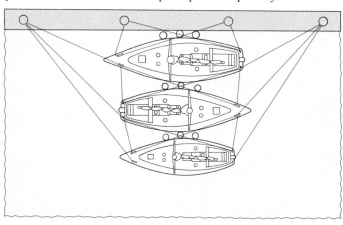

Above, boats correctly rafted up with bow and stern lines from each boat to the pier, and breast ropes and springs between the boats. The boats are positioned so that the masts are staggered to prevent fouling of the rigging.

Left, boats rafted up to a pier: a small boat is rafted up alongside large ones which will prevent it from swaying about.

Leaving a raft

When leaving from the middle of a raft you must always depart with the strongest element: wind or tide. If you are leaving from the outside of a raft, you can simply maneuver as if you were leaving from a float or pier. If, on the other hand, you find that you are on the inside the process will be a little more awkward. If you leave with the strongest element, the boats outside you will tend to close up. Never attempt to leave against the strongest element from the inside of a raft of several boats — the outside boats will drift on the tide and you could find yourself dealing with four or five craft drifting uncontrollably away from the rest of the raft. Some of your own crew may have to stay on the raft to make fast the remaining boats.

Once a boat has made fast outside a raft, the shore lines must be rigged. Here the stern line is led ashore clear of other boats.

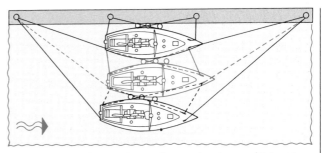

1 Unfasten your bow and stern lines and springs and bring them on board. Unfasten the springs and breast lines of the boat outside you.

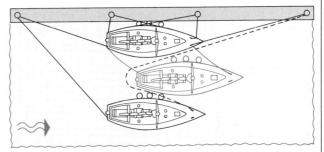

2 Unfasten the appropriate bow or stern line of the outside boat and lead it around your boat and back to the shore.

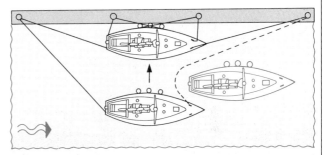

3 Let go of the breast ropes of your own boat and allow it to move out with the stronger element. If your crew are still on the raft, turn and come alongside the outside boat in the raft to pick them up.

Rafting up around a mooring buoy

Some harbors have large mooring buoys around which a number of boats can moor up bow-on. The main advantage of this system is that a boat can leave relatively easily — it simply departs stern first and, if necessary, a crew member stays on board the raft to refasten the springs and lines of the other boats. Mooring buoys are not used in waters with a strong tidal current, as a lot of strain would be placed on the buoy.

When rafted up around a mooring buoy, breast lines and springs will be necessary to keep the boat in position. A bow fender is essential, to protect the bow from banging into the mooring buoy.

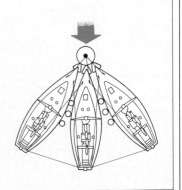

Marina berths

Marinas are becoming more and more popular in many harbors. They provide a complex system of piers or floats and usually have good amenities ashore. They are very popular and tend to get very crowded in summer. As the berths are close together, you have to be able to control your craft properly if you are not to damage either your own or other people's boats. Space to maneuver is limited, and there will be occasions when you can only dock or leave by making a three-point turn. This means that your boat has to handle well in reverse gear, and that you know what its handling characteristics are. It would be a mistake to try and dock a boat with a lot of windage and a weak engine in a confined space. It would be better to take an outside berth first and warp the boat around to a more suitable berth afterwards. The same rule applies if, by any chance, you have to sail in. In normal circumstances, though, it would probably be a mistake to try to dock under sail in a marina.

In most marinas, you do not normally have to worry about the tide—they are often constructed away from the main tidal stream. However, if there is a tidal stream, the float may

well be jutting into it, and you should consider the direction of the tide before planning your departure or approach. Always thoroughly brief the crew well before any maneuver is started, as mistakes could be expensive.

In a crowded marina it is often safer to warp the boat out of the berth into the open water, rather than to attempt to leave under power.

Handling a difficult berth

In some berths you may find that your room for maneuver is too limited for you to attempt to leave under power. The best solution is to use lines to move the boat away from the others into open water. It is not possible to lay down rules as to which lines should be used, but the skipper has clearly got to work out for himself how to put the boat in the best position from which to leave. It is, in fact, very easy to move a boat by using lines but remember that once the boat has started moving, it will take time to stop. The other alternative in confined spaces,

particularly when reversing out of a berth, or when a strong wind is blowing, is to use springs. The boat below has limited turning room and a strong wind could prevent her bow from going up to windward. If the stern line is rigged as a slip line, the boat can be motored out astern, leaving slack on the line (1). Once the stern is clear of the berth (2) a turn can be taken on the cleat to hold the stern until the bows clear the berth (3) and then the line can be freed and allowed to slip as the boat motors off forward into clear water.

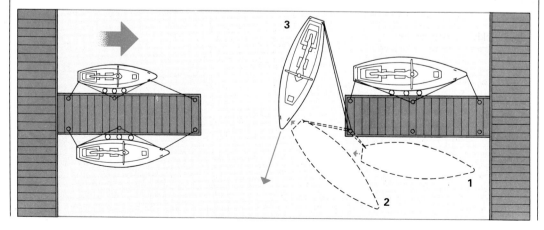

Leaving

Before the boat's lines are cast off the skipper has to decide on his method of leaving. You need to check around first to see if there are any other boats in the process of leaving or arriving which may interfere with your proposed course of action. Not only should you consider the effects of wind and tide at the berth itself, but also on your path out of the marina. Your exit from the marina will probably be very slow and you need to be sure that you can control your craft properly.

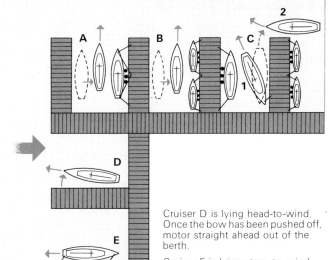

Cruisers A and B have simple slips to leave from. Put the engine in neutral before the lines are cast off, then let the boat drift clear of the berth. Motor out into open water. If there is not enough wind to push the boat clear, push the bow off.

Cruiser C has a more difficult leaving situation, as it is berthed bow-on in a windward berth. Either spring off the stern (1) or warp the boat onto the end of the slip (2) so that it can leave with the bow facing into the wind.

Cruiser D is lying head-to-wind. Once the bow has been pushed off, motor straight ahead out of the berth.

Cruiser E is lying stern-to-wind and, provided it has an adequate engine, you can motor clear of the berth in reverse, using prop walk (with a clockwise-rotating propeller) to take the stern clear of the slip. The crew could help you by walking the boat out using the stern line and aft spring, and climbing aboard as the boat passes the end of the slip.

Arriving

As a visitor, when planning to berth in a marina, you should first try and find out if there are special visitors' berths, or whether a visitor is expected to find his own berth. Usually, the pilot book for the harbor will give you the information you need. Before you come into the marina you should brief the crew. It is unlikely, however, you will know in advance which side of the boat will be alongside the berth and so the crew must be ready to rig the lines quickly as soon as the skipper himself knows the answer. If there are enough fenders to go around, hang them over both sides of the boat. The skipper should keep a watch for other boats entering or leaving the marina and control his own speed accordingly.

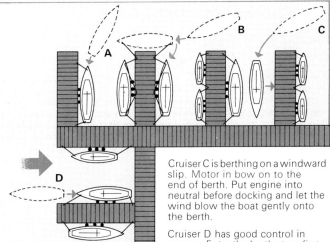

Cruiser A is berthing in a leeward berth. If your boat has good maneuverability and little prop walk on the engine, you can berth astern, allowing the stern to lie upwind slightly of the berth. Stop boat alongside and secure it.

Cruiser B is less maneuverable. Bring the boat alongside the end of the slip head-to-wind, and once the bow and stern lines have been secured, the crew can walk the boat into the berth.

Cruiser C is berthing on a windward slip. Motor in bow on to the end of berth. Put engine into neutral before docking and let the wind blow the boat gently onto the berth.

Cruiser D has good control in reverse. Enter the berth stern first and use forward gear to stop. This leaves the boat lying head-to-wind and prevents drafts in the cabin.

Cruiser E has less control in reverse. Enter with the engine in neutral (if the wind is strong enough). As the boat arrives at the berth, the crew attaches the stern line and aft spring first to slow the boat down. (With good astern power, a final burst astern could be used instead.)

Docking stern-to

In some marinas, boats have to be berthed stern-to, and secured at the bow with an anchor to hold the boat at right angles to the shore (right). These berths are easier to leave from than to berth in, unless the boat has good handling characteristics astern. Boats berthing regularly in this type of marina will usually have an opening in the stern rail and a gangplank aboard to make boarding easier. The stern of the boat is secured to the shore by lines rigged like springs (see page 176—7). A tripping line on the anchor (see pages 200—1) is a good safety precaution.

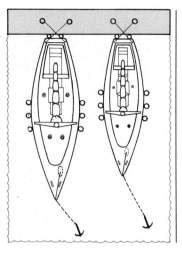

Leaving

When leaving a stern-to berth, the routine is essentially the same whatever the direction of wind or tide. The stern lines are released first and the boat is motored forward while the anchor rode is recovered. Once the boat is over the anchor, the anchor is broken out and the boat taken clear of the berth before it is stowed. With a strong cross-wind or tide, a stern line should be rigged first as a slip and the boat motored out of the berth with the crew controlling sideways slip by pulling on both stern and anchor lines. Once the anchor is broken out, slip the stern line and motor clear.

Arriving

Prepare the anchor and rode well in advance and if you are attempting to berth between two other boats, have the fenders rigged on both sides. Lay the anchor (see pages 200—1) and reverse into the berth, while a crew member lets out the anchor rode as you do so. If the boat swings out of line, straighten it up by snubbing the anchor rode briefly (see page 198). Once berthed, attach the stern lines and adjust the anchor rode to hold the boat clear of the shore. If there is a strong cross-wind, and your engine is weak, you may find that the boat drifts sideways, or the bow blows downwind. The best solution is to motor in bow-on first, attach a line to the shore and then reverse out again paying the line out as you go. When you reach the anchoring position, lay the anchor, take the slack line to the stern and reverse into the berth, berthing stern-to in the normal way.

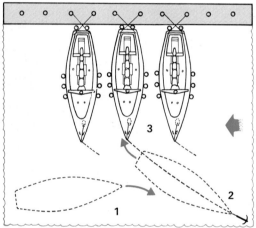

Motor in parallel to berth, clear of anchor lines (1), lay anchor rode (2), reverse into berth and attach stern lines (3).

Strong cross-winds

In strong cross-winds work in two stages. In the first stage (right) motor up to berth (1), come in bow-on and fasten bow line ashore (2), reverse paying out bow line and lay anchor (3). In the second stage, far right, turn boat on the anchor (4), take bow line to stern and reverse into berth using stern line and anchor rode to keep boat straight (5). Fasten stern springs (6).

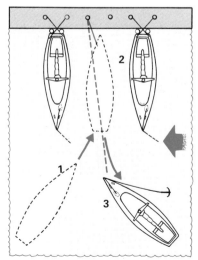

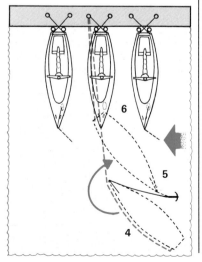

Pile and float berths

Some marinas use pairs of piles instead of finger floats to secure the boat. Most permanent berths have permanent lines attached to the piles, to make leaving and arriving easier. If there are no permanent lines attached you will have to rig your own lines and remove them as you leave. Although boats with strong engines will be able to berth stern-to, most sailing boats with weaker engines will find it easier to berth bow-on.

Leaving

When leaving a berth between marina piles, the method you use depends on the effect of the wind on the boat. If it is from ahead or astern, assuming the boat is berthed bow-on, the stern lines are taken forward to the shrouds and rigged as slip lines, and the bow lines cast off. By pulling on the stern lines, the boat can be taken smoothly straight out. As the bow comes level with the piles the lines are released. With permanent lines at the float and piles, simply let them go as necessary. With strong cross-wind blowing, assuming you are berthed bow-on, you will first have to ease out the windward bow and stern lines, letting the boat drift to leeward until you can reach the leeward pile, letting go the leeward stern and bow lines. Then pull the boat back up to windward and rig an extra line as a slip from the windward pile to a point near the bow.

The windward bow and stern lines (whether they are permanent lines or ones you have rigged yourself) are then released and the boat motored out astern. If the bow starts to blow to leeward, tighten the slip line briefly to pull the bow back to windward. As the bow passes clear of the piles, the slip line is released. If the boat is berthed stern-to, reverse the instructions for bow and stern and motor forwards out of the berth.

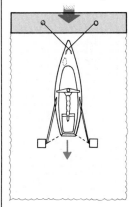 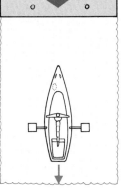 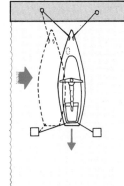 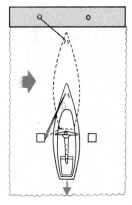

Wind ahead or astern
1 Rig stern lines as slips and cast off bow lines.

2 Reverse boat out of berth, and when level with piles, release slip lines.

Cross-winds
1 Ease windward bow and stern lines to release leeward lines.

2 Rig slip line from bow to windward pile. Reverse out using slip line to guide you.

Arriving

The crew should rig two bow lines and two stern lines, the ends of which are led forward to the shrouds. If there is a cross-wind come in close to the windward pile. As you reach the piles the crew members attach your lines to the mooring rings (see page 176). Motor in while the crew pay out the lines. If the wind is on the beam, keep the bow up to windward. As you reach the float, two bow lines are taken ashore, and the lines adjusted to keep the boat just away from the float and between the piles. Permanent lines are rigged in the same way.

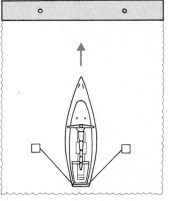 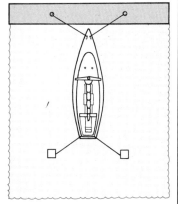

1 Rig stern and bow lines. Bring stern lines to shrouds and attach stern lines to piles.

2 Motor forward, paying out stern lines and fasten bow lines on pontoon.

Pile moorings (dolphins)

In many harbors, sets of piles (large wooden or metal stakes driven into the seabed) are used to provide fore and aft lines along the edge of a channel. These have special fittings to which the boat's lines can be attached. Quite often, several boats will raft up to the same set of piles, although most harbors will limit the number of boats allowed on each pair. When rafted up on piles, all the boats should be secured to the piles as well as to the neighboring boat in the same way as when rafting up alongside a pier (see pages 186–7). Boats which are to be left for any length of time on pile moorings should be left facing into the ebb tide which is normally stronger than the flood, but if strong winds are expected, the boat should be turned to point into the wind.

Tying up

Mooring piles are fitted with a metal bar on each side on which runs a large metal ring to which you attach your lines. When a boat is moored, the rings move up and down with the rise and fall of the tide. This means that you do not need to adjust your lines. A retrieval line is tied between the ring and the top of the bar to enable you to pick up the ring at all states of the tide. When securing lines to the rings, the best knot to use is a round turn and a bowline with a long loop (see below and page 331).

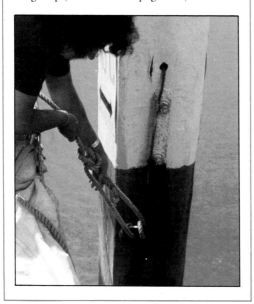

Leaving under power

The procedure for leaving a pile mooring under power will depend on whether you are lying alongside another boat or in the middle of a raft, or on your own, and the direction and relative strength of the wind and tide. If you are lying in the middle of a raft, you can use the methods for leaving described on pages 186–7. If you are on the outside you can recover your lines in the tender and leave using the methods described for alongside berths (see page 182). If the boat is between the piles on its own, you must use one of three methods described below, depending on the strength and direction of the wind and tide, and whether your boat handles well in reverse.

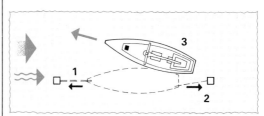

Bow into strongest element
Pull the boat forward to the forward pile while letting out on the stern line (1). Rig the bow line as a slip and allow the boat to drop back to the aft pile (2). Release the stern line and motor away forwards as you slip the bow line (3).

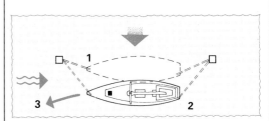

Wind abeam
If the bow is pointing into the tide, rig both bow and stern lines as slips (1) and allow the boat to drift to leeward of the piles by slackening the lines and steering away (2). Once clear, slip both lines and motor off forwards (3). If the boat is stern-to-tide, see below.

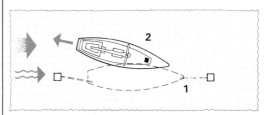

Stern into strongest element
If the boat handles well in reverse, rig both lines as slips (1) and motor out astern (2), preferably in the direction favored by the prop walk. If the boat does not handle well in reverse, turn the boat by use of lines (see page 181) and leave using the method for bow into strongest element.

Arriving under power

When planning on picking up a pile mooring under power, the same factors need to be taken into account as when approaching other mooring and berthing situations. The skipper must work out a course of action depending on the relative effects of the wind and tide and the boat's handling characteristics. A dummy run is always useful for both the skipper and the crew. The bow and stern lines, boat-hook and fenders, if needed, must all be ready before the actual approach is made. It is best if two crew members cooperate to secure the boat to the piles as it can be awkward for one person. If there are other boats on the piles, the approach will be the same as for an alongside berth, with the bow and stern lines rigged to the piles later using the tender. If there are no other boats you must use one of the methods described below. If after having tied up you find that you are facing away from the ebb tide, you should turn the boat using lines (see page 181).

One crew member holds the boat steady near the pile, while the other ties the knot.

Wind and tide together
Approach into the wind and tide and stop with the bow alongside the forward pile and attach the bow line (1). Let out the line to allow the boat to drop back to the aft pile and secure the stern line (2). Pull the boat forwards until it is equidistant from the two piles and adjust the lines. Alternatively, the stern line could be taken to the pile in the tender, or the method for wind and tide opposed could be used.

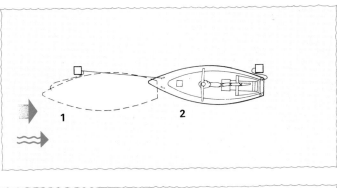

Wind and tide opposed
Approach into the strongest element. Stop at the aft pile first and attach the stern line, but keep it slack (1). Motor forwards to the forward pile and attach the bow line (2). Drop back and adjust the lines to position the boat. It is important that a crew member is delegated to tend the stern line throughout the maneuver to prevent it fouling the propeller. This method is known as a "running moor".

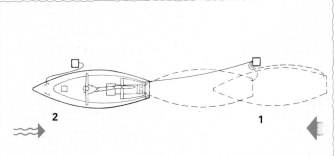

Wind abeam
The method is basically the same as the running moor described above, but the boat approaches the aft mooring to windward (1). After securing the stern line, motor slowly forward, keeping the bow pointing slightly into the wind so that the boat moves crabwise to the forward pile. Secure the bow line (2) and centre the boat in between the two piles.

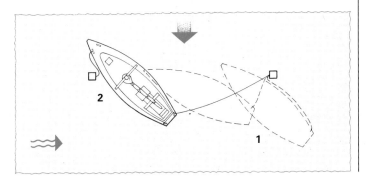

Leaving under sail

Leaving pile moorings under sail presents no particular problem but, in common with other maneuvers in and out of berths, it is usually best not to attempt it if the area is crowded. As pile moorings are usually situated on the edges of channels where there is a tidal stream, when under sail, it is usually best to leave bow to tide as this gives better control over your speed and steering. This means that you may have to turn the boat between the piles first by the use of lines. If yours is the only boat moored to the piles, leave using one of the methods shown right, according to the direction of the wind. If you are lying on the outside of other boats moored to the piles, recover your lines to the piles in the tender and leave using one of the methods for leaving an alongside berth described on page 183. If, however, you are in the middle of the raft you will have to wait for the other boats to leave first.

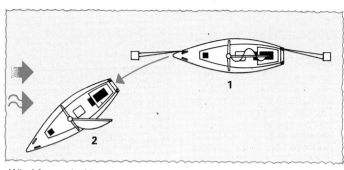

Wind forward of beam
Turn the boat bow-to-tide and prepare both sails for immediate hoisting. Rig the bow and stern lines as slips. Hoist the mainsail (1). Sheet in and steer onto your chosen course, preferably to leeward of the forward pile. Slip the stern line as the boat gathers way, and then slip the bow line (2). Once clear, hoist the headsail.

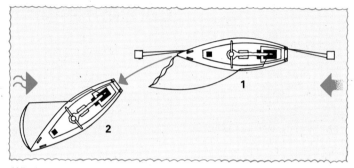

Wind on or aft of beam
Turn the boat bow-to-tide and prepare both sails for hoisting. Rig both lines as slips and hoist the headsail (1). Sheet in the sail and steer onto your chosen course, preferably to leeward of the forward pile, as the boat gathers way (2). As soon as you are clear, turn head-to-wind and hoist the mainsail.

Arriving under sail

When arriving at a pile mooring under sail you must choose an approach according to the strength and direction of the wind and tide. It is normally best to approach into the tide unless there is a much stronger opposing wind, in which case you should approach upwind. The sail you use will be determined by whether the wind is forward or aft of the beam as you approach. As the approach must be slow and controlled, you must adjust the speed by letting out the sheet. The aim will be to secure the boat to the upwind pile first, stopping so that it is near the shrouds. It is important to secure the line immediately and if the crew cannot tie the knot quickly enough, it is best to rig the lines temporarily as slips and tie permanent knots later.

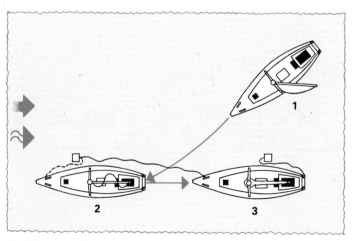

Wind forward of beam
When approaching against the tide with the wind forward of the beam, or into a strong wind with an opposing weak tide, approach the forward pile under the mainsail only on a close reach. Stop the boat with the pile near the shrouds and secure the bow line (2). Lower the mainsail and allow the boat to drop back to the aft pile and secure the the stern line (3). Adjust the lines.

Fore and aft buoys

Some harbors and rivers have fore and aft moorings (right). They secure the boat at the bow and stern to prevent it swinging in the wind or tide. The methods you use for leaving and approaching are the same as for pile moorings. Before picking up fore and aft mooring buoys, it is important to check that they are suitable for the size of your boat (see also Anchoring and mooring, pages 198–9).

Pick-up buoys
Sometimes the main buoys will have smaller pick-up buoys attached to them by a rope or chain. These are easily picked up and secured on board when mooring up. When you approach such a berth (right), pick up the buoys together (1) and bring them on board taking the forward one to the bow and the aft one to the stern (2). When a boat leaves the mooring the two pick-up buoys are often left joined together in the middle of the berth.

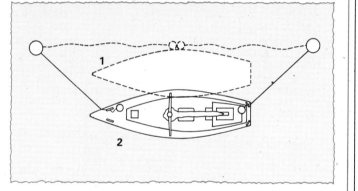

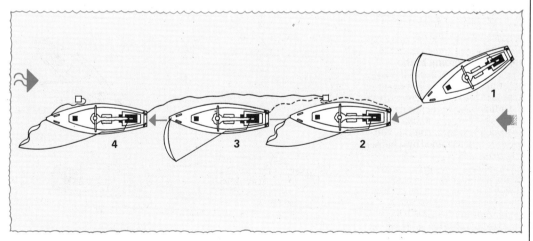

Wind on or aft of beam
When a relatively strong tide is opposing a weak wind, approach into the tide under the headsail alone and use a running moor. After lowering the mainsail, sail towards the aft pile under the headsail (1). Stop by allowing the sail to flap or lowering it partially or totally when the pile is near the shrouds and attach the stern line (2). Then sheet in the sail and approach the forward pile while letting out the stern line (3). Stop the boat against the forward pile and secure the bow line (4). Lower the headsail and adjust the lines so that the boat is positioned equidistant from both piles.

Drying out

Few of the ports you will visit in North America will dry out at low water, but you may want to tie up alongside a wall or pier in a harbor which does dry out, in order to examine or maintain the boat hull and keel. It may be perfectly safe to take the ground but the right precautions must be taken.

Firstly, it is important to realize that different hull forms behave in quite different ways when they go aground. The most stable, of course, is a catamaran, while a boat with bilge keels is also stable: the two keels will support the boat and, unless the ground slopes very steeply away from the wall, there will be no need to worry about it falling outwards. A yacht with a long straight keel will also take the ground comfortably though precautions must be taken to ensure that it heels towards the pier. With a boat which has a fin and skeg profile, care must be taken with the balance – the weight of the crew too far forwards can easily result in the bow tipping

down. If you own a boat which is deeper aft than forward you will have to watch out that the bow does not swing in towards the wall, as this will result in the boat lying in a precariously upright position.

Do try and find out the nature of the ground on which you intend to dry out. If it is strewn with rocks and rubbish the damage done to your boat could be considerable. If the ground slopes very steeply away from the pier it is likely to cause your craft to slip outwards. This fate could result in as much damage as a fall away from the wall. It may well prove best to take up some temporary mooring and study the ground at low tide. If it seems suitable you can then go alongside on the next flood. Advice from a pilot book or the harbor master will also assist you.

Having found what, to all intents and purposes, seems a suitable stretch of wall, you must prepare your boat to take the ground. In order to ensure that it leans inwards against the wall,

Attaching lines and springs
Bow and stern lines should be made fast a long way fore and aft of the boat so that their angle is not too acute at low water. They will not need to be adjusted with the rise and fall of the tide. If you are remaining on board, you will adjust the springs to ensure that the boat lies comfortably. If leaving the boat, the springs must be long enough to accommodate low water.

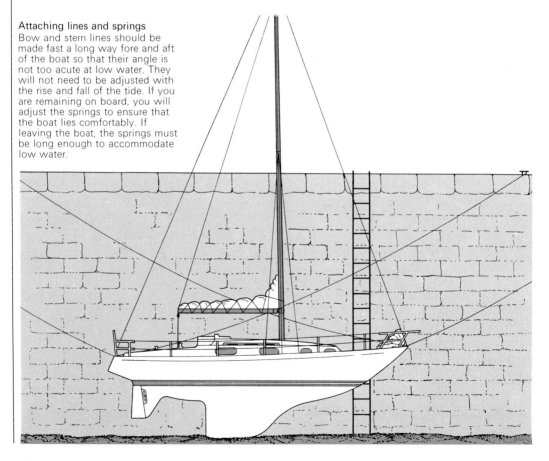

you will have to shift some ballast (either anchor chain, fuel or water containers) onto the deck so that it will lean (with no one on board) at about 10° towards the wall. As the tide begins to fall, further precautions must be taken. Fenders should be strong and plentiful. If they are not, or if the surface of the wall is very uneven, you will need to use a fender board.

Then you must make sure that the boat is lying fairly close to the wall. If it strays away it will heel at an alarmingly steep angle and the damage done to the rails, rigging or mast, if not all three, could be extensive. As the tide falls, make sure that a smaller boat does not raft up alongside you because, when you take the ground, it will pull you over. Equally, remember that your dinghy must drop to the ground when the tide is out. If the painter is not long enough, then it will hang in mid-air.

You must also check that the springs won't become fouled by rails or fenders and if you have open fairleads, ensure that the lines are lashed into them otherwise they may easily slip out as the tide falls.

When drying out in an unfamiliar harbor you must watch the boat closely. Once you have seen that it can take the ground comfortably you will then be able to leave her unattended. Some boats take the ground better than others and you will learn from experience how capable your boat is at looking after itself.

Weighting the lines
To stop your boat straying away from the wall, you can attach an anchor or a weight to both the bow and stern lines. In sinking, they will pull down the slack of the lines thus ensuring that these remain taut and hold the boat close to the wall.

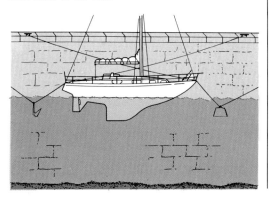

Attaching a running block
Though you will have to trim the boat by placing ballast on the shoreside deck, a further precaution should be taken by attaching a line with a running block extending from the wall to a taut halyard by the mast. As the tide rises and falls, the block will move up and down the halyard so that the line always remains at a constant tension.

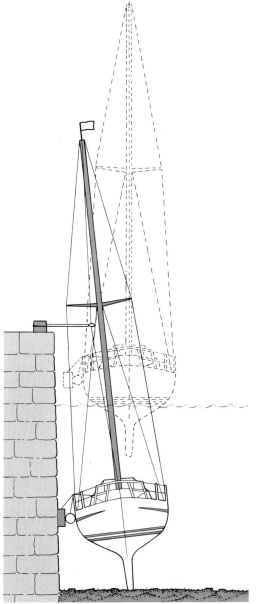

Anchoring and mooring

Anchoring and mooring are related techniques in that they both involve securing the boat to a fixed point surrounded by water. In both cases the way you approach and leave the site will be the same but when mooring the means of securing the boat is provided by the buoy, and when anchoring you have to provide it yourself. This involves additional equipment and preparation and more complicated crew routines.

Anchoring is a skill which is becoming less used as harbors are filled up with moorings, piles and, of course, marinas. Nevertheless, there are many times when the ability to anchor correctly can be a great asset, whether for a lunchtime stop in a quiet cove or to ride out a gale. It is in the latter case that you need to have complete trust in your equipment. The size of the anchor is critical. A small anchor may well hold in a good holding ground and light winds, but will drag or break loose if the wind increases. Different types of anchor are shown below and on page 94; different types of mooring are described on page 82.

The anchor and rode are prepared by the crew before stopping at the anchorage.

Choosing an anchor and rode

There are several different types of anchor on the market. The type you choose will depend on the seabed in the area you will be sailing in most often. Recent developments in anchor design include the Plow (illustrated on page 94), the Danforth (below right) and the Bruce (page 94). All of these are designed to bury themselves in the seabed and can hold up to 30 times their own weight. The traditional Fisherman's anchor (below right) will hold up to ten times its own weight in a sandy bottom. It will also hold on rocky and weedy ground on which other anchors may not hold. Whichever type you choose, it must be heavy enough to hold your boat in all conditions. Most boats are supplied with anchors which are the minimum weight needed and, since you should always carry at least two anchors, it is often best to keep the one supplied as a second, or kedge, anchor and to invest in a heavier one for the main, or bower, anchor. If you need an anchor which is too heavy for your crew to handle, it may be necessary to fit an anchor winch on the foredeck. You will also need a sturdy bow fitting to take the anchor

rode. The type of rode and its length will greatly affect the holding power of your anchor. Chain is usually recommended because it is resistant to chafe and because its own weight creates a curve between the anchor and the boat. This helps absorb the shock of the boat jerking (snubbing) on the anchor. It also helps to keep the pull on the anchor near horizontal which provides the best hold. However, the weight of a chain rode can be a disadvantage. Nylon rope used for anchor rode solves the problem of weight, but is subject to chafe and does not assume a natural curve between the boat and the anchor. Its stretch properties do, however,

help prevent the anchor from being pulled free. A compromise is to use chain for the first 10ft from the anchor, and nylon rope for the remainder. It can help to reduce snubbing if you lower a weight about halfway down the rode. The length of the rode (scope) is important and is usually described as the ratio between the length of the anchor line and the height of the bow fitting above the sea-bed. Under favorable conditions, a minimum scope for an all-chain rode would be 3 : 1, while if a nylon and chain rode is used, the minimum scope would be 5 : 1. In rough conditions it will probably be necessary to increase the scope to 10 : 1 or more.

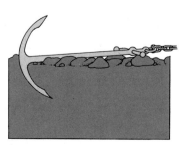

Fisherman's anchor

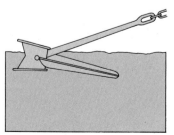

Danforth anchor

Choosing an anchorage

When planning on lying to an anchor, it is important to choose the site with care if you are to have a trouble-free stay. There are several considerations to take into account before the anchor can be dropped. It is important to know what the holding ground is like. Information on the type of seabed can be found from a chart or, once *in situ*, by the use of a lead line (see Navigation, page 239). If the ground is not suitable for your anchor, you should look for another spot. The water must be shallow enough for you to be able to lie to the correct amount of rode, but you must make sure that it will be deep enough at low tide to keep you afloat. If you anchor at any time other than high tide, you must calculate what the depth will be at high water (see pages 244 – 5) and allow sufficient rode for that depth. To ensure that the boat lies as still as possible, try to choose an anchorage sheltered from the wind (bearing in mind possible wind shifts) and out of a strong tidal stream. A spot away from busy traffic will give a more comfortable stay, as the boat will not be rolling around in the wash of passing boats. If the anchorage is a crowded one, you must ensure that the boat has room to swing a full circle without colliding with other boats or obstructions (below left). Different types of boat react in different ways to the effects of wind and tide. Boats with a lot of windage and little underwater area will be affected more by wind than current, but deep keel boats with less windage are more likely to swing to the tide. If the boats are all of a similar type, their swinging circles may intersect slightly without danger of collision, so always try to lie near boats similar to your own. Where this is not possible you must calculate the swinging circles of nearby boats to make sure yours will not intersect. To do this you will need to find out where their anchors are laid. If there is no one on the boats to ask, you must estimate by looking at the direction and angle to the surface of their anchor rodes. Should you find that you are in danger of fouling another boat, then it is up to you to move.

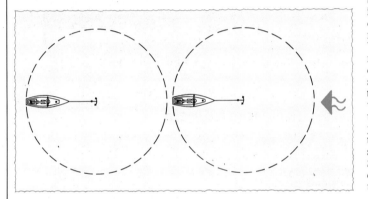

Choosing a mooring

When choosing a mooring, the considerations of water depth, and shelter from wind and traffic, that apply to anchorages must also be taken into account. In addition, you must make sure that the mooring you choose is not a private one, and that it is designed to take the weight of your boat. Many moorings are marked with the maximum size of boat they hold. If you pick up a mooring that is too light for your boat and it breaks while you are there, you will be responsible for the damage caused. When picking up a mooring, it is best if you check immediately with the harbor master that it is both suitable and available for you to use. Swinging room on moorings is not usually a problem, as they are laid with regard to the size of boat that will pick them up. Also the mooring line has a shorter scope than that of an anchor.
(Instructions for leaving and approaching fore and aft moorings are given on page 194.)

Having picked up the mooring, the crew inspects it to make sure it is large enough for the boat.

Dropping anchor

All the preparation for dropping anchor must be completed before you approach the anchoring spot, so the skipper must brief the crew well in advance. You must remove the anchor from its stowage and hang it over the bow fitting with the rode made fast on a cleat or bollard. Pull the amount of rode that is likely to be needed from its locker and flake it down carefully on the deck (see page 95). This ensures that the rode will run out without snagging when you let the anchor go. Once you have pulled the right amount, make the rode fast at this point. When the boat has reached the anchoring spot, the skipper will give the instruction to let go. Because it is often quite difficult to hear spoken orders along the length of the boat, it is best if a pre-arranged signal is used. When signalled, uncleat the part of the rode which is holding the anchor on the bow fitting and lower the anchor into the water. Allow the rode to run out under control until you feel the anchor hit the seabed. Then let out the remainder of the rode previously flaked out and when it is used up, you will feel the strain on the rode as the anchor bites into the seabed. The skipper must then decide if he wants to let out more rode. Once the correct amount has been let out, make fast the onboard end. If, for any reason, the anchor does not bite straight away, try letting out more rode. If this doesn't work you may have to pull it up and move to another spot.

The correct length of rode is flaked out on deck ready for the anchor to be dropped.

Laying an anchor from a dinghy

There are some occasions, such as when planning to lay a second anchor or when leaving an alongside berth in an onshore wind, when you will need to drop an anchor from a tender. It is easier to lay an anchor from a rigid rather than an inflatable dinghy and you should use a rope rode as chain is difficult to handle in a dinghy. As it will probably be the kedge anchor you are using, the rode is likely to be of rope anyway. Bring the dinghy alongside the boat and tie it fore and aft. Hang the anchor over the stern of the dinghy and secure it with a length of light line tied to the anchor and to the thwart. This will enable you to release the anchor while seated. Next flake the anchor rode in the stern of the dinghy, starting at the anchor end. When sufficient rode for the depth is in the dinghy, make the other end fast on board the boat. Row away in the direction in which you want to lay the anchor, and when all the rode has run out, undo the light line and allow the anchor to drop. Someone on the boat then takes in the slack to set the anchor.

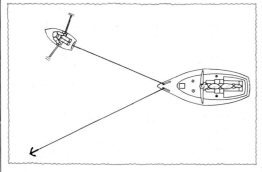

Having dropped and set the main anchor, the kedge can be laid from the tender.

Retrieving an anchor from a dinghy

It may sometimes be necessary to retrieve your anchor from a dinghy: for example, if you are lying to two anchors and wish to retrieve the kedge. However, you should only attempt to do this if you have a fairly large, preferably rigid, dinghy. One person sits in the dinghy and pulls it along the anchor rode until the rode dips into the water vertically, indicating that the anchor is directly beneath. The buoyancy of the dinghy and the pull of the person holding the rode over the stern should break out the anchor and it can then be pulled into the dinghy. The person in the dinghy returns by pulling the dinghy back along the rode.

Tripping line

There is always the danger that the anchor may become fouled in the seabed and it may be impossible to free in the normal way. Motoring around the anchor and pulling from several directions sometimes helps, but it is best to avoid the problem by securing a tripping line to the anchor. The anchor can be released by pulling on the line.

A tripping line is a light line attached to the crown of the anchor (right). The line is either attached to a buoy or secured on board.

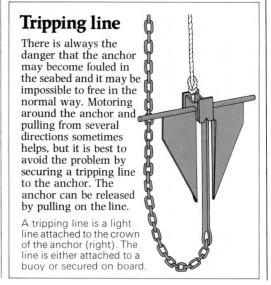

Laying two anchors

If a boat will not lie steady to a single anchor, it can be secured by two anchors, as shown below left. This reduces the boat's movement and divides the strain between the anchors. However, if the wind or tide changes and the boat is tending to lie at a different angle, you may have to re-lay the anchors. Another method of using two anchors is shown below right. This is often used in a crowded anchorage when you need to

reduce the swinging circle of the boat. The main anchor is dropped and the boat is allowed to drift back to set it. When twice as much rode as you need is let out, the kedge can be dropped. The boat is pulled forward on the main rode as the kedge rode is let out until you are positioned midway between the two. The two rodes are then joined and the ends secured so that the strain is only on the main rode.

The main and the kedge anchors (A and B respectively) have been laid. The kedge rode is joined to the main rode with a rolling hitch (see page 332) and the join lowered well below the keel.

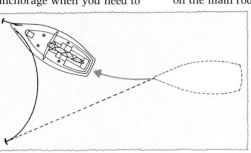

Drop the main anchor as usual (see opposite) and allow the boat to drop back to set the anchor. Motor forwards at an angle of about 45° to the line of the first anchor and drop the kedge abeam of it. Allow the boat to drift back and adjust the rodes.

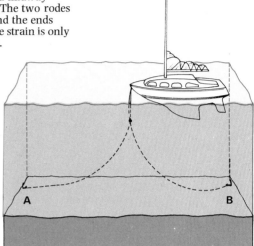

Weighing anchor

The ease with which the anchor can be retrieved will depend on the conditions, the weight of the anchor and rode, and the strength of the crew. The first stage of retrieval is to bring the boat over the anchor. In light winds or in a weak tide this can be achieved by hauling on the anchor rode, but it is usually best to sail or motor to the right position, as the crew takes in the rode. As soon as the angle of the rode from the boat to the anchor is vertical, the crew must signal to the skipper so that he knows that the anchor will soon break out. The crew continues hauling on the rode until they feel the anchor break out of the seabed and they signal to the skipper. The anchor is then brought to the surface but care must be taken to prevent it swinging against the hull. If there is time, the anchor should be cleaned off before bringing it on deck. Once on board, the anchor and rode should be stowed as soon as possible.

Picking up and leaving a mooring

Before the mooring is approached, the crew must have the boat-hook and a line ready on the foredeck ready to catch hold of the mooring as the boat stops with the buoy alongside the bow. The way in which the boat is secured to the mooring will depend on the type (see page 82), but the skipper will usually decide how he wants it done in each case. The crew routine for leaving a mooring will depend on how the boat has been

attached to it. If the boat is made fast with its own mooring line to a ring on top of the buoy then it is best to rig the line as a slip first so that it can be easily dropped when the skipper gives the order to let go. If the mooring buoy has been brought on deck, and the chain underneath attached to a cleat or bollard, it can be uncleated and held with a turn around the cleat until the skipper is ready to leave and it can be released.

The crew are ready to pick up the buoy with the boat-hook.

Arriving and leaving

Whether you are dealing with a mooring or an anchorage, the methods you use for arriving and leaving are the same. Only the crew routines for handling the equipment will differ (see pages 200–1). When arriving, the aim of the skipper is to stop the boat in the required position, so that the crew can either drop anchor or pick up the mooring. If you are anchoring, you must make sure that the boat has stopped or is moving backwards before you give the signal to drop the anchor. This will prevent the cable landing on top of the anchor and possibly fouling it. You must then check that the boat is not dragging on the anchor by taking a range as described on page 105, or by taking compass bearings on fixed objects (see page 249). When leaving an anchorage or mooring, it is important to plan your route carefully, especially if the area is crowded. You will need to assess what effect the wind and tide will have on the boat once the anchor is raised or the mooring dropped so that the boat does not drift away out of control. In all cases the crew must be briefed and given enough time to prepare the necessary equipment. If you are going to maneuver under power the engine must be switched on and given a few minutes to warm up before it is needed.

If the skipper judges the approach accurately, the boat will stop at the buoy so that the crew on the foredeck can easily pick it up and secure it.

Arriving under power

After choosing your anchoring spot or mooring buoy, you must decide from which direction to make the approach. The direction you choose will be heading into the element which has the strongest effect on your boat. This will help to slow the boat down once the engine is put into neutral and will therefore give you greater control. A convenient way of deciding on the direction of your approach is to look at the way other moored boats similar to your own are lying — they will be facing the strongest element. Once an approach has been decided the crew should be thoroughly briefed and given time to prepare the anchor and rode or boat-hook and line.

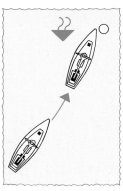

How to approach
Once the crew has the equipment ready on the foredeck, motor gently forward into the strongest element (in this case the tide) towards the anchoring (or mooring buoy). Gradually reduce speed until you stop at the chosen position. The crew can then either drop the anchor (or pick up the mooring).

Leaving under power

When leaving under power, the first thing to consider is the route you will take away from the anchorage or mooring buoy. Since the boat will be pointing into the strongest element you will normally leave heading in that direction unless an obstruction forces you to reverse away and turn onto another course. Once you have decided in which direction to leave, you must brief the crew. If you are moored up to a buoy, it can simply be dropped (see page 201) and the boat will drift clear, or you can reverse away before steering the boat onto your chosen course. If you are anchored, you must retrieve the anchor before you can leave (see page 201).

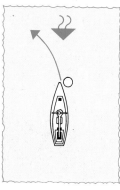

How to leave
Having planned your course and briefed the crew, drop the mooring or motor forward to break out the anchor. Once the boat is free, you can motor off in your chosen direction.

Arriving under sail

When arriving at an anchorage or a mooring under sail, your final approach will be under either the mainsail or headsail alone. As the choice of sail depends on whether the wind is forward, on or aft of the beam when the boat is lying to the anchor (or mooring), you must determine how your boat will eventually lie in relation to the wind. It is a good idea to spend some time sailing around the area first to assess the situation and brief the crew. They will need plenty of time to prepare the deck gear and to lower whichever sail is not going to be used. Your speed can be controlled by letting out the sheet in the final stages. If you are mooring, aim to stop with the buoy towards the strongest element.

Leaving under sail

The way to leave a mooring or an anchorage under sail will depend, as when arriving, on the angle of the wind to the boat when it is lying to its anchor or mooring. When the wind is forward of the beam, you can leave under the mainsail alone. The headsail should however, be ready for immediate hoisting. If you are at a mooring the boat can be turned in the direction in which the skipper wishes to leave and at the same time, it can be given steerage way by pulling the mooring buoy past the shrouds before releasing it. If recovering an anchor, the steerage way is provided by pulling the boat forward on the rode. When the wind is on or aft of the beam you must leave under the headsail.

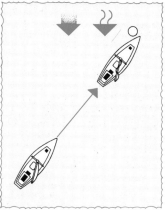

Wind forward of the beam
Approach under the mainsail alone to keep the foredeck clear for the crew to work. Sail in on a close reach. Let the sail flap to stop.

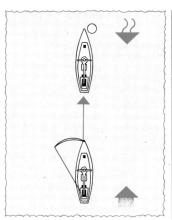

Wind aft of the beam
Lower the mainsail and sail in under headsail alone. In the final stages, lower the sail and complete the approach under bare poles.

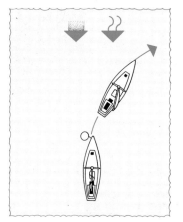

Wind forward of the beam
Hoist the mainsail. Release the mooring by pulling it along the side of the boat (or pull forward on the rode to break out the anchor) and turn the boat. Sail off.

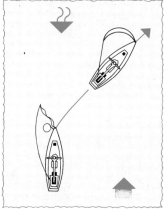

Wind aft of the beam
Hoist the headsail and immediately drop the mooring (or raise the anchor). Sail well clear before hoisting the mainsail.

The crew of the boat, left, are preparing to sail off their mooring with the wind forward of the beam. The mainsail has been hoisted and the headsail is being rigged ready for hoisting once clear of the mooring.

Basic handling under sail

The deck equipment on a cruising boat and the methods of leaving and arriving at various berthing and mooring situations have been discussed assuming a knowledge of sailing principles on the part of the skipper. The following pages all deal with how to handle a cruising boat under sail with the emphasis on crew routines. While the way a cruiser reacts to the wind is much the same as a small boat, any sailor of one-designs who is new to cruising will feel a great difference between the two, mainly because of the greater strain taken by the equipment and the effect of a ballasted keel. For your first practice sessions, motor out of harbor and find a quiet stretch of water. When you are ready, slow the boat down and turn so that it is almost, but not quite, head-to-wind and hoist the mainsail and then the headsail. Switch off the engine and start to practice the basic maneuvers. Standard methods for sail hoisting and lowering, tacking and jibing and heaving-to are described on the following pages.

Handling the headsail

The headsail can be hoisted and lowered on any point of sailing. It is easier if two people work together. Assuming that the sail is already rigged and removed from stowage, check that the sheets are attached and correctly led outside the shrouds with stopper knots in the ends. Make sure that the halyard is not twisted around the forestay and shackle it to the head. Take the end once around the winch. Hoist most of the sail by hand, finishing off using the winch handle. Remember that it is possible to over-hoist the sail so watch the luff as you work. When lowering the sail, ease the halyard out while someone else gathers in the sail.

Above, a crew member hoisting the headsail using the winch handle in the final stages.

Tacking

Tacking a cruising boat is basically the same as tacking a one-design (see pages 66–7). However, because a cruising boat is much heavier, the maneuver will be much slower. Also, because the sails are bigger, there will be more work for the crew. A cruising helmsman must tack slowly enough for the crew to perform their tasks. It is best if one crew member mans each headsail winch, if enough crew are available. Once the decision to tack has been made, the helmsman calls, "Ready about". One crew member checks that the new headsail sheet is ready with a couple of turns around the winch. The other then uncleats the working headsail sheet, but keeps the tension on it. Once they have told the helmsman they are ready, he calls, "Hard-a-lee" and puts the tiller over to leeward to start the tack. The crew on the working sheet, eases it (see page 207), and then releases it completely, as shown on page 170. In some boats with a lot of windage, the skipper may prefer the headsail to be allowed to back

before releasing the sheet and you will have to decide which method suits your boat best. As soon as the sheet has been released, the crew on the other winch must start to pull the new sheet in by hand as quickly as possible. It is at this stage that the helmsman can help the crew by slowing down the turn

Left, as the boat starts to turn, the crew releases the working headsail sheet, by lifting it off the winch.

Above, having released the old sheet, the crew member helps to sheet in on the new side by winching while the other person tails.

slightly. This gives the crew time to finish sheeting the sail with the winch handle before it fills completely and becomes difficult to pull in. While winching, the crew must be careful to watch the sail so as not to damage it by over sheeting which may cause it to chafe on the leeward spreader.

Handling the mainsail

It usually is better if two crew members work together to hoist the mainsail. The wind must be forward of the beam so that the sail doesn't fill. One person shackles the main halyard to the head, having checked that it is not fouled aloft and takes up the slack on the halyard. The other person removes the sail ties and eases out the mainsheet. The sail is then hoisted as described right. When the sail is fully hoisted, the halyard must be stowed and the topping lift slackened. To lower the mainsail the procedure is basically the reverse of hoisting. The wind must be forward of the beam and the mainsheet eased, to allow the sail to flap. Always remember to tighten the topping lift before releasing the halyard, or the boom will crash on top of the cabin top. As the person on the halyard eases the sail down, the other gathers it in and stows it. The mainsheet should then be tightened.

Hoisting the mainsail
The person by the halyard puts one turn around the winch and takes up most of the sail by hand until it is too difficult to continue (left). A few more turns can then be put on the winch and the sail fully hoisted with the assistance of another crew member using the winch handle. It is important for the person winching to watch the luff of the sail so that it is not over tightened.

Jibing

Jibing a cruising boat is basically the same as jibing a one-design (see pages 68–9). But the crew must remember the weight of gear on a cruiser and make sure that they do not get in the way of the boom sweeping across the boat. It is therefore particularly important that the boat is not allowed to jibe accidentally. It is also essential to check that the mainsheet traveller is firmly secured in the middle of the track. The mainsheet is usually sheeted in before a jibe but in light winds this is not often necessary and the boat can be jibed "all-standing". The crew routine shown is a standard one.

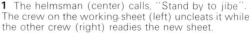

1 The helmsman (center) calls, "Stand by to jibe". The crew on the working sheet (left) uncleats it while the other crew (right) readies the new sheet.

2 Having sheeted in the mainsail, the helmsman moves the tiller to windward and calls, "Jibe—oh". The crew releases the old sheet.

3 As the boom moves across the boat, the helmsman centers the tiller and eases out the mainsheet. The crew starts to sheet in the headsail on the new side.

Heaving-to

Heaving-to is one of the most important handling techniques. It allows you to stop or slow down the boat under full control. This can be useful when you want to change sail, reef or steady the boat for any reason. Because of the effect of tidal streams and the boat's windage, the boat will not lie completely stationary but will drift, and the navigator must take this into account. The way in which a boat will lie steadiest depends on the weather conditions and the boat's drifting characteristics. No definite rules can be given about the method to use and the skipper must experiment until he discovers which method suits his boat in various conditions. For short stops, you can use the method for one-designs on page 64 and lash the tiller to leeward. The boat will then drift slowly to leeward and move ahead as the boat alternately luffs and bears away. However, this method should only be used for short stops, as the flogging of the sails puts a great deal of strain on them and the rigging. A method suitable for longer stops is to back the headsail, ease out the mainsail and lash the tiller to leeward (right and below). It works best in long-keeled craft; fin-keeled boats may not lie steadily and you will have to experiment with the sail and tiller positions. If you are heaving-to in order to ride out rough weather, you may find it necessary to lower one of the sails to reduce sail area. Which sail you choose to lower will depend on the boat and you will have to find out the best method by experimenting. If you heave-to under the headsail alone, try sheeting it to leeward and lash the tiller to leeward. If you are using the mainsail, allow it to flap a little and lash the tiller amidships. (For additional rough weather sailing techniques, see pages 226–7.)

The boat shown above and below is safely hove-to with the headsail aback and the mainsail eased. It need not be constantly tended by the crew.

Riding turn

Sometimes, when winching, the coils of sheet on the barrel become crossed (known as a riding turn). This is usually a result of taking too many turns on the winch. It cannot be undone unless the tension is removed. Another line is first tied to the sheet, between the winch and the sheet lead, using a rolling hitch. The new line is then taken around a spare winch and wound in until it is taking the strain from the first winch and the riding turn can then be released. If you find that riding turns are occurring frequently, you should check the angle of the sheets to your winches.

A riding turn forms when a turn on a winch rides up over the one above it.

To ease a riding turn, another line is tied to the sheet to take the tension off the winch.

Learning about your boat

When sailing in an unfamiliar boat or with a novice crew, it is important to spend some time practicing the basic maneuvers under sail. This will help you get to know how your boat will behave in a variety of situations, and will give your crew an opportunity to practice the routines in a relaxed way until they are able to carry them out fluently. It will also help you, as the skipper, to decide which handling methods are most suited to your boat and crew. Once you have found a quiet place to practice and have hoisted your sails, drop a fender (with a weight attached) overboard and use it as a reference point for your maneuvers. First try to stop your boat by the marker on different points of sailing until you can control it accurately in varying wind and sea conditions. This will help you when maneuvering in crowded harbors. To develop your skill in approaching a mooring, practise sailing up to an anchored marker on a close reach. Adjust your speed by easing out the sheets and stopping with the "buoy" alongside. You can also try stopping the boat to leeward of the marker and turning head-to-wind to allow the boat to be carried towards it under its own momentum. Using two fenders as markers, you can sail a figure eight course which gives you an opportunity to practice tacking and jibing. You must also find out which of the methods of heaving-to, opposite, is most suited to your boat. Try each of

the methods in turn, adjusting the positions of the sails and tiller until you find an arrangement which reduces the boat's movement to a minimum. You can estimate the rate of drift by looking at the boat's wake – the more marked it is, the faster the drift. You should not forget to spend some time practicing the man overboard recovery routine described on pages 208–9. Throw the weighted fender or dan buoy overboard while sailing on each of the different points of sailing and recover it using the recommended method until it becomes second nature to all of the crew. It is important that all the members of the crew are given an opportunity to take the helm. On a long cruise the skipper will not be able to steer continuously and other crew members will have to take over from time to time. In addition, if the skipper falls overboard someone else must be capable of carrying out the recovery routine, or if he is ill or injured, the boat must be brought safely back to port. While practicing these maneuvers, you must learn to set your sails correctly for the conditions in order to get the best performance from your boat. The guidelines for setting sails on one-designs on pages 58 and 102 can also be applied to cruiser sailing. If you practice these maneuvers each time you go for a sail, you will soon learn a considerable amount about boat handling which will always be of use to you.

Easing a rope on a winch

It is important to know how to ease the tension of a sheet or halyard on a winch. The tail of the line is taken off the cleat but the tension must still be kept on it. One hand should then be placed on the turns of the line around the winch barrel and the heel of the hand used to feed the line around the barrel, as the other hand eases the tension on the line. It is most important that the fingers are kept well out of the way.

The tension of a sheet on a winch is eased by using the palm of a hand to control the movement of the sheet around the barrel.

Man overboard

Losing a member of the crew overboard is one of the worst things that can happen on a boat and, as with one-designs, it is essential that all members of the crew are familiar with a set routine for finding and recovering the person in the water. All crews should practice a man overboard recovery regularly, under sail and power, and in varying weather conditions using a dan buoy and drogue (see page 227) as a substitute "man". Remember that it may be the skipper who goes overboard, so at least one other person must be capable of taking charge in such a situation. If you are skippering an unfamiliar boat it is advisable to spend some time practicing the recovery maneuver, even if you are normally able to do it perfectly well. The drill described below is suitable for all boats and is straightforward to learn. If it is practiced as a set routine it will reassure you and your crew that you can return to a person in the water and regain contact with them quickly. Always make sure that you have at least two lifebuoys and a dan buoy in the cockpit ready for immediate use in such an emergency.

Recovery under sail

Whenever a person falls overboard there are several things which must be done very quickly. Someone must throw a lifebuoy and the dan buoy overboard. He should aim the lifebuoy upwind of the person in the water so that it has a greater chance of blowing towards him. He must alert the rest of the crew with a cry of "Man overboard", throw in a second lifebuoy (if there is more than one left) and a dye marker or any floating objects, such as torn up paper, which will mark the position. One crew member must immediately be detailed to watch the man overboard to minimize the risk of losing sight of him. Even a momentary distraction could result in his being lost from view among the waves. While the crew is carrying out these tasks, the person on the helm must immediately start to steer the course described below. If the spinnaker is set, it must be quickly lowered. The navigator or helmsman must note the time and course steered—if the person is lost from sight, it may be necessary to use this information to return to the spot. A crew member must prepare two lines to throw to the person in the water when the boat returns. A boat-hook should also be available. Once there is sufficient searoom, the helmsman should tack. (If sailing under the headsail alone, the boat's handling characteristics may dictate that you jibe instead.) It is particularly important that the person watching the man overboard should not take his eyes off him during the turn, as everyone else is likely to become disoriented. Once the boat has turned, the navigator must note the time and the new course. The helmsman should aim to stop the boat to windward of the man in the water so that he is alongside the cockpit area, near enough to be reached.

During a practice drill, one person watches the "man overboard", while the helmsman concentrates on the course sailed to bring the boat back to the right position.

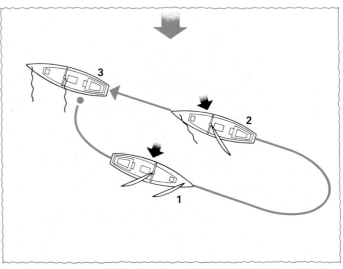

Sailing the course
Steer onto a beam reach to the apparent wind (1). When you have enough searoom (about ten boat lengths), tack onto a close reach to the apparent wind, the reciprocal course (2). Let the headsail fly to slow down and stop the boat to windward of the man overboard (3).

Recovery under power

If someone falls overboard while you are motoring, the immediate danger is that he will be caught by the propeller. If the helmsman sees the person falling overboard, he should steer at once towards the side over which he fell, to move the stern away from him. The same crew procedures for recovery under sail should be carried out but the course steered will be different. To bring the boat back to the person in the water, turn a tight circle and stop head-to-wind with the person in the water forward of the cockpit. Once you have secured him to the boat, turn off the engine and get the man out of the water as fast as possible using one of the methods described below. If the boat is under sail when the person falls overboard and the remaining crew are not confident that they can complete the recovery maneuver under sail, it may be advisable to lower the sails and continue under power. However, it must be remembered that the noise of the engine will make it difficult to hear the shouts of the person in the water. So if you have lost sight of him, you will have to turn off the engine periodically to listen.

Getting the person on board

Once you are alongside the person in the water, the first thing to do is to secure him to the boat. The method you use will depend on whether he is able to help himself or not. If he is able to help himself you can throw him a line with which to secure himself. If the person is unable to help himself, you will have to catch hold of him or part of his clothing by hand or with a boat-hook while you secure a line around him. You must then devise a safe method of getting him on board, bearing in mind any injuries he may have sustained. If the person is fit, he may manage to get aboard using a boarding ladder, if available, or by clambering up assisted by ropes. If he is weak or unconscious a strong crew may be able to lift the person under the arms facing him away from the side of the boat. If this is not possible, you may be able to improvise a pulley on the end of the boom to lift the man out of the water (right). Alternatively, lower the mainsail so that the boom rests in the cockpit and the sail hangs in the water. The person can then be scooped up inside and hoisted into the boat. You may have to cut or loosen the lifelines around the cockpit to make recovery easier.

To lift the person out of the water the boom vang can be attached to the boom end and used as a tackle.

Person out of sight

If you lose sight of the person in the water, the safe recovery of a man overboard is dependent on the ability of the helmsman to sail an accurate course. If the time when the man was lost and the course sailed noted, the navigator should be able to calculate the direction of the reciprocal course and the length of time to sail it to bring the boat back to the right place. If you cannot see or hear the person in the water when you reach the place, then you must start a square search (right). As this depends on accurate control of speed and direction it is often best done under power. The aim is to cover the area systematically so that you will pass within a set distance of the man overboard. The navigator must plan the course as shown, right, calculating the legs in terms of distance travelled at a given speed for a set time. The length of the legs will depend on the conditions. In average daylight conditions, you should plan to be no further than 50 m (165 ft) from the person in the water; at night the distance should be less.

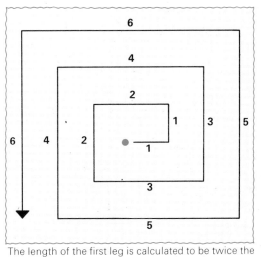

The length of the first leg is calculated to be twice the maximum distance you want to be from the man. The following legs are increased as shown.

Sails

The types of sail used on a boat will depend on the rig, and on the use to which the boat is put. Some boats are simple cruising boats, others are intended for both cruising and racing, and yet others for racing only. Needless to say, the needs of an out-and-out racing boat are very different from those of a cruising boat, as the essence of yacht racing is the search for speed, and all other considerations, such as comfort or ease of handling, are secondary to it. On a racing boat, maximum speed has to be maintained in all wind conditions; this dictates that the boat carries a number of sails, each cut to suit a very small range of wind conditions. In practice, this often means frequent and rapid sail changing. Although cruising yachtsmen naturally seek efficient sails, they are not primarily concerned with speed. They would prefer to sacrifice some speed to comfort and ease of handling. They therefore tend to carry fewer, but more versatile sails aboard which take up less stowage space below. As many sail with a relatively inexperienced crew, any attempt to make numerous sail changes would be both time-consuming and arduous. As they do not expect their crew to behave like a crack racing team, they organize their boat and its sail wardrobe accordingly.

Rigs with fewer sails are much easier to handle than others. The growing popularity of alternative rigs, such as the junk rig, is probably because they can be managed easily by a relatively inexperienced crew. A Marconi-rigged

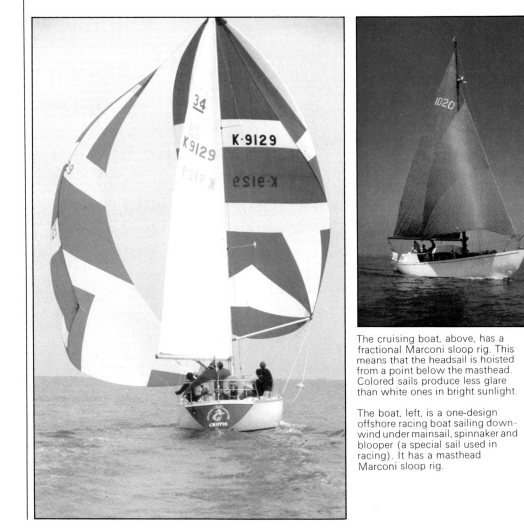

The cruising boat, above, has a fractional Marconi sloop rig. This means that the headsail is hoisted from a point below the masthead. Colored sails produce less glare than white ones in bright sunlight.

The boat, left, is a one-design offshore racing boat sailing downwind under mainsail, spinnaker and blooper (a special sail used in racing). It has a masthead Marconi sloop rig.

sloop tends to rely on a spinnaker for good downwind performance, and not every crew can cope with the setting and trimming of a spinnaker, except in very light winds.

Although alternative rigs are becoming more common, the average small- or middle-sized mass-produced boat is normally equipped with a Marconi sloop rig. Whatever the rig, the sails must be both easy to handle and do their job in a wide range of wind conditions. The type of sailcloth used in their construction is important. The weight of cloth in different types of sail varies — those for heavy weather are made of heavier cloth. For most sails, polyester is the standard fabric; polyester sailcloth can be coated with a layer of filler which helps the sail hold its shape. All sails should be of the best quality, ordered from a reputable sail maker.

On the Marconi ketch, above, the headsail has a high foot for good visibility, but unfortunately the sails are not well-cut, so the performance of the boat will be impaired.

Both boats, left, are gaff rigged. The one, far left, is a gaff cutter, the other a gaff ketch. Both carry two headsails and a gaff mainsail but the ketch is also setting a topsail and a mizzen.

The cruising boat, below, is rigged as a junk schooner with two unstayed masts.

Sail wardrobe

Every cruising boat needs to
carry a selection of sails to
keep the boat sailing
efficiently in all wind conditions. The number and sizes
of sails needed will depend
on the kind of sailing you
wish to do, the type of area
you will be sailing in and, of
course, the rig of the boat.
A Marconi-rigged sloop for
coastal cruising would need
a full suit of sails which
includes a genoa, a lapper,
working jib, storm jib, mainsail and, if possible, trysail
(a rough weather sail rigged
instead of the mainsail). A
spinnaker may also be
carried. A cutter would
need to add one or two
staysails and a ketch would
need to add a mizzen and
maybe a mizzen staysail.

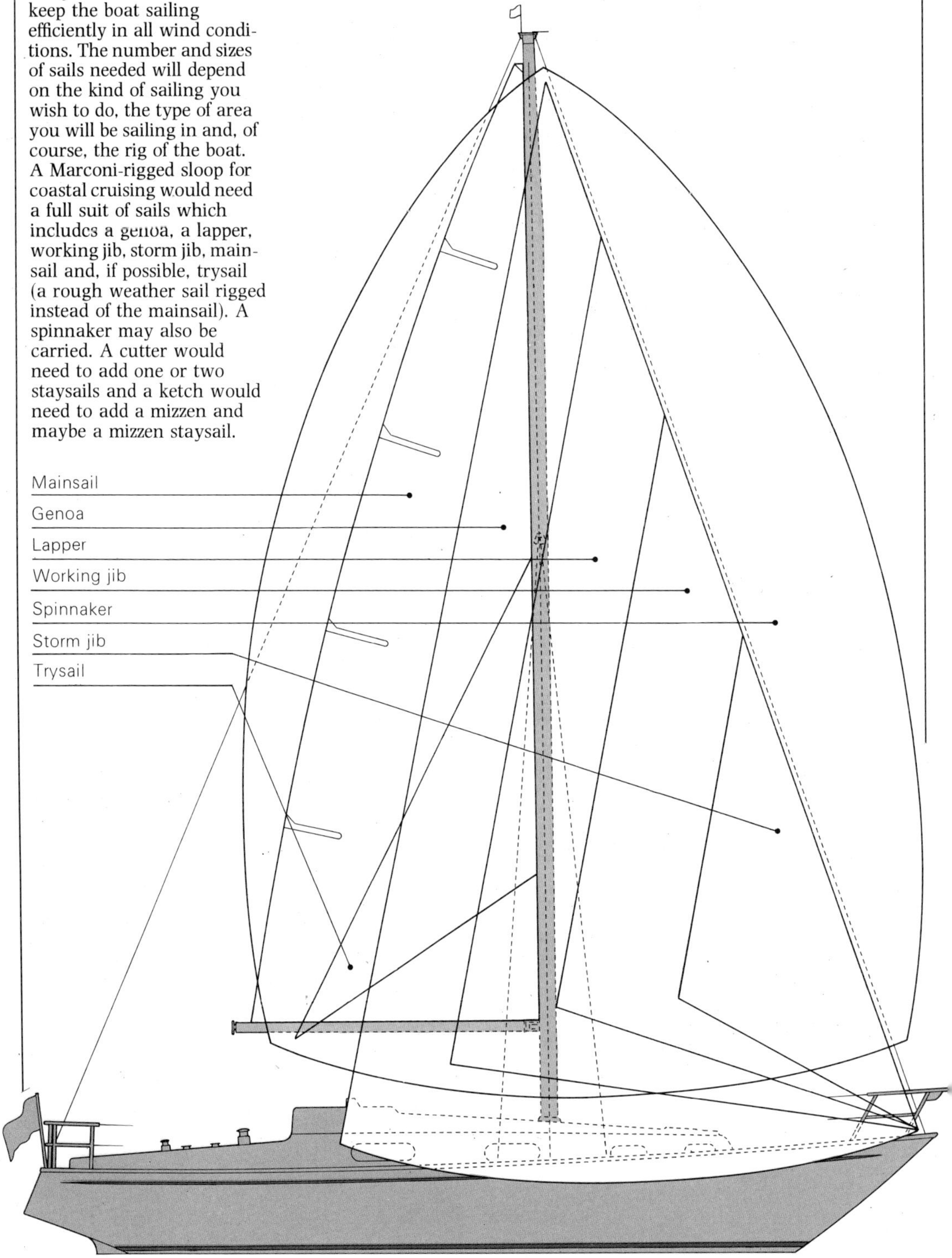

Mainsail

Genoa

Lapper

Working jib

Spinnaker

Storm jib

Trysail

Headsails

The type of headsail you rig will depend on the strength of the wind, the size of the waves, and the capabilities of the crew. The rougher the weather and the more inexperienced the crew, the smaller the headsail you will need. Racing headsails are cut with a low foot to prevent the wind escaping underneath and wasting power. However, the cruising skipper may be happy to sacrifice the extra drive for the increased vision that a higher-footed sail allows, both forward and to leeward. Not only should the headsail be sheeted at the correct angle to the wind (see pages 64–5), but the angle of the sheet to the sail should also be correct. The aim is to keep the tension on the leech and the foot balanced, and to keep the clew at the right height. Adjustable sheet leads help you to maintain a constant sheeting angle with different sizes of headsail (below right). They also allow you to adjust the sail shape according to the conditions. The further aft the sheet is led, the greater the tension on the foot and the more the leech will twist, resulting in excess wind being spilled. If the sheet is eased when sailing off the wind the clew tends to rise so the lead should be moved forward to prevent this happening.

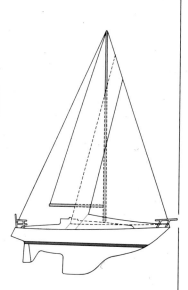

For cruising, headsails cut with a high foot, like the jib above, are best.

Racing headsails, like the large genoa carried here, provide great power, but restrict vision.

A small jib needs to be sheeted further forward than a genoa to keep the correct sheeting angle.

Mainsails

Most cruising boats are only equipped with one mainsail, with any adjustments in the sail area being achieved by reefing. However, a trysail should be carried for use in very strong wind conditions. The sheeting angle of the mainsail can be controlled by the use of the mainsheet traveller, if fitted. When sailing upwind, in medium-strength winds, the traveller is generally kept fixed in the middle of the track. But in stronger winds it should be allowed to move to leeward to reduce the heeling force. In very light winds the traveller can be moved to windward and the mainsheet eased, to keep the boom on the centerline without putting tension on the leech. When sailing downwind the traveller will be allowed to move to leeward.

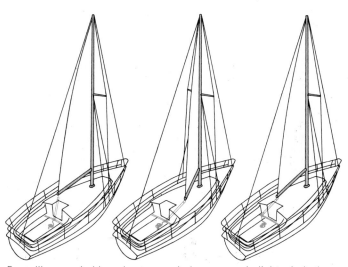

For sailing upwind in medium-strength winds, the traveller is positioned amidships.

In strong winds or when sailing off the wind, the traveller is moved to leeward.

In light winds the traveller is brought to windward and the mainsheet is let out.

Reducing sail

For all boats there is a certain wind speed beyond which the full-sized sails need to be reduced in area if the boat is to be kept sailing efficiently. There are no firm guidelines which can be given to help you decide when to reduce sail; it is a decision for the skipper to make on the basis of the type of boat, the experience of the crew and the conditions. The only advice which can be usefully given is that the boat should be sailing with no undue strain on any part of it. If it becomes clear that the boat is overcanvassed for the conditions, the sail area must be reduced. The headsail area can be reduced either by changing to a smaller sail or by reefing, but the mainsail can only be reduced by reefing unless the conditions are very rough when a trysail can

be rigged instead. It is essential to plan changes in the sail area carefully. The areas of the headsail and mainsail must be kept in proportion so that the boat maintains its balance and continues to handle well (see page 58).

There are different methods of headsail changing and reefing the headsail and the mainsail, according to the equipment fitted on your boat and the most common are described on the following pages. These are basic seamanship skills and should be practiced until they can be carried out quickly and efficiently.

A basic method for changing sails is given below. However, techniques developed by racing crews to speed up the procedure have led to the development of new methods and equipment for

Moving the sails on deck

The sail stowage is often in the fore cabin and the easy route to and from the foredeck is via the forward hatch. However, in some conditions opening the hatch could result in water getting below and if this is the case the sail should be taken via the main companionway. Once a sail change has been completed, the old sail can either be bagged on the foredeck, or be taken below to be packed. If the forward hatch cannot be opened, it will have to be taken along the windward side deck with great care.

Changing the headsail

The basic method of changing the headsail, used when the boat is fitted with a simple forestay and hanked on sails, requires that the old sail be lowered and completely removed before the new sail can be bent on and hoisted. Two crew members are generally needed to operate the halyard and to handle the sails. Bring the new sail onto the foredeck and secure it. Lower the sail as described on page 204. Remove the halyard and stow it on the

pulpit. Unhank the sail and remove it from the tack fitting and pass it back to be stowed, after having removed the sheets and secured them to the guardrails. Take the new sail and attach the tack while the sail is still in its bag. Then hank it on and attach the halyard to the head. Meanwhile the other crew member attaches the sheets and adjusts the sheet leads. Once the foredeck is clear, the sail can be hoisted.

When moving a heavy sail bag along the deck, it should be dragged rather than carried.

The crew member responsible for gathering in the old sail braces himself in the pulpit.

Having hanked on the new sail the crew checks that the halyard is not fouled aloft before it is hoisted.

changing headsails. A variation on the basic method using a simple forestay, is to hank on the new sail between the tack and the first hank of the old sail before the latter is lowered. Twin headfoils, a recent development, allow the headsail to be bent on without the use of hanks.

Both reefing and headsail changing are best carried out before leaving your berth or anchorage. However, it is often difficult to predict changes in conditions and you will frequently have to make these adjustments at sea. The best course to sail when reefing is a close reach, while sail changing is easiest when hove-to or when sailing downwind. When changing sails the crew should always clip on their harness lifelines to allow both hands to be used for working in safety. It is a golden rule never to stand to leeward of a flogging sail.

A twin headfoil in use during a sail change. The new sail is being fed into the groove, ready to be hoisted before the old sail is lowered.

Jiffy reefing

One of the most common methods of reducing the area of the mainsail on modern boats is by jiffy reefing. This is a variation of the points reefing principle used on many one-designs and older boats (see page 92). It is a convenient method of reefing as the equipment is cheap and easy to fit and can be managed by one person. The reefed sail shape is also much more efficient than that produced by roller reefing (see page 216). The equipment for jiffy reefing is described right. Instructions for how to reef are given below. The reef is shaken out by reversing the procedure.

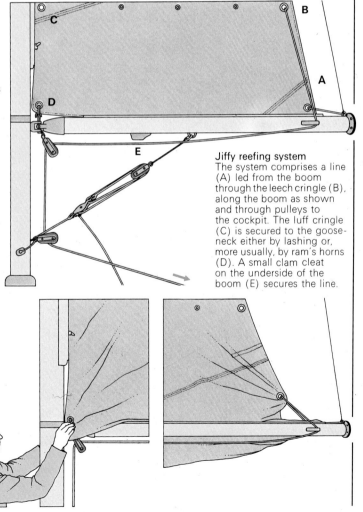

Jiffy reefing system
The system comprises a line (A) led from the boom through the leech cringle (B), along the boom as shown and through pulleys to the cockpit. The luff cringle (C) is secured to the gooseneck either by lashing or, more usually, by ram's horns (D). A small clam cleat on the underside of the boom (E) secures the line.

How to reef
When you are ready to reef, tighten the topping lift and lower the halyard to bring the luff cringle to the height of the gooseneck. Remove the lower slugs from the mast and hook the cringle onto the ram's horns (right). Then lower the leech cringle to the boom by pulling on the reefing line and cleat the line on the boom (far right). Tension the luff with the main halyard and release the topping lift. The fall of the sail should then be neatly gathered.

Roller reefing

Many cruisers are fitted with a roller reefing system for the mainsail. This works in the same way as rolling the sail round the boom for one-designs (page 93), but the equipment is more sophisticated. In many systems, a handle on the mast turns the boom and wraps the sail around it. The advantage of roller reefing is that the sail can be reduced by any amount, unlike points reefing, where the steps are predetermined. However, there are considerable disadvantages. It is hard to make the reefed sail set well and the boom, unless tapered, is inclined to droop. A further problem when roller reefing is rigging the boom vang, as the rolled sail covers the attachment point on the boom. A common solution is to attach it to a claw which clamps around the boom. When roller reefing it is important to make sure nothing gets caught in the reefing gear and that the slugs are not rolled into the sail. Once the sail area is sufficiently reduced, tighten the halyard and release the topping lift. To shake out the reef, reverse the process.

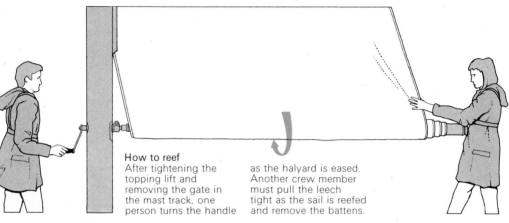

How to reef
After tightening the topping lift and removing the gate in the mast track, one person turns the handle as the halyard is eased. Another crew member must pull the leech tight as the sail is reefed and remove the battens.

Stowing the mainsail

The way in which you stow the mainsail will depend on whether the sail is to be left attached to the mast or removed from it. If the sail has no slugs you will always use the latter method. If the sail is to remain attached, lower it and arrange the bulk of it on one side of the boom. Then take a section of the leech about 1 m (3 ft) from the clew and pull it out to form a pocket. Bundle the rest of the sail into the pocket as neatly as possible and pull the pocket tightly around the sail and secure it with sail ties or shock cord. If the luff of the sail is to be removed from the mast, lower the sail, pulling the luff out from the track. Then either pull out a section of both the luff and the leech to form a pocket and pack in the bulk of the sail as before, or flake out the sail neatly over the boom (right).

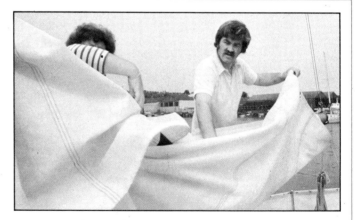

Above, in this method the luff is left attached to the mast. Two crew members then pack the bulk of the sail into a pocket formed by pulling out a section of the leech.

Left, in this method, after lowering the sail and removing the luff from the mast track, the sail is flaked out over the boom and then secured.

Headsail furling

Furling, a method of stowing the headsail by winding it around the forestay, has been in use for many years but recently, furling systems have been developed to allow the headsail to be roller reefed. When deciding on a headsail reefing system of this kind, it is a good idea to seek the advice of your sailmaker to make sure that your sails are suitable. The most effective system uses headfoils (see pages 214–5). The whole headfoil is rotated by a wire fitted to a drum at the base of the forestay so that the sail is wound evenly around the foil from tack to head. Always make sure that a headsail stowed on its stay for any length of time is protected from sunlight with a cover.

The headsail is furled by pulling on a wire which rotates the drum and the headsail.

Furling the headsail completely around the headfoil, above, is a neat method for stowing it.

Points reefing the headsail

Some boats carry headsails which are designed for points reefing. The sail may have one or two rows of cringles or reefing points running parallel to the foot. If the sail has only a single row of cringles, the amount by which the sail can be reduced can still be varied (see below). When reefing the headsail it is necessary to remove and re-attach each of the sheets in turn. First remove the lazy (windward) sheet and attach it in the new position and then heave-to with the headsail aback to move the leeward sheet. If you are reducing the luff, rig a reefing line through the luff cringle as shown below. The sail should be allowed to flap slightly. Ease out the halyard so that the cringle can be brought down to the tack by pulling on the reefing line. Use the halyard to tension the luff.

An unreefed headsail with one row of reefing cringles. The area to be reefed is shown shaded.

The sail is partly reefed by attaching the sheets to the leech cringle.

The sail is fully reefed by lowering the sail and securing the luff cringle to the tack.

The reefing line is led from the bow fitting through the cringle and the tack to a cleat.

When the halyard is eased, the reefing line is pulled to lower the luff cringle.

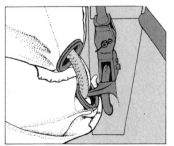

When the sail is lowered sufficiently, and the cringle pulled tightly down, the line is cleated.

Once the sail is reefed, the foot of the sail should be secured by lacing cord through the cringles.

Increasing the sail area

The modern Marconi sloop, while very efficient to windward, is generally underpowered when sailing downwind in light winds. In order to improve performance when sailing off the wind it is often necessary to increase the sail area. Racing crews use large spinnakers together with other downwind sails such as the blooper (see pages 210–1), to increase boat speed as much as possible. There is a disagreement among cruising yachtsmen about whether the spinnaker is a seamanlike sail for a cruising boat. It is argued that for cruising purposes the spinnaker requires too much ancilliary equipment to control it and that it can easily become difficult to manage if the wind increases. However, the cruising skipper need not be deterred from carrying a spinnaker and using it in light and moderate winds as his own and his crew's experience permits. As long as the skipper and the crew understand and practice how to use the sail there should be no control problems. In stronger winds most cruisers will sail fast enough downwind under the mainsail and headsail and it will not be necessary to hoist the spinnaker. If you do not choose to use a spinnaker, there are several

Hoisting the spinnaker

You must make sure that the spinnaker is properly packed in the bag without twists. It is hoisted straight out of the bag, which is secured to the pulpit or, if you have a hanked-on headsail, to the leeward guardrails. Then attach the halyard to the head and a sheet and a guy to each clew, as shown right and below. Each guy is led outside all the rigging to a block forward of the cockpit and back to a winch, and each sheet is led to a block aft of the cockpit and to a spinnaker sheet winch. (When the spinnaker is hoisted, the windward sheet and leeward guy are left slack, or "lazy".) Steer onto a broad reach with the headsail still up and clip the pole onto the mast fitting and the windward guy into the pole end. Then raise outer end of the

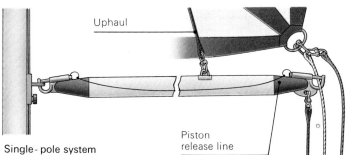

Uphaul

Piston
release line

Downhaul

Guy

Lazy sheet

Single-pole system
A common system for cruisers is shown. Both the uphaul and down-haul are led aft, via the mast and a block on the foredeck respectively.

pole using the uphaul until it is horizontal. Then adjust the downhaul. Hoist the sail by pulling on the halyard as fast as possible keeping a turn on the winch. Once the sail is hoisted, trim the guy and sheet and lower the headsail.

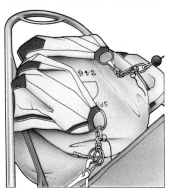

The sail bag is secured in the pulpit. The corners of the spinnaker protrude, with the halyard, sheets and guys attached.

The spinnaker pole is raised, but is still against the forestay, as the spinnaker is hoisted.

The sail is fully hoisted and the guy and the sheet are trimmed to fill the sail.

different ways of improving performance in light winds on a downwind course which are described on pages 220.

Cruising boat spinnakers are similar to one-design spinnakers (see page 112), although they are obviously larger and are made of heavier cloth, and require more sophisticated control systems. The handling techniques are also broadly similar. Basic methods of hoisting, jibing and lowering using a common single-pole system are shown. For methods of trimming and playing see pages 118–9.

These cruising-racers are carrying spinnakers on a reach in perfect conditions.

Jibing the spinnaker

The method you use to jibe the spinnaker will depend on the system fitted. If your boat is fitted with a double-ended pole (one which can be fitted to the mast or guy at either end), you will use the method shown on pages 118–9 for one-designs. However, most larger cruising boats are fitted with a system similar to the one shown opposite, where the uphaul and downhaul are attached at the outer end of the pole, and you will need to use the dip-pole method of jibing described here. Detach the pole from the guy using the piston release line and lower the outer end of the pole by letting out the uphaul so that it can clear the forestay and swing the pole around to the new side. Bring a bight of the new guy forwards and clip the pole onto it. Raise the pole to the correct height, as the helmsman jibes the mainsail. Adjust the downhaul and trim the spinnaker for the new course.

One crew member lets out the uphaul, while the other person guides the pole across.

The crew on the foredeck clips the pole onto the new guy.

The mainsail has been jibed and the pole is being hoisted and trimmed for the new course.

Lowering the spinnaker

Before lowering the spinnaker, hoist the headsail to make sure that the spinnaker cannot wrap itself around the forestay. Next, the helmsman must steer onto a broad reach and ease out the guy until the pole is nearly touching the forestay. A crew member then disengages the guy from the sail. As soon as the sail is free, a crew member in the companionway must pull in the leeward clew by hauling out the lazy guy, then ease out the halyard and bundle the spinnaker down the companionway. It is important not to let out the halyard too quickly or the sail could fall in the water.

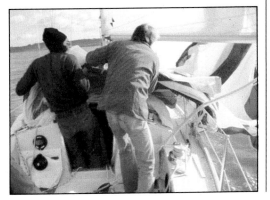

Once the halyard is eased out, the spinnaker must be bundled below as quickly as possible.

Alternatives to the spinnaker

If you do not wish to use a spinnaker for any reason, there are various other methods for improving downwind performance in light and medium winds. The genoa can be goosewinged, so that it is not blanketed by the mainsail and poled out to keep it set to windward (below). Another solution is to hoist two headsails. When using this technique offshore it is usual to lower the mainsail to stop it chafing on the shrouds and to prevent it from blanketing the leeward headsail. This method of increasing downwind drive is best suited to boats with headfoils. However, if your boat has a single forestay you can set two headsails by attaching the hanks of each sail alternately to the forestay or by attaching one by

the head and tack only. When carrying two headsails it is usually advisable to pole out the windward sail to keep it set. One disadvantage with this technique is that if the mainsail is lowered your maneuverability and control are limited. This could be critical in the event of a man overboard emergency. A further alternative is to use a boomless spinnaker. Unlike the conventional spinnaker, it is assymetrical. It is set from the spinnaker halyard and its tack is attached to the foredeck. As it does not require a pole or guy, it is much simpler to control than an ordinary spinnaker and is a good choice for a cruising skipper, providing plenty of extra drive on courses downwind of a broad reach.

Poling out the headsail
To pole out the headsail, clip the spinnaker pole to the mast and attach the uphaul and the downhaul. Take a spinnaker guy through its fairlead, outside all the rigging and attach it to the downhaul fitting on the pole. Clip the lazy headsail sheet into the pole end. Raise the pole to the height of the clew and position the pole about 50° from the forestay. Goosewing the headsail by pulling in the lazy sheet.

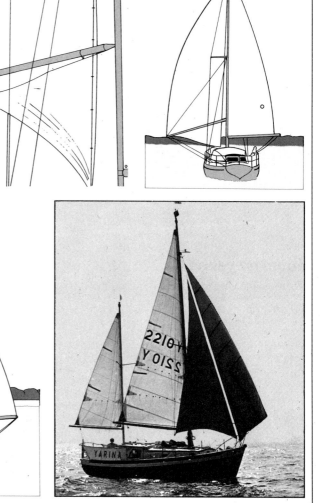

A boomless cruising spinnaker reduces the amount of equipment needed. It is set flying with its tack attached on the foredeck.

A cruising ketch sailing downwind in light airs has added to its sail area by hoisting two headsails set on twin forestays.

Mainsail control

When sailing downwind in light winds, once you have rigged enough sail, the next thing you should consider as a way of improving downwind performance is the set of the mainsail. For maximum drive the mainsheet should be eased out as much as possible without allowing the boom to touch the shrouds and subject the mainsail to chafe against the rigging. One of the most common faults in sail control when sailing downwind is an over-slack boom vang. If the boom is allowed to rise, the mainsail will form an inefficient curve resulting in a loss of power. It is also likely to chafe on the shrouds and twist at the top of the sail causing the boat to roll sometimes violently, resulting in a possibility of broaching (right). You can avoid these problems by using an efficient boom vang with an adequate purchase or winch. On larger boats it is often advisable to take the boom vang from the under-side of the boom to the deck instead of the base of the mast.

Broaching

Broaching is when the boat turns violently to windward, out of control. It is most common when broad reaching or running but can happen on any point of sailing. A common cause of broaching is rolling, which gives the hull an assymetrical underwater shape causing the boat to move in the opposite direction to the way it is heeled (see page 57). When this force is great enough to overcome the effect of the rudder the boat will broach. If the mainsail is too large in proportion to the headsail or spinnaker this will contribute to the tendency to broach, as once the broach has started the mainsail will assist the turn (see page 57). If a broach occurs, the mainsheet should be eased out immediately and, once the boat is back under control the mainsail area should be reduced.

The yacht, above, has just started to broach while attempting to jibe, probably as a result of sheeting in the mainsail.

Boom preventer

When sailing downwind there is always the danger of an accidental jibe. One way to prevent this occurring is to rig a boom preventer which fixes the boom on one side of the boat.
Once you have rigged the line, ease out the mainsheet until the boom is out slightly too far and then pull in the boom preventer until it is just taut and secure it. The mainsheet is then pulled in to fix the boom in position. To jibe deliberately you must of course remove the boom preventer first and then fix it in position on the new side after the jibe. Another practice is to shackle the boom vang to a pad-eye abaft the shroud or to a toe rail or stanchion ring.

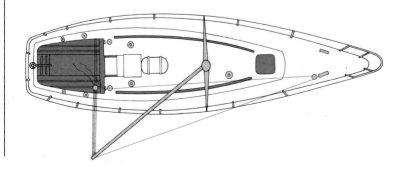

Rigging the line
To rig a boom preventer, attach a line to the end of the boom, preferably with a snap shackle. Lead it forward outside all the rigging and make it fast to a forward deck cleat. Alternatively, lead the line through a forward fairlead and back aft as shown.

Night sailing

A night passage should only be attempted if there is a sailor on board with experience of sailing at night (see Planning a cruise, pages 156–7). The helmsman must learn to be able to judge distances and direction with only the compasses, the stars and other boats' lights as a guide. The crew must be familiar enough with the sail handling routines and stowage systems to be able to use all the equipment in the dark. It is essential to have a good watch system (see pages 156–7), to make sure that the boat is properly manned by an alert and capable crew at all times. Safety procedures must be adhered to and a careful watch kept for all potential sources of danger. It must be a strict rule that nobody goes on deck unless they are clipped on with a safety harness, even if the weather is

very calm. When preparing for a night sail, try to get as many jobs completed before dark as possible, including any sail changes that may be needed later. A change down to a smaller headsail is often advisable, as it will be easier to handle and is less likely to restrict visibility. Only an experienced night sailing crew should attempt to sail with a spinnaker at night, so it is usually best to substitute a poled-out headsail which will be easier to control. After carrying out these adjustments, the decks should be cleared of all unnecessary equipment and the remainder neatly stowed. As soon as the light starts to fade, the navigation lights should be switched on.

Although the boat's behavior doesn't alter in the dark, your impression of the conditions may be different. It will often seem rougher than

Lights

At night, the principal way of detecting the presence of other boats is by their navigation lights. It is important to display the correct ones on your boat and to learn how to recognize other boats by theirs. Different combinations of lights show whether a boat is under sail or power, anchored or under tow. They also give a rough indication of boat size. It is difficult to remember all the variations, and the Rules of the Road governing the waters in which you are sailing, so it is essential to carry a reference book aboard which describes them. A selection of the most common light formations is shown right. The basic lights which are used are a white stern light, a red port side light and a green starboard side light. Boats under power must show one or two forward masthead lights according to size. The regulations specify the angle of the arc through which each light must be seen. As the lights can easily move out of adjustment, you must check them from time to time. Sailing boats under 7 m (23 ft) are not required to carry more than a simple white torch. Small vessels under power (under seven metres and travelling at less than seven knots) need only show an all-round white light. But in both cases, in the interests of safety, it is better to show the proper lights if possible.

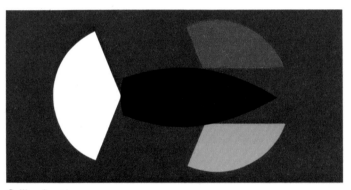

Sailing boats
Sailing boats over 7 m (23 ft) are required to show a stern light covering a 135° arc, and side lights covering an arc of 112.5° each, from dead ahead. The arcs are the same for lights on boats under power.

Large boats under power
Boats over 50 m (164 ft) when under power must show, in addition to the normal power boat lights, a second masthead white light shining forwards over the same arc, but higher and further aft than the first.

Boats at anchor
Any boat at anchor must show a single all-round white light forward in the boat. Vessels over 50 m (164 ft) must also show a second all-round white light lower and further aft than the first.

in daylight and inexperienced night sailors may feel nervous and disoriented. The helmsman depends on the compass for steering at night, but it is important for him not to stare at it continuously – his night vision will be impaired and it may give him eye-strain. When steering, try to use the stars or moon, or any other reference points, for periods of time, using the compass only to check the accuracy of the course. At night it is, of course, much more difficult to judge the setting of the sails. You will need to check the luffs occasionally with a flashlight. Be careful not to use unnecessary light on deck – it could impair your night vision for up to 20 minutes. Red lights should be used at night below decks. For navigating at night, see the section on buoyage, pages 260–2.

The crew on a boat, right, in the "Wight by Night" Race, 1975.

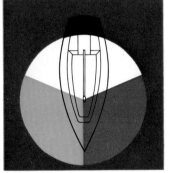

Sailing boats under 12 m
Sailing boats under 12 m (39 ft) may combine the lights in one masthead unit, unless under power.

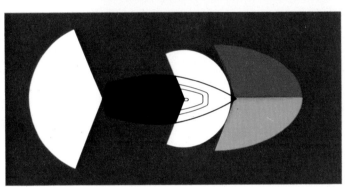

Power boats
In addition to stern and side lights, a white masthead light is shown forwards over a 225° arc. Boats under 20 m (66 ft) under power or sail may have combined side lights (above).

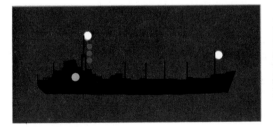

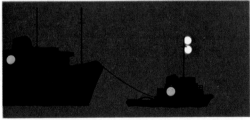

Vessels in special circumstances
Above, a vessel constricted in its ability to maneuver by its draft may show three all-round red masthead lights, in addition to standard power boat lights. Above right, a tug and tow of a combined length of under 200 m (660 ft). The tug must show standard power boat lights with an additional masthead white light over the first and a yellow towing light over the stern light. The towed vessel shows side and stern lights. Right, a vessel trawling must show side and stern lights and green over white all-around lights.

Sailing in fog

Fog, even more than rough weather, presents a great danger to a small boat. Reduced visibility increases the possibility of a collision with another vessel, since even lights cannot easily be seen. There are several different types of fog (see pages 278–9), but all types cause problems for the small boat. If fog has developed or is expected when you are in harbor, you should not begin a passage until it clears. The skipper who deliberately sets out in reduced visibility is courting danger. If already out at sea when fog starts to form, the skipper must put into action a well organized procedure to minimize the risks as far as possible. The navigation of the boat is important and, at the first hint of reduced visibility, the navigator must use every means at his disposal to verify his position and then to plot a course to avoid shipping traffic and dangerous waters. He must constantly update the position and aim to keep the boat in safe waters even at the expense of completely altering the original passage plan (see pages 156–7).

When visibility is poor, other boats or ships may appear with little or no warning, resulting in a serious risk of collision.

Preparation

As soon as fog starts to appear or there is a threat of fog, the skipper and crew must start to make preparations to make the boat as noticeable as possible. A radar reflector should be hoisted, if it is not kept permanently hoisted in position (see opposite) and you must start to make the appropriate fog signals and turn on the boat's navigation lights. Crew members acting as lookouts, should be stationed fore and aft to watch and listen for other boats. All the crew must wear lifejackets, but they should not clip on their safety harnesses. This is because, in the event of a collision, the crew may have to jump clear and must not be attached to the boat. Even those crew members resting or asleep in the cabin should wear lifejackets and remain fully clothed. Anybody in the fore cabin should move to the main cabin because of the risk of damage to that part of the boat in a collision. If possible, the dinghy should be towed behind the boat so that it is immediately available. Have the liferaft ready, and red and white hand flares to hand, to use to draw attention in an emergency (see pages 314–5). It is useful to have a rough idea of your visibility.

One way of estimating this is to drop a bundle of paper overboard and to note the length of time it takes for it to disappear from view. The navigator should then be able to work out how close another boat can be before it is seen. It is important that the boat is kept moving so that it has enough steerage way to maneuver out of the way of other boats, but you should not go so fast that there would not be time to react if you were to see another boat. In light winds it may be better to use the engine, but it must be switched off from time to time to listen for signals from other boats. If you have to cross a main shipping lane do so at right angles and as quickly as possible. One way of reducing the risk of collision is to head for shallow water which large boats cannot negotiate. You must remember that other small boats are likely to have the same idea, so look out for them. If possible, anchor once you have reached the shallow water and make the appropriate signals while maintaining a careful lookout. Although you will be signalling yourself, and listening for other boats, you must not rely on sound

signals and must keep a careful watch at all times. Lookouts on large ships may be deafened by the noise of their own engines and may well be unaware of your presence, so never stand on your rights and depend on another ship to take avoiding action first. If you see another boat you must take the responsibility of moving out of the way. The first glimpse you may have of another boat on a collision course with you may be the white bow wave. If you are heading straight for it, try to turn the boat so that it is end-on to the other boat. This gives the greatest chance of being pushed aside by the bow wave. Similarly, if you are on a converging course turn so that you are facing in the same direction as the other boat, to result in a glancing blow.

Radar reflector

Large ships and many fishing vessels carry radar equipment to help them detect obstacles. To stand a good chance of being spotted by a large ship, a sailing boat needs to have a correctly mounted radar reflector of a suitable type. A radar reflector operates by returning radar waves along the path on which they arrived, resulting in your boat showing up distinctly on a larger boat's monitoring screen. The best position for the reflector is the masthead, where it cannot be masked by the sails. Alternatives include hoisting it up on the backstay (right) or on a flag halyard near the spreaders.

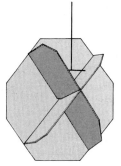

A radar reflector must be large enough if it is to be effective. A reflector about 60 cm (2 ft) in diameter is the minimum size.

Sound signals

In fog, the normal way of detecting the presence of another boat, and advertising your own, is by the sound of fog-horns, bells and gongs. Different combinations of these sounds are used to indicate boats making way (travelling under sail or power), under way (not at anchor or moored but not moving through the water), at anchor and aground. The pattern of sounds also gives a broad indication of the size of the boat. Boats under 12 m (39 ft) need only carry an "efficient sound signal", usually an aerosol fog-horn, illustrated below. (It is important to remember that the cannisters run out fairly quickly, so spares must always be carried.) If required, other sounds can be made by improvisation. Boats over 12 m (39 ft) must carry a bell in addition. Boats over 100 m (328 ft) may also be required to make gong signals. Horn signals can be either short (one second)

or long (four to six seconds) and bells can either be sounded as a single ring or as rapid ringing for five seconds. Gongs are always sounded singly. Each set of sounds must be repeated at specified maximum intervals. As with lights, it is important to familiarize yourself with the most common signals (shown below) but you must also keep a reference book aboard to remind you of unusual ones, and the Rules of the Road governing the waters in which you sail. In a crowded channel, it is easy to be confused, and you may have difficulty discerning the direction of the signals, as fog can distort the sound. The sounds made by navigation marks also add to the complications but it may be essential for the navigator to recognize them. The equipment on the buoy will be marked on the chart and a description of the sound made can be found in a nautical almanac.

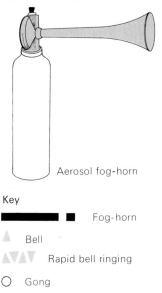

Aerosol fog-horn

Key

▬▬▬▬ ▪ Fog-horn

▲ Bell

▲▼▲▼ Rapid bell ringing

◯ Gong

Under sail
One long horn blast and two short ones every two minutes. This also applies to a boat with restricted maneuverability.

Making way under power
One long blast on the horn every two minutes.

Under way
Two long horn blasts at two minute intervals.

Aground – under 100 m (328 ft)
Three bells followed by rapid ringing and another three bells at one minute intervals.

Aground – over 100 m (328 ft)
Three bells, followed by rapid ringing, three bells and a gong sounded aft every minute.

At anchor – under 100 m (328 ft)
Rapid ringing of the bell forwards in the boat at one minute intervals.

At anchor – over 100 m (328 ft)
Rapid ringing of a bell forwards, followed by a gong sounded aft at one minute intervals.

Pilot boat on duty
Normal signals for a boat under power, followed by four short horn blasts every two minutes.

Rough weather sailing

Most cruising boats are better able to cope with prolonged periods of strong wind and large seas than one-designs, as they are more robust and rarely capsize. They also provide a refuge for the crew from the wind and sea in the cabin below. There is no strict threshold beyond which a moderate to strong breeze becomes rough weather. It depends on the type of boat, the experience of the crew and the course being sailed. A crew without much first-hand experience of sailing in rough weather may feel that they are in strong wind conditions when a crew with a wide experience of bad weather are enjoying an exciting sail. As a general rule, you need to consider using heavy weather techniques when you, your boat or crew begin to find the conditions too great a strain.

Every cruising skipper should be alert to the possibility of being caught out at sea in rough weather, and he must be aware of the strain the increased force of the wind will put on his boat and also the debilitating effect the conditions will have on the crew. He will need to consider the various courses of action open to him; whether to make for a sheltered harbor or anchorage, or to attempt to ride out the bad weather at sea. In order to prevent the crew from being surprised by the new situation, the skipper should make sure that they practice rough weather techniques, using the appropriate safety equipment, in moderate breezes, even when such measures are not strictly necessary. If you have never sailed in rough weather it is difficult for you to imagine the effect of heavy seas and strong winds. However, when fitting out your boat you must try to appreciate the strength of the forces the equipment may have to endure. It is a help if your sail wardrobe includes a really small storm jib and, if possible, a trysail (see pages 212—3).

Preparation

As soon as you are aware that there is likely to be rough weather ahead, it is important that you start to make preparations, even if you are planning to make for a sheltered harbor. The deck area should be cleared of loose equipment, and other items, such as the tender and liferaft, checked to ensure they are securely lashed down. The cabin must be preserved as a place where the crew can take turns to rest, so you must try to arrange that it is kept as tidy and dry as possible. Everything must be securely stowed so that it will not fall around the cabin if the boat heels violently. All hatches must be securely bolted shut and any ventilators, which may let in water, blocked. The companionway washboards must be securely fitted in place and only opened for access, if necessary. The crew on deck must be dressed in warm and waterproof clothing and each person must wear a properly adjusted safety harness. It is vital that the skipper emphasizes the importance of clipping on lifelines before emerging from the companionway. As some water is bound to be shipped, the bilges should be pumped dry before the bad weather arrives and at regular intervals thereafter. It is a good

The crew must be secured by a safety harness when working on deck or in the cockpit.

idea to eat before the boat starts to react to the increasing wind and seas because it is likely to be difficult to cook later on. Some easily eaten food should also be prepared for later and seasickness pills passed around. If visibility is likely to be poor, the navigation lights should be switched on and the radar reflector hoisted.

Tactics

When there is a threat of bad weather at sea, the skipper must decide on the course of action on the basis of severity of the expected conditions, the experience of the crew and the strength and reliability of the boat. If you are close to a sheltered port with known safe berthing or mooring facilities, it is advisable to head towards it. However, possible that entering a harbor on a lee shore or where the wave pattern is likely to be irregular, or where the water may be shallow, could be far more dangerous than staying out at sea. Always try to make for shelter to windward. Once in harbor, or if you are there when bad weather is forecast, double up all lines and do not attempt to leave until the weather is clear. If you are not within reach of a safely approached harbor, or if you are anchored near an exposed lee shore, you have no choice but to ride out the gale at sea. Your efforts must then be concentrated on gaining as much searoom to leeward as possible.

Procedure

As the wind increases, no matter which point of sailing you are on, you will have to reduce the sail area by degrees by reefing and using smaller sails. If you are beating to windward, the deterioration in the weather will be particularly noticeable and you will have to reduce sail quickly. Sailing offwind in rough weather places less strain on the boat and is more comfortable. However, you must not allow yourself to underestimate the strength of the wind and in most circumstances it is better to use less sail than you think you can handle. There is also a danger of sailing too fast when travelling downwind, as the effect of the boat moving quickly through the water can disrupt the waves coming up from behind and cause them to break over the stern. Often the boat can be made more comfortable by sailing under the headsail alone. On all points of sailing take account of the way you approach the waves using the techniques as described for one-designs on pages 131−3. If you wish to avoid going off course, or if you want to give the crew a rest, you should stop the boat as much as possible by heaving-to, using one of the methods described on page 206, or by lying a-hull. Heaving-to is a useful way of riding out rough weather as it is the best way to reduce drift to leeward. However, the fact that there are sails up means that unless you have a very small storm jib and a trysail, there may be considerable strain on the boat. In addition, waves may be breaking over the boat and the hull and rigging will be prone to damage. If the strain on the equipment becomes too great while hove-to, and if you have sufficient searoom to leeward, the next thing to do is to take off all the sails and either lie a-hull, or run before the wind. Lying a-hull has the advantage that the drift to leeward, while greater than when lying hove-to, is much less than while running and it will normally be your next course of

The cruising boat, above, is carrying a small jib and a deeply reefed mainsail.

action. Once the sails have been lowered, the tiller should be lashed to leeward, and the boat will lie at its natural angle to the wind. The boat will heel over and the danger is that it may be flung to leeward by the waves and capsized if the seas are very large. If this seems likely to happen, you will have to run before the wind or, if there is insufficient searoom, try to lie to a drogue (below). When running under bare poles, the boat must be steered constantly.

In strong winds the boat may travel too fast causing the waves to break over the stern and an attempt will have to be made to slow the boat down using one of the methods described below. If the conditions continue to deteriorate and you feel that your crew are in real danger, it may be necessary to take emergency measures and summon assistance (see pages 314−7).

Slowing the boat

When riding out a gale at sea, you will need to devise ways of slowing down the boat. The best method is to trail a heavy line of sufficient length − 45 m (150 ft) minimum − in a bight behind the boat. Each end is led through a stern fairlead and around a winch before being cleated. Another method is to trail a sea-anchor (an open-ended conical canvas bag) behind the boat but this may hold the boat too well and prevent it giving way in large waves. A sea anchor can also be let out from the bow to try to make the boat lie head-to-wind and reduce drift. However, this often results in the boat lying beam on.

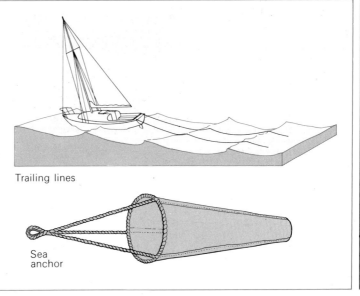

Trailing lines

Sea anchor

Rules of the road

There are international rules which apply to the rights of way of all sizes of craft using the high seas and other waters – The International Regulations for Preventing Collision at Sea, 1972 (72 COLREGS) which replaced rules set down in 1960. In addition there are three sets of Rules of the Road in effect in U.S. waters: the Inland, Great Lakes, and Western Rivers Rules. You must know which of the four governs the waters in which you are operating, and the demarcation lines are defined in the Coast Guard publications, CG 169–1.

There are others, pilot rules or speed limits, for example, laid down by the Coast Guard and by state and local authorities. For any sailor, it is important to realize that the skipper of a pleasure craft, however small, has the same responsibility as the captain of a large tanker.

The regulations are not as complex as they look at first sight, but it takes time to learn them thoroughly. A good commercial skipper clearly knows the regulations thoroughly from constant practice but a pleasure boat owner normally knows only the common ones and will need to have appropriate reference on board to check on others. One simple way of doing this is either to buy or make a set of check cards which contain the information you are likely to need in simplified form. This is a great help if a problem does arise, because if you had to hunt through the reference books, the solution might be produced too late.

Courses of action

For the skipper of a small cruising boat there are several points to consider when sailing in areas used by both small and large vessels. One of these is how to keep an adequate lookout. On most small- or medium-sized cruising boats, the crew is usually fairly small and often relatively inexperienced. If you are the skipper you need to know if an approaching vessel is likely to be a danger, but an inexperienced crew member may well not be able to determine this. The simplest solution is for you to stipulate that all vessels sighted should be reported to you. You also need to know rapidly where the vessel is, and the simplest way for the crew to report the information is by using the clock notation system (shown below).

Once a vessel has been sighted, the skipper has to determine whether there is any risk of collision. The best and quickest way to do so is to take a series of bearings of the other vessel, normally by using the hand bearing compass. If the bearings change significantly (that is if there is a difference of several degrees between each bearing) there is no danger of collision, but if they remain constant, the risk still exists. If a hand bearing compass is not used, you simply line up the other vessel with a fixed object on the boat, such as a stanchion, to see if these stay in line. If they do, the boat is on a collision course. If the other vessel appears to move ahead in relation to the stanchion (provided, of course, that you have not moved and altered your own sight line) then it will cross your bows. If it appears to move behind the stanchion it will pass astern of you.

If there is any risk of collision you have to decide quickly whether you have the right of way under the regulations. A handy reference guide is the only way of checking unless you happen to know the rules very thoroughly. If you decide that you have to give way, take action immediately, normally by altering course; you need to do so to an extent where your actions are clear to the other vessel. Often, when a large vessel is approaching, most skippers prefer to alter course even if they have right of way. In any event, the other vessel may not have noticed you because your boat is too small to be seen in time or to have shown up on the radar. If from your bearings you realize that you will clear the larger vessel, beware of crossing ahead of it even if the bearings show you he will pass astern. It is much safer to pass astern of him yourself. If you alter course to go astern of the other vessel (that is, not to stand on your rights) keep your new course consistent and make sure he realizes what you are doing. Otherwise, the other vessel may be confused by your intentions. Continue to keep an eye on the other vessel afterwards; large ships have radar and may well have to alter course to avoid a danger which you cannot see.

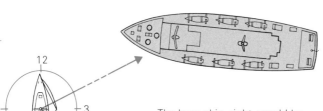

The large ship, right, would be described to the skipper as "large ship at two o'clock, moving from right to left". (In practice the vessels would be considerably further apart when sighted!)

Steering rules

These define which vessel, in a given situation, has the right to hold its course and speed, and which vessel has to give way. The three basic rules covering sailing boats meeting were shown in the one-design section (page 94) but some others are shown here, right and below. Reference should be made to the full regulations for a more complete understanding of the rules. Before a rule can be applied, the other vessel has first to be identified. This is normally easy but where confusion may occur certain shapes are displayed by day (see page 230) and special lights by night (see page 222).

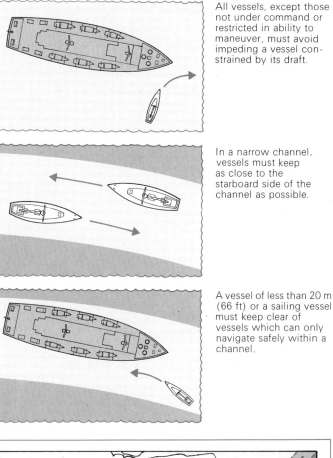

All vessels, except those not under command or restricted in ability to maneuver, must avoid impeding a vessel constrained by its draft.

In a narrow channel, vessels must keep as close to the starboard side of the channel as possible.

A vessel of less than 20 m (66 ft) or a sailing vessel must keep clear of vessels which can only navigate safely within a channel.

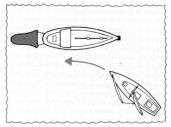

A vessel fishing or trawling (but not using trolling lines) in open water has the right of way except over a vessel not under command or with restricted maneuverability.

Traffic separation

Schemes to separate vessels are used in areas of dense traffic. Through traffic is separated from local traffic and the through traffic is split into two streams. Traffic lanes are separated by areas where no movement is allowed except in specified cases. Boats joining a through lane should normally do so at either end of it, but if this is not possible they should enter the lane at as shallow an angle as they can. Local traffic keeps out of the lanes and uses the inshore zones. Any vessel crossing a traffic separation scheme should do so at right angles to the flow of traffic, and should take great care not to cross in front of passing boats. Only vessels fishing, crossing over the lane or in a state of emergency can enter the separation zone.

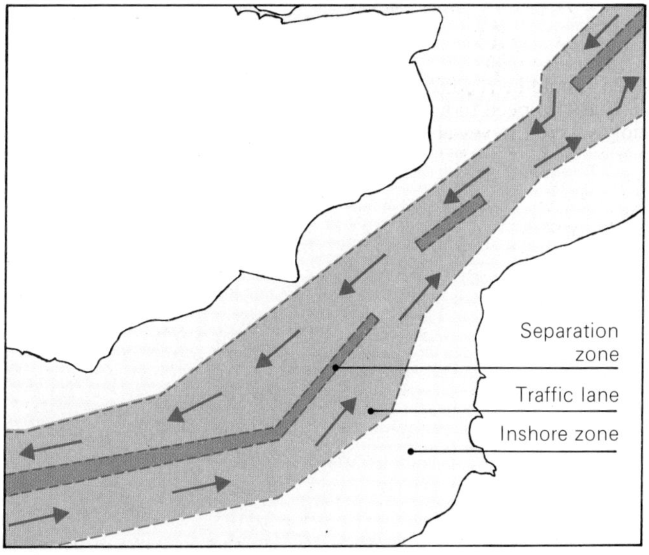

Separation zone

Traffic lane

Inshore zone

A traffic separation scheme, above, consists of inshore zones, two traffic lanes and a separation zone.

Sound signals

Sound signals are used in fog to identify vessels (see page 225) but are also used in clear visibility when vessels are in sight of one another, and wish to indicate that they are carrying out a maneuver. Normally small boats carry an aerosol foghorn with which to make the signals but a bell, whistle or gong are also used in some cases. When vessels under power are in sight of one another, and if one of them is altering course or maneuvering it must indicate its intentions by the use of whistle signals (below). At night, as well as, or instead of, the whistle an all-round white light can be flashed for the appropriate number of times. When a vessel is approaching a blind bend or an obstruction in a channel it should give one prolonged blast. This has to be answered by a prolonged blast from any approaching vessel which is similarly obscured from view. In a narrow channel if a vessel wishes to overtake another, and can only do so if the vessel ahead takes some avoiding action, then the over-taking boat must indicate its intentions as shown below. The answering call from the vessel being overtaken is either the permission to pass signal or one which indicates that the intentions of the other vessel have not been understood (below).

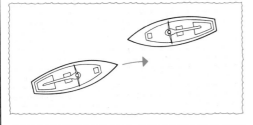

One short blast
Signal for vessel (far left) which intends to alter course to starboard.

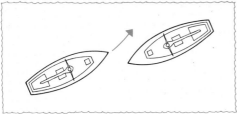

Two short blasts
Signal for vessel (far left) which intends to alter course to port.

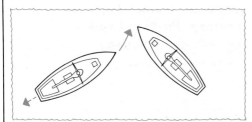

Three short blasts
Signal for vessel (far left) which has its engine in reverse.

— — •

Two long blasts, one short blast
The signal for a vessel wishing to pass another vessel to starboard in a narrow channel.

— • — •

One long blast, one short blast, one long blast, one short blast
Signal for leading vessel which agrees to being overtaken.

— — • •

Two long blasts and two short blasts
Signal for vessel wishing to pass to port in a narrow channel.

• • • • •

Five short blasts
Signal for vessel which wishes to indicate that another vessel's intentions are not clear.

Daylight shapes

To make identification easier during normal daylight hours, vessels often carry specific shapes, normally made of metal, attached where they can best be seen. These demonstrate the type or purpose of a particular vessel. At night, lights are always used instead (see page 222).

Vessel under sail and power

Vessel fishing or trawling (not trolling) over 20 m (66 ft)

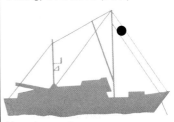

Vessel at anchor

Vessel constrained by its draft

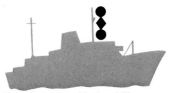

Vessel restricted in its ability to maneuver

Navigation

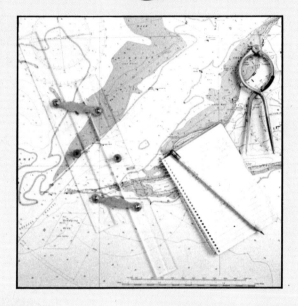

Basic terms · Instruments and equipment · Using compasses
Tidal calculations · Shaping a course · Position fixing
Radio aids · Navigating in fog · Windward sailing
Errors · Pilotage · Planning a passage · Buoyage

Starting to navigate

Man is as much a natural navigator as migratory birds or animals. The difference is that whereas birds and animals use their navigational skills to survive, modern man no longer needs to do so and the natural skills are dormant. Anyone used to living and working in the countryside usually has a good sense of direction coupled with an ability to gather information from natural signs. In fact, everyone unconsciously uses some basic navigation techniques in everyday life: moving around the landscape they navigate by eye from one identifiable landmark to the next.

Pilotage

For many yachtsmen, who never venture far from their local area, navigation at sea is a very similar process to finding their way around on land. This particular type of navigation is known as pilotage (see page 256). It is used when sailing in protected or familiar waters, or in estuaries and bays where there are easily recognized landmarks, as well as for entering and leaving harbors in good visibility. All that is needed for piloting your way around is a chart, a steering compass, basic plotting instruments and a depth sounder.

As you go further afield and attempt short passages along a coastline, your navigation skills have to improve. To begin with, you should plan to undertake short cruises in good weather in sight of landmarks. You will have to consider the state of the tides and bear in mind that if the weather deteriorates, or if visibility decreases, you may need to rely solely on your ability to navigate by instrument alone. You will need additional navigational equipment: a nautical almanac, a tide table of the area, a handbearing compass, a radio receiver and a pair of binoculars. As your navigation becomes more proficient you can undertake passages out of sight of land. On these, you rely on pure navigational skills alone to find your way, and you will need more sophisticated equipment on the boat. Navigation is often regarded, quite wrongly, as a highly mathematical subject. In fact, the only mathematical skills needed are those of simple addition and subtraction, with some division and multiplication at times. If you have enough intelligence to work out your weekly shopping bill, there is no reason why you can't learn to navigate.

The way the subject is sometimes taught can confuse the potential navigator. Sitting at a well lit desk in night school, solving hypothetical navigational problems, is a far cry from crouching over the chart table of a boat, feeling seasick and with a number of other problems to tackle, all demanding immediate attention.

Preparation

For the average skipper of a small boat with a family crew, learning to understand the priorities and how to satisfy them as quickly as possible is the key to success. One way you can make the task a lot easier is to do as much preparation as you can before starting a passage: look up sailing directions, plot rough courses on the charts and make lists of buoys and lights in the order you are likely to meet them, and mark the tide table with the appropriate times. If you do all this before starting out, in the comfort of your own home, you will reduce your workload considerably when at sea as well as building up a picture of what to expect on the voyage.

It is important to realize that your navigation can only be as good as the information you have at your disposal. Spare no effort to make sure that it is constantly updated. Only experience will give you the knowledge to handle the information properly, reliably and accurately; but when navigating a small boat, do not expect to eliminate errors. Even the best navigators make mistakes and understanding how errors occur, and making allowances for them, is probably the least recognized part of the whole subject. Minor errors waste time and effort and major errors, at the worst, are potentially dangerous. The way to reduce them is to double check every calculation before you rely on it and where possible to double check every piece of information you use.

Practice and experience

When you begin to navigate, you will find that all your calculations take time and effort but as you become more practiced, you will find the process much simpler. It is surprising how after only a few passages you will rapidly develop your skills. Navigation, like any other aspect of boat handling, is largely a matter of common sense, practice and experience. Before you begin, however, you need to be familiar with the basic terms used in navigation and these are explained opposite. The following pages explain the elements of navigation needed in off-shore cruising.

Position

The system used in navigation to describe position on the earth is a grid with sets of lines running from east to west and north to south. These lines are called parallels of latitude (when east to west) and meridians of longitude (when north to south). The position of any place can be given by naming the exact longitude and latitude (see pages 240–1 for chart information). Longitude and latitude lines are formed as shown below, and measured in degrees (°), minutes (′) and tenths of a minute. There are 60 minutes in one degree.

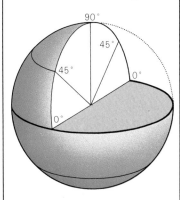

Latitude
Lines of latitude are drawn parallel to the equator by measuring from the center of earth in degrees, using the equator as 0°. Lines of latitude run 0° to 90°N and 0° to 90°S.

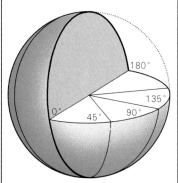

Longitude
Lines of longitude are drawn from the north to south poles by measuring from the center of the earth along the equator using the Greenwich meridian (0°) as the starting point. Lines of longitude run 0° to 180°E and 0° to 180°W.

Direction

In navigation terms, a direction is given as the angle between that of the direction itself and north. When the direction is one along which your boat is sailing, it is known as a heading or course. When it is a direction between your boat and another object, or between two objects, it is known as a bearing. Both bearings and headings are measured in degrees clockwise from north. The meaning of north varies, however, and can be described either as true, magnetic or compass north (see below and page 238). A bearing of 120° from true north will have the suffix T added (120°T); a bearing using magnetic north has M added (120°M) and one using compass north has C added (120°C).

To give the direction of a heading (above right) or a bearing (right), measure around from north (0°) clockwise, in degrees.

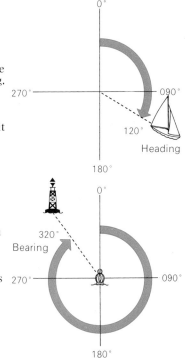

Heading

Bearing

Distance, speed and depth

For all purposes of navigation, distances at sea are measured in nautical (or sea) miles—one **nautical mile is equal to 1′ of latitude** (averaging 6080 ft — longer than a standard mile). The symbol is NM. A nautical mile is divided into 10 cables, written as tenths of a mile. Thus the standard abbreviation for 5 miles 2 cables is 5.2 NM. The unit of speed is the knot and the symbol used is Kn. One knot is defined as one nautical mile per hour.

The current unit to measure depth is the foot. The original unit of measurement, the fathom, is found on older charts and is indicated as fm. A fathom equals 6 ft.

Magnetic variation

When lines of longitude are described as running from north to south, this refers to true north and south, that is the geographic poles. In a boat, a compass is used but this shows magnetic north and south, and aligns itself along the earth's magnetic field which runs between the magnetic poles. These differ in position from true north and south—the amount of the difference is known and is called variation.

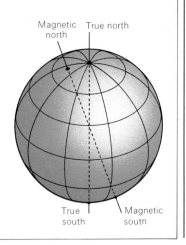

Magnetic north   True north

True south   Magnetic south

Navigation equipment

Before you start on the practical aspects of navigation, you need certain items of equipment. The essential ones do not need to be elaborate or expensive. Where plotting instruments are concerned, you have the choice between traditional instruments, such as roller or parallel rulers, and proprietary instruments, such as the two simple plotting instruments (below). One of your first priorities if you have a small boat is to make sure that you have a reasonable size chart table to work on. It should measure 58 cm by 75 cm (24 in by 30 in) minimum – any smaller and it will not accept an Admiralty chart folded once. If you don't have a permanent chart table, use a flat board which can be stowed away when not in use.

It is important to make sure that you have adequate stowage space for all the equipment used at the chart table, together with a shelf for navigation books. The charts themselves need to be stowed flat, folded once only. The boat's navigation instruments are usually arranged around the table where they can be easily read by the navigator. The whole area must be adequately lit and the lighting arranged in such a way that it doesn't disturb the rest of the crew at night. One solution is to have a small bulb, covered with a hood, on the end of an adjustable stalk. It can be moved to provide either focused or a more diffused light.

The position of the chart table in the boat is important. Whenever possible it should be in the middle, where there is less motion, but close enough to the cockpit for the navigator to be able to talk to the helmsman.

The chart table, above, is well arranged with the equipment and instruments ready to hand.

Plotting instruments

There are many types of plastic plotting instruments on the market but the two shown below are probably the most commonly used. One, a simple rectangle of transparent plastic, engraved with semi-circular scales and a set of parallel lines, can be used to plot a line in a required direction, to measure the direction of an existing line or to draw lines parallel to one another. The other consists of a square of transparent plastic engraved with a grid of parallel lines, a rotating plastic circle marked like a compass card and a swinging arm. Because the circle rotates, variation can be allowed for before plotting or measuring directions. This allows the navigator to do all his plotting in degrees magnetic if he so wishes thus helping to eliminate possible errors. In use the square is lined up with a line of latitude or longitude and the arm is swung to line up with the required direction on the compass scale, and the line drawn. Alternatively the arm can be lined up on the chart and the direction read off.

The simple rectangular plotter (top) is a convenient size and is robust with no moving parts to break, but it only enables directions to be measured or plotted in degrees true. Also it can be inconvenient to use when the lines of latitude or longitude are widely spaced. The plotter shown below, on the other hand, has the advantage that plotting and measuring can be done in degrees true or magnetic equally conveniently. It is, however, larger and, because it has two moving parts, more likely to get broken.

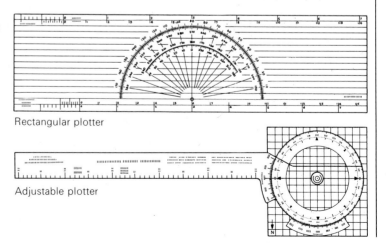

Rectangular plotter

Adjustable plotter

Parallel rulers

There are two types of parallel ruler, one version has two arms arms which enable the ruler to be walked across the chart without altering the angle at which they were positioned. The other type has two knurled wheels which enable the ruler to be rolled across the chart, while achieving the same result. When in the correct position the wheels can be locked to prevent movement. Parallel rulers are the traditional plotting instrument and people learning navigation for the first time are usually taught to use them. They are not, however, the easiest instrument to use accurately and for this reason many experienced navigators use a protractor instead.

The roller parallel ruler is simply rolled across the chart. With the sliding type, one leg is held firmly while the other extended, and the movement repeated.

Roller parallel ruler

Sliding parallel ruler

Dividers and compasses

You will need a pair of compasses and dividers for marking off and measuring distances on a chart. Buy the best quality in either brass or stainless steel. They should be at least six inches in length so that they have a reasonable span. The compasses need only be simple ones.

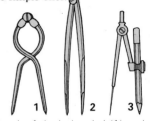

A pair of single-handed (1) and straight dividers (2), and a simple pair of compasses (3).

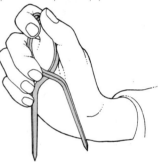

To use single-handed dividers, hold them as shown. Pressure on the upper part opens them; on the lower part, shuts them.

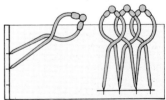

To mark off a greater distance than the dividers' span permits, measure the distance in stages by rotating the dividers.

Pencils

You will need some soft pencils (2B are ideal) which do not permanently mark the charts. They should be hexagonal, as the round ones roll off the table. You will also need a good eraser and a pencil sharpener.

Logbook

A logbook is an essential part of the boat's equipment. You will need it for recording events, as they occur. It must be kept as neatly as possible as you will need to refer to it from time to time, particularly on longer passages. Most navigators use a simple exercise book or loose-leaf sheets (below). Some navigators keep a second log book which is used by the watch on deck (see page 157) and the information is then transferred by the navigator to the main logbook. A rough notebook is useful for working out any rough calculations before they are transferred to the main logbook. Should you enter into a dispute of any sort over your rights at sea, your logbook can be used in evidence and it is therefore important to keep it accurate.

Time	Log	Course required	Course steered	Wind	Baro.	Remarks
12:30	0.0	‑	-	S 4	1005	Departed Yarmouth under power.
12:45	0.8	240°C	240°C	S4	.	Sconce Buoy, full main, No. 2 Jib.
13:00	2.4	240°C	240°C	S4		Warden Buoy.
13:30	5.2	285°C	285°C	SW 5	1004	SW Shingles. Reefed 1 slab, No. 2 jib.
14:20	10.9	285°C	310°C	WNW 5/6	1003	2 slabs and No. 2 Jib. Fix, see chart. Wind veering.

Compasses

One of the most vital parts of a cruising boat's equipment is the compass. The boat should have at least three: one for steering by, another for taking hand bearings and a third in the radio direction finding set (see page 252). All compasses work on the same principle: they show the direction of compass north (see page 240) on a circular card with degrees around its circumference, from 0° to 359°, usually with a mark every 5° and a figure at every 10°. Compass markings vary to some extent according to type – occasionally they are marked on the edge of the card as well as on the top.

The card itself is suspended on a pivot point and has two or more small bar magnets fixed to its underside. The whole assembly is supported in a bowl which is usually filled with a mixture of water and alcohol. This fluid is used to float the compass card and to damp out any violent oscillations.

A line, called a lubber line, is used as a reference point from which to read any movement of the compass. The lubber line is usually painted or engraved on the inside of the bowl but its position depends on the type of compass. With most compasses, the bowl assembly is mounted in a gimballed fitting to keep it horizontal as the boat heels. Some compasses, especially those mounted on a pedestal or on the bulkhead, have a gimballed frame on which the card and the lubber line are mounted. Thus the bowl itself does not need gimbals and tilts with any movement of the boat while the card and lubber line remain level.

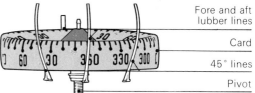

A top and edge reading compass card with pivot, and fore and aft lubber lines. Also shown are two 45° lines used for viewing from the side.

Steering compasses

There are a number of different types of steering compass but whichever you choose, you should make sure it is a good quality one. Pick the one with the largest and most clearly marked card. The compass should have some form of illumination so it can be used at night, and it should be sited where the helmsman does not have to peer sideways at it when steering. Make sure the compass is at least 2 m (6 ft) away from the engine. Take care also to keep any movable items of metal away from it. If you have a wheel-steered boat the compass is usually mounted in front of the helmsman in a case on a pedestal (known as a binnacle compass – below). In the case of tiller-steered boats, it is best to have two compasses, one on each bulkhead (right), so that the helmsman gets a clear view of the compass from either side of the boat. If you use a grid compass (below), which is read from above by lining up parallel lines, the siting is less vital as the reading does not distort when the helmsman sees it at an angle.

Bulkhead compass
This is mounted on the bulkhead. Make sure that the center line of the compass is parallel with the centerline of the boat.

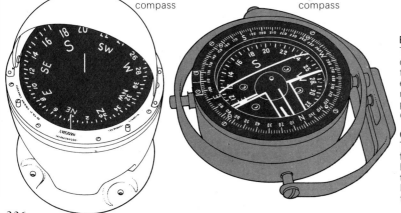

Binnacle compass

Grid compass

Binnacle compass
This has a large glass dome which magnifies the card and makes it easy to read. It is normally mounted on a pedestal directly in front of the steering wheel.

Grid compass
This need not be sited in front of the helmsman. It is used by lining up the two sets of marked lines and always keeping them parallel

Hand bearing compasses

A hand bearing compass is used when the navigator wishes to find the bearing of an object from the boat. Very few steering compasses are situated where they can be used for this purpose and a separate small compass, easily hand-held, is used instead. It needs to have electric or radiant illumination for night use. Traditional types are mounted on a handle. The bowl has a prism on top which makes it possible to read the compass when held at eye level. There is usually a sighting "V" in the prism and a line down its face. When these are lined up with the object, the bearing is visible on the prism. This type of compass should be held steadily at arm's length when taking a bearing. Modern developments in sighting optics have introduced new types of hand bearing compass which can be held close to the eye, and the object and compass card viewed together but with the eye focused at infinity. An even more recent development in this field is the completely solid-state hand bearing compass. It electronically senses the lines of magnetic flux and quickly gives a read-out in digital form.

Traditional hand bearing compass
A traditional type of hand bearing compass, right—there is a prism on top with a sighting "V".

Mini-compass
This is a small, compact compass (right and below) with a sighting device that allows it to be held close to the eye when taking sights.

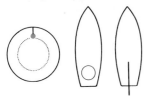

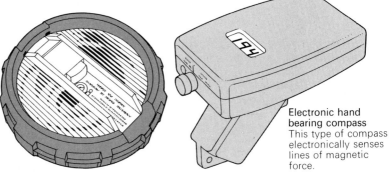

Electronic hand bearing compass
This type of compass electronically senses lines of magnetic force.

Steering a compass course

When steering a compass course in a small boat, the best that can be expected of the helmsman is to steer on a 5° or 10° compass mark, and a sensible navigator would realize this in issuing steering instructions. Never ask the helmsman to steer a very accurate course to windward in shifting winds. Instead, leave him to steer the best course he can and ask him what course he is averaging.
Steering a compass course is largely a matter of practice. Beginners tend to find it tiring because they steer with their eyes fixed on the compass. One solution is to put the boat on course, then steer for a particular object, such as a landmark, cloud or star, and check your course regularly on the compass. Beginners often compound any steering errors they make by pushing the tiller or turning the wheel in the wrong direction (see diagrams below for instructions on how to steer).

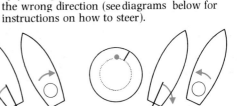

On course
The required course (represented by the dot) is against the lubber line. No movement of the tiller or wheel is necessary.

Off course to port
Compass reading has decreased and the boat must be turned to starboard. The tiller is put to port; the wheel is turned to starboard.

Off course to starboard
Compass reading has increased and the boat must be turned to port. The tiller is put to starboard; the wheel is turned to port.

Magnetic deviation

In theory, the needle of a compass points to magnetic north but in practice it is often influenced by the boat's own magnetic field. When this happens, the compass points to what is known as compass north and the difference between this and magnetic north is called deviation. The amount of deviation varies on different headings (see right) and, like variation, may be westerly or easterly. To reduce the deviation to a minimum, position the compass away from large metal objects such as the engine, and keep all small metal objects away from it as well.

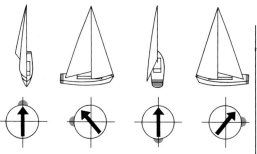

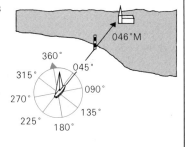

Large amounts of metal affect the compass: as the boat, turns, the metal moves in relation to the compass card, causing varying deviation on different headings.

Swinging for errors

A compass should never be used until the amount of deviation on all headings is known. To determine the deviation, the compass must be "swung". To do so, choose a calm day and stow all gear in its normal place. Then steer the boat to where you can watch a range between two fixed charted objects. Establish the magnetic bearing from the chart and sail slowly across the range on eight different headings all around the compass (right). Every time you cross the range, take the observed bearing from the compass and note it down, together with the heading at the time. For accuracy, the process should be carried out under both power and sail. If the deviation is significantly different under both, two deviation cards should be made (see below).

Recording errors

To record the headings and bearings you should make up a tabulated sheet, as shown right. The figures on the right are the result of three separate crossings of a range on each of eight points of the compass. Deviation is labelled E (east) when the observed bearing is less than the true bearing and W (west) when it is greater.
The deviation can be left uncorrected on the compass. However, if the amount is too great, the compass should be adjusted accurately by a professional.

Boat heading as shown on compass	Range bearing known	Range bearing observed	Deviation
000°C	046°M	043°C	3°E
045°C	046°M	048°C	2°W
090°C	046°M	052°C	6°W
135°C	046°M	053°C	7°W
180°C	046°M	050°C	4°W
225°C	046°M	045°C	1°E
270°C	046°M	042°C	4°E
315°C	046°M	040°C	6°E

Deviation card

If the compass is uncorrected, you should make out a deviation card. The best method is to plot the figures as a curve so that the deviation is read off accordingly. By inserting both compass and magnetic readings on the card you can use the card to read from compass to magnetic and vice versa. If the reading you require is in between two readings given, then you can use the graph to interpolate. To correct for deviation, the same rules are applied as in correcting for variation (see page 242).

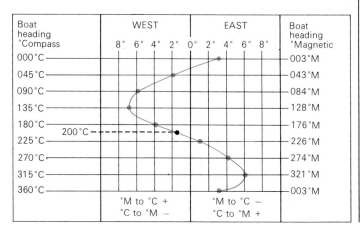

Navigation instruments

Very few instruments are needed for safe, accurate navigation. You will, however, need some kind of log to measure speed and distance. Simplest of these is the chip log which is used when other instruments fail or, more usually, as a check on the accuracy of more sophisticated instruments. All logs should be calibrated against the chip log or over a measured mile so that any errors can be allowed for. Most complex of all are pressure logs which measure the speed of water past the hull using electronic sensing devices and then convert it to give speed and distance read-out.

Apart from a log, you will need a depth sounder, a portable radio with long and medium wavebands and a stop watch for timing light sequences (see page 262). A pair of 7 × 50 binoculars, a cabin clock with alarm, and a barometer or barograph (see page 283) are also necessary.

Chip log

The chip log consists of a weighted plywood triangle attached to a line knotted at 7.71 m (25.3 ft) intervals. The log is dropped over the stern of the boat and the number of knots which run out in 15 seconds are counted to give you your speed (1 knot = 7.71 m per 15 secs).

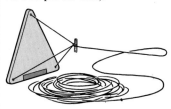

Impeller log

Impeller logs are hull-mounted below water level. The turns of the impeller (a small propellor) are transmitted either electronically or mechanically to a remote speed and distance read-out. Small paddle wheels are sometimes used instead of an impeller because they are less easily fouled by weed.

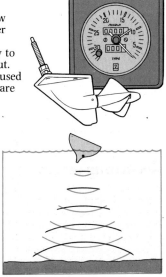

Depth sounder

The depth sounder, after the compass, is probably the commonest instrument found on cruising boats. It measures the time taken by a sound pulse to reach the bottom and bounce back (right), and converts the time into a depth reading on a pointer dial, neon or digital display.

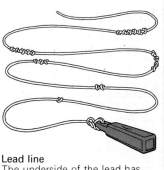

Some echo sounders, like the one shown left, have a neon display which can help you to determine the nature of the seabed. A sharp line display indicates a hard surface, while a fuzzy line indicates a muddy one.

Patent log

The patent log is one of the simplest, cheapest and most reliable distance-measuring devices. But, because it is towed behind the boat, it cannot be used in crowded waters. A recording head at one end of the line registers the number of revolutions of the spinner in the water and expresses them in miles and tenths of a mile. The latest models have a separate speed read-out dial but speed is usually estimated, noting the tenths of a mile covered in six minutes.

Lead line

The traditional measure of depth is the lead line. Modern lines are calibrated in feet or fathoms, using knots (right) or with materials of a different type and color for each depth. In use, the lead and some of the line is held in one hand and cast ahead of the thrower. As the boat "catches up" with the lead, the line will run perpendicular from the deck to the seabed and the mark at water level is read off.

Lead line
The underside of the lead has a shallow depression which, when filled with grease, brings up a sample of the seabed.

Charts

An up-to-date chart is essential. Without it you have little hope of navigating safely from place to place unless you happen to know the area already from long-term, first-hand experience.

Charts are issued by various agencies of the Federal Government and can be obtained from them or from retail sales agents. The majority of sailors use charts issued by the National Ocean Survey (NOS) of the National Oceanic and Atmospheric Administration. These charts cover the coastal waters, harbors and tidal rivers of the U S. Charts of the high seas and foreign waters are issued by the Defense Mapping Agency.

The job of the chart is to represent the earth's surface on paper. As the paper is flat and the earth's surface is not, some distortion naturally occurs. Various types of projection are used when making charts but the Mercator projection is most commonly used by small-boat sailors.

Charts are made in a variety of scales, and the size you buy depends on the intended use. For general chart coverage most sailors use the NOS conventional charts, but supplementary cover can be obtained from small-craft charts, where available. These are useful for recreational sailing, as they are accordion-folded, take up less space and emphasize additional useful information.

The conventional charts come in a range of scales. The smallest scale ones, known as sailing charts, cover long stretches of the coastline. The next size, known as general charts, cover a more limited area, and are intended for general coastal navigation. The next largest scale, the coastal charts, are used for close-in coastal navigation and the largest scale harbor charts, give the necessary detail for entering or leaving harbor.

Whichever type of chart you use, conventional or small-craft, you will find it contains a great many symbols and a lot of information. As it is impossible to carry the symbols in your head, the best solution is to keep a copy of Chart No. 1 on board. This is a comprehensive guide to all the symbols used and is produced jointly by the NOS and the DMA.

Like land maps, sea charts are the result of surveys taken at regular intervals. Information from these surveys is also used to up-date existing charts or to issue new ones.

Detail of NOS conventional chart, No. 13223, of Narragansett Bay, Rhode Island.

Compass rose
At various places on the chart are found true and magnetic compass roses. These can be used in conjunction with parallel rulers for measuring directions in either degrees true or degrees magnetic. Directions can also be converted easily from true to magnetic and vice versa.

Symbols
A great number of symbols are used on a chart to indicate hazards or reference points of various kinds. A typical example is the one shown which indicates a submerged rock over which the depth of water is unknown.

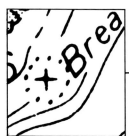

Latitude and longitude
The horizontal and vertical lines marked on the charts are lines of latitude and longitude and provide a grid reference system for measuring position. They can also be used as the reference point from which directions are measured using plotting instruments.

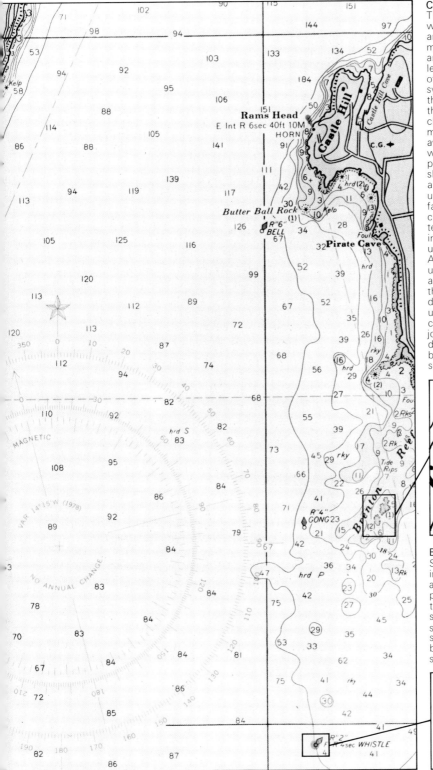

Chart datum

This is the level from which all water depths and drying heights are measured (see pages 244 and 286—7). Different levels are used on charts of different areas and the system used is shown on the chart. In the case of the chart, left, the level of chart datum is that of mean low water (the average of all the low waters over a certain period). Depths are shown above chart datum and at present are usually shown in feet or fathoms. Some newer charts use meters and tenths of a meter. It is important to check which unit is used on the chart. Any areas which are uncovered at chart datum are marked in green, and the height above chart datum is marked with an underlined figure. Most charts have contour lines joining places of equal depth, the actual depth being determined by the scale of the chart.

Buoyage

Some of the most important information on a chart is the type and position of buoys. Here the symbol for a lit, starboard-hand buoy is shown, with the additional symbol showing that the buoy carries a whistle signal.

241

Magnetic variation on charts

As has already been shown, the position of magnetic and true north are not the same. The directions shown by a magnetic compass will vary, therefore, from the true directions marked on the chart itself. This difference, known as variation, is measured in degrees; the amount differs according to the location. The compass rose, printed on the chart, gives the correct amount of variation for the year of publication and is used to convert degrees true to magnetic or vice versa. If magnetic north lies to the east or west of true north it is known as easterly or westerly variation, respectively.

You can convert directions from magnetic to true (and vice versa) in one of two ways. The simplest method is to lay a ruler across the compass rose, making sure that one edge of the ruler lines up both the centre of the rose with the direction that you wish to convert. You then read off the new direction from the compass rose. If the chart is an old one, your calculations may be slightly out, but normally the error is small enough not to be of any significance.

The other method is to use calculation. However, it is not entirely to be recommended as it can be difficult to ensure that your calculations are accurate. It seems simple but if you add where you should have subtracted, you end up with a figure which could give a disastrously wrong reading. However, as there may be times when calculation is necessary, you should know how. When the variation is westerly, to convert from true to magnetic you add the amount of variation, and from magnetic to true you subtract the variation. When the variation is easterly, you do the opposite: to convert from true to magnetic you subtract the variation and from magnetic to true you add the variation.

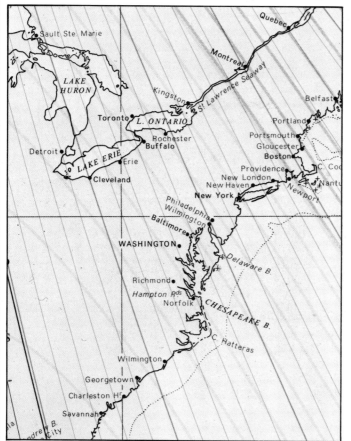

Isogonic charts (detail of British Admiralty chart 5375) show magnetic variation over large areas. These charts are used in long-distance cruising.

Working on charts

When working on a chart, plotting directions, you can work in either true or magnetic, but you must be consistent. Traditionally, navigators are taught to work in degrees true but, in a small boat at sea, working in magnetic has many advantages. All the compass bearings and headings can be plotted directly having allowed for any deviation (see page 238) using the magnetic compass and a parallel ruler, or by using a plotting instrument. By eliminating the stages of conversion from one set of figures to another, the risk of error is minimized and time is saved. Publications normally give direction in degrees true, so these figures will have to be converted before plotting on the chart. However, this is only likely to be a small part of the work. If other crew members of your boat help you, make sure they know which system you are working in. Keep any calculations you make on rough paper with the chart so that you can check them again if the need arises.

Tides and tidal currents

If you are making a passage in tidal waters the rise and fall of the tide and the direction and rate of flow of the tidal current will affect your progress. In certain areas, the tidal current could be strong enough to set a boat off-course by a considerable amount, if it were not allowed for.

The information needed for navigation in tidal areas is published annually by the U.S. Department of Commerce in the form of tide tables (which detail the rise and fall of the tide, see pages 244–5) and the tidal current tables and tidal current charts. The latter publications give information on the direction and rate of flow of the tide, but whereas the tidal current tables are a comprehensive tabular guide to tidal currents, the charts, although easier to work from, only cover certain areas.

The system used by the tidal current tables is to give information about the times, directions and strengths of maximum flood and ebb currents plus the time of slack water for major reference stations around the coast, with corrected information for subordinate stations. A table is supplied for calculating the strength of the current between slack and high water.

The tidal current charts consist of a booklet containing a set of 13 reproductions of small-scale charts of particular areas, in which the direction and strength of the tidal current for each hour of the tide cycle is shown using arrows and numbers. Although some of the charts must be used in conjunction with the tidal current tables, others relate to the tide tables. The numbers indicating the strength of the current are those which apply at the time of the mean range of the tide. At other times, conversion has to be made using a table supplied at the front of the booklet.

The navigator should use the information contained in the tidal current tables and charts with care. Unusual conditions could vary the current strength and direction from that predicted. As the predictions are generally for a spot location, the situation could well vary considerably, even at another close location.

How to use tidal current charts

To use the tidal current chart you must first check whether the chart has to be used with the tide tables or the tidal current tables and to which reference port the chart relates. In the example shown right, the chart refers to Newport, Rhode Island, and is used in conjunction with the tide tables. This information is given on the first page of the booklet, as is information on how to use the charts. Using the chart shown, you should then consult the tide tables to discover the time of high water at Newport on the day in question. The page marked "High Water, Newport" then gives you the direction and strength of the current at this time. The succeeding pages give you the current information for any hour after the time of high water. You should use the table provided on the first page to correct the strength of the stream for the range of the particular tide you are interested in.

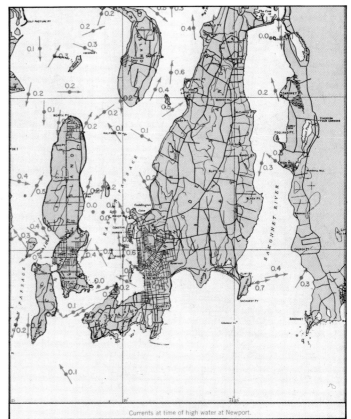

Currents at time of high water at Newport.

Estimating tidal height

When sailing in shallow water or when leaving or returning to harbor, you will need to know how much water you have under the boat. Your first responsibility is, of course, to know how much water your boat requires (its draft) and then to work out whether the depth of water is adequate. You should never take unnecessary risks and, if in doubt, should wait for the tide to rise. The area chart will give you the depths at chart datum (known as soundings) but to find out the height of tide above or, in some cases, below chart datum, you will need to use the tide tables. These are published by the National Ocean Survey.

Formal calculation

The National Ocean Survey publish four volumes of tide tables which between them cover the world. Volume 2 covers the East coast of North and South America and Greenland, while volume 3 covers the West coast of North and South America. The tide tables give the predicted times and heights of high and low water for each day of the year for a number of important points known as reference stations. Extra information is then tabulated showing the difference in time and height between these reference stations and many other points known as subordinate stations. This information enables you to find the tidal information for almost any point along the coast. The heights given in the table are all related to a plan of reference known as chart datum (see below). The time in the tide tables is the local standard time and is indicated at the foot of each page. If you are in an area which uses daylight time you must remember to apply the necessary correction. Once you have extracted the necessary information on the times and heights of high and low water for the place you are interested in, you can use another table to find out the height of tide at any intermediate time between high and low water.

Using the tables
This example is a guide to the use of the tables. Let us assume that you wish to know what the height of tide above chart datum will be at 13.30 Local Standard Time on the 16th August 1980 at the entrance to Cuttyhunk Pond, Mass. From the index to Vol. 2 of the tide tables you find that Cuttyhunk Pond is listed as a subordinate station. Turning to the appropriate page we find that the relevant reference station is Newport, R.I. The first step in the calculations is to extract from the predictions for Newport (Fig. 2) the time and heights of the high and low water which straddle the time you are interested in. Write these down as shown below then turn to the page on which are shown the time and height differences which must be applied for Cuttyhunk Pond entrance (Fig. 1). Write these down as shown. By applying the differences to the times and heights for Newport you now have the time and height of high and low water at Cuttyhunk Pond entrance.

Newport HW		LW	
time	height	time	height
11.23	3.4ft	16.33	0.6ft
Correction			
+0.04	−0.1ft	+0.06	0.0
Cuttyhunk Pond			
11.27	3.3ft	16.39	0.6ft

To find out what the height of tide will be at 13.30 you can use table 3 in the tide tables (Fig. 3) but first we need to work out the range of the tide, the interval from the nearest high or low water of the time we are interested in, and the duration of the rise or fall of that particular tide.
The range of the tide is simply the height difference between high water and low water. In this case it is 3.3−0.6, that is, 2.7ft. By inspection you can see that 13.30 is closer to the time of high water than low water and the time interval is HW+2hrs 03mins. Finally the duration of the fall of this tide is the time interval between high water and low water which in this case is 5hrs 12mins.
Using this information you can now enter table 3 (Fig. 3) by first finding the figure in the column marked Duration of rise (or fall), nearest to 5hrs 12min. Then follow this line across the page until you come to the figure closest to the time interval of 2hrs 03min. The correction figure you are looking for is now in the column below in line with the range of tide closest to the actual range of 2.7ft. The correction figure we obtain in this example is 0.9ft and it is subtracted from the height of high water to give a height above chart datum at 13.30 to 2.4ft. Note that if the time of low water had been nearest to the time you were interested in, then the correction figure would have been added to the height of low water. You must also realize that the figure you have obtained is the height above chart datum. To get the depth you must add to this figure the sounding shown on the chart of the area.

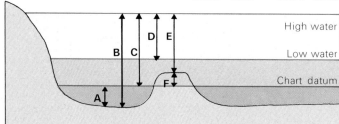

A common level for chart datum is the level of mean low water. A represents the depth at chart datum, B is the total depth at high water, C the height of high water, D the range of the tide, E is the total depth and F is the drying height.

TABLE 2.—TIDAL DIFFERENCES AND OTHER CONSTANTS

No.	PLACE	POSITION		DIFFERENCES				RANGES		MEAN TIDE LEVEL
				Time		Height				
		Lat.	Long.	High water	Low water	High water	Low water	Mean	Spring	
		°N.′	°W.′	h. m.	h. m.	feet	feet	feet	feet	feet
	Vineyard Sound Time meridian, 75°W.			on, NEWPORT, p.40						
	Quicks Hole									
1099	South side ·	41 26	70 51	−0 07	+0 14	−1.0	0.0	2.5	3.1	1.2
1101	Middle ·	41 27	70 51	+0 03	+0 15	−0.5	0.0	3.0	3.7	1.5
1103	North side ·	41 27	70 51	−0 05	−0 03	0.0	0.0	3.5	4.4	1.7
	Buzzards Bay									
1105	Cuttyhunk Pond entrance · · · · · · · · · · · ·	41 25	70 55	+0 04	+0 06	−0.1	0.0	3.4	4.2	1.7
1107	Penikese Island · · · · · · · · · · · · · · ·	41 27	70 55	−0 14	−0 11	−0.1	0.0	3.4	4.2	1.7

Fig 1 Tidal differences related to Newport, RI.

TIMES AND HEIGHTS OF HIGH AND LOW WATERS

AUGUST

HEIGHT		TIME	HEIGHT		TIME	HEIGHT		TIME
		DAY			DAY			DAY
ft.	m.	h.m.	ft.	m.	h.m.	ft.	m.	h.m.
0.1	0.0	1 0422	-0.4	-0.1	16 0409	0.3	0.1	1 0016
3.5	1.1	F 1115	4.2	1.3	SA 1123	3.4	1.0	M 0547
0.4	0.1	1654	-0.1	0.0	1633	0.6	0.2	1251
3.5	1.1	2339	3.9	1.2	2338	3.1	0.9	1856
0.3	0.1	2 0515	-0.3	-0.1	17 0446	0.4	0.1	2 0120
3.4	1.0	SA 1213	4.2	1.3	SU 1210	3.3	1.0	TU 0652
0.6	0.2	1757	0.1	0.0	1718	0.7	0.2	1353
3.3	1.0							2022
0.4	0.1	3 0037	3.6	1.1	18 0027	2.9	0.9	3 0224

Fig 2 Times and heights of HW and LW for Newport, RI.

TABLE 3.—HEIGHT OF TIDE AT ANY TIME

	Time from the nearest high water or low water																		
h. m.	h. m.	h. m.	h. m.	h. m.	h. m.	h. m.	h. m.	h. m.	h. m.	h. m.	h. m.	h. m.	h. m.	h. m.	h. m.	h. m.	h. m.	h. m.
4 00	0 08	0 16	0 24	0 32	0 40	0 48	0 56	1 04	1 12	1 20	1 28	1 36	1 44	1 52				
4 20	0 09	0 17	0 26	0 35	0 43	0 52	1 01	1 09	1 18	1 27	1 35	1 44	1 53	2 01	2 10			
4 40	0 09	0 19	0 28	0 37	0 47	0 56	1 05	1 15	1 24	1 33	1 43	1 52	2 01	2 11	2 20			
5 00	0 10	0 20	0 30	0 40	0 50	1 00	1 10	1 20	1 30	1 40	1 50	2 00	2 10	2 20	2 30			
5 20	0 11	0 21	0 32	0 43	0 53	1 04	1 15	1 25	1 36	1 47	1 57	2 08	2 19	2 29	2 40			
5 40	0 11	0 23	0 34	0 45	0 57	1 08	1 19	1 31	1 42	1 53	2 05	2 16	2 27	2 39	2 50			
6 00	0 12	0 24	0 36	0 48	1 00	1 12	1 24	1 36	1 48	2 00	2 12	2 24	2 36	2 48	3 00			
6 20	0 13	0 25	0 38	0 51	1 03	1 16	1 29	1 41	1 54	2 07	2 19	2 32	2 45	2 57	3 10			
6 40	0 13	0 27	0 40	0 53	1 07	1 20	1 33	1 47	2 00	2 13	2 27	2 40	2 53	3 07	3 20			
7 00	0 14	0 28	0 42	0 56	1 10	1 24	1 38	1 52	2 06	2 20	2 34	2 48	3 02	3 16	3 30			
7 20	0 15	0 29	0 44	0 59	1 13	1 28	1 43	1 57	2 12	2 27	2 41	2 56	3 11	3 25	3 40			
7 40	0 15	0 31	0 46	1 01	1 17	1 32	1 47	2 03	2 18	2 33	2 49	3 04	3 19	3 35	3 50			
8 00	0 16	0 32	0 48	1 04	1 20	1 36	1 52	2 08	2 24	2 40	2 56	3 12	3 28	3 44	4 00			
8 20	0 17	0 33	0 50	1 07	1 23	1 40	1 57	2 13	2 30	2 47	3 03	3 20	3 37	3 53	4 10			
8 40	0 17	0 35	0 52	1 09	1 27	1 44	2 01	2 19	2 36	2 53	3 11	3 28	3 45	4 03	4 20			
9 00	0 18	0 36	0 54	1 12	1 30	1 48	2 06	2 24	2 42	3 00	3 18	3 36	3 54	4 12	4 30			
9 20	0 19	0 37	0 56	1 15	1 33	1 52	2 11	2 29	2 48	3 07	3 25	3 44	4 03	4 21	4 40			
9 40	0 19	0 39	0 58	1 17	1 37	1 56	2 15	2 35	2 54	3 13	3 33	3 52	4 11	4 31	4 50			
10 00	0 20	0 40	1 00	1 20	1 40	2 00	2 20	2 40	3 00	3 20	3 40	4 00	4 20	4 40	5 00			
10 20	0 21	0 41	1 02	1 23	1 43	2 04	2 25	2 45	3 06	3 27	3 47	4 08	4 29	4 49	5 10			
10 40	0 21	0 43	1 04	1 25	1 47	2 08	2 29	2 51	3 12	3 33	3 55	4 16	4 37	4 59	5 20			

(left side label: Duration of rise or fall, see footnote)

	Correction to height														
Ft.	Ft.	Ft.	Ft.	Ft.	Ft.	Ft.	Ft.	Ft.	Ft.	Ft.	Ft.	Ft.	Ft.	Ft.	Ft.
0.5	0.0	0.0	0.0	0.0	0.0	0.0	0.0	0.1	0.1	0.1	0.1	0.2	0.2	0.2	0.2
1.0	0.0	0.0	0.0	0.0	0.1	0.1	0.1	0.1	0.2	0.2	0.3	0.3	0.4	0.4	0.5
1.5	0.0	0.0	0.0	0.1	0.1	0.1	0.2	0.2	0.3	0.4	0.4	0.5	0.6	0.7	0.8
2.0	0.0	0.0	0.0	0.1	0.1	0.2	0.3	0.3	0.4	0.5	0.6	0.7	0.8	0.9	1.0
2.5	0.0	0.0	0.1	0.1	0.2	0.2	0.3	0.4	0.5	0.6	0.7	0.9	1.0	1.1	1.2
3.0	0.0	0.0	0.1	0.1	0.2	0.3	0.4	0.5	0.6	0.8	0.9	1.0	1.2	1.3	1.5
3.5	0.0	0.0	0.1	0.2	0.2	0.3	0.4	0.6	0.7	0.9	1.0	1.2	1.4	1.6	1.8
4.0	0.0	0.0	0.1	0.2	0.3	0.4	0.5	0.7	0.8	1.0	1.2	1.4	1.6	1.8	2.0
4.5	0.0	0.0	0.1	0.2	0.3	0.4	0.6	0.7	0.9	1.1	1.3	1.6	1.8	2.0	2.2
5.0	0.0	0.1	0.1	0.2	0.3	0.5	0.6	0.8	1.0	1.2	1.5	1.7	2.0	2.2	2.5
5.5	0.0	0.1	0.1	0.2	0.4	0.5	0.7	0.9	1.1	1.4	1.6	1.9	2.2	2.5	2.8
6.0	0.0	0.1	0.1	0.3	0.4	0.6	0.8	1.0	1.2	1.5	1.8	2.1	2.4	2.7	3.0

Fig 3 The height of tide at any time between high and low water.

Twelfth's rule

The method previously outlined is an accurate means by which the state of the tide can be estimated. There are many occasions when a rule-of-thumb method is needed. This one, probably the most commonly used, assumes that the tide rises and falls at a rate which is proportional to the time between high and low water. It also assumes that the time difference between high and low water is six hours. (There are many cases where the latter assumption is not true and in such cases the rule must be used with caution especially if the difference is large.) The rule assumes that in the first hour after high or low water the tide rises or falls by 1/12th of its range; in the second hour 2/12ths; in the third hour 3/12ths; in the fourth hour 3/12ths; in the fifth hour 2/12ths; and in the sixth hour 1/12th. Using the example opposite we know that the time we are interested in is approximately two hours after high water so, using the twelfth's rule, the tide should have dropped by 1/12th+ 2/12ths or 1/4 of its range. This gives us a figure of 0.7ft. Deducting this figure from the height of high water gives a height at 13.30 of 2.6ft. The difference (0.2ft) between this result and the calculated one is really insignificant for the purposes of practical navigation.

Shaping a course

The basis of navigation is to get from one place to another with the help of any equipment available. To do so you must determine in advance which heading to steer so that you reach your destination. This is known as shaping a course. When the appropriate heading is obtained, and the boat set on it, you will still have to check periodically to make sure the boat is actually continuing on the correct course, or if you wish to find out where it is at any given time. This checking procedure is done by one of two means: by fixing (see page 249) or by plotting the position. The former is the more accurate, but it is not always possible to do it. Plotting involves using a similar technique to shaping a course. Using a past position and recorded information, the boat's latest position is worked out. Both shaping and plotting courses require the use of a chart, tidal information from a tidal atlas, chart or pilot book, and information from the log and compass as well as basic plotting instruments. Since shaping and plotting courses are the corner-stones of navigation, you should practice laying off courses and measuring distances until you are thoroughly familiar with them, and can use the plotting instruments accurately. You have the choice of doing all your chartwork using degrees true or degrees magnetic for your plotting (see page 242). The choice is yours, although working in magnetic is to be recommended for small boat navigation since it simplifies your work.

Whichever method you use, make sure that you are consistent, or mistakes will occur. Another area in which you must also be consistent is in the use of symbols and abbreviations, so that your course plotting is clear both to yourself and to anyone who may be helping you.

Symbols

Symbols are normally used when plotting or shaping a course, or when fixing a position, as it is quicker and easier, and takes up less room on the chart. The ones shown below are those which are commonly used. Time is most conveniently written using the 24 hour clock: 21.30, for example; but it is vital that you identify the time zone you are using.

Key

°T	Degrees true
°M	Degrees magnetic (°T corrected for variation)
°C	Degrees compass (°M corrected for deviation)
X	DR (deduced position or dead reckoning position)
△	EP (estimated position)
→	Wake course
→→	Track
→→→	Tidal stream or current
⊙	Fix
←→	Position line
←←→→	Transferred position line

Marking the track

The first stage in shaping a course is to pencil in a line on the chart from your point of departure to the destination. This line is known as the track. In many cases, it will not be possible to sail a direct line because of having to tack but this is dealt with on page 254. Here the situation under consideration is when you can steer a direct course under power or with a fair wind. In the diagram, right, a line is drawn between two points, the departure point, A, to the destination, B. To shape a course properly you have to take into consideration any factors which might cause the boat to deviate from the required course, and then make the appropriate allowance so that you can steer the boat as necessary to arrive at B.

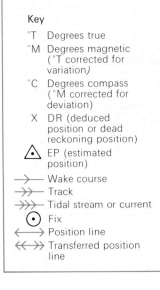

Leeway

One of the factors which will cause the boat's actual track to differ from the required direction is leeway (also described on page 73). The amount of leeway depends on the relative direction of the wind to the boat. A boat on a close-hauled course will make more leeway than on a reach. The type and shape of boat also affects the amount of leeway. Modern boats, well-sailed, will not make much leeway although small cruisers with high topsides and shallow hulls may do so. To assess the amount of leeway, take a bearing on the wake of the boat using a hand bearing compass and compare this with the heading being steered (see right). Most modern boats make an average leeway of 2° to 6° when close-hauled. The course the boat travels through the water is known as the wake course, and the difference between this and the course steered should be noted. A wake course, when plotted on the chart, is marked with a single arrow.

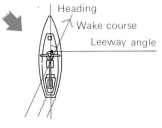

Note the difference between the heading and the wake course

Allowing for tides

Tidal streams and currents are usually the major cause of a boat not actually following the heading steered. When a boat is sailing in tidal waters or in strong currents it will affect the boat's speed and/or direction over the ground. The slower the boat sails, the greater the effect of the tidal stream or current. In the simple cases, right, the tidal stream is flowing parallel to the boat's course but in both cases makes a significant difference to the boat's speed over the ground. In both cases we can assume the boat's speed through the water is 4 Kn and the tidal stream is running at 1 Kn. When the tidal stream is against you your speed over the ground is only 3 Kn – whereas with the tide with you it will be 5 Kn. The cases where the tidal stream is flowing parallel to the track means that the wake course and the track will be on the same straight line but of different lengths. To find out how long a particular leg will take, you need to divide the total distance by the speed over the ground. When the stream is not setting parallel to the required track the effect is as shown, bottom left.

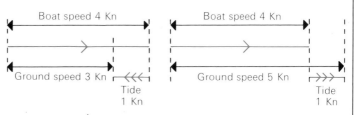

Boat speed 4 Kn   Boat speed 4 Kn

Ground speed 3 Kn   Tide 1 Kn   Ground speed 5 Kn   Tide 1 Kn

How to shape a course

To shape a course, draw a line on the chart between the departure point, A, and the destination, B. Mark the line with two arrowheads. Look up the direction and strength of the tidal stream for the appropriate time; in this case, the tide is flowing at 120°M at 1 Kn. From point A, draw a line along 120°M and measure it for 1M (to C). Mark the line with three arrowheads. The point C is the one where the tide would take the boat if it drifted for one hour. Decide what the likely speed of the boat will be, in this case 4 Kn, and, using the same scale as for A–C (normally the latitude scale), open the compasses to 4M. With the point of the compasses on C, draw an arc to cut A–B or its extension at D. Join C–D and mark the line with a single arrowhead. Measure the direction of C–D with a protractor or parallel rulers. This is the wake course or the direction the boat is required to travel through the water. Note that the boat never goes near C – it follows the track line. The speed of the boat over the ground is given by the length of A–D. A correction must be applied to windward of the wake course to allow for leeway (if necessary) to get the course to steer and this is then converted to °C, before it is given to the helmsman to steer.

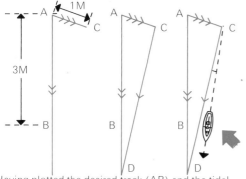

1M
3M

Having plotted the desired track (AB) and the tidal vector (AC) to find the wake course (CD), leeway must be allowed for if it is present. This gives the heading which is converted to a course to steer in °C.

Allowing for more than one tide

In most cases more than one hour of tide will affect you during a passage and this can be allowed for in one of two ways. Having drawn the required track on the chart check to see if there are any dangers to either side which mean that you must keep to the track line. If so, proceed as follows (see right) Find the direction and speed of the tide for the first hour. Lay this off from A. Find the wake course (C–D). Repeat the procedure for each subsequent hour of the passage. Each course has to be converted into courses to steer allowing for leeway and any variation or deviation. Where there are no dangers to be avoided an alternative method can be used. Estimate how long the passage will take. From A, draw in the tidal line for the next hour. Repeat for each subsequent hour of tide to get point C in the diagram on the right. Open the compasses to the distance you estimate the boat will sail through the water during the number of hours of tide allowed for (in this example it is boat speed times 4 hours). With the point of the compasses on C, inscribe an arc to cut A–B. This gives the line C–B, which is the wake course for the entire passage. This is converted as before to a course to steer.

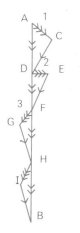

A wake course is found for each hour so the boat follows the track.

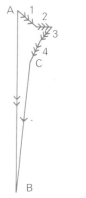

One wake course is found but the boat will not follow the track.

Plotting procedure

As we have seen the navigator shapes a course to sail from A to B, allowing for various factors which may set the boat off course. However carefully this is done it is quite likely that when the actual leg is sailed one or more factors may differ from their assumed direction or speed. For instance, the boat's speed through the water may be greater or less than estimated, leeway experienced may not be as predicted, the tidal stream may be at variance with the available data or the helmsman may not hold to the planned heading for various reasons (see Errors page 255). Because of these discrepancies between planned and actual events, the navigator must periodically plot his position, which will be his best possible estimate of the boat's position at the time. The most accurate way of determining actual position, apart from sailing alongside a navigation mark, is to fix the position by using observation of fixed objects (as described opposite). When this is not possible, the navigator must be able to plot the boat's estimated position using all the

information at his disposal. To do this it is vital that a record of all the courses steered, and times and distances travelled, is kept in the logbook. Without this record, it is impossible to plot an estimated position. The other necessity is to have a firm reference position from which to work. This means the log should be put back to zero, or the reading noted, and the time and course steered should also be noted, when at a fixed position at the departure point. If, during the passage, you obtain a new reference position, either by closing with a mark or by obtaining a fix (which can be confirmed by another shortly afterwards), the original reference point becomes irrelevant and all future plotting (or shaping) can be done from the new reference position. You should always make an appropriate entry in the log book whenever any new information is available. When beating to windward, make sure that every tack is logged immediately, with the new heading, the time and log reading, as well as any other relevant information.

How to plot a course

To plot the course the following procedure is followed. From the logbook obtain the course steered (see Errors, page 255) and convert this to °M by applying deviation (if chart work is done in °T also apply variation). Estimate the amount of leeway and apply to leeward of the course steered. This gives the direction of the wake course. From the reference point, lay off this line. Measure the distance sailed through the water since leaving point A using the

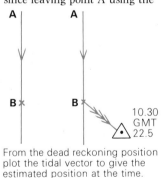

From the dead reckoning position plot the tidal vector to give the estimated position at the time.

latitude scale at the side of the chart and mark this position with an X and the time. This position is known as the dead reckoning (DR) position. Strictly speaking, the DR position should not take into account the effect of leeway but for practical purposes it is easiest if it is allowed for before plotting the wake course. (The term dead reckoning can also be used in a general way to mean the general business of plotting position, but this must not be confused with the DR position.) From the DR position, lay off a line in the direction of the tidal stream experienced since leaving point A, and mark the line with three arrowheads. Measure along the tide line the distance the tide has pushed the boat in the time since leaving A using the latitude scale. (If you are working in °M remember to convert tidal stream information to °M before plotting.) Mark this position, as shown and write the time and log reading alongside it. This is the estimated position at that time.

Estimated and actual position differences

There will be some instances when the information used to plot the EP varies from the actual situation. For this reason the boat's position should be fixed at regular intervals (see page 249). If this is done, and the fix differs from the EP, the difference between them can give useful information. If you are sure that the difference is not caused by other errors (see page 255), you can use the difference to compare the actual tidal situation with what was predicted. For instance, at 1100 hours a fix is obtained and the EP is plotted (below). Having checked for errors, the difference between them suggests that the tidal stream is running about 50 per cent more strongly than was thought. You can then correct the tidal information accordingly.

In this example the EP has been plotted at 1100 hrs and a fix has been taken at the same time. The difference between the two can give information on the actual tidal stream.

Once the first estimated position, or EP, has been plotted, further EPs are plotted from the first:

Fixing position

Being able to fix the position of your boat is an essential part of navigation. Having obtained an estimated position of the boat by plotting the position using logged information in relation to a reference point, the next step is to check the accuracy of your course. This is normally done by taking a fix—in other words by taking a position line from the boat to a visible object, marked on the chart, and by crossing this line with at least one other similar position line. The intersection point will give you the boat's position. There is a choice of method for securing a position line. On most cruising boats, one of the commonest ways is to use visual bearings, normally taken with a hand bearing compass. Other methods are shown on the following pages and a radio direction finder which can also be used is described on page 252. With two of the methods, the position can be assessed differently. In one it is done by finding the range of a given object from your boat. From this range you will get a circular position line. Whichever method you use, you must positively identify the chosen object on the chart. Make sure no error is made, because it will invalidate your findings. Depth soundings can also be used to give a good position fix, either by following a contour line (shown on page 253) or by taking a series of them and comparing them with the soundings marked on the chart. There is no reason why ranges should not also be used for position fixing. They are explained in detail on page 257.

Fix by compass bearings

The most common type of fix is one obtained from crossing two or three position lines found by compass bearings on charted objects. If using only two position lines try and make sure that they cross at about 90° to each other. Three position lines should preferably cross at about 60° to each other. The great advantage of using three objects is that any error is likely to be obvious. In practice, the three lines are unlikely to meet at one point but will form instead a "cocked hat" or error triangle, the size of which is a good guide to the accuracy of the bearings. If the triangle is large the bearings must be checked. The position of the boat is usually taken to be at the center of the triangle but in fact the actual position need not be in the triangle at all. If you are close to any danger a safer procedure is to draw a circle around the center of the triangle with a radius equal to twice the length of the longest side of the triangle. Then take your position at the point on the circle most badly placed in relation to any possible danger.

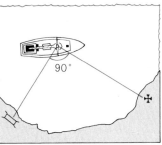

When only two positions lines are used to obtain a fix they should cross at a 90° angle for accurate results.

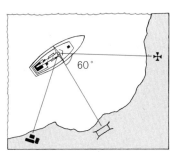

If three objects can be used accurate results will be obtained if they cross at an angle of about 60°.

Taking a compass bearing

Most cruising yachtsmen use the hand bearing compass for obtaining a position line. To make position fixing accurate attention should be paid to how the bearing is taken. Choose a place on the boat at least 2 m (6 ft) away from any large ferrous metal object and brace yourself as securely as possible: in the companionway of the boat, or in front of the mast. If the latter, use your safety harness and sit down, so that both hands are free. Having identified the object on the chart, line up the compass with the object using the sighting "v" or ring. Let the compass card settle down before noting the bearing. Take three bearings on each object and average them out for the final bearing. If possible, get someone to record the bearings as you call them out, and get him to repeat them back to you. To plot the bearing on the chart, using your chosen plotting instrument lay off a line from the object in the reciprocal direction of the bearing obtained from the boat and mark it with a single arrowhead. Correct from magnetic to true, if you work in true on the chart.

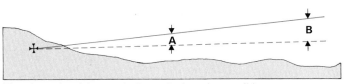

The closer the object to the boat, the less the possible error. At A, a small error is considerably less than at B.

Single position lines

Sometimes only one object suitable for a visual bearing is in sight which means that only one position line can be obtained. This is not a serious problem as there are several ways of checking your position even if you can only get one position line. If it is parallel, or nearly parallel, with the required track of the boat, it will show whether or not the track is being followed. Alternatively, if the position line cuts the track at an angle of approximately 90°, the point where the position line crosses the track can be used to check upon your estimated speed over the ground. A single position line from a range can be used to enter or leave a harbor, or to act as a clearing line. A single bearing can also be used as a clearing line to avoid a danger by keeping to one side or other of the line, as appropriate.

Running fix

When you use a single object from which you take several bearings at specific intervals it is known as a running fix. It is not as accurate as the simultaneous fix described earlier but it can be useful. A first bearing is taken on the object and plotted on the chart, together with the time and the log reading. When the bearing of the object has altered enough to give a good angle of cut with the first line (between 50° - 100°) you take a second bearing of the same object and plot it, with the time and log reading. Between taking the bearings, the boat has to be kept on a steady, accurately steered course, which is also recorded. If it is assumed that there is no tidal stream to contend with then, when both bearings have been plotted, the course sailed over the ground between the bearings is laid off, allowing for any leeway (the wake course) from any point on the first position line. You measure along the wake course the distance sailed in the time between taking the bearings, as measured with your log recordings. Then, using a parallel ruler or other plotting instruments, draw a line through this point, parallel with your first position line. This is known as an advanced position line and is marked as such with two arrowheads. Where the transferred line crosses the second line is the position of the boat at the time of taking the second bearing and it is marked with a circle and the time. Of course, the accuracy of this type of fix depends on the accuracy of the estimation of direction and distance travelled over the ground between the bearings. When a tidal stream complicates the issue, as is often the case, the fix is suspect because the accuracy of the tidal information is usually in doubt. You have to work out from the tidal atlas the direction and rate of the tidal stream during the period between taking the bearings, and add it to the wake course to get your actual movement over the ground. However, the running fix is a useful technique to know about and the accuracy can be improved if two bearings can be transferred up to the time of a third bearing so that you then obtain a triangle of error, the size of which can be used to assess the accuracy of the information you have obtained.

The running fix can be used even when the bearings cannot be obtained from the same object. For instance, you may be sailing along a coast in bad visibility but still manage to obtain a single position line on one object before it disappears from view again. Sometime later you may sight another different object and take a bearing of that and plot the position line. The first position line can then be transferred up to the time of the second, as before.

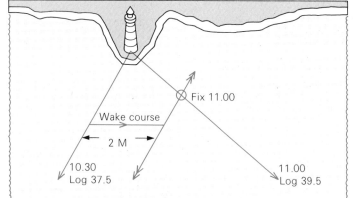

When a tidal stream does not complicate matters, the first position line is advanced through the end of the wake course.

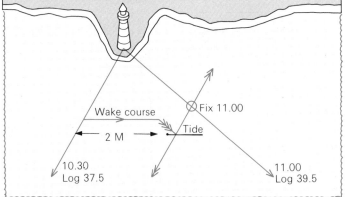

If a tidal stream is present, its effect must be allowed for, before transferring the first position line.

Rising and dipping horizon

It can be very useful on occasions to be able to gauge your distance from a particular object, such as when closing or leaving a coast at night on which a lighthouse is situated and the height of which is marked on the chart. The distance is obtained by noting the time when the light just appears over the horizon (when approaching it) or dips below it (when sailing away). It is the direct light that you are interested in, and not the reflected light or loom from the sky which is often visible further afield from the light. If the height of the object and your height of eye are known, you will be able to use the table of rising and dipping distances given in a nautical almanac to find how far away you are from it (the light has to be powerful enough to be visible at its geographical range – its power is normally shown on modern charts as nominal range – broadly 10 nautical miles visibility). The heights are given as above mean high water springs so you will have to make a correction if the tide level is below this by calculating the difference in height and adding it to the height of the charted object. You need to be aware of two things – firstly, that when you see the light it is just rising over the horizon (check it by lowering your own sight line and seeing if it disappears straight away) and secondly, that you have positively identified the object. If a compass bearing is taken on the light an absolute fix is obtained.

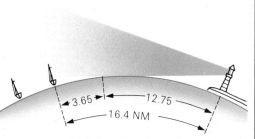

The distance off a light is found by using published tables, once your height of eye and the height of the lighthouse is known.

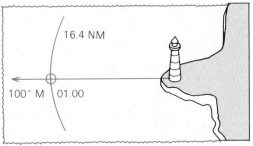

With the distance off the light known, and a bearing taken on it, an absolute fix is obtained.

Depth soundings

The depth sounder tends to get neglected by the navigator but it can be extremely useful. Firstly make sure it is accurate and reads the depth from the surface. In tidal waters you will have to make any necessary corrections for the height of the tide above chart datum and then subtract it from all depth readings. You can use the depth sounder to confirm an estimated position or a position obtained by a fix if the depth agrees with that given on the chart at the fix position. The depth sounder can also be used on its own, either to follow a contour line (very useful in fog) or to take a series of depth readings, corrected to chart datum, so that they can be compared with the depth soundings on the chart. To make use of this method, the boat has to be held on an accurate course at a steady speed, if possible, and any tidal stream needs to be known. What you do is simply to note the depth readings at specific times and the log readings at the same time. Take a piece of tracing paper and stick it over the chart so that the edges line up with the grid lines. On the tracing paper, plot the boat's track between the times of the first and last depth reading. Along the wake course, mark the distance intervals between the soundings, then from these points draw lines, parallel to the tide line, to cut the track line. Where these lines cut the track mark the appropriate depth readings. Now move the tracing paper, keeping the edges parallel to the grid lines, until the first sounding is at the estimated position at the time the sounding was taken. Check if all the soundings along the track line correspond with the depths marked on the chart. If they do not, move the paper, keeping it lined up, until a good fit is obtained between the actual soundings and those marked on the chart. If no other place exists which provides a good fit the position of the last sounding should be the boat's position at that time.

Time	Log reading	Distance between soundings	Soundings
1600	20.1		22m
		0.5	
1610	20.6		23m
		0.5	
1620	21.1		25m
		0.5	
1630	21.6		12m
		0.5	
1640	22.1		5m

To work out your position using a line of soundings, a record is kept of the time, the log reading and the sounding at regular intervals. The soundings are marked on the track line and compared with soundings printed on the chart to find the position at the last sounding.

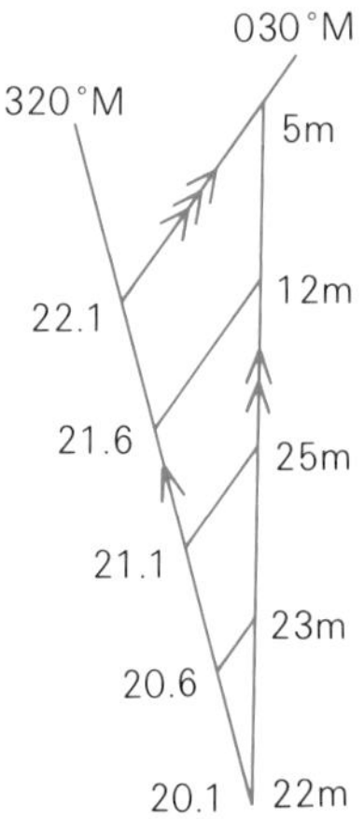

030°M
320°M
5m
22.1
12m
21.6
25m
21.1
23m
20.6
20.1 22m

Radio aids

The principal radio aid to navigation is the radio direction finding (RDF) set. This is a simple system which enables you to take a bearing on a signal from a transmitting station and cross it with bearings from other stations to help you fix your position. Marine transmitting beacons are positioned around many coastlines and on light ships. A maximum of six beacons, each with their own identification signal, transmit a continuous tone in turn on the same fre-quency. Information relating to the location of these beacons and the frequencies on which they transmit can be found in nautical almanacs and radio lists, and they are often marked on charts. The usefulness of an RDF set is limited by its inability to determine the distance from the radio beacon. Some sailors nowadays, however, use Loran-C, a long-range aid to navigation, which is more expensive than traditional RDF equipment but more accurate.

RDF equipment

Your RDF set should ideally be one, such as the model shown right, which provides a quick and accurate bearing on a station. If your boat is constructed of steel you will need a set with an automatically operating loop aerial fitted to the mast head.

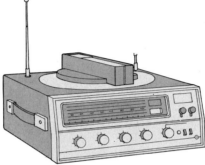

The RDF set, left, is a four-band unit which provides navigable fixes on both AM and Beacon bands. It has a dial which can be illuminated for night-reading and works both on battery and on the boat's power supply.

Using RDF

To fix your position using RDF, first find out which beacons are nearest and on which frequency the group of beacons transmits. Tune in the receiver and the aerial to the given frequency and identify the code signal. When the continuous tone starts, take the aerial unit and start to turn it in a horizontal plane. Listen to the sound and note the position of the aerial when the signal is at its weakest or disappears. This point is known as the null. When the aerial is in this position it is pointing either towards or away from the source of the signal. Use the compass to take a bearing and plot the line on your chart from the beacon. Usually it will be obvious which side of the beacon you are on. Repeat the process with at least one, but preferably more, beacons and plot the bearings. Your approximate position is where all the lines intersect.

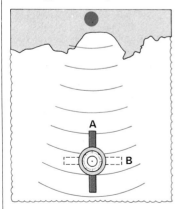

A is the null. B is where the signal is strongest.

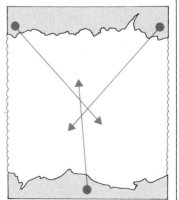

To fix your position, plot the bearings of two or more beacons.

Loran-C

Loran is a long-range aid to navigation which has been in use for a number of years. The original system, Loran-A, is now being replaced by the more accurate Loran-C. To use this system a special receiver is needed which is relatively complex and expensive. In use a pair of on-shore transmitters send out signals that are received and processed by the receiver to give a position line. A second position line is obtained in the same way to give a fix. The position can be found by the use of tables or by plotting on a special chart. More expensive automatic receivers are available which, when started at a known location, give a direct position in latitude and longitude, as well as direction and distance to a pre-set point and other useful information. Loran-C can give very precise positions accurate to within 200 yds at a range of up to 1200 miles. This means that it is a valuable supplement to celestial navigation, providing full-time, all-weather fixes. It does, however, rely on the accurate operation of electronic equipment on board and ashore.

Navigating in fog

Fog is as much a problem to the navigator as it is to the skipper. If you are the navigator, you need to know in advance whether to expect fog, and you should make any necessary preparations before it sets in. The most important point is to determine your position as accurately as possible before visibility is impaired. As pilotage is impossible, you can only find your position by dead reckoning (see page 248) and by using non-visual fixing techniques. Because fog is usually accompanied by lack of wind, your dead reckoning could easily be innaccurate. Most logs tend to under-read when the boat is sailing slowly, and the course steered by the helmsman may also be incorrect, as with little steerage way on, he has less control over the boat. Although motoring would ease the problem from the navigator's point of view it would exacerbate it from the skipper's, because the noise of the engine makes it impossible to hear if other vessels are approaching.

If you are using dead reckoning, you need to take great care to check all the tidal information to make sure that your estimated positions are as accurate as possible. Steering errors can be minimized by putting a crewman as a watch on the course steered. If fog suddenly descends in navigable water, near a navigation buoy, the boat should be sailed over to it where it can be kept in sight (known as closing with a buoy), either by heaving-to close by or by sailing around it in circles until you have time to sort out your plotting and to plan the next move.

Obtaining a fix

In fog there are very few ways of obtaining a position fix. If you have a Loran C receiver on your boat, it can be used to obtain an accurate fix. If you only have a radio direction finding set, however, it pays, when fog is forecast, to check it for accuracy against a number of visual fixes. If you have failed to do this in time, use the method of closing with a buoy, if possible, and take bearings from this point to check the accuracy. Take as many bearings in fog as possible as it will help show up any wrong ones, and compare the RDF fixes with your estimated position, starting to check them if they appear to differ appreciably. RDF can be used as a homing aid to enter a harbor or to arrive in the approaches of one, as some harbor entrances have directional radio beacons which will guide you in provided you pick up a continuous signal. Non-directional beacons can be used by taking repeated bearings and lining up your headings on these. However, check that the line of approach obtained is a safe one.

Closing with a mark

In some situations, such as when forced to negotiate a harbor entrance in fog or when clarifying a position, you may have to find and identify a navigation mark. This may bring the boat into areas frequented by other shipping which should be avoided where ever possible. Many navigation marks have fog signals and the navigator should have a list of these handy, so that the mark can be identified accurately. Sometimes it is possible to follow a contour line (see below). Using dead reckoning is a more risky operation. If the buoy has not appeared at the expected time, the only solution may be to institute a square search for it, see page 209. Do not just carry on sailing blindly in the hope you will find the next buoy — you almost certainly won't!

Using a depth sounder

A depth sounder (see page 239) can be very useful in fog. Obviously, this is only true if the equipment is accurate and it should therefore be calibrated at the start of each season, and any errors noted. When using the following methods, you must also know the exact height of the tide so that you can reduce the soundings to chart datum for comparison with the chart. You can use the depth sounder either to check a position by confirming that the depth is correct for your position or by using it on its own to take a fix from frequent soundings (see page 251). Another very useful method is to follow a contour of the seabed. As you take the soundings, the boat sails a slightly wavy course (right) to come back onto the contour line. It can be useful as a method for finding a required mark or buoy, or a harbour entrance, but make sure the route is a safe one.

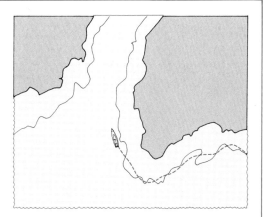

Find an appropriate contour line on the chart of the area and take soundings continually, keeping the boat as near as possible to the position marked by the contour line.

Navigating to windward

There is usually nothing a navigator of a small yacht dislikes more than a beat to windward, except perhaps fog. On all other points of sailing you shape a course towards your objective which the helmsman steers. But when beating, the heading is determined by the direction of the wind and you can only record the information and keep a plot of the boat's position. You are also reliant on the helmsman's ability to steer a consistent close-hauled course. You need to take account of the possibility of wind shifts which could affect the situation significantly for better or for worse (see page 104 and below). The presence of a foul tidal stream is another element you may have to allow for when beating to windward, especially in light winds.

Tack limiting lines

The further a boat sails from a line directly downwind of the objective, the more likely it is to be adversely affected by a wind shift. You must therefore aim to stay as close to this line as possible if you are to gain from a change in the wind direction, or at least to be not too greatly disadvantaged by one. The best way to make sure you do not sail too far from the downwind line is to draw tack limiting lines between which the boat tacks. Draw the downwind line on the chart from the objective, according to the true wind direction. There are two ways of drawing the limiting lines according to whether the beat is expected to be short (near right) or long (far right); they may also be combined.

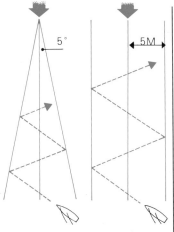

Tack limiting lines can be drawn either diverging from the objective (above left) or parallel to the downwind line (above right).

Taking advantage of wind shifts

There are many situations where you can predict a wind shift from your own observations or from weather forecasts. If you do not expect the wind to shift significantly or consistently, draw the tack limiting lines the same distance or angle from the downwind line on either side. If you are expecting a long-term shift in a particular direction you can plot your tack limiting lines, as shown below, to enable you to use it to the best advantage.

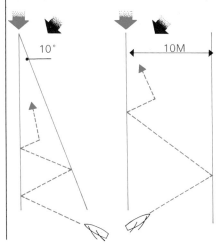

To take advantage of a change in the wind direction, use the downwind line as your first tack limiting line and draw the other on the side of the expected wind shift. When the wind shifts you may be able to steer directly towards your objective.

Tidal streams

The effect of a tidal stream is a significant factor when navigating on any point of sailing, but can be crucial when sailing to windward. If you are in a small boat sailing to windward against a strong tide, it can often prevent you making any headway at all and it may be best to enter a port or anchor until the tide or wind changes direction. If this is not possible, you should try to keep to shallow water, away from the strongest stream. The presence of a strong tide will also affect the strength and direction of the apparent wind. When the boat is beating against the tide the apparent wind speed will be reduced because the boat is being carried downwind. The converse also applies. When the tide is running across the wind on the lee bow an advantage can be gained because it increases the speed of the apparent wind and alters its direction so that the boat is effectively freed and can point higher (see page 104). When the tide is on the windward bow the effect is the reverse, so try and tack when the tide changes to keep it on the lee bow.

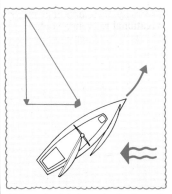

When the tide is on the lee bow the apparent wind shifts to allow the boat to point higher.

Navigational errors

With the resources available on a small boat, it is not possible for any navigator to ensure complete accuracy. Errors are something that you must accept and understand. It must be made clear that there is a difference between errors, with which we are dealing here, and mistakes. Errors are usually associated with inherent inaccuracies in instruments or in navigation methods and are unavoidable but, to some extent, predictable. Mistakes are the result of a miscalculation or a misinterpretation of correct information, and are essentially unpredictable. Every attempt must be made to eradicate mistakes by attention to detail and meticulous checking. It is important to make every effort to find out where errors are likely to exist in your calculations and to what extent, so that you can allow for them and produce accurate results.

Sources of error

Of the instruments, the log and the compass, being the most used are the likeliest sources of error. Compass deviation and errors are discussed on page 238. Error occurs in the log reading, not only as a result of faults in the instrument, which must be checked and allowed for, but also according to the conditions. In light weather the log may under-read, but in large waves it is likely to over-read (below). Towed logs are particularly prone to this type of error. Error may also arise in the reading of instruments, although some may consider this a mistake. This occurs when the dial is not read from directly in front and is known as parallax error (right). The helmsman can also be a source of error. An inexperienced helmsman may steer a zig-zag course which causes the log to over-read. A steering error to windward is also common, especially when on a run in strong winds. The best way to reduce this error is to ask the helmsman which course he estimates he is averaging and make your calculations accordingly. Information given in navigational reference books, particularly for tides, is subject to

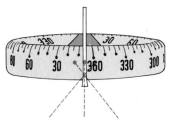

Parallax error occurs when you read the card at an angle as the lubber line will indicate a reading along your line of vision.

error. To prevent your calculations being upset by this type of inaccuracy always check the actual conditions against those predicted in the reference source wherever possible. However, careful the navigator is, some errors in plotting are bound to occur. If rigorous steps are taken to reduce the amount of error, your calculations are still likely to be as much as 3° out, and on small-scale charts distance measurements could be up to half a mile in error. You must also remember that in rough weather, and when the wind has been blowing in the same direction for some time, the surface of the water drifts to leeward and this will affect the course you sail.

Allowing for error

Once you accept that errors exist and understand their causes, and the likely amount, you can allow for them when shaping and plotting a course and fixing your position. Make a list of all the possible errors and estimate their maximum amount. Some errors will cancel each other out and some will be cumulative. Plot the results on your chart. You will end up with a box (see below) in which your estimated position must lie if you have assessed the amount of error honestly, a much better situation than having a single dot of your estimated position.

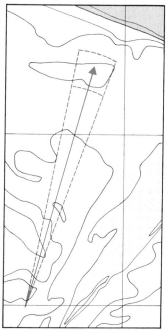

The solid line marks your intended course. With no tide, the possible error in bearing and in distance sailed is marked. Your estimated position is shown by the dotted box.

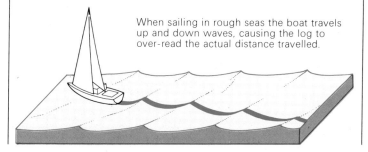

When sailing in rough seas the boat travels up and down waves, causing the log to over-read the actual distance travelled.

Pilotage

Pilotage, the technique of navigation by eye, uses no navigation equipment, apart from charts, pilot books and binoculars and maybe a hand bearing compass. It is used in good visibility when in sight of land. However, although other instruments are not used, they should be on board the boat in case visibility deteriorates, and in case your passage should take you out of sight of land.

If you are to become a good pilot, you need to be able to read a chart and relate the information to what you see about you. One of the pitfalls of pilotage is that many sections of the coastline look remarkably similar when seen from the sea and it is often easy to convince yourself, quite erroneously, that the coastline in front of you is the part you wish to see. You need to be careful about identifying navigation marks for the same reasons. If you expect to see a particular buoy, it is surprising how quickly you convince yourself that the buoy you can see is the one you want. You need to be very disciplined about checking your information and guarding against errors of this nature. The art of successful pilotage is to move from one known safe position to the next, by checking and rechecking the information you have. Needless to say, the process naturally breaks down if you start to work on assumptions rather than facts. Pilotage in familiar waters is usually much easier but even here errors can occur from false assumptions. A harbor which you know well in daylight may appear to have different characteristics at night, and you could be confused unless you have done your homework on light sequences of buoys and so on beforehand (see page 262). One of the main problems for pilots is trying to make accurate judgments of distance at sea. Even the most experienced find it difficult and the inexperienced can be hopelessly wrong, so if you have an inexperienced crew aboard, be wary about asking them to judge distances.

One of the main ways of establishing your position when piloting a boat is to take ranges (see also page 105). When the navigator sees two objects which are in line with each other he knows his boat must be somewhere on an extension of the line drawn through the objects. You can use ranges in several different ways (see opposite). However, you must ensure that the objects are shown on your chart. If you are piloting your boat along a channel or in and out of harbor, for example, you should have checked beforehand on the chart which object

Using binoculars

Binoculars are a useful aid when piloting but only if they are correctly used. They must be kept clean and dry, and if a sachet of silica-gel is put in the storage space it will keep the binoculars moisture-free. Make sure that the pair you have is not too heavy for you to hold comfortably, or your hands will shake when using them. The binoculars should have a magnification no greater than seven times; anything larger is unsuitable for use on a boat. Adjust the neck strap so that the binoculars sit high on the chest and always use the strap or you will lose them sooner or later. Your binoculars may have individual adjustments on each eyepiece. If so, adjust them for clarity, using your strongest eye first. The binoculars will also probably have a scale measuring the distance or angle between the eyepieces which also have to be adjusted. When the eyepieces fit closely to each eye, the binoculars are opened by the correct amount. You can determine whether your binoculars are functioning properly by trial and error or you could consult your optician. When using binoculars do not keep them to your eyes for too long at a time, or you may suffer eyestrain.

might be useful to you for taking ranges. The objects you use should conform to certain criteria: they should be clearly visible; they should not be easy to confuse with any other object; they must be on the chart; they should be in a fixed position and they should neither be too close together nor too close to your boat. Although buoys can be used for LOPs, they move slightly with the wind and tide and are not really satisfactory. Certainly, they are better than nothing, but they shouldn't be used where accurate pilotage is required, as for example in rock-strewn waters. Marks on land are often used – lighthouses, beacons, buildings or prominent natural features. Lighthouses and beacons are shown on the chart and are readily identifiable but buildings, although shown on the chart as conspicuous, may be obscured on the skyline by newer buildings. Natural landmarks are often useful but they must be prominent – a large rounded hill is less useful than a unusually shaped rocky outcrop. Although isolated rocks can be useful, their height, size and shape should be studied on the chart to check their position, and in tidal waters it must be remembered that the appearance of the rock could change markedly between high and low water. The background could also obscure a rock or similar object and this can be checked beforehand on the chart.

Using ranges

When choosing two marks as sources for lines of position, make sure they are on the same side of the boat, or it will be impossible to line them up. Landmarks behind the boat are just as useful as those ahead. A beam bearing is often used to check progress against a foul tide or for indicating a point at which to alter course. Ranges at a harbor or river mouth are usually known as leading marks. They are normally marked on charts and in pilot books with the bearing given (usually in degrees true) for when they are in line. Landmarks not quite in line can be used as a clearing line, provided you know whether to keep them "open" or "closed".

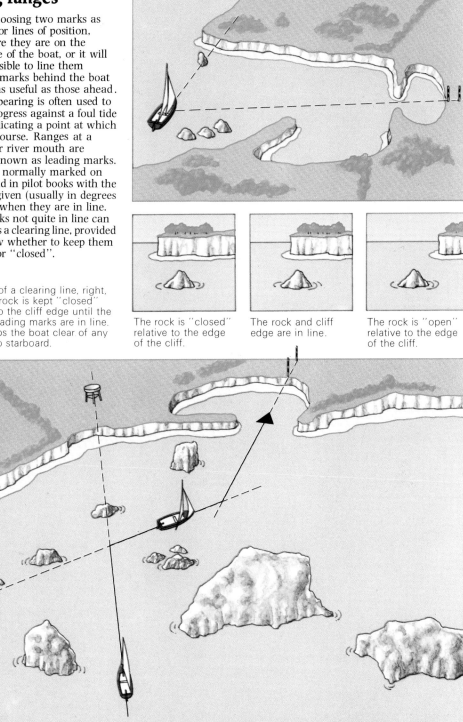

The use of a clearing line, right, where a rock is kept "closed" relative to the cliff edge until the harbor leading marks are in line. This keeps the boat clear of any danger to starboard.

The rock is "closed" relative to the edge of the cliff.

The rock and cliff edge are in line.

The rock is "open" relative to the edge of the cliff.

Ranges can often be used in rock strewn waters to ensure safe pilotage. The boat, above, sails first on a line from ahead, between the water tower and the rock, then turns to starboard when on the line between the two rocks on the left. When the boat is on the leading line it can turn to enter harbor.

Passage planning

Although it is possible to set off on a passage without first having made a passage plan, it is certainly not to be recommended. At the very least, it is almost bound to result in an inefficient passage, and at worst, it may put you, your crew and your boat in danger. Laborious and painstaking though it may seem, planning will pay dividends when you are on the passage. Most people only have a limited amount of time to devote to sailing, and it therefore makes sense to use that time as effectively as possible. When undertaking a cruise – a series of passages over a period of several days or more – it is essential to spend time ashore planning the trip out first,

so that you leave more time afloat for the actual business of sailing. Working at leisure at home also helps reduce the likelihood of mistakes.

A lot of small boats sail with a family crew where the skipper is also the navigator. In these circumstances, it is essential for him to reduce the navigation work load as much as possible, so that he can perform his role as skipper efficiently and safely, and so he himself can get as much pleasure as possible from the cruise. In any harbor it is all-too-common to see a small boat arrive with an exhausted and irritable skipper-cum-navigator in charge, and a glum and resentful family as crew.

Making the plan

Having armed yourself with all the reference material and a notepad, pencil, and eraser, your first task is to check all your reference material (charts, pilot books and so on) to make sure that you have all you need, and that it is up-to-date. If the charts are not, correct them. You need to make sure you have any supplements that have been issued to your almanac, and see that you have the full chart cover for the area in which you intend to make your passage or cruise, together with any emergency cover you may need for areas around the chosen one, in case of bad weather or a change of plan.

It helps to make the initial plan using a small-scale chart which shows both the departure point and the destination. Draw in pencil lightly, the proposed track of the boat between your departure point and your destination.

Plan to keep a good distance, say five nautical miles, off any possible lee shores or other dangerous coastlines. Avoid any area where tidal races or overfalls (shallow water with short, breaking waves) could be expected, such as around headlands. If there are any unmarked dangers, give them a wide berth by day and an even wider one at night. Having drawn in the first track lines, go over them again from end to end in conjunction with the sailing directions or pilot books, checking for any possible dangers on or near the route, or anything else that may require a change to the

planned track. If there are any traffic separation schemes on the route, plan to use the inshore zone; if it is necessary to cross the lane, plan to do so at right angles to the lanes (see also page 229). Having settled on a track, using dividers, measure the full distance, and that of any intermediate legs between turning points, if any. Then you must decide on a likely average speed on which to base your passage plan. At this point, many navigators become wildly optimistic and use an average speed which they are highly unlikely to sustain. Be honest with yourself instead and set a speed which you can reasonably expect to average, either by motoring or motor-sailing if the wind drops. If a beat is likely during the passage, the speed made good to windward may only be half of what it would be on a "free" (offwind) leg. You may prefer to make two separate plans for two possible speeds. Using the expected speed, work out the approximate time for the passage and for each intermediate leg. Add on to this a time for clearing the departure harbor and entering the destination harbor (another common source of under-estimation – it can take two or three hours to get into or out of a harbor and to tie up or leave). The tide tables should then be referred to, and the days and dates of the planned passage pencilled in on the margin of each page together with the appropriate times from the tide table, starting

with the page relating to high water, and then working forwards and backwards page by page (see also pages 244–5). Check to see whether the tides for the days in question are at springs or neaps or in between, and if necessary, work out a correction factor for interpolation between springs and neaps and include this in the pencilled notes. (It helps to preserve the atlas if clear plastic is stuck on the margins and the notes written with a chinagraph pencil.) The next step in improving the plan is to see if there are any critical times at which you must arrive at specific points. Check whatever information there is available about your destination. Read the information in the pilot books and on the charts, and make notes of relevant details. You need to know, for example, if there are any restrictions to entry, such as bars at the harbor entrance, which limit the times of entry. With this information organized you will have a preferred time (or several times) for arrival at your destination. Another consideration is the landfall (when you sight the coast) itself. You may prefer a landfall at night if the coast is well lit and difficult to identify by day, or it may be better to make the landfall in daylight. Also you may decide to approach the coast to one side or the other of the harbor. This is useful on a coast with few landmarks as it means the navigator knows in which direction to turn when the coast is sighted. Otherwise, if a course is set for the harbor and your dead-reckoning is slightly out, the coast may appear with no sign of the harbor. In this case the navigator is unlikely to know on which side of it he is. If this method is used for making a landfall, allowance must be made for any extra distance involved and the time it involves. Having sorted out any landfall considerations, see how these affect the best times of arrival at the destination. If, having checked on the arrival situation, there are limits to the time you can arrive, this will affect the time you need to plan your departure. Another thing which may affect departure times is the existence of tidal gates *en route*. This may be a headland or channel which is impossible to pass on a foul tide. If any of these restrictions exist, it will be necessary to work your departure time backwards from these points, using the distances already measured and the estimated speed or speeds. If other restrictions don't prevent it, try to time your departure to get the maximum amount of fair tidal stream, and the minimum of foul, during the passage. The tide tables should be consulted in conjunction with the estimated boat speed to determine a suitable departure time. Once you have a departure time (from the harbor entrance or where-ever you set your first course), add to it the time necessary for reaching the departure point from your moorings to find the latest time by which you must leave the mooring. Having decided on a firm time of departure, work forwards again through the whole passage, using the tide tables, and work out times and distances for each leg and, say, at three hourly intervals along legs, correcting the boat speed by working out the effect on it of the tidal stream, if any. Allow safety margins in both distance and speed and also be pessimistic when allowing for tidal streams.

Passage notes

One of the most useful things that can be done during the planning stage is the compilation of quick-reference check lists to save work during the passage. These should include a list and description of land or sea marks to be passed on the way starting from the departure point, marking the distances between them and the magnetic bearing of the track line. The latter will enable you to set a rough preliminary course when you reach a turning point while you work out your actual required course with reference to the tidal information. This list can also include an approximate ETA for each point, based on the planned speed or speeds. Another list should be made for all the navigational marks you expect to sight in the order in which they should appear. Include full information of the marks in each case including shape (you could draw each buoy), color and so on. For the parts of the passage to be covered at night, include all navigation lights, noting the full information available. Also include information on any fog signals near the track. Having drawn up a list covering the required track, make another of any marks, lights or fog signals which may be seen or heard if you are off course, or if you have to enter another harbor for any reason. Make sure the two lists cannot be confused. Make another list of RDF beacons

which you could use during the passage and group together those which have the same frequency. Note the call sign, range and time of transmission of each. You should also have a list containing any useful information on harbors you will, or may have, to enter during the passage, not forgetting the destination. Use a pilot book and a large scale chart to make this list. Typical information would normally include safe entry times and weather conditions, restrictions to entry, approach bearings, traffic control signals, port radio frequency (if you have VHF) and useful transits or leading marks together with their bearing.

Emergency plan
You must next consider any possible occurrence that may result in your having to change your plan while on passage. The usual reason for this would be bad weather but there could be other unforeseen ones. Consider your track, leg by leg, and list all possible refuge ports, bearing in mind the likelihood of bad weather from all or any direction. Check that your chart list is sufficient for these ports, and make sure it includes a large-scale chart of each port and its approaches, and that your sailing directions or pilot books cover these ports. Make a similar list of those mentioned to cover any such possible change of plans.

Passage planning at a well lit desk at home is much easier than working in a pitching boat and greatly simplifies the work.

Buoyage

Aids to navigation are used to show the sailor where he is, and where it is safe for him to go. These aids are represented on charts by the use of symbols (the full list of the symbols and their explanation can be found in the booklet Chart No. 1 published by the Department of Defense) and range from lighthouses, buoys and day beacons, to Loran and other electronic systems. The various aids can be identified by their shape and color, and, if they have them, their light characteristics. The lights are also marked on the chart using symbols. Some have a sound signal, while others are designed to reflect radar signals.

The United States has more than one buoyage system but the one described and illustrated here is the main one. Others include the buoyage system used on the Intracoastal Waterway, the Western Rivers and the Uniform State Waterway Marking System. In many foreign waters agreement has been reached to introduce the system known as IALA A, and it is likely that in the next few years the United States will introduce a similar system to be known as IALA B.

A typical example of the aids to navigation seen when approaching a river from seaward.

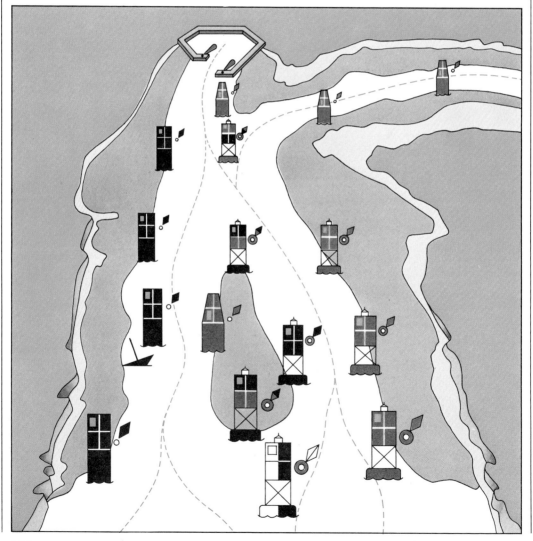

Lateral marks

The basic system used in the United States is a lateral system whereby the type of buoy is determined by its place relative to the navigable channel. It depends on there being an easily recognizable direction of buoyage. Thus the buoys are placed as they should be seen when entering a channel from seaward. Obviously this is not always possible and for coastal waters the direction of buoyage is basically clockwise around the United States.

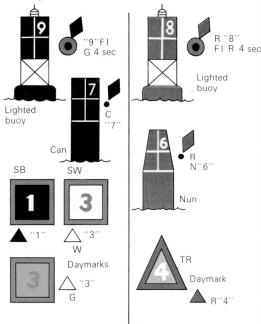

Port-hand buoys
Black can buoys mark the port side of a channel when entering from seaward. They may have odd numbers.

Starboard-hand buoys
Red nun buoys mark the starboard side of a channel when entering from seaward. They may have even numbers.

Other marks

Red and white buoys with horizontal bands mark junctions in a channel or wrecks or obstructions that may be passed on either side. This may only apply when travelling from the sea and if going in the opposite direction you must check on the chart if you can pass on both sides or if there is a danger to one side of the buoy. These can also be lit or unlit buoys or daybeams (see below). These buoys are not numbered but are identified by a letter.

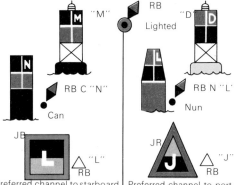

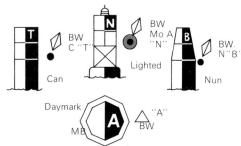

Preferred channel to starboard | Preferred channel to port

Mid-channel and junctions
Mid-channel buoys mark the fairway while junction buoys show the preferred channel.

Non-lateral buoys

As well as the lateral system of buoys the navigator may also encounter several types of special purpose buoys which do not have any lateral significance. These buoys may be lit or unlit and if the latter may be any shape. They are used to signify several things such as a quarantine anchorage, a fish-net area, a dredging area, a survey area, an anchorage, or for other purposes. The one marked "special purpose" (right) is used when no other buoy of either the lateral or non-lateral type is applicable.

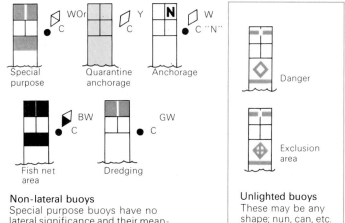

Non-lateral buoys
Special purpose buoys have no lateral significance and their meaning is indicated by their colour.

Unlighted buoys
These may be any shape; nun, can, etc.

Buoyage at night

At night many navigational marks are lit to enable the navigator to identify them. Lighthouses have the most powerful long distance lights. Onshore beacons are usually lit and generally tend to use medium-range lights; leading lights—pairs of beacons used to guide vessels into narrow channels or through harbor entrances—are usually in this group. Buoys are generally lit with short-range lights. Because it is quite easy to confuse lights at night, the different marks are all lit in ways which help to distinguish one mark from another. The characteristic of each light—its color, period and flashing sequence—is marked on the chart in an abbreviated form. Full explanation is usually given in the official list of lights or in a navigator's almanac. Four main colors, white, red, green and yellow, are used for lights but purple, blue and orange are also used. Where possible, the color of the light is the same as the buoy itself, so a red port-hand lateral mark would show a red light at night, and a green buoy a green light and so on.

The other way to identify the light is by its flashing characteristic. The patterns of the main ones are shown below, together with their abbreviation as seen on the chart. The third way of identifying the light is by the timing of the flashing sequence, known as the period. This is the time for one complete cycle of the light characteristic and is shown, below right. The color, flashing characteristic and period of a light will be shown on the chart alongside the symbol for the mark, written in the abbreviated form shown below. Medium- and small-scale charts often only give brief details of a light and reference needs to be made to the list of lights or to the almanac.

Light pattern	Abbreviation	Description
	F.	Fixed continuous light
	Fl.	Flashing (light shorter than dark)
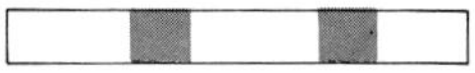	Occ.	Occulting (dark shorter than light)
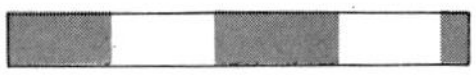	Iso.	Isophase (light and dark equal)
	Gp. Fl. (3)	Group flashing (3 in this case)
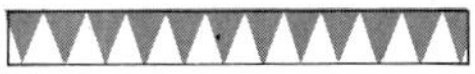	Qk. Fl.	Quick flashing 50 or 60 per min.
	V. Qk. Fl.	Very quick flashing 100 or 120 per min.
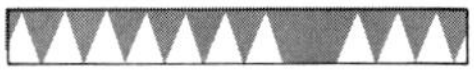	Int. Qk. Fl.	Interrupted quick flashing
	Gp. Occ. (2)	Group occulting (2 in this case)
	Alt.	Alternating (changes color)
	Mo. (U)	Morse code (U in this case)

Period of light
The period of the light is the time required for one complete sequence from the start of the pattern to the start of the next pattern. The time is always given in seconds and appears on the chart written after the number of flashes (shown in brackets).

←10 seconds→

Fl. 10s.

Gp. Fl. (3) 10s.

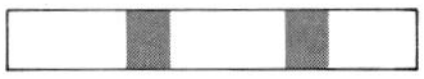

Occ. 5s.

Gp. Occ. (2) 10s.

Observing lights

To an inexperienced navigator, the array of lights in different colors and sequences can be very disturbing. One of the most important factors in identifying a light is the period it is lit. Although some people can count off seconds quite accurately, it is much better to use a stopwatch. When timing a light sequence, remember that the period is from the start of one sequence to the start of the next—that is the whole cycle. The light should be timed through three full cycles before you can positively identify it. Never assume the buoy is the one you want until you have confirmed it with a stopwatch. It can be particularly confusing approaching a harbor at night when the shore lights mingle with the navigation mark lights. In any passage, the navigator and crew should memorize the characteristics of the buoys they are looking for and establish their relative position to that of the boat. Once the first buoy has been identified, the rest will not be so hard to establish. When close to the first buoy, look along the bearing.

Light sectors

Some lights, such as lighthouses and some beacons, use color sectors to indicate safe or dangerous areas. These sectors are indicated on the chart and are also shown in the list of lights and in the almanac. When the edges of the sectors are given in degrees, this is the reading from the ship, not the lighthouse. The figures are always given in degrees true and if you work in magnetic on the chart you will have to convert these to degrees magnetic (see page 238).

Meteorology

Daily weather changes · How weather develops
Passage of weather · Winds · Storms · Fog
Weather forecasts · Causes of tides

Introduction

Of all sports, sailing is one of the most weather dependent. Very few other sports rely quite so heavily on the weather for their whole existence, and it is the interaction between wind, water and boat that makes sailing such an enthralling pastime.

Some sailors tend to take the weather for granted and apart from listening to weather forecasts, show very little interest in finding out how weather works. Inland sailors, in particular, often feel that there is not a lot of point in learning about the weather but they are quite wrong. Anyone who races a one-design regularly, and does well, has almost certainly started to think about the race and the tactics for it, the day before. They make sure that they see or hear a weather forecast and they start to think about how the weather will affect the race. Although the final planning will be done on the day itself, near the time of the start, the overall strategy will have been worked out the day before and modified later, when necessary.

For cruising sailors, whether coastal or offshore, some knowledge of likely weather patterns is vital. Planning a cruise of any sort demands some knowledge of what the weather is likely to do: even cruising yachtsmen who do not go far from home will meet considerable changes of condition. It helps to know how the weather will change during the day: when to expect sea breezes, for example, and when fog might occur.

Both cruising and one-design sailors need to have some knowledge about the weather so that they can make reasonably accurate guesses as to how it is going to develop. It can help, for example, if you hear on the forecast that a depression is approaching and know enough about its character to predict that the wind will back and increase as it arrives. You may be racing a one-design when a depression is passing, and it would be to your advantage to know about the veering wind shifts that occur when a front passes.

Most sailors do not have the time or patience to acquire a detailed knowledge of meteorology, but an understanding of the basic concepts will improve their sailing performance and help to make their sailing safer. Many sailors spend a great deal of time on tuning their boats, and buying expensive gadgets to improve the performance, but in fact a little time spent studying the wind and weather patterns could be more profitable.

Daily weather variation

When you go sailing, the conditions you may encounter will differ according to the time of day. In the morning, there may well be quite clear skies and light winds, but as the time passes and the sun rises, puffs of cumulus cloud (1) may appear. At the same time, you may find that wind strengthens and might even change direction a little. Later on, these cumulus clouds may grow larger (2) and sometimes they get so big that they can produce rain showers or even thunderstorms. Shower clouds often have big rounded tops and dark heavy bases (3). Thunderstorms do not often occur and most clouds do not grow big enough to produce the

1 Shallow cumulus (the Latin name for heap) cloud means good weather. If it is to continue, the clouds must not be deep. You can expect the wind to be variable underneath this type of cloud.

4 A cumulonimbus cloud which has produced a thunderstorm. You can expect to get very strong winds from the direction of the storm and for the temperature to drop rapidly.

weather shown in (4). If they should do, it will often be late afternoon or early evening when thunderstorms break out (see page 276). The afternoon produces the strongest wind but in the evening, as the skies clear (5) the wind becomes less strong and not so gusty and overnight it may drop almost to a calm. When that happens and the skies have broken cloud, fog patches can form (6).

This daily change in wind, cloud and temperature is known as the "diurnal" variation and the main attributes of this daily change are shown in the diagram on page 266. These changes occur because the sun heats the land but hardly heats the sea (as the sea reflects a great deal of the sun's radiation and absorbs the rest in depth). The heat of the day is then absorbed into the air from the earth's surface

and works its way upwards by convection currents — rising and sinking currents of air caused by warm air rising, cooling and sinking again. The normal state of the atmosphere is for the temperature to drop as you ascend. Higher up, the wind is going to be stronger because it is free from any friction with the earth, which slows it down.

Because the upper wind is brought down by the sinking parts of convection currents, stronger winds appear during the day. So, when the convection currents stop in the late afternoon (when the land temperature falls) so the strong wind also tends to drop. The light winds of the night can be explained if it is understood that in the same way that the air was heated by the sun from the ground upwards, so the night air is cooled from the cooler land surface

2 When cumulus clouds grow considerably, as above, they may produce rain. If the rounded tops push upwards, you can expect to get showers accompanied by strong winds.

3 When a cumulonimbus cloud (nimbus means rain bearing) grows amongst smaller cumulus, you can expect to get heavy showers of rain, snow or hail. Thunderstorms can also occur with this type of cloud.

5 You often find that the skies clear at sunset, as the convection cloud formed during the day disappears, or when, as here, a front (see page 268) is in the process of passing over.

6 Coastal regions are prone to fog patches and more extensive areas of fog form near them when moist air lies over colder sea. This type of fog may not clear when the sun rises, as fog over land does.

upwards, leaving warmer air over colder surface air. This occurrence is exactly the opposite of the normal one (where lower temperature should be found higher up) and is therefore known as an "inversion". The effect of an inversion is to prevent winds above it from mixing with, and speeding up, the winds below it. Cut off from help above, the surface wind, colliding with surface obstacles, begins to slow down. The lowest wind speed is found around dawn when fog patches can form and the temperature is at its lowest. It is not until the sun rises the following morning that the land once again can be heated, convection currents occur and the daily cycle repeated. Changes arising from major weather systems can upset this pattern, which is one that occurs normally in settled weather.

How weather develops

Before you can begin to make any predictions about the weather, you must first understand how weather patterns develop.

All air contains some water vapor and the maximum amount it can contain depends on the temperature of the air. Warm air can hold more water in the form of vapor than cold air. When warm air which contains a lot of water vapor is cooled, the vapor condenses into water droplets and forms clouds.

There are two main ways by which air cools: firstly, warm air ascends, expands and so shares its heat over a larger volume. Alternatively, it can come into contact with something colder, such as the earth's surface. When the latter occurs, fog is often the result (see page 278). There are three main ways by which air rises. One is the slow lifting of warm air over cold air, as happens along fronts (see page 268), another is the rapid lifting of air in convection currents and the third occurs when air is forced to ascend the slopes of hills or mountains (see below).

Cloud forms in three main layers: low clouds which form from the earth's surface up to about 2 km (7,000 ft) and include cumulus (photo 2, page 265) and stratus (photo 12, page 269); medium level clouds between 2 to 8 km (7,000 to 25,000 ft) and include altocumulus and altostratus (photo 10, page 269); high level clouds between 8 to 15 km (25,000 to 45,000 ft) and include cirrus (photo 7, page 268), cirrostratus (photo 8, page 269) and

Key

Inversion layer

Convection currents

Cooling air

High speed wind

Low speed wind

How an inversion forms
Radiation cools the air near the surface but not the air higher up. The division between warm and cold air is known as an inversion.

How air rises
Because warm air is less dense than cold air, it will lift over a wedge of colder denser air.

How an inversion breaks
The sun's heat causes convection currents to form which break through the inversion layer, and the wind becomes more variable.

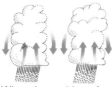

When the earth's surface is heated, it warms the air above it which rises, cools and sinks again as convection currents.

When the air meets an obstacle such as a hill or a mountain, it is forced to rise over it.

cirrocumulus. Knowledge of the different types of cloud formation is important for helping to predict the weather.

Not all clouds produce rain and the amount of rain is dependent on the depth of the cloud. Low cloud, for instance, which is no more than a thin layer, will not produce rain. Heavy cloud, which reaches up high and which is composed of ice-particles at the top, will, on the other hand, produce heavy rain.

The amount of water vapor in the air (and hence the amount and type of cloud) depends largely on where the air comes from originally. Air that has travelled a long way over oceans will have picked up a large amount of water *en route* while air that has blown over land for a long period will be relatively dry. Although you feel this air when sailing as wind blowing over the boat, it stretches upwards for 16 km (45,000 ft) or more. Any such airmass has particular characteristics. In the simplest terms, it can be warm or cold, wet or dry. Cold air is denser than average while warm air is less dense, so a column of cold air weighs more than an equal sized column of warm air. The weight of air spread over a unit area is what is known as pressure, hence dense, cold air creates high pressure and, conversely warmer, less dense air, low pressure.

These warm and cold airmasses are semi-permanent in origin, created originally in the equatorial and polar regions which receive the most and the least heat respectively. The difference in pressure between the airmasses causes the air to be drawn from areas of high pressure into areas of low pressure. Although, in theory, the air should move outwards from an area of high pressure into one of low pressure, another factor enters in. The earth rotates and causes the movement of air to be deflected – to the right in the northern hemisphere and the left in the southern hemisphere (see page 270). At the equator the spinning effect changes and the air tends to move directly from high to low pressure. These movements of air, which we feel as winds, are semi-permanent also. The patterns they form are shown below. More information on winds and how they form is given on pages 272–275.

Once an airmass is on the move it becomes known as an airstream. The kind of weather you experience depends to a large extent on where the airstream flowing over you originated from. A sub-tropical high pressure airmass, once it moves polewards, will get progressively cooler at the surface and the water vapor contained in it will form low cloud – often covering most of the sky. In extreme cases, the cloud forms at sea level to give extensive fog. This sort of airstream is known as a stable one. On the other hand, a high pressure mass originating over the poles and moving towards warmer areas will be a cold airstream which gets progressively warmer nearer the surface. This is an unstable airstream and the warm air below tends to lead to convection currents and hence to cumulus

Prevailing winds

Generally speaking, the worldwide wind patterns are those illustrated on the right. However, land masses and different pressure systems will cause these patterns to be altered so that this basic pattern becomes distorted. The blue arrows indicate warm air streams while the black arrows show cold ones.

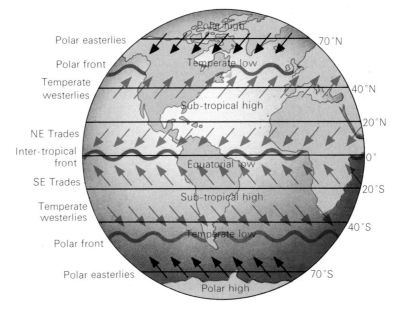

cloud. Obviously, there are times when these warm and cold airstreams meet, and when they do they form a well defined boundary zone, which may form a sort of battleground in which complex weather situations develop, as the airstreams confront each other.

The line, or frontier, where cold and warm air masses meet is termed the polar front. Sometimes, a wedge of warm air will penetrate the cold air mass along this front. The cold air, which circulates around this wedge or kink, distorts and increases its size until it reaches the proportions of a wave (see stage 1 of the diagram below). It is this wave of warm air, lower in pressure than the surrounding cold air, which forms what is known as a depression. Because of the westerly jet stream, a band of high speed winds, depressions move in an easterly to north-easterly direction.

The diagram below illustrates three stages in the life cycle of a depression. At the second stage the kink is well developed and the wedge of warm air, known as the warm sector, is sandwiched between cold air both behind and in front of it. The leading edge of the warm air mass is known as the warm front while the back edge of the wave is known as the cold front. As the depression develops into stage 3 in the diagram, the occluded stage, the cold front catches up with the warm front and results in the wedge of warm air being squeezed up off the surface of the earth. This stage heralds the end of a depression.

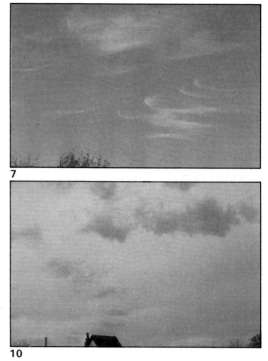

7

10

7 A cirrus cloud. It is composed of ice crystals and often is the first sign of a coming depression.

8 Cirrostratus usually follows cirrus across the sky when bad weather is in the offing.

9 When there are holes in altostratus cloud the coming weather should not be too bad.

The diagrams right illustrate the three stages of a depression. The diagram beneath is a cross-section taken along the dotted line of the diagram above. The numbers refer to photos 1 to 12.

Key

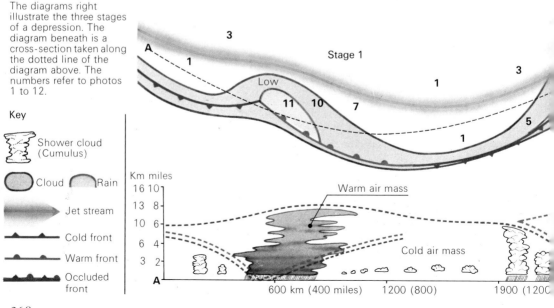

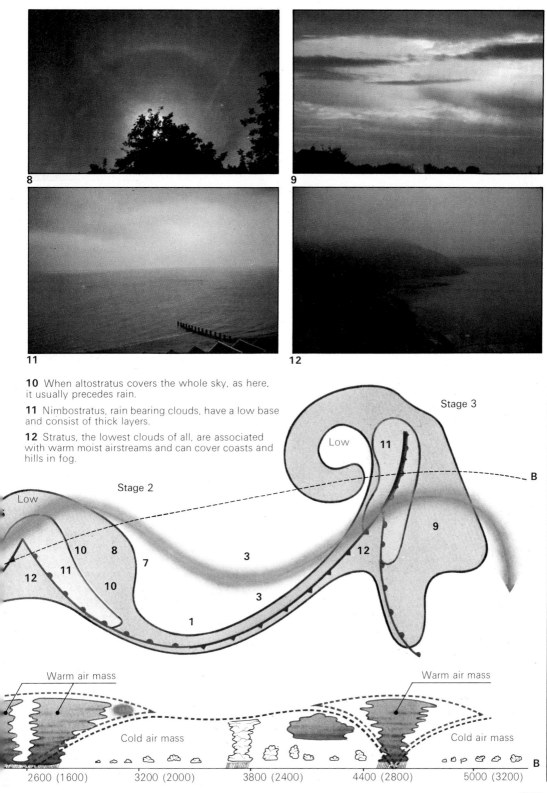

10 When altostratus covers the whole sky, as here, it usually precedes rain.

11 Nimbostratus, rain bearing clouds, have a low base and consist of thick layers.

12 Stratus, the lowest clouds of all, are associated with warm moist airstreams and can cover coasts and hills in fog.

Stage 3

Stage 2

Low

Low

Warm air mass

Cold air mass

Warm air mass

Cold air mass

2600 (1600)   3200 (2000)   3800 (2400)   4400 (2800)   5000 (3200)

B

269

The passage of weather

In temperate latitudes most of the major weather changes are brought by a succession of depressions with intervening high pressure areas between them. Depressions are of greater significance to sailors because, in severe depressions, gale force winds usually develop and even in lesser depressions, there are major changes and shifts of wind direction.

The high pressure areas (or anticyclones as they are called) are areas where cold dense air sinks and becomes warmer. They are inherently more stable than areas of low pressure (see page 267) and are responsible for long periods of warm, dry weather in summer. There is little high altitude cloud, but there may be low level cloud, especially over the sea. Generally, the winds experienced in high pressure areas are fairly light. From the local point of view, the coastline can modify the effects of a high if the wind is blowing onto a hilly shoreline or if sea breezes occur (see page 275) causing the wind to alter in strength and direction.

Depressions

The diagrams on pages 268–9 explain how a depression is caused in the first place and the development from a small kink in the polar front to a full-scale depression. Clearly the weather the observer sees and feels will depend on his position in relation to the center of the depression. The closer he is to the center, the more severe the weather is likely to be.

The following is the description of a typical depression passing slightly to the north of the observer: the first sign is a fall in pressure (which will be shown on the boat's barometer,

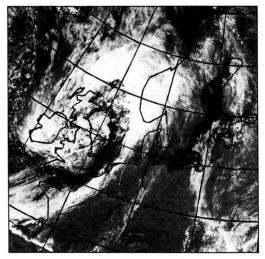

The satellite cloud photograph above of the storm that ravaged the Fastnet yacht race in 1979 was taken during the afternoon of Tuesday, August 14th. The long band of cloud marks the cold front leading out from the center of the depression.

see page 283) and the appearance of thin high cirrus cloud (photo 7, page 268). The faster the cirrus cloud is travelling and the denser it is, the stronger the depression and the more likely that gale force winds will blow. These thin high clouds can give a yachtsman about 12 to 24 hours warning of an approaching gale, depending on how fast the depression is travelling. The cirrus cloud thickens into cirrostratus which covers the sky at high altitude. The sun or moon may develop a halo (photo 8, page 269), pressure will fall, and the wind will back or shift counter-clockwise so that a westerly wind, for example, changes to a south-westerly or south-south-westerly. In a severe depression the cirrostratus thickens quickly into altostratus, but in a less severe one, the clouds look more

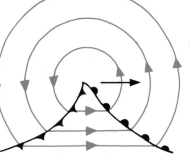

A low pressure system in the northern hemisphere (right) and the southern hemisphere (far right). The blue lines (isobars) join points of equal pressure and give the directions of the wind.

Key

→ Wind direction at 670 m (2000 ft)

→ Movement of low pressure area

Warm sector

Warm sector

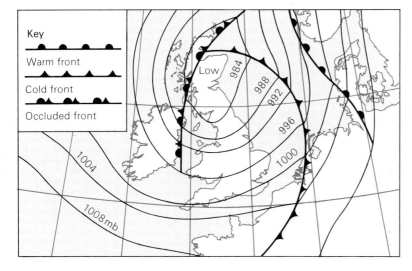

The weather map, left, showing the depression over Scotland at noon on August 14th; the close isobars over the Irish Sea indicate the strong winds which, at times, reached 60 knots. Further information on weather is given on pages 279–83.

like photo 3, page 265. Gradually the cloud thickens and nimbostratus (photo 11, page 269) forms. Visibility decreases, the cloud base is much lower and heavy rain falls. The pressure continues to fall and the wind may back further around to the south, or even slightly east of south. As the warm front passes over, the rain turns to drizzle or stops altogether. The pressure usually stabilizes and the wind veers back more to the west. If you are well away from the center of the depression, you may then see the cloud break up.

Cold fronts

With the approach of the cold front (which follows behind the warmer air of the low pressure area), the pressure may start to fall again (owing to a trough of low pressure which often occurs near the front) and the wind may back again a little. In fact, there is very little visible warning of the approaching cold front because the uppermost part of the wedge of warm air will still be above you.

When the cold front does come, it can be very active. The extra energy of cold fronts comes about because the cold air is sweeping in under the warm air, causing the warm air to lift rapidly. This produces heavy showers and accompanying gusts and squalls. The convection of the warm air causes great heap clouds (cumulonimbus, photo 4, page 264) to form. The cloud patterns of the cold front run in reverse order to those of the warm front but are less easy to distinguish as the front usually passes twice as rapidly.

As the cold front passes over, the wind usually veers, often sharply, to the north-west

and the pressure will start to rise. Clouds disperse and visibility improves rapidly. The passing of a cold front at night often produces a sky like the one in photo 5 on page 265 – in which case the old adage, "red sky at night is sailor's delight", actually comes true. High cloud clearing at nightfall nearly always leads to a fair night, while high clouds moving in from the east at dawn, producing a "red sky in the morning", are usually the forerunners of a warm front and its associated depression.

Depending on where you are and how close you are to the depression, there will obviously be wide variations in the weather and wind strength you experience. Some depressions are more active than others and the wind shifts and pressure changes are consequently greater. The speed at which a low pressure area travels can be anything up to about 60 knots. Clouds can be up to 960 km (600 miles) ahead of the warm front and the warm front rain may fall 160 km (100 miles) ahead of the front.

A severe depression can cause havoc at sea with strong winds building up large waves. The signs the yachtsman has to look out for are: a rapidly falling barometer and the approach of thin high cloud. However, gale warnings are broadcast on the radio and most boats sailing in coastal waters can usually get to port before a storm occurs. More information is given on different types of storm on page 276, and weather forecasting is dealt with on pages 279–83. Should your forecasting fail and should you get caught out in a gale, you may have no option but to ride it out. Special precautions should be taken and these are dealt with on pages 226–7.

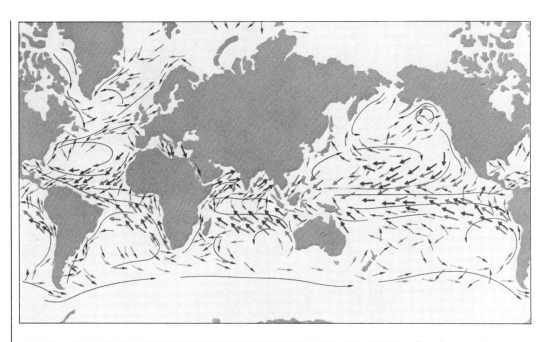

The diagram, above, shows the direction of the prevailing winds and the major ocean currents. The diagram, left, gives a more detailed picture of these elements in the North Atlantic

Key

The arrows give the direction of the winds—the blue ones for January and the orange for July. Where the winds are particularly steady, as in the Trades, the arrows have been strengthened. The purple arrows show the location and direction of the main currents.

→	Winds
➤	
→	
⌣	Limit of pack-ice in January
▽	Limit of icebergs in January
▼	Limit of icebergs in July
→	Currents
1	Labrador
2	North Atlantic
3	Irminger
4	Gulf stream
5	Canary
6	North Equatorial

Winds

As we have seen, winds are caused by differences in temperature and pressure. We also know that high pressure is where cold, heavy air is sinking while low pressure is located where warm, light air is rising. Winds are caused by air trying to move from high pressure areas to lower pressure areas. In the low latitudes (areas between the equator and 30° north and south) the earth receives most heat while in the high latitudes (areas between the poles and 60° north and south) the earth receives very little of the sun's heat. Owing to these global temperature contrasts, complex air motions are formed (at heights which do not affect the yachtsman) and result in bands of high and low pressure around the world. It is these bands which cause the world's wind patterns (see page 267). At about 30° north and south and over the poles there are immense semi-permanent anticyclones while at 60° north and south and at the equator there are bands of low pressure. The global winds are caused by the air flowing out of the high pressure areas to feed the areas of low pressure. From 30° north and south the air blows back to the equator. These winds are known as the trade winds. Other winds blow towards the low pressure areas at 60° north and south. These winds are known as the temperate westerlies. The outflowing airmasses from the high pressure areas over the poles are cold and are known as the polar easterlies.

We have also seen how the earth's rotation distorts the winds. Instead of blowing directly northwards and southwards towards the poles and the equator the winds in the northern hemisphere bend to the right while in the southern hemisphere they bend to the left. Alternatively, airstreams that move polewards become westerlies while those that move towards the equator become easterlies.

Now, where these winds meet there are the mobile dividing walls known as fronts which we have already discussed (see page 270).

Where the north easterly and south easterly trades meet is a line known as the inter-tropical front. Most of the world's pleasure boating is done where the temperate westerlies hold sway so it is essential that a sailor has a rudimentary knowledge of temperate latitude meteorology.

Tropical meteorology (relating to the inter-tropical front) is a difficult science and anyone sailing in these climes must study local conditions very carefully for, should they have gained their knowledge of meteorology in temperate latitudes, they will find that the "rules" they know do not often apply on the equator. For example, though depressions will form, the winds will not necessarily follow the rules of rotation which are discussed on pages 270–1. Local winds become crucial and should be learnt about while there is a greater incidence of thunderstorms in these latitudes.

The diagrams (opposite) show the trends of the prevailing winds over the oceans in January and July. Both the Atlantic and the Pacific have well-defined cells of anticyclonic winds in their northern waters and less well-defined ones in their southern waters.

In the Atlantic these semi-permanent winds in their turn entrain the ocean surface beneath them and create such drifts as the Gulf Stream, the Canaries Current and the North Equatorial Current. A similar situation exists in the north Pacific where a semi-permanent wind causes the Kuro-Siwo and the North Pacific Drift. These drifts, constrained by land masses and "thrown" by the rotation of the earth, develop into clockwise-rotating cells in the northern hemisphere and counter-clockwise ones in the southern.

The wind directions in the two diagrams opposite represent the basic pattern to which winds will always try to return. However, they are vulnerable to modification through smaller pressure systems which move through the areas, the varied topography of the coastlines, and land and sea breezes.

Weather systems

We have mentioned earlier how depressions affect the weather. The next step is to understand how high and low pressure systems within the overall global systems modify the prevailing winds. Pressure, which varies from place to place, can be plotted on a map. This is done by drawing lines, called isobars, which join areas of equal pressure. They form closed concentric patterns around the centers of high and low pressure areas. We know that air tries to move directly from high pressure areas to low pressure areas. However, because of the earth's rotation this does not occur and the air is forced to move in a circular fashion, parallel with the isobars. In the northern hemisphere winds rotate in a counter-clockwise fashion around low pressure areas and in a clockwise direction around high pressure areas. The opposite happens in the southern hemisphere. A simple rule will help you locate the position of high and low pressure areas. If you stand with your back to the wind in the northern hemisphere the low pressure will be on your left and the high pressure area on your right while the opposite applies in the southern hemisphere.

This is what occurs at 7km (20,000ft) above ground level and the wind at this height is known as the gradient wind. On the surface, and this is what matters to yachtsmen, the direction and speed of the wind will be distorted. For reasons too complex to explain here, the surface wind around a depression is bent in towards the centre while the wind circulating around an anticyclone is bent outwards from the centre (see below). The angle depends on the surface roughness. Over the sea, it tends to be bent by about 15° and over land by about 30°. There can be wide variations. Often there will be gusts of wind with speeds and direction which are more like those at 7km (20,000ft).

Local winds

Not only should yachtsmen know about global winds, cyclonic and anticyclonic winds, but also, and this is particularly important for dinghy sailors, local winds. The causes of local winds are the same as for global winds: namely, temperature differences. As we have seen, the very fact that cold air is heavier than warm air determines that there is wind. In order to understand how local winds work it is important to realize that air is not heated by the sun's rays but by the surfaces over which it travels. Consequently, because different surfaces heat up at different speeds and reach different temperatures, it is inevitable that on any day there will be variations in air temperature and these will in turn cause winds to blow.

The most well-known local wind is the sea breeze. As the sun rises in the morning the land heats up and warms the air above it. Over the

The diagrams (right) show the direction of the winds around low and high pressure areas in the northern hemisphere. The blue arrows represent the direction of the gradient wind (parallel with the isobars) while the black arrows show the direction of the wind on the earth's surface.

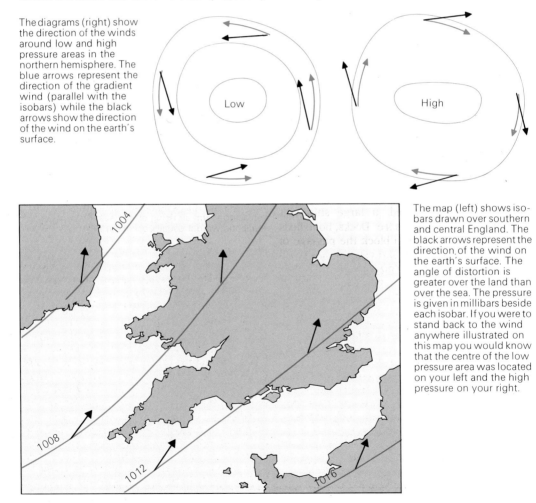

The map (left) shows isobars drawn over southern and central England. The black arrows represent the direction of the wind on the earth's surface. The angle of distortion is greater over the land than over the sea. The pressure is given in millibars beside each isobar. If you were to stand back to the wind anywhere illustrated on this map you would know that the centre of the low pressure area was located on your left and the high pressure on your right.

sea the air remains cooler as the water absorbs the sun's rays and does not warm up as does the land. As the warm air rises over the land a supply of cool air pours in underneath from the sea. It is this wind which is known as the sea breeze. On a hot summer's day a sea breeze may have blown many miles inland by mid-afternoon. During heat waves you may often witness a breathless calm first thing in the day but you can still be confident that there will be an onshore wind by mid-morning.

At night the reverse will tend to occur. Just as the land warms up quickly during the day so it loses its heat rapidly at night. Often the temperature of the land will fall below that of the sea and this will result in a light offshore wind brought about by the air over the land cooling, sinking and pushing out to sea. If the coastline is very hilly or mountainous the cool air is drawn down by gravity and causes a strong down-slope wind which is known as a katabatic wind. Sometimes these winds may blow for several miles out to sea. They occur most frequently at night in conjunction with land breezes and are usually light.

If you are sailing on an inland waterway, whether it be a lake or a river, the same principles of cause and effect can be taken into account. The air over the land is warmed and rises, allowing the colder air over the water to drift off the river. If you are a one-design sailor you will find that considerable progress can be made by exploiting these light winds.

When you start sailing you will notice how features on the shore interfere with the wind. Obviously, when moored, a large ship will produce a dead area in its lee. Docks, boatsheds and warehouses will also block the passage of the wind. Trees along the shoreline can cut wind speeds by almost half. You should either sail close to the trees where the wind is blowing through them, or a long way away where its passage is unaffected.

Always remember that winds experienced on land can be most deceptive. Wind speeds are reduced considerably by their contact with the land and, around boatyards and marinas, a strong wind will often seem no more than a gentle breeze. Once at sea you may regret that you ever left your comfortable berth. Nevertheless, the Beaufort scale (see page 282) will help you to evaluate wind speeds even when you are not at sea, as it lists the effects of winds on land bound objects such as trees. Only with experience will you be able to anticipate the actual wind strength you will find at sea.

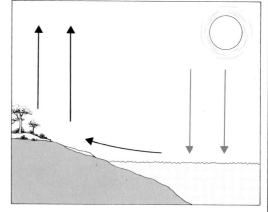

The warm air which is rising over the land is being replaced by the cooler air sinking over the sea. This onshore wind is known as a sea breeze.

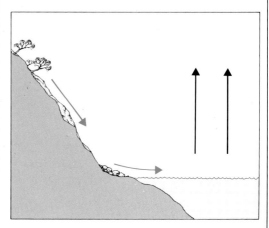

Cool land air is sinking down a mountainside and replacing warm air rising off the sea. Known as a katabatic wind, it usually occurs at night.

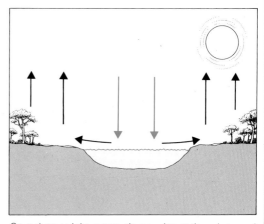

On a river or lake warm air may rise at the edges and be replaced by cooler air over the water. The Zephyr winds resulting can be used by one-design sailors.

Storms

Low pressure areas, as we have seen, are the major cause of bad weather. They are comparatively large and their influence in terms of time and area is quite considerable. As well as these there are small-scale disturbances such as thunderstorms, tornadoes and hurricanes. Though they are of short duration and cover only a small area at a time their intensity is often great, causing heavy rain and very strong, destructive winds.

There are three basic requirements for the formation of a thunderstorm. Firstly, there must be strong upward currents of air. This explains why thunderstorms occur most frequently on hot humid days and towards the late afternoon or early evening after the earth has had time to heat up the air. Secondly, this air must be buoyant enough, relative to the surrounding air, to keep ascending higher and higher, until it passes the freezing level. Thirdly, the air must have a large concentration of water vapour.

Thunderstorms far out to sea are relatively rare. When they do occur they are located along fronts. Only over land do they occur on their own in the middle of a stable air mass.

A thunderstorm occurs only where there is cumulonimbus cloud (see page 265). The prime danger signal is a cumulus cloud growing larger. An approaching thunderstorm will have four distinct features (see below). At the top there will be a layer of cirrus cloud, shaped like an anvil, and consequently called an anvil top. This anvil will point in the same direction as the wind is blowing and will thus indicate the direction in which the storm is moving. The second feature will be a large body of cumulus cloud underneath. It will have cauliflower sides and extend upwards, towards the anvil top to a great height. The third feature will be the roll cloud formed by violent currents of air along the leading edge of the base of the cloud. The final feature is the dark area extending from the base of the cloud to the earth. This is where there is precipitation. It is in this area that you will experience the storm.

Thunderstorms often appear in the late afternoon or early evening. But if you are sailing across an ocean where they are far less common, you can expect them between midnight and dawn. Thunderstorms are most common in

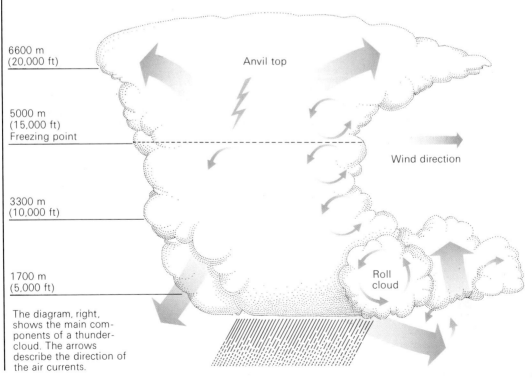

6600 m
(20,000 ft)

Anvil top

5000 m
(15,000 ft)
Freezing point

Wind direction

3300 m
(10,000 ft)

1700 m
(5,000 ft)

Roll
cloud

The diagram, right, shows the main components of a thundercloud. The arrows describe the direction of the air currents.

tropical latitudes. In higher latitudes they are both less common and less intense.

When a thunderstorm draws near, the wind will drop and become variable. As the roll cloud passes overhead, you will experience violent shifting winds and strong downdrafts. Just behind the roll cloud will come the heavy rain or hail. However, after the passage of the storm the weather will clear quickly leaving both the temperature and the humidity lower.

Wind speeds can reach 40−50 knots in the worst cases which occur most frequently over large land masses. Indeed, in the United States such wind speeds are not uncommon. The higher the anvil the more violent will be the storm. In higher latitudes, in autumn and winter, storms tend to be less violent than in summer. Though they last for a comparatively short time, sailors should take care if a storm approaches. One-design sailors are advised to make for the shore; on cruising boats, sails should be reefed and the boat headed into the storm. If you sail in the same direction as the storm you will simply lengthen your period of discomfort. Lightning is a danger and boat owners should get advice about lightning conductors. If you find yourself in a thunderstorm in a one-design which has a metal mast it is advisable to trail the boom in the water over the side, while at the same time keeping it in contact, via the gooseneck, with the mast.

You can gauge the distance between yourself and the thunderstorm quite easily. If you are at the actual point of a lightning discharge, the thunder will occur simultaneously but if you are any distance from the storm you will see the lightning before you hear the thunder. You should time this interval in seconds and then multiply the number of seconds by 0.2. The result will be the approximate number of miles between yourself and the thunderstorm.

Tornadoes

A tornado is an exceptionally violent, but small-scale, whirl of air. If a number of thunderstorms are associated with a cold front, the storms are likely to be organized in a long, narrow band. It is along the forward edge of this line that cold downdrafts from the series of thunderstorms meet the warm air. Sharp drops in temperature and vicious gusts sometimes spawn this most destructive type of storm. Few countries are free of them though some suffer more than others. The large land masses, notably North America, always suffer the worst from tornadoes. The very worst whirlpool of wind which they create,

usually experienced ashore, may only have a diameter of some 185 m (200 yards) but their wind speeds may exceed 150 mph, leaving havoc in their wake.

Hurricanes

A hurricane is the name given to a large tropical revolving storm. On the Beaufort scale (see page 282) any wind which exceeds force 12 is classed as a hurricane. Generally, in the northern hemisphere, they travel in a north-westerly direction before turning towards the north-east. In the southern hemisphere, they travel in a south-westerly direction before turning to the south-east. This is their usual path which, of course, is open to variation. They are known as hurricanes in the Atlantic, north-east and south-west Pacific, typhoons in south-east Asia, cyclones in the Arabian Sea and Bay of Bengal, and willy-willies in north-west Australia. In the Caribbean, hurricanes are most prevalent in September. In the Arabian Sea and the Bay of Bengal, there are two peaks, during June and July, and October. The typhoons of the China sea and the hurricanes of the north-east Pacific tend to blow in September. South of the equator, the peak of the season tends to come in January.

The best warning of a hurricane now comes from weather bureaus via the geostationary satellites that revolve over fixed points over the equator. Regular warnings of the movement and intensity of a storm are given by radio. The best avoiding action is to simply steer clear of those areas mentioned above during the seasons when hurricanes are prevalent. If, by some misfortune, you find yourself in the path of one of these storms you should make for a hurricane hole (a sheltered lagoon which is marked for such use on charts) or try to sail away from its path. If you suffer really bad luck and are unable to avoid the storm you will have no choice other than to go below decks, batten down and hope that your boat survives. Because of the force of the winds which are associated with hurricanes, however, there is no guarantee that your boat will be safe except perhaps in the most sheltered harbors. Indeed, unless you are able to find a hurricane hole your boat may be no safer in port than it would be out in the open sea. In the northern hemisphere, the northern half of the storm is the most navigable while the opposite applies in the southern hemisphere. Sailors should know that old tropical storms can travel across to the Atlantic coasts of Europe in September and October and rejuvenate themselves as dangerous storms.

The causes of fog

Fog is simply cloud, the base of which rests on the land or the sea. It consists of water droplets which are far too small to be seen individually but can be so numerous that objects close at hand become obscured. For fog to form, there has to be sufficient water vapour in the air and it must fall below the temperature of the dew-point (the temperature to which unsaturated air must be cooled in order to become saturated). Further cooling usually results in condensation of the water vapor. Dew-point varies according to the temperature and the water content of the air. The higher the temperature of the air the more water vapor it can hold before it becomes saturated. Moist air can therefore become saturated by either cooling it down or by causing more water to evaporate into it. Dew-point can be calculated (using a psychrometer) and when the temperature falls below this fog will form. There are four different types of fog and three of these are caused by factors causing the air temperature to be reduced below its dew-point. The fourth type, Arctic sea smoke, is caused by cold air absorbing more moisture.

Radiation fog
Radiation fog is caused by the air radiating its heat into space until its temperature falls below that of its dew-point. This happens on clear nights when there are no clouds to trap the heat. Radiation fog will only occur where there is rapidly cooling land, moist air which will probably have travelled over water, and very little wind so that the air cannot be heated up by being mixed with the air above. It generally occurs in high pressure areas where there is little wind and clear skies, and tends to form in valleys where the mixing of air of different levels is least likely. During the early hours of the morning it may spread out to sea for several miles. However, it seldom extends further than

about five miles and is normally dispersed by about noon. This is because, as we have already seen, it usually occurs in anticyclones and the fair weather gives the air a chance to warm up. It may persist during the morning if extensive cloud cover has moved in. Radiation fog is most common during spring and autumn and can cause problems in busy harbors.

Advection fog
Advection fog is caused by air being carried over a surface whose temperature is below the dew-point of the air. Advection fog which occurs at sea is known as sea fog. It can occur in a number of different circumstances. In spring and early summer, when the temperature of the sea is still cold, warm land air may move over cold sea. Evaporation takes place, the dew-point rises, the temperature of the air falls and fog forms. Air moving from over a warm sea to a colder sea can be another cause of sea fog. This occurs most frequently on the Grand Banks of New-foundland where the warm air from the Gulf stream moves over the colder sea of the Labrador current. A third cause of sea fog is the movement of air over a sea which becomes gradually colder. A warm, humid air mass moving into higher latitudes and over cold water is cooled, becomes saturated and fog forms. Sea fog can be very thick and irritatingly persistent. Often a complete change in the weather pattern is required for it to disperse.

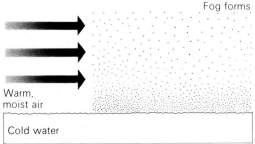

Advection fog forms when warm moist air lies over cold water.

Frontal fog
The third type of fog is frontal fog. As its name implies, it occurs where a warm, moist front meets a colder polar front. The temperature of the former airmass is cooled to below its dew-point and fog forms. This type of fog is usually experienced as low cloud which sometimes falls to sea level. The primary danger associated with

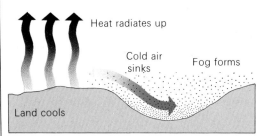

Radiation fog forms on a still, clear night, when the heat of the day has radiated into the atmosphere.

this fog is that, although it is often clear at sea level, it is misty at higher levels, so land masses, lighthouses and other crucial landmarks may be obscured when the air around your boat is quite clear. This form of fog, by its very nature, exists as a thin belt along a front.

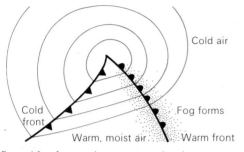

Frontal fog forms where warm moist air encounters colder air.

Arctic sea smoke

Arctic sea smoke is the fourth and last type of fog. As its name implies, it usually forms inside the Arctic circle. Unlike the fogs which we have already outlined it is not caused by warm moist air being cooled, but by cold air absorbing moisture through the evaporation of warmer water. Because the air in this part of the world is very cold, its dew-point is correspondingly very low. Therefore any moisture which is absorbed is almost immediately transformed into fog. However, almost as soon as the fog has formed the air is warmed by the sea, the dew-point rises and the fog immediately above the surface of the sea disperses. This warm air which then rises is cooled again by the cold air above so that fog forms again higher up. It is this continual process of fog forming, dispersing and reforming which creates the strange effects by which it acquires its name. Sea smoke lasts only a short time for the conditions bringing it about are quickly balanced out. The cold air becoming sufficiently warm to reduce the likelihood of fog.

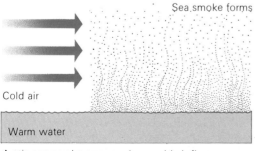

Arctic sea smoke occurs where cold air flows over warm water.

Weather forecasting

Monitoring and interpreting the weather is an essential part of the sailor's art. It should be looked upon as important as, say, trimming the sails. The type of knowledge you need depends, of course, on the sort of sailing which you do. A one-design sailor will want to know about the weather in specific areas, over short periods of time, whereas the cruising man will be concerned with the weather over a period of days and its behavior over wider areas. We have already talked in general terms about the world's weather and weather systems but those sailors who venture out in the latitudes where weather is variable (i.e. along polar fronts) rather than merely seasonal (i.e. in the tropics) must learn to monitor the weather forecasts, make their own meteorological maps (see pages 283—85) and forecast the weather themselves.

The first job which needs to be done before even thinking of going to sea or making your own met map is to observe and log the actual weather which you are experiencing in port or at your anchorage. You need to record the barometric pressure and if you have heard a shipping forecast beforehand you can record the change. You will then know if the pressure is rising or falling and this will give you some indication of whether the conditions will improve or deteriorate. Also record the direction and the speed of the wind. If you do not have instruments for gauging these you will have to judge them by looking at the condition of the sea. The direction of the wind can be judged by regarding the wave line (not the swell) on the water. They are nearly always at right angles to the actual direction of the wind. Record the direction by compass points. The speed of the wind can be judged by the sea state (see pages 280—1 on which the six photographs show the sea state in moderate and very strong winds). If you are in a sheltered anchorage, watch how trees and other objects behave (see Beaufort scale, page 282). You must also take into account the visibility, the proportion of the sky which is covered by cloud as well as the type of cloud. Just as you make these observations before setting out to sea, so you should continue to make routine observations during any passage, as necessary. You will need to develop a form of shorthand to make quick, easily written notes, both of your own forecasts and those of the meteorological stations. Some of the standard abbreviations, normally used by meteorologists, are shown on page 285.

Force 3: gentle breeze
Wind speed will be between 7 and 10 knots. Waves will be small and crests will begin to break. Average wave height will be 0.6 m (2 ft).

Force 4: moderate
Wind speed will be between 11 and 16 knots. Waves will be small with some white horses. Average wave height will be 1 m (3 ft 3 in).

Force 5: íresh breeze
Wind speed will be between 17 and 21 knots. The waves will be moderate with frequent white horses occurring and some spray. Average wave height will be 1.8 m (6 ft).

Force 7: near gale
Wind speed will be between 28 and 33 knots. Seas begin to pile up and much foam is blown from breaking waves.
Average wave height will be 4 m (13 ft 6 in).

Force 9: strong gale
Wind speed will be between 41 and 47 knots. Waves are high and dense foam blows from the tops of breaking waves.
Average wave height will be 7 m (23 ft).

Force 11: violent storm
Wind speed will be between 56 and 63 knots. Waves will be exceptionally high and the sea will be completely covered with long patches of foam and the edges of all the waves will be turned to froth.
Average wave height will be 11.3 m (37 ft).

Beaufort scale	Description and wind speeds (knots)	Land signs	One-design criteria	Cruising boat criteria
0	Calm less than 1	Smoke rises vertically. Leaves do not stir.	Drifting conditions. Heel the boat to reduce the wetted surface and enable the sails to assume an aerofoil shape. Make no sudden movements.	Often unable to maintain steerage way. Use engine.
1	Light air 1–3	Smoke drifts. Weather vanes do not respond.	Sufficient to maintain gentle forward motion. Sails should be flattened. Crew balance boat to keep it slightly bow down and heeled to leeward.	Spinnaker may fill but collapses in lulls. Use engine.
2	Light breeze 4–6	Wind felt on the face. Leaves rustle. Light flags not extended. Weather vanes respond.	Sufficient to sail at an even speed with the boat upright. Sails can be full but must be adjusted to changes in wind speed and direction.	Spinnaker may fill but collapses in lulls. Use engine.
3	Gentle breeze 7–10	Light flags extended. Leaves in constant motion.	Most small boats will sail at hull speed. Planing possible for thoroughbred one-designs. Ideal conditions for learner.	Sufficient to fill sails and progress at a leisurely pace. Spinnaker fills and sets. May need to use engine to maintain good speed.
4	Moderate breeze 11–16	Most flags extend fully. Small branches move. Dust and loose paper may be raised.	Crew fully extended. Planing on most points of sailing. A learner's gale— make for shore.	Most cruising boats sail at hull speed. Full use can be made of larger sails. One reef in some mainsails.
5	Fresh breeze 17–21	Small trees in leaf sway. Tops of all trees in noticeable motion.	Ideal sailing conditions for experienced sailors. Capsizing common amongst the more inexperienced crews.	Large headsails may be changed for smaller sails. Ideal cruising wind. Heavy, traditionally built boats sail at hull speed. Lighter boats change headsails and reef mainsails.
6	Strong breeze 22–27	Large branches in motion. Whistling heard in wires.	Small-boat sailor's gale. Often difficult to make progress without reefing only experienced crews race.	Most crews begin to seek shelter or remain in harbor. Mainsails will be double reefed. Wear and clip harnesses.
7	Near gale 28–33	Whole trees in motion. Inconvenience felt when walking against wind.	Most one-designs remain on shore. Those which go afloat risk gear failure and being overpowered.	Family crews, unless very experienced, have problems coping. Seek shelter, or if gale is forecast sail away from land in order to ride out the storm.
8	Gale 34–40	Twigs broken off trees. Generally impeded progress on foot. Rarely experienced on land.	Small boats should be securely tied down to prevent them blowing away.	Deep reefed mainsail and small headsail. Close and secure hatches and companionways. Be prepared for seas to break over boat and flood the cockpit. Only essential crew should be on deck.
9	Strong gale 41–47	Chimney pots and slates removed. Fences blown down.		Danger of knockdown. Some crew continue to sail. Others must lower sails and lash the tiller. Much depends on the sea state. In open conditions with large regular waves you could set a trysail.
10 and upwards	Storm 48 upwards	Very rare inland. Trees uprooted. Considerable structural damage.		Survival conditions, especially when near shelving coasts. Danger of 90° knockdowns and capsizes. Stay well away from coastlines.

Weather maps

Since weather is of such vital and continuous concern to the sailor, it is important to use every means available for keeping up with weather forecasts and possible changes. "Local knowledge" gained by observation and experience comes first when in home waters. Most areas have a distinct pattern of weather behavior that follows a daily routine, especially in settled summer weather, and anyone who spends time living by and with the weather, as sailors do, should make a habit of studying this pattern. Keeping a log of wind directions, temperature, barometer and cloud conditions by time of day can build up valuable data that reveals the local pattern. Once this becomes familiar, the signs that herald a shift of wind or the approach of a front or storm system become quite apparent. After a while, log keeping might even become superfluous, as the conditions would be seen to repeat themselves fairly predictably.

In most coastal areas, a sea breeze that is basically a local thermal condition (see pages 274–5) will spring up sometime between late morning and early afternoon on fair weather days. At night, the thermal breeze is likely to be a much lighter one, blowing from the land towards the water. If the sea breeze persists strongly at nightfall, with cloudy conditions developing, it is very often a sign that a weather change is coming. The approach of thunderstorms, usually in late afternoon on a warm summer day, should be watched for with care in most areas of continental North America, and these usually follow a set path as they develop and move. In most cases, there is a danger sector from which storms approach and this should be carefully noted. Thunderstorms associated with a cold front can behave differently and are not confined to afternoons like the thermal storms on fair weather days, so the approach of a cold front should be watched with care. Since most weather in North America moves from west to east (hurricanes are an exception), knowledge of conditions to westward can be especially helpful. For instance, if the wind is southerly locally and the temperature is warm with clouds building up, while a station 200 miles to the west reports cool north-west winds, it is a good indication that a cold front is approaching from that direction.

Nowadays there are so many public aids to weather forecasting that no sailor need be caught unawares by a front or by more serious disturbances, such as coastal storms or hurricanes. Commercial TV and radio abound with weather broadcasts and there is no area of North America that lacks these sources of information. The National Weather Service provides a continuous broadcast of conditions at many places with the emphasis on marine use. These are pre-recorded tapes which are updated every few hours. The frequencies used are 162.550, 162.400, and 162.475 MHz. These forecasts can be received on inexpensive transistor radios, as well as on regular VHF sets and MF-band radio-telephones. The broadcasts

Barometers

The most important, indeed the one essential item of meteorological equipment, is the aneroid barometer. Pressure is now measured around the world in millibars so avoid acquiring one which is marked only in inches. One defect of the aneroid barometer is that the spring tends to settle down and during only one season's sailing the barometer can become increasingly inaccurate. This is not as disastrous as it sounds as it is the change in pressure rather than the pressure itself which is of greatest interest to the sailor. Remember that a rise or fall of three millibars or more in an hour spells very bad weather for the sailor. Adjusting your barometer is simply done by speaking to the nearest weather station, telling them your position, and asking for the pressure reading, in millibars, at mean sea level. You then adjust the screw at the back by turning it very gently.

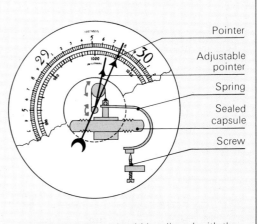

Pointer

Adjustable pointer

Spring

Sealed capsule

Screw

The adjustable pointer should be aligned with the pointer after recording the pressure. In this way it is easier to keep an eye on the rise and fall of pressure.

are of excellent quality and are probably the single most valuable means of keeping up with the weather situation. In addition, aviation weather reports can be heard in most areas, giving present conditions at selected airports over a wide area, and these provide a good picture of the approach and development of fronts and other systems.

The weather map provides the reader with a picture of the weather over a large area but its many figures, lines and symbols can lead to confusion for the uninitiated. However, after a little study, the map can give you a good idea of the causes of the current situation as well as enabling you to predict future changes. Some boatmen may receive the weekly compilation of daily weather maps provided by the National Weather Service but the majority depend on the weather maps printed in newspapers for their information. These maps are drawn by the weather service from master weather charts which are updated four times each day and show surface and upper air weather. The problem with most newspaper weather maps is that they are too simplified and thus only give a broad picture, although they are of use in showing the location of fronts and storm systems. Another drawback of the newspaper maps is the delay between the time they are drawn and the time they reach the reader. Despite these disadvantages, the boatman should make use of them to give him an overall picture. For sailors on long offshore passages, the U.S. Coast Guard broadcasts wide-range forecasts for ocean areas on single sideband radio. These are quite general and cover large areas, but they can be a help in giving the general state of the weather at sea, and all services step into high gear during the hurricane season. All tropical disturbances are given code names and tracked in careful detail, and there is a long interval between the warnings and the arrival of the disturbance. Perhaps the most dangerous storms are the ones that develop in a few hours on a wave along a front, building to hurricane strength quickly, and catching weather services unawares. It is in this sort of situation that local communications with the Coast Guard and airports, via a two-way radio, can be a great advantage.

In all, a personal "weather eye" based on experience and backed by a means of picking up commercial radio and VHF, remain the best means of keeping in touch with the weather situation. Also the prudent sailor is always aware that the unexpected, unusual development that breaks a normal pattern is the major cause of weather related problems. It is very important that you are ready at all times for the unexpected.

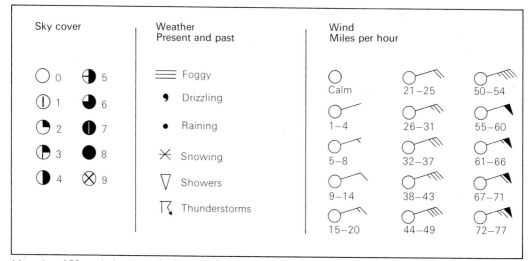

More than 150 symbols are used when weather maps are drawn but it is unnecessary for the sailor to know them all. In most cases the selection of symbols shown above will be enough to help you interpret and understand the weather maps which appear in newspapers. The map shown right is an artist's impression of a weather map which contains all the information necessary for you to predict changes in weather.

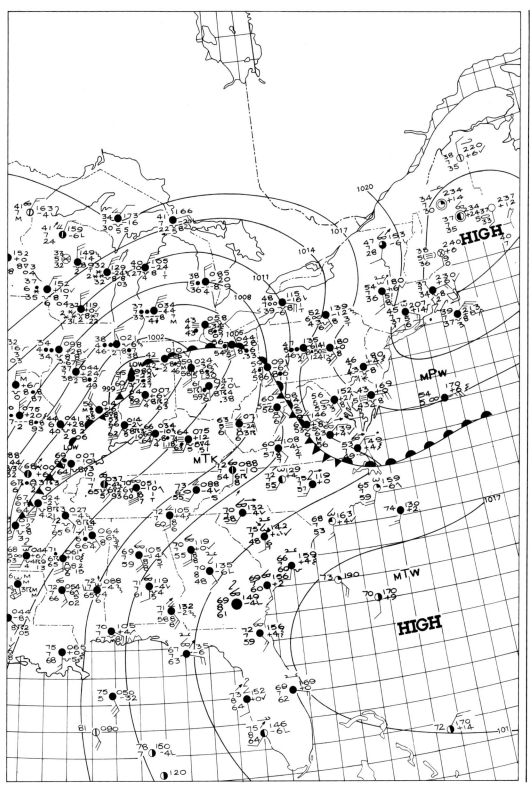

The causes of tides

The causes of tides have exercised man's curiosity for many centuries and there are few other subjects which have created so much speculation and so many far-fetched theories, even in relatively recent times. Darwin himself wrote in 1911, "it is not necessary to search ancient literature for grotesque theories of the tides". However, sailors have managed to gauge their effect and to use the tides to advantage without any real idea of the cause. The information about tides that the navigator needs to know is given in the chapter on navigation, but an attempt is made here, in layman's terms, to give a simple explanation of how tides occur. To understand the causes precisely requires a knowledge of mathematics and physics well beyond the scope of most people, and the following explanation, is, of necessity, a simplified one.

Gravitational pull

Because of the gravitational pull exercised on the earth by certain celestial bodies (principally the moon and the sun), the water on the earth's surface is drawn into two distinct "heaps". The gravitational pull is in a direct line, so one of these heaps occurs on the side nearest the moon and the other on the opposite side (where there is less pull on the water but more on the earth, drawing the earth moonwards and leaving the water behind). Two troughs occur

on the opposite axis as a result (see below). The heaps of water are referred to as tidal waves. They are not stationary, as the earth rotates causing the moon's gravitational effect to be felt over any meridian once in every 24 hours 50 minutes (the lunar day). The effect is to produce two high waters (the heaps) and two low waters (the troughs) at any place every 24 hours 50 minutes. Because there is a time lag in the effect that the moon has on the water, the actual high water is experienced up to six hours after the moon has passed over, and low water occurs when the moon is roughly over the meridian.

The pattern of two high water and two low waters a day is known as a semi-diurnal one. In some parts of the world (partly because of the path travelled by the moon) you only get one high and one low water a day—diurnal tides. The range of these diurnal tides is not very great and they occur mainly in the tropics. In certain areas you will get mixed tides, where a combination of diurnal and semi-diurnal tides

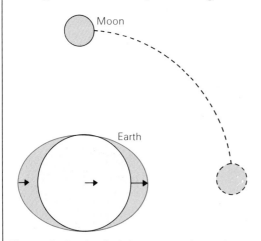

The gravitational pull of the moon on the earth causes two tidal humps and troughs but because of a time lag the effect at any place on the earth's surface is not felt until up to six hours afterwards. This is shown above where the apparent movement of the moon is caused, in practice, by the rotation of the earth under the moon.

←—24 hours —→

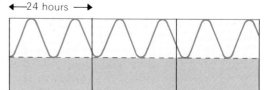

Semi-diurnal tides
A semi-diurnal tide gives two high and two low waters every lunar day.

Diurnal tides
A diurnal tide gives only one high and one low water every lunar day.

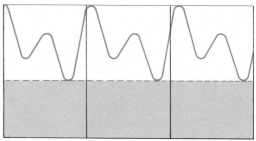

Mixed tides
Mixed tides gives two high and two low waters every lunar day, but with a great difference between the heights of successive low and high waters.

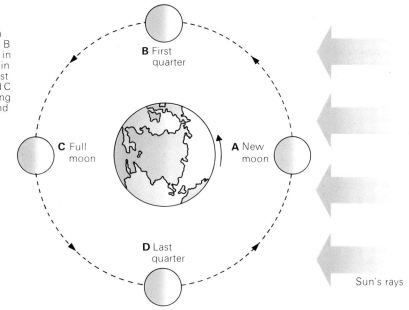

When the moon is in position A it is called a new moon, in position B it is in the first quarter, in position C it is full, and in position D it is in the last quarter. Positions A and C are associated with spring tides and positions B and D with neap tides.

occurs, so that there are two high and two low waters every lunar day, but with a large difference between the heights of consecutive high and low tides.

Spring and neap tides

The moon is not, of course, the only celestial body to exert a gravitational pull on the earth. The sun also does, but to a lesser extent. Thus the position of the sun relative to the moon and the earth will affect the height of the tide. Twice every month when the sun, moon and earth lie in a straight line (when the moon is either full or new) the pull of the sun is added to that of the moon so you get far higher and far lower high and low waters than average (above). When this happens (top right), it is known as a spring tide (not to be confused with the time of the year — it has nothing to do with it). In between the spring tides when the sun and moon are at right angles to each other, the effect of the sun is to minimize that of the moon. This results in a lower than average high tide and a higher than average low tide. This is known as a neap tide (bottom right). The time lag effect occurs also with spring and neap tides, so the actual effect is not felt for some time afterwards (approximately two days).

Despite the fact that the rise and fall of the tides has been charted for many years, to the point where predictions of tidal rises and falls are fairly accurate, freak weather conditions can disrupt the pattern and tidal surges are some-

times caused, creating higher or lower tides than predicted. It is these tidal surges which, when they occur at a spring tide, cause so much havoc in the shape of flooding and damage. While it is fairly safe to go by a tidal timetable to estimate the expected height of a tide, it would be unwise to assume that the timetable is infallible.

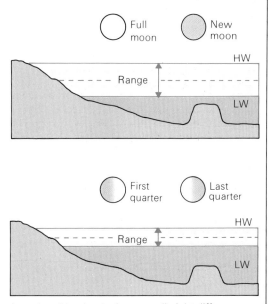

At spring tides (top), the range (height difference between high and low water) is large while at neap tides (above) the range is small.

Tidal flow

The direction of the tidal stream is, of course, determined to some extent by the obstacles it encounters in its path. When the tidal wave meets an isolated land mass, it has to split and travel around the coastline (right). Once it reaches the end of the landmass the streams will join to form one single stream again. The effect of the tide being forced through a narrow channel increases the rate of flow, hence the tidal races which occur in certain areas (of which the sailor needs to be aware).

One factor which has to be borne in mind when observing the tidal stream is the effect of the rotation of the earth. This deviates air or water from its normal path, to the right in the northern hemisphere, and to the left in the southern hemisphere. In the case of a channel in the northern hemisphere lying on an east to west axis, the range of the tide will be less on the northern shore and greater on the southern shore as a result. A good example of this is in the English Channel where the range on the French coast is greater.

An interesting phenomenon which is also caused by constricted water and shallow seas is the development of areas where the tidal range is zero—there is no fluctuation in tidal height. Such an area is known as an amphidromic system and is shown on charts known as co-tidal and co-range charts which can be useful for finding tidal heights when offshore.

In narrow channels, which run on the same axis as the flow of the tidal stream, an interesting effect may occur. The tide simply runs backwards and forwards along the channel so that when it is high water at one end, it is low water at the other. It can be compared with the effect of placing a marble on a curtain rail, which is supported centrally like a seesaw; when one end of the seesaw is high (at high tide) the other

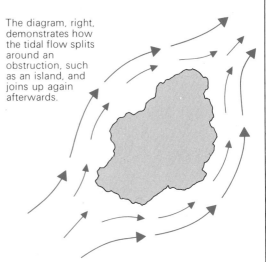

The diagram, right, demonstrates how the tidal flow splits around an obstruction, such as an island, and joins up again afterwards.

end is low. The ball (the tidal flow) runs along the seesaw, slowing down after it crosses the half way mark as the other end starts to rise. Thus in a channel like the English Channel, the tidal range will be greater the closer the area is to the ends of the channel.

Obviously the sailor is more interested in being able to find practical information about tides than in knowing their causes. Fortunately, the information has been charted by official hydrographers. It is important to understand that the chart and tide tables refers all tidal heights to what is known as chart datum. This is the lowest astronomical tide, that is the lowest level to which any tide could be predicted to fall under average meteorological conditions and under any combination of astronomical conditions. This level will not be reached every year, but the depths of water measured on most charts measured from this base figure. Information on calculating tidal heights and streams is dealt with in Navigation, pages 243–5.

The diagram, right, illustrates the seesaw effect created when a narrow channel lies in the path of the main tidal flow, when high water is at one end of the channel, it will be low water at the other and vice versa.

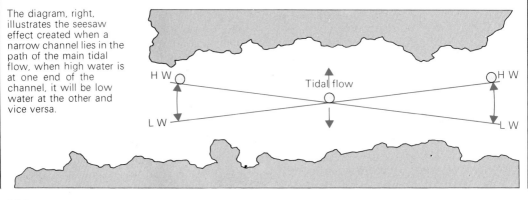

Maintenance
and Safety

General maintenance · Laying up and wintering
Engine, fuel, electricity and water systems
Emergency repairs · Safety requirements
Coping with emergencies · Stranding · Towing a cruiser
Abandoning ship · First aid and medical care

Maintenance

For most people, buying a boat represents a substantial financial outlay. Maintaining the boat and all its equipment in good working order not only safeguards your investment, it also allows you to enjoy the pleasure of being afloat as safely as possible. Neglect will not only cost you money, but it could also put you and your crew in grave danger. How much maintenance you do yourself will depend on your financial resources, your skill and the amount of time you have available – or a combination of all three. Experience will help you to do more of your own maintenance and as you build up a knowledge of construction and materials, you will probably become skillful enough to undertake most repairs yourself. Regular maintenance is a must. It should never be regarded as a once-a-year chore, but as an integral part of sailing a boat. You must get accustomed to the idea of checking your boat over each time you use it for any signs of general wear or damage. Each boat owner will develop his own system of maintenance checks. How and when regular maintenance is carried out will depend on your sailing pattern and the area in which you live.

At the end of the sailing season, when the time comes for laying up the boat for the winter, you will need to carry out a very thorough check of the boat and all its equipment. Whenever possible it is best to get your boat out of the water. One-designs present no great problem – they can be laid up at home and covered with a tarpaulin (see page 97). A cruiser needs to be placed on special chocks (see opposite) – any boatyard will give help and advice. If you have to leave the boat afloat, you must first make sure you have removed anything from the boat which could collect moisture and get moldy. Scrub out lockers and leave open. The sails should be taken ashore and cleaned and repaired, as should all lines. Lubricate all the moving parts of the boat, and remove any electrical equipment. Pump out bilges and pour in antiseptic solution. Make sure all fittings are attached securely. If possible, remove the mast and rigging, and keep it under cover. Finally, protect the deck area with a waterproof cover.

If you own a cruising boat, you will probably have to have any major repairs carried out by a boatyard. Most boatyards will also carry out maintenance inspection work and if you get a boatyard to do this for you, try to make a point of going around the boat with the manager or

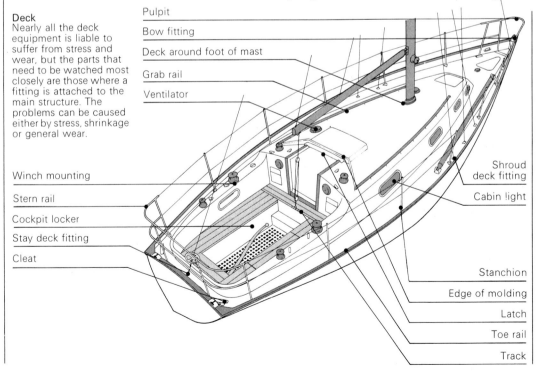

Deck
Nearly all the deck equipment is liable to suffer from stress and wear, but the parts that need to be watched most closely are those where a fitting is attached to the main structure. The problems can be caused either by stress, shrinkage or general wear.

Pulpit

Bow fitting

Deck around foot of mast

Grab rail

Ventilator

Winch mounting

Stern rail

Cockpit locker

Stay deck fitting

Cleat

Shroud deck fitting

Cabin light

Stanchion

Edge of molding

Latch

Toe rail

Track

foreman, so that you can learn what to look for yourself in the future. Any work done by a boatyard should be on quotation, and unless you know the yard well, it may be a good idea to get more than one estimate for the work to be done. Always inspect the work after it is finished, and if you feel uncertain of your ability to check the work, take a knowledgeable friend with you if possible.

If parts are replaced on the boat by a boatyard, always ask to see the faulty part; it helps you to understand what to look for next time. If the yard makes any alterations to the fuel or electricity systems, for example, make sure you get the details so that any future work is made more easy.

If the boatyard carries out an inspection and gives you a list of repair work necessary, or if you carry out the inspection yourself, make a list of the priorities and see that the repairs which affect the seaworthiness of the boat take precedence over any cosmetic repairs, such as repainting the galley. Never economize on jobs high on your priority list.

Should you decide to tackle repairs yourself use a reliable do-it-yourself manual or watch someone experienced to find out how to carry out the repair. Get an expert to inspect your work afterwards. The skills needed to

repair a cruising boat, for example, are often wide ranging – you need to be shipwright, carpenter, electrician, plumber and mechanic in one.

Even if you cannot manage the repairs yourself, the more experience you have of what may go wrong the better – you will be able to detect where faults will occur and save a potentially dangerous situation from occurring. The following pages explain the most likely causes of wear and tear and where to look for them.

Cruising boat laid up for the winter on special chocks and covered with a tarpaulin.

Hull

The main areas of the hull that are likely to show signs of wear are annotated below. The boat will have to be taken out of the water at least once a year to inspect the parts below the waterline.

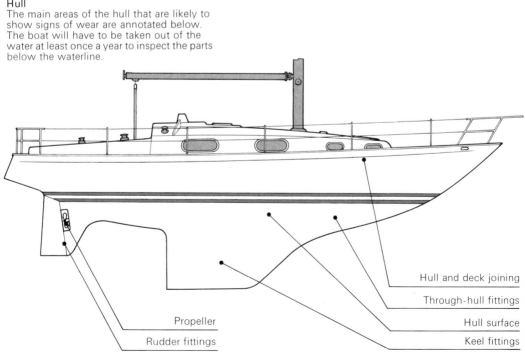

Hull and deck joining

Through-hull fittings

Propeller

Hull surface

Rudder fittings

Keel fittings

Maintaining hull and deck areas

The type and extent of the maintenance your boat needs will depend on the kind of construction. There is no such thing as a maintenance-free material despite what you may hear to the contrary – every material is subject to wear and tear to some degree and all types will be affected if water seeps through the fabric, particularly around joints and fittings. The hull is particularly prone to damage around chain plates, inlets and outlets for heads and engines, and the rudder, propeller shaft and keel (see pages 290–1). Screws, nuts and bolts corrode and wear. Most boats are made throughout of one material, but you will find boats with the hull made of one material and the deck of another – such as a ferrocement boat with a wooden deck, for example. Although you will be able to carry out inspection for deck maintenance on board, you will have to get the boat out of the water to look at the hull and hull fittings.

Most of the construction of the hull is hidden on the inside by the joinery needed for bunks, lockers and so on. However, where possible, check the inside for signs of structural damage, particularly where the bulkheads join the hull. The limber holes – notches at the bottom of the bulkhead which allow water to drain into the bilge – should be kept unblocked.

Wood

With wooden boats, you need to check the seams and joints very carefully for deterioration in the fastenings and for rot. Be thorough and check each plank on the outside and, where possible, on the inside as well. If the hull is painted, the rot will show as a crinkling of the paint surface.

Check all suspect timbers by prodding with a sharp instrument like a marline spike. The further it goes in the deeper the rot. The fastenings should be firmly attached and the wooden plugs which are used to cover the screws should be in good condition – not shrunken or distorted.

In this wooden hull the rot has become so extensive as to have demolished parts of the hull. Clearly, regular maintenance would have prevented this occurring.

Ferrocement

Ferrocement boats are usually fairly easy to maintain. However, the hull construction is reinforced with steel rods and wire mesh, so examine it for signs of corrosion. Check all areas around fittings attached to the hull and scrape away any rust to see how deep it goes.

Rust stains on the hull are a sign that the internal construction is damaged and needs attention.

Varnish

Wooden hulls and deck surfaces which are varnished will need to be regularly maintained if the wood is not to rot. You should check that all the varnished areas are neither flaking nor discoloured. If they are, the old varnish should be stripped off down to the bare wood and the surface revarnished – either with a natural linseed oil-based varnish or a synthetic variety, such as polyurethane. Varnishing is probably one of the least difficult tasks for the amateur to undertake – the instructions in most reliable do-it-yourself manuals are easy to follow.

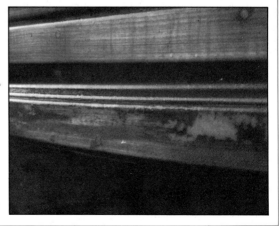

The varnish on the hull, right, has started to flake off. It needs scraping down and renewing if the wood underneath is not to rot.

Fiberglass

A large number of modern boats are composed of fiberglass which is often regarded as a trouble-free material. Like any other material, though, it has its own special problems arising from the way it is constructed. When a fiberglass boat is constructed, a gelcoat is first laid on a mold of the hull shape. This outside coat is not merely a cosmetic finish – it is intended to be a waterproof layer. However, it is never entirely resistant to water penetration. Occasionally small voids, in which air is trapped, occur between the gelcoat and the first layer of the fiberglass material. If water, or water vapor, gets through the outside coat, it is then trapped in pockets between the layers. This liquid turns to acid and builds up pressure which in turn causes the gelcoat to swell and the bond to fail. You then get blisters on the gelcoat (see right). In time, this delamination and weakening will affect the whole structure. However, it is not a rapid process and treatment need not be carried out immediately – the repair can normally be left until the end of the sailing season. In warmer climates, the heat can speed up the process of deterioriation, so if you are sailing in tropical waters, for example, you should get any problem treated straight away. The gelcoat can crack for a number of other reasons – the most usual cause is a sharp blow to the lower part of the hull from a rock or a jetty, for example. Damage can also be caused by scraping alongside another boat or a harbor wall. If the indentations

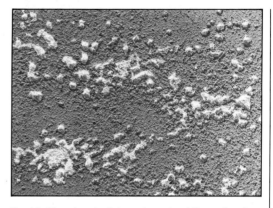

On this fiberglass hull the gelcoat has blistered owing to the build up of acid between the layers of the fabric.

are deep they need to be properly filled in quite quickly to prevent deterioration of the whole fabric, but even surface scratches should not be neglected for too long. Cracks and indentations are not difficult to repair – they simply need to be scraped clean and then filled in and sealed. Materials for carrying out fiberglass repairs can be obtained in ready prepared packs. The instructions must be followed carefully, and the color matched as accurately as possible to that of the repaired part of your boat.

Metal

The main danger to metal hulls and fittings is a process known as electrolysis. This occurs because a purer metal will progressively eat into any baser metal it comes into contact with, if both are in water. The warmer the water and the higher the salt content the more the process of deterioration is speeded up. You need to examine the hull and fittings carefully. If, for example, a steel plate is attached with a brass screw, the brass (pure metal) will damage the steel (base metal). However this is not going to create as much damage as, say, will be done to a

steel bolt through a brass plate, where the steel bolt would be eaten away completely.
The base metal can be protected by a properly installed system of sacrificial anodes – small zinc plates which attract the damage in an area where electrolysis is likely to occur.
Inspection of metal hulls and fittings should be carried out regularly and the problem, if it occurs, dealt with quickly by professional treatment. Fitting this type of protection to a metal hull is a skilled operation where expert advice should be sought.

Exposure to salt water has caused the corrosion which has badly affected the metal hull.

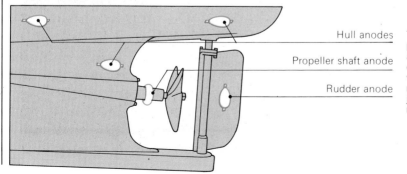

Hull anodes

Propeller shaft anode

Rudder anode

The exact size and positioning of sacrificial anodes is a matter for experts – they are used where base and pure metals are found in juxtaposition, and should not be painted over.

Sails and rigging

Sails and rigging are expensive to replace, so it is worthwhile trying to prolong the life of such equipment by taking good care of it. All modern synthetic sailcloth is more resistant to salt water than the natural materials formerly used, but it can still be damaged by chafe and stretching and prolonged exposure to sunlight. Attention to all aspects of sail care is essential (see opposite). You must inspect all sails regularly and systematically for signs of wear when they are set and when they are ashore. Sheets and lines are also susceptible to chafe and must be checked often. Metal spars and fittings are subject to metal fatigue and corrosion and must be examined at frequent intervals to prevent a defect going unnoticed and possibly leading to an accident at sea. The standing rigging, which is normally made of metal wire, takes a lot of strain and will rust or possibly break if not properly maintained.

Sail maintenance

Most people are not sufficiently expert to be able to carry out any but the most minor repairs to their sails and it is better not to attempt to mend sails yourself. They should be sent back to the manufacturer or to a professional sail repairer. However, it is essential to learn how to spot signs of wear so that you can deal with it before it gets worse. The easiest way to inspect your sails is to lay them out flat on an even clean surface and work around the edges and over the belly of the sail. Pay special attention to the points where the sail is attached to the spars and rigging.

The head
Examine the headboard (the reinforced part at the head of the sail) and make sure that the rivets are in place and that the stitching is not weak anywhere. The latter may well wear around the head and you will need to check the reinforcing patches in this area.

The tack
The tack is subjected to a great deal of strain and can distort. If the stitching breaks the whole sail will become misshapen. On a mainsail, look out for signs of wear on the bolt line (rope edging) where it rubs on the boom and for damage to the stitching on it.

The clew
The clew is subjected to the same type of wear as the tack, but on headsails is particularly vulnerable to chafe against the standing rigging.

The luff
On a mainsail, check that all the slugs are properly attached and not broken and that the reefing cringle is not distorted. Look out for chafe along the bolt line on a mainsail and for strands of broken wire on a headsail luff. The hanks on a headsail must be firmly attached and free from any corrosion.

The foot
On a mainsail with a roller reefing system, check for signs of chafe where it has been rolled around the boom. If there are slab reefing points or eyelets check that these are not pulled or torn.

The leech
Examine the batten pockets for damaged stitching and if there are any leech line attachments make sure they are in position. Genoa leeches on cruising boats are particularly vulnerable to chafe against the lifelines or shrouds.

General points
Always be alert to the possibility of deterioration of the fabric due to sunlight. If the cloth is thin or brittle over a small area it can be patched, but with larger areas the sail should be replaced.

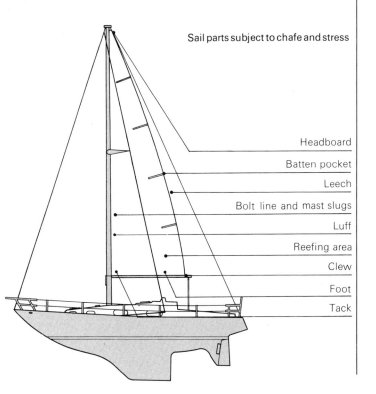

Sail parts subject to chafe and stress

Headboard

Batten pocket

Leech

Bolt line and mast slugs

Luff

Reefing area

Clew

Foot

Tack

Spinnakers

Spinnaker cloth is more delicate than that used for other sails and has to be treated with care. It is particularly susceptible to damage by sunlight and you must check it regularly for signs of deterioration. Spinnaker fabric is also liable to stretch and if this happens the sail may become unusable in all but light winds. From time to time compare the leeches to make sure one has not stretched more than the other. Pay special attention to the stitching on the corners and look out for chafe. The foot may show signs of wear where it rubs against the forestay.

Looking after sails

Sails are expensive to repair and replace so it is worthwhile following the hints on sail care below to help them last longer.

• Hose down sails after a wet trip and allow them to dry. Fold each one carefully and stow the bags in an airy place. Remove all dirt and stains as soon as possible and, at the end of the season, wash and dry them, following the sailmaker's instructions, before storing them.

• Never pull on the leech of a sail or it will distort.

• When hoisting a mainsail, support the boom as you pull on the halyard, with the topping lift on a cruising boat, or by hand on a one-design.

• Avoid putting unnecessary strain on sails and don't allow them to flog any longer than you can help it.

• Don't oversheet sails, especially headsails, which may rub against the ends of the spreaders.

• Never hoist sails in wind strengths higher than those for which they were designed.

• Use covers to protect sails left on spars for any length of time.

Sheets and lines

All your sheets and lines should be checked regularly. A broken or badly worn line, in particular, could be very dangerous. Laid rope can be spliced (see page 335), but if damaged, sheets and uphaul and downhaul lines which are normally made of plaited rope, will have to be replaced. You can prolong the life of sheets and lines by washing them in fresh water at least once a year to remove the salt and grime. The whipping on the ends of all ropes should be checked and, if necessary, reworked.

Spars and standing rigging

The majority of masts fitted to modern production boats are constructed from extruded aluminum. They are usually designed to take more strain than they are likely to be subjected to in order to make sure they last the life of the boat. Older boats or those built with a traditional design have wooden masts and spars. Aluminum spars should not need regular maintenance apart from a wash down with soapy water occasionally. However, you should

Cracking in an aluminum mast can result in it snapping when under strain if not properly treated.

Fraying near a shroud terminal can be caused by corrosion or fatigue, or by the terminal fitting pinching the wires.

inspect them regularly for signs of cracking and if you discover any fault in the metal, you should take expert advice. The spreaders, which take a great deal of strain, must be checked at intervals to make sure their fittings are secure. Load bearing fittings attached to the mast are made from marine grade stainless steel which does not corrode but is prone to stress fractures due to metal fatigue. If this occurs the fitting should be replaced. The standing rigging supporting the mast is normally made of 1 by 19 stainless or galvanized steel wire (that is 19 strands of wire twisted together). Galvanized wire needs to be treated annually with a linseed oil dressing to prevent rusting. The weakest parts of the standing rigging are the terminals where the shrouds are attached to the mast or deck. These should be checked regularly for signs of corrosion and lightly greased at regular intervals.

Halyards

Halyards can be made of rope or wire and run either inside or outside the mast through pulleys known as sheaves. If the halyard is wire, you must have a metal sheave, but some older boats with rope halyards have wooden ones. The sheaves are fitted into boxes at the top and bottom of the mast. The wear on halyards is concentrated in the areas where they rub on the top and bottom sheaves when the sail is hoisted. To ensure that the wear on the halyard is even it is a good idea to dismantle all the halyards and lay them out end-to-end at the end of each season so they can be inspected.

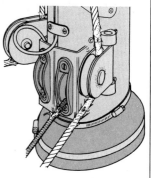
The wire and rope halyards above are both chafed where they enter the sheaves.

Engines

Crowded harbors, strong tides and the general need to be back at your permanent mooring or berth at a fixed time, have made it necessary for virtually all cruising boats to be fitted with an auxiliary engine. Boats can have one of two types (sometimes both): an outboard (a self-contained engine unit mounted on the stern of the boat) or an inboard (an internally mounted engine, usually situated under the cockpit floor).

Both types of engine need proper attention and regular servicing and maintenance. As with all rotating machinery, great care should be taken when working on or near it. If you are working on an inboard engine, make sure the cabin is properly ventilated.

Not so long ago most engines, and inboards in particular, were regarded by their owners with some suspicion. Inevitably, the engine failed to start or cut out at an inopportune moment. The present generation of engines have solid state ignitions and improved combustion, and are more resistant to the corrosive effects of salt water. Although the boat you buy will usually be fitted with an engine, if it is not, seek expert advice before installing one.

Every engine normally has a handbook which gives detailed illustrations of the parts and the main servicing points. You should keep the handbook on board in case you need it when afloat. You must also make sure that the engine is regularly and properly serviced. There may well be times when it is vital for the safety of you and your crew. You should also keep an adequate stock of spares on board (see opposite).

Outboard engines

Many small cruisers and most tenders are fitted with an outboard rather than an inboard engine. The advantage of an outboard is its light weight compared with an inboard, the small amount of space it requires and, of course, its relative cheapness. The engine can be removed easily for servicing and for laying up. Outboards can either be two- or four-stroke engines. The two-stroke (right) is the more common. It runs on a predetermined ratio of gas to oil the exact ratio being a vital part of the correct functioning of the engine. Any alteration in the fuel type or mixture will lead to the engine seizing up or overheating. The starting procedure recommended in the handbook should be followed and care taken not to flood the engine. Outboards respond to good treatment so be careful to operate yours according to the instructions.

Fuel filler

Ignition coil

Flywheel

Starter

Twist grip throttle

Generator

Connecting rod

Crankshaft

Water cooling system

Piston

Spark plug

Gear case

Main drive shaft

Water pump

Cavitation plate

Rubber shock absorber

Lock nut

Maintenance

In order to keep your outboard running efficiently it will need to be serviced at regular intervals, either by you if you are sufficiently skilled or by an expert mechanic. First of all the propeller needs to be inspected for damage or distortion. The starter cord should be checked for wear or the starter pinion movement examined. Look for any leaks or signs of overheating. Check the water pump is working (water should emerge from the outlet) and all fastenings are tightened. Spark plugs should be fitted with new washers and burnt or worn plugs cleaned or replaced. Make sure plug leads are in order.

If fitted with a battery charging system, make sure that it is working. Spray the electrical parts with damp-proof fluid and smear with silicone grease. Remove and clean the fuel filter bowl, rinse it in clean gas and clean the carburetor float.

Grease all moving parts and exposed cables. Change the oil in the lower drive unit, and clean and coat battery terminals with Vaseline. Drain and flush the gear case and refill to the correct level with recommended lubricant.

If, despite your efforts, your engine does not run properly then you will have to take it to an approved dealer. As a rough guide to the health of your engine, the tip of a spark plug of the correct type in an engine burning the right fuel mixture should look clean. There should be no build up of deposits and the electrodes should not be burnt away. Don't forget that you must have the correct fuel which should be fresh, and recently mixed. If the fuel has been standing around for a week or so, shake the can to mix it in. If refilling a can always put the oil in first – the gas will mix with the oil as it is added. When you connect the tank to the engine, make sure the air valve on top of the filler cap is undone, otherwise the engine will eventually stop as a vacuum builds up in the tank.

Installation

If you use a small outboard engine on a tender, you will have to take particular care when positioning it on the boat. It is important to get the mounting angle correct because otherwise the trim of the boat will be wrong. You can also use the position of the engine to adjust the trim of the boat if necessary and most engines have a special fitting which enables you to adjust the angle of the engine to the boat.

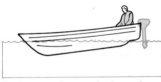

Engine too close to the boat. Stern rises out of the water and bows dip.

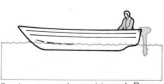

Engine too far away from boat, bows rise out of water and stern therefore dips.

Engine correctly positioned. Bows and stern level. Engine functions most efficiently.

Laying up

For the winter months the engine needs to be taken off the boat. If it needs servicing, get that done before laying up the engine, not at the beginning of the next season. Store properly in a warm dry place on a stand (right) and covered. The handbook for your engine should give you the appropriate information for your particular engine, but the general principle is, after flushing the engine out according to the instructions, to insert rust inhibiting oil into the air intake, and to coat all the outer moving parts with rust inhibiting oil. All other fluid should be removed from the engine. Cover the whole engine with cloth. When it comes to recommissioning, refill the fuel tank and run the engine in fresh water before use.

Fix the engine securely onto a trestle or similar support. Cover with cloth not plastic, which will cause condensation and possible rust. If possible store it under cover in a warm and dry place – a garage, for example.

Checklist and spares

Make sure your boat carries spares in case of trouble. Much will depend on the type of engine but generally you need spark plugs, spare fuel, shear pins, spare starter cord, wrenches, plug leads and parts, filters, damp start, grease and oil. Always take care

● to disconnect the battery when working on the electric starter.

● to disconnect the battery when leaving the boat.

● to disconnect and earth spark plug leads when working on manual starter.

● not to tilt the motor head down so that water runs into the power head.

● not to run the engine out of water – it will overheat.

● to use correct oil/fuel mix.

Diesel engines

Diesel engines are probably the simplest type of inboard engine. Some people, therefore, think that they are more suited to marine use than gasoline engines (opposite). Diesel engines also tend to be larger than gas engines and more subject to vibration. The diesel engine fires by compression of the fuel rather than by an electrical spark like the gas engines. The injector inserts the fuel at the right time in the compression cycle. Diesel fuel can cause problems if it is allowed to accumulate dirt and rust particles which then block up the fuel injectors (see below). Diesel fuel is less volatile than gas, and is therefore less dangerous to have on board.

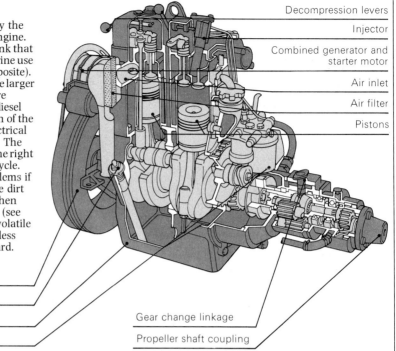

Decompression levers

Injector

Combined generator and starter motor

Air inlet

Air filter

Pistons

Flywheel

Oil dipstick

Oil sump

Fuel filter

Gear change linkage

Propeller shaft coupling

Fuel injection

The most likely source of trouble in a diesel engine is the fuel injection system, and the fuel injectors themselves in particular. An injector has a spring-loaded valve with a needle which fits exactly into the main nozzle body. It is held in place by a coil spring. As the fuel from the injection pump enters the gallery around the bottom of the needle, its pressure rises and causes a metered dose of fuel to be sprayed into the combustion chamber through the hole in the nozzle body. If an injector blocks, it will have to be stripped down. This is really a job for experts but can be dealt with on board if essential. The injector should be taken apart, and the parts soaked in finely filtered fuel or kerosene to clean them, using brass wire to unclog any small holes. Only non-linting cloth should be used to clean the parts which are reassembled wet.

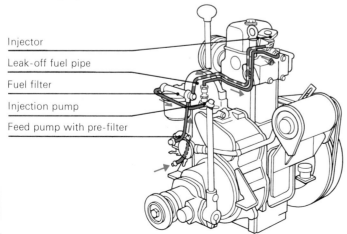

Injector

Leak-off fuel pipe

Fuel filter

Injection pump

Feed pump with pre-filter

Laying up

Laying up an engine, diesel or gas, is not complicated. The engine and gearbox oil should be changed, as should the filter elements. Drain and clean the water separating and sedimenting unit. All moving parts inside and outside the engine should be coated with rust inhibiting oil or grease. The engine should be drained (unless anti-freeze is being used). Batteries should be brought home, cleaned and protected from freezing. Starter motors should be sprayed with a moisture repellent (WD40, for example) and covered with a plastic bag. Crank the engine over periodically through the winter and oil the bores from time to time. Keep it covered with cloth to protect it.

Never leave water in the cooling system. Run the engine dry for a minute or two until no more water comes out of the exhaust pipe. Remove all impeller pumps, place the impellers in a plastic bag and tie them to the pump housing. Place a warning card on the engine to remind you what needs to be replaced before you try to start it again.

Gasoline engines

In some respects, a gas engine is easier to look after than a diesel engine, because although it takes more maintenance time, its workings are so similar to those of a car engine. A marine gas engine has certain special features: it has a two-stage cooling system which makes use of sea water. Because gas is highly volatile, great care needs to be taken that the fuel does not leak into the bilges of the boat. Frequent and thorough maintenance is a must, and the electrical system should be checked regularly.

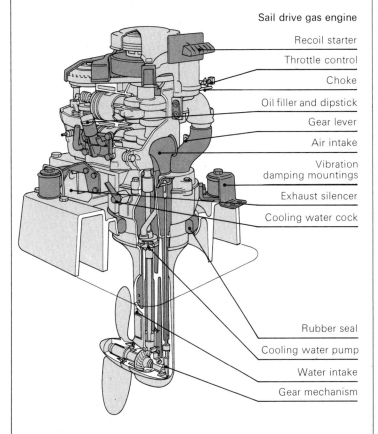

Sail drive gas engine

Recoil starter
Throttle control
Choke
Oil filler and dipstick
Gear lever
Air intake
Vibration damping mountings
Exhaust silencer
Cooling water cock

Rubber seal
Cooling water pump
Water intake
Gear mechanism

Spares

If you are sailing offshore, it is a good idea to take spares for your engine in case of an emergency. What you carry will depend on the space you have available. However, when sailing around your own waters, you can probably get whatever spares you need at a nearby port. It might be sensible to carry the smaller, more lightweight spares on board for the sake of convenience (below).
For a gas engine you would need: drive belt, water pump impeller; head and exhaust gaskets; cooling hose and clamps; propeller nut and pin; filter elements; length of fuel pipe and clips; spark plug set; distributor cap; coil; high tension lead; condenser.
For a diesel engine you would need: a filter, an injector; fuel pipe and clips; copper sealing washers; fuel pump; drive belt; water pump impeller; water hose and clips; head and exhaust gaskets; propeller nuts and pins.
If you are going to do any repairs yourself, you need a good tool kit on board. Keep it somewhere accessible and make sure that it contains the wrenches and screwdrivers that fit the nuts, bolts and screws on your particular make of engine.

Maintenance

The maintenance requirements for both gas and diesel engines are not dissimilar. Both should be serviced regularly in accordance with the instructions in the handbook for the particular type of engine. As an unreliable marine engine could put the lives of both you and your crew in danger if it failed at the wrong moment, it is vital that you should take all possible steps to make sure your engine is going to run smoothly. Regular inspection will help — look for possible oil, fuel or water leaks before they develop into serious trouble. The cleaner you keep the engine the easier it will be to spot any faults. You should make sure that you use only clean fuel in the engine. All tanks should be fitted with inlet filters. A large filter will normally be supplied

with the engine, but it is desirable to fit a water separation/sedimenter in the fuel line to make sure that only pure fuel reaches the engine. Both filter and sedimenter should be cleaned regularly. Air filters should also be cleaned and replaced regularly. As engines often operate at an angle, particularly if you are motor sailing, make sure the oil level is correct. In both diesel and gas engines, the stern bearing (the part where the propeller shaft passes through the hull) should be looked after carefully. The bearing prevents water from coming into the boat and needs to be greased at regular intervals. Make sure the water cooling system is working properly (simply check to see if water is coming out of the exhaust system) or the engine will overheat.

Electrical system

Recent developments in electronic navigational aids and their increasingly widespread use, even in relatively unsophisticated boats, have given added importance to the electrical system on a boat. No longer is the battery just a means of starting the engine and of providing interior lighting as a bonus, it is an integral part of the boat's sailing equipment. While it is unlikely that most owners will have sufficient knowledge to design and fit an electrical system themselves, it is important to learn the basic principles of the system in your boat and how to maintain the batteries and wiring in good condition so that you can always be sure of their safety and efficient operation. It is worthwhile familiarizing yourself with the wiring plan so that any fault can be quickly traced and repaired.

Nearly all boats are fitted with a basic DC (direct current) system as it is the only type suitable for starting a marine engine. In addition to a DC system, some boats are also fitted with an AC (alternating current) supply, which can either be operated from a shore-based power supply or from an onboard generator. An AC system gives a higher voltage current and allows you to use domestic appliances which cannot be operated on DC electricity. The AC and DC wiring systems are totally separate.

A correctly wired boat will have a bonding system which grounds any current which may build up in a metal fitting. All large metal parts of the boat, such as the fuel tank, and appliances using a lot of current should be connected via heavy-duty, insulated, braided, copper wire to a bonding plate or anode fixed on the underwater part of the hull. This will discharge any electrical current and will prevent anyone receiving a shock from a fitting and will also inhibit damage from corrosion caused by electrolysis (see pages 292–3).

Basic DC system
In a DC system, the charge is generated in the engine by a dynamo or, more usually, an alternator, and is stored in the battery. This supplies current to the starter motor when required, and to the electrical fittings on the boat via a distribution panel. All appliances wired to the DC system are connected to the distribution panel by a live wire and a return wire to complete the circuit.

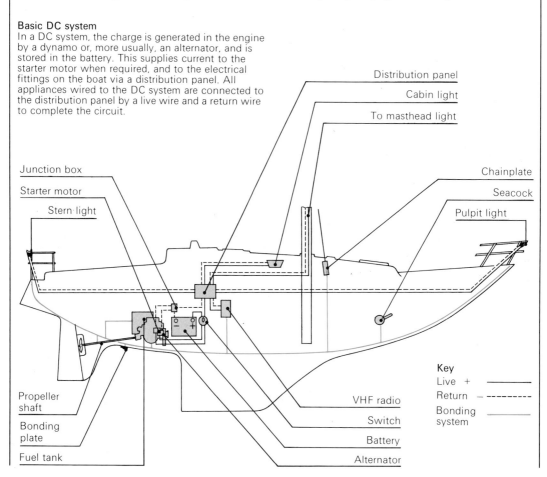

Distribution panel

Cabin light

To masthead light

Junction box

Starter motor

Stern light

Chainplate

Seacock

Pulpit light

Propeller shaft

Bonding plate

Fuel tank

VHF radio

Switch

Battery

Alternator

Key
Live +
Return −
Bonding system

Wiring

The wiring on a boat should be of well-insulated, tinned-copper, stranded wire which is more flexible and less subject to fatigue than solid wire. It is very important to make sure that wiring is sufficiently thick for both the load and the distance the current must travel from the power source to the appliance. If the wire used is too thin it will overheat and cause a drop in voltage. The route that the wires follow from the distribution panel must be planned to protect them from chafe, heat, water and oil. It is often a good idea to run them through plastic conduits. Live and return wires from each appliance, which are separately insulated, must be twisted together to prevent the formation of electromagnetic fields which may adversely affect navigation instruments. The wiring must be checked at the beginning and end of each season for signs of deterioration in the insulating casing and for corrosion at the terminals. Any damaged parts should be replaced. If a new length of wire needs to be fitted, always join it with a specially made terminal fitting, instead of by splicing, as wires joined in this way may separate and corrode in the vibration of the boat. If a metal part is lost from a terminal do not substitute a part of a different metal as this will result in corrosion due to electrolysis. Never secure wiring runs with metal staples as these may pierce the insulation, but use plastic loops or cleats instead. Cleanliness is vital, and dirt and grease must not be allowed to accumulate around terminals. This is particularly important in the case of the battery lead terminals. If they show signs of corrosion they should be removed and scrubbed with a wire brush and then refitted tightly and coated in silicone grease or petroleum jelly.

Batteries

Most boats operate on a 12 or 24 volt system supplied by a battery, usually of the lead and acid type. You will need to make sure that your battery is of a suitable capacity (in terms of amp/hours) for your needs and, if necessary, link up another battery using one of the methods shown below. Your battery must be carefully fitted, preferably in a special ventilated box which keeps it in position even in a 360° roll and prevents acid leakage. It should have vents leading outside the boat to prevent hydrogen accumulation. You must check the level of the electrolyte fluid in the battery regularly and keep it topped up with distilled water. The acid content must be checked twice a year with a hydrometer.

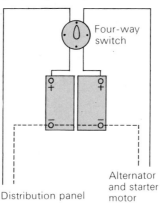

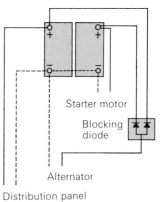

Linking two batteries
There are two methods of linking batteries. The first, above left, makes use of a four-way isolating switch which allows you to use either of the two batteries separately or both at once. An alternative method (above right) is to fit a blocking diode which charges the batteries separately and allows you to use each battery for a different function.

Installing new equipment

When fitting a new DC appliance you must first make sure that it will not overload your system. If necessary, consult an expert first. The next step is to turn off the power at the battery. Then remove the cover of the distribution panel which will reveal two bars to which the pairs of wires from existing fittings are attached. These are the positive (live) and negative (return) bus bars. Join the live and the return wires on your new appliance to vacant terminals on the appropriate bus bars. Replace the panel cover and secure the wires at regular intervals between the appliance and the distribution panel.

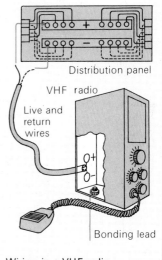

Wiring-in a VHF radio
The live and return wires are fitted to the distribution panel. A third wire links the appliance to the bonding system.

Water systems

There are usually four separate water systems on a boat, all of which require maintenance if they are to work efficiently. One system is used to pump the water out of the bilges, the second is the fresh water system which can be as simple as a plastic can or a sophisticated assembly of plastic piping, with pumps and filters. Another system provides the heads with salt water and takes away waste, and yet another cools the engine. The type of system will depend to some extent on the size and design of the boat. Quite a few boats have a waste discharging system which includes a special holding tank so that any foul water can be retained and discharged at recommended places or waste-treatment areas.

As far as maintenance goes, your principal tasks are to check that all the pumps are working. The system should be drained at the end of the season, the pipes and tanks cleaned, the moving parts lubricated.

The illustration shows the main water systems on board an average-sized cruising boat. The plan of your boat's plumbing will depend on its design: the position of the heads, and the type of waste disposal system direct — direct into holding tank or treatment device.

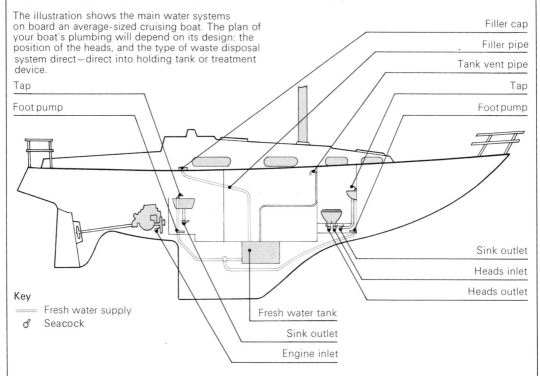

Filler cap

Filler pipe

Tank vent pipe

Tap

Foot pump

Tap

Foot pump

Sink outlet

Heads inlet

Heads outlet

Key

=== Fresh water supply

♂ Seacock

Fresh water tank

Sink outlet

Engine inlet

Seacocks

Seacocks are the means by which your boat is prevented from flooding should a pipe or connection break. They control the flow of sea water into the boat, and have a rotating valve which can be opened or closed. This valve needs lubricating about once every three months or so. It is important to make sure it functions properly for obvious reasons. It is a good idea not to leave a seacock permanently open or shut for too long at a stretch or it may well jam in that position. When your boat is laid up for the winter, it would be advisable to dismantle the seacocks and inspect them. Debris which catches in the filter can be removed from the inside when the boat is afloat, but make sure the seacock is firmly closed.

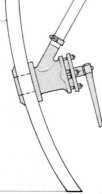

The seacock is a special valve fixed through the bottom of the boat. It enables water to be taken in for engine cooling, flushing the heads and washing up. It should be constructed of metals suitable for use in sea water and should be kept closed except when in use. Flexible hoses are attached to seacocks with stainless steel clips.

Water tanks

If you are going to leave your boat for any length of time, the water tanks should be drained, although for any period under a month the water will last without any undue risk of contamination. When you are laying up the boat for the winter you clearly will have to empty the tank to stop it from freezing. When you drain the tank you should check the inside surfaces for algae or slime. As there is no inspection cover in some water tanks, the best solution is to cut your own and fit a removable lid. Shine a flashlight inside and use a mirror to examine the inner top surface. The best way of cleaning a contaminated tank is to pour in some bicarbonate of soda solution (approximately 1 tsp per liter) and then flush the tank out with fresh water before refilling. Check the pumps, pipes and joints at the same time. Plastic pipes will harden and crack after a time, and should be replaced as necessary. Pumps should be stripped down, cleaned and have the washers replaced, and, if you don't have a filter already, you could insert one into the system. Keep a supply of water purifying tablets on board in case the water source is suspect.

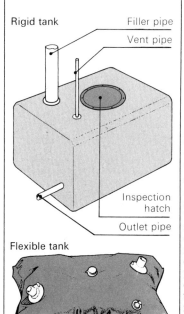

Rigid tank — Filler pipe — Vent pipe — Inspection hatch — Outlet pipe

Flexible tank

Heads

Lavatories on board, known as heads, use sea water pumped through pipes to discharge effluent. (Check the new regulations for approved MSDs for your type of boat and the waters you sail in.) Unless you take care of the heads, their presence will dominate the boat. Make sure that the bowl and the pipes are kept clean by using an approved disinfectant and pumping it through the system. The heads will block easily; unless you want to spend time afloat unblocking them, make sure all new crew members understand how the heads work (see below). Some lavatories have manual, and some electrical pumping systems – if the latter, take care that the electric system on the boat is properly maintained.

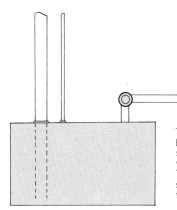

The most common system is a bowl with a sea water inlet and raw sewage outlet into a holding tank which can be pumped out ashore. The inlet and outlet both have seacocks. A pump is used to flush the bowl.

Bilge pumps

Keeping the bilges of the boat dry and in good condition is vital. It would take a great amount of water in the bilges to sink the boat and it is unlikely you would ever accumulate so much water that this could occur. However, damage caused by even quite small amounts of water can be considerable. The engine, and other metal equipment, will begin to rust and corrode and mildew will grow, leaving an unpleasant smell in the boat.

There are several types of pump with which to empty the bilges. They can be manual, electric or engine operated. The electric type can be fitted with an automatic switch to turn on the pump, if the water level rises to a predetermined level. Engine operated and electrically operated pumps should not usually be allowed to run while dry or they may burn out. All pumps need regular servicing, and every boat should have at least two bilge pumps on board. One must be operable by the helmsman and one ought to be a manual type in case the electric system on the boat fails.

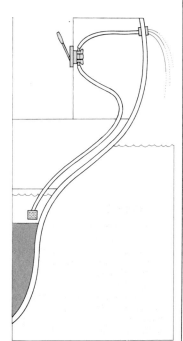

One of the most common types of bilge pump is the manual diaphragm type, above. The end of the hose should have a filter to prevent debris blocking the system. The handle is stowed when not in use.

Emergency repairs

Accidents to the boat and its equipment usually occur through lack of maintenance or sailing skill, or through straightforward negligence. A well-maintained boat, handled by a competent crew, should face few real emergencies except those caused by freak weather conditions. Nonetheless, you have to be prepared for any emergency, should it occur.

In most boats, failure of one of the fittings is the most likely cause of an emergency. The most common problems arise when some part of the rigging snaps in heavy weather, or a sail tears. One of the difficulties you, as skipper, have to face in dealing with an emergency is the circumstances in which it happens – nearly always in freak weather. Not only do you have to deal with the emergency but you also have to contend with heaving seas, strong winds, driving rain, and a seasick crew into the bargain. Your main objective is to make the boat seaworthy again, as quickly as possible, so that further damage does not occur and so that the boat can make to port, and safety, as quickly as possible.

Clearly, you can only make a good job of the repairs if you have whatever tools you need to do the job, and it would be a mistake to economize on a proper tool kit. The one, listed below, should be adequate to cover most of the repairs.

Repair equipment

Engines: spares according to manufacturer's instructions, such as gaskets and seals; oil filter; spark plugs and coil (for a gas engine) and injectors (for a diesel one); fuel and water pumps.

Sails: sailmaker's palm; sail needles – assorted sizes; waxed sail thread – assorted weights; piston hanks; mast track slugs; marline spike; sailcloth (same weight as principal sails); self-adhesive sail mending tape.

General: blocks and shackles; turnbuckles; bulldog clamps; screws and nails – assorted sizes; split pins and rings; washers; fuses; bulbs; corks and rubber plugs; insulating tape; epoxy adhesive; sealant; Vaseline; oil; waterproof grease; solder; wire cutters; bolt cutters; small vise; hack-saw; wood saw; drill and bits; brace and bits; files; spanners; pliers; screwdrivers; hammer; mole wrench; spare cord; wire rope; flashlight (batteries and bulb spares); assorted pieces of plywood; a wooden plank (for gang-plank or fender board if necessary).

Sail repairs

On the principle that prevention is better than cure, you need to take care of your sails when in use and inspect them regularly (see pages 294–5). Any weakness in the cloth, or any minor damage, will immediately worsen considerably in a strong blow and a useless sail in certain conditions could be dangerous. You will help preserve the life of your sails if you make sure you do not over-canvas your boat for the conditions – if the wind increases, you should change down to a smaller sail or take in a reef. Your passage may be slower but it will certainly be safer and you will prevent undue strain and stress on the sails, rigging and fittings.

If a sail does tear in use, lower it at once to prevent further damage and hoist an alternative sail if possible. If the mainsail alone is damaged, sail under the headsail or the headsail and the mizzen

Mending a tear
If you have to mend a tear or split in a sail, it is best to use a stitch, like herringbone stitch, right, which is very strong. Make sure you do not stitch too close to the tear. Insert the needle at A. Reinsert it at B and take it across the back of the work, through the gap and over the thread A–B and then across the back of the work to C. Reinsert needle, repeat steps as required and finish off.

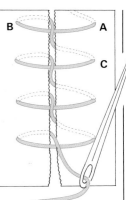

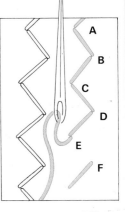

Sewing a seam
When restitching a seam which has pulled apart, you should follow the original stitch pattern. Make a row of stitches, B–C, D–E, and so on, in one direction. Then work back in the intervals, A–B, C–D, E–F and so on, until complete.

(if applicable), or hoist a headsail in place of the main by fixing the head to the mainsail halyard, and the tack and clew to the boom – it will serve as a loose-footed sail. By doing so, you will keep the boat better balanced than by sailing under headsail alone. Once the boat is sailing properly, you can then put the sail repairs in hand.

Most sail repairs done at sea are only intended to serve as a temporary measure and the damaged sail should be taken to a sail repairer on your return to have it repaired permanently. However, the temporary repair must be sewn securely enough to make sure it holds in strong winds. You will need a sail marker's palm (a leather thong, with a metal insert, which is strapped across the palm of one hand) to exert pressure on the needle. It is important to make sure the stitching is properly secured at the beginning and end of the work.

Restitching a bolt rope
If the bolt rope on the sail comes adrift, it will have to be stitched back on using a stronger needle than usual and with doubled thread. Stitch across the lay of the rope and take care not to let the sail curl around the rope.

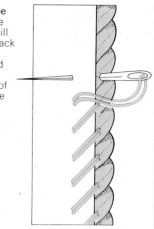

Joining cloth
If you need to seam two pieces of cloth together, turn under the adjacent edges of both pieces of cloth by an equal amount (1), overlap the edges (2) and then seam down each new edge in oversewing stitch as shown to make the final seam (3).

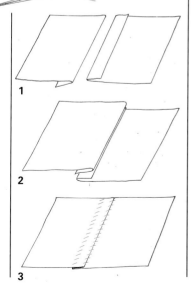

1

2

3

Patching a sail
When making a patch, be careful to position the new fabric centrally over the tear. If you do not, the patch will distort under the strain and cause more damage. You need to cut the fabric patch large enough to allow for turnings and to cover the tear or hole with room to spare. Cut off an appropriate size rectangle and trim off the corners (1), turn the edges under and place the patch over the centre of the hole (2), oversew around the turned edges of the patch (3) and then turn the work over, trim the hole to a rectangle and oversew around the raw edges (4) to produce a neatly finished patch (5).

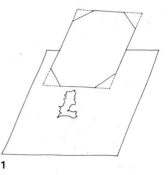

1

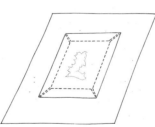

2

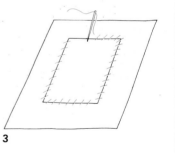

3

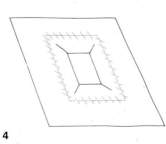

4

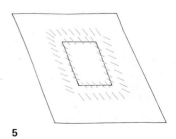

5

Hull damage

Should you have the misfortune to tear a hole in the hull of your boat, your first job is to stem the flow of water which will pour in if the boat was holed below or near to the waterline. This area is the most likely to be damaged as the boat will, in all probability, have collided with a hidden obstacle beneath the surface of the water.

If the hole is around the waterline mark, you must try to lift the damaged area out of the water. The simplest way of doing this is to get the boat to heel over so that the damaged part is on the windward side out of the water. You can also try to raise the damaged part further by moving a weight in the boat onto the leeward side (though not, of course, to the point of capsizing it, if a dinghy, or causing the boat to broach, if a cruiser).

The next task is to block the hole temporarily. A very small hole can be plugged with a cork or screwed-up piece of cloth. A larger hole will need to be stuffed with a much thicker piece of cloth — a sail bag or cushion, for example. The wadding will have to be kept in place with an object, such as a fender board or boat-hook, which in turn is wedged

into position. It helps to seal the hole if an additional stout piece of cloth (such as a spare sail) is bound over the damaged part of the hull (see below). Once the hole is plugged, the crew must be organized to bail out the water using pumps and buckets. The size of the hole will determine your ability to plug it, and if there is absolutely no way you can plug the hole, prevent water from coming in and the boat from sinking, then you may find you have to abandon ship (see pages 316–7).

If you happen to be cruising offshore in a wooden boat which is accidentally holed you could manufacture a more permanent repair. Plug the hole in the usual way with cloth, and then anchor the boat while you screw or nail a piece of wood over the hole on the inside and if possible another piece of wood over the outside as well. Most other constructions are more difficult to repair at sea, unless you happen to be carrying extensive spares and tool kit. However, repairs at sea are not very easy to tackle and you may be better advised to make for the nearest port and professional help as soon as possible.

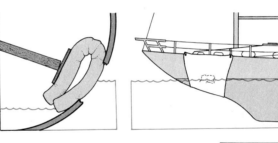

A cushion has been used, right, to plug the hole in the hull. It can be wedged with a board or broom handle.

The hull, far right, has been bandaged with a sail which is lowered over the bow. Lines attached to each corner of the sail are secured on cleats.

Broken rigging

If some part of the rigging snaps, it can in turn lead to the mast breaking if action is not taken immediately. Should a shroud break (usually when sailing to windward in heavy weather) you should put the boat onto the opposite tack immediately, to take the strain off the remaining shroud and the mast. A spare halyard can be used to take the place of the broken shroud; if the shroud deck fitting is undamaged, attach the halyard to it, but if it is broken or weakened, attach the halyard to a deck eye or other strong point. Should the forestay break, you can use a spare halyard as an immediate temporary repair. The luff wire of the headsail helps support the mast so it is less likely to snap. The forestay can be secured temporarily if it snaps near the deck fitting by making an eye in the end (see right) and then attaching a line from the new eye to the deck fitting. The backstay

can be repaired in the same way. If a fitting high up on the mast breaks, it will not be easy to repair until back in harbour. It is possible to go up the mast on a bosun's chair (right) but, at sea, this is strictly for the experienced.

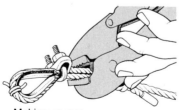

Making an eye
Bend the end of the broken wire or halyard into a U-shape. If you have a thimble, put it inside the U and then clamp the two ends of the U together with a plier wrench. Attach a bulldog clamp to the base of the new eye, and tighten up the nuts so that wires are securely gripped. This forms the new eye.

Climbing the mast
To go up the mast, you need a bosun's chair — a canvas harness. Clip the belt to the shackle of a halyard. A second halyard can also be clipped on and kept taut as a safety precaution, and a line around the waist and mast used as well. You are then winched up the mast.

Dismasting

If you maintain your mast and rigging in good repair, you are less likely to run the risk of being dismasted. Masts usually break owing to failure of the standing rigging but in a small boat a capsize could also easily cause the mast to snap. When it does break, it most commonly snaps off at the spreaders where the load on it is at its greatest.

When it snaps, the mast will usually go overboard on the leeward side. You may be able to turn the boat so that the wreckage is to windward, preventing the boat from riding over the lost mast and thereby damaging the hull. Whatever you do, do not run the engine while the mast and rigging are lying in the water – the propeller will almost certainly become fouled.

Your first task once the mast has broken is to try and recover the wreckage if possible or, failing that, to cut it all away with a hacksaw. If sailing offshore, you may well need to put up temporary replacement rigging (known as jury rigging).

How the boat is jury-rigged depends to some extent on your own ingenuity, on the construction of the boat and, more particularly, the type of mast, the amount of equipment you have on board, and on how much of the mast is left

On this boat, which has lost half its mast, new shrouds have been jury rigged onto the stump and a jib hoisted in place of the mainsail.

standing. With a wooden mast, the job of jury rigging is made simpler because you can screw and bolt fittings into the stump from which temporary rigging for the sails can be attached.

You can make a temporary mast from the boom or spinnaker pole stepped in the mast step (or lashed to the stump of the mast) on which to hoist a makeshift sail. Shrouds can be jury-rigged to keep the new mast in place using spare lines and a jury rig knot (see page 336). You will have to tension the new lines using winches. A small jib, used loose-footed, can be set in place of the mainsail.

Steering failure

Loss of steering gear requires some ingenuity on the part of the skipper. If the rudder breaks, an oar, ladder or spinnaker pole can be strongly lashed to the stern to provide some sort of temporary steering gear. In addition, the crew can try to trim the sails so that, by altering the balance between jib and mainsail, the bow of the boat can be made to move towards or away from the wind. However, in many modern designs, the boat, once rudderless, tends to swing around the keel. The solution for these types of boat is to tow a board, ladder or small bucket from the leeward quarter of the boat, which will help to pull the bow away from the wind.

Fouled propeller

All too often, and too easily, a propeller is fouled by a rope, wire or fishing line, for example, catching in the propeller and winding itself around the shaft. Freeing the line can be difficult. There are several methods for trying to free the rope (other than going overboard in a wet suit, armed with a hacksaw, which can be both difficult and dangerous). If one person catches the free end of the line, while another turns the blades of the propeller by manipulating the flywheel by hand (see right), the line may free itself.

Whatever you do, make sure the engine is switched off and the plugs disconnected if it is a gas engine (or, if a diesel, decompressed) before you start trying to free the jammed propeller.

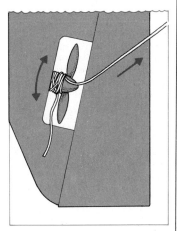

To free a line caught around the propeller, one person turns the flywheel in the opposite way to that in which it was turning while the other gives a sharp tug on the line in the opposite direction.

Safety

Safety afloat often has as much to do with the attitude of the skipper as the amount of equipment on board the boat. A good skipper will be aware of the likely dangers and organize himself, the crew and the boat so that these are reduced as much as possible, without spoiling the enjoyment of the trip. He must accept responsibility for the welfare of all those on his boat and make every effort to make sure they come to no harm.

Everybody who sails knows that there is an element of danger involved and many would argue that this is an integral part of the enjoyment of the sport. However, it would be foolhardy not to take every reasonable precaution to prevent your boat becoming involved in accidents which could endanger your crew and those on other boats. The other major point to bear in mind is that if you are involved in an accident at sea, many others will automatically be involved The Coast Guard or Coast Guard Auxiliary could be called out to your assistance, and people could well risk their lives to save yours.

Safety precautions

There is a great onus of responsibility on the skipper's part not to put to sea with an unseaworthy craft or an inexperienced crew, or to take unnecessary risks. Too many people decide that sailing is easy after a few trips in good weather in someone else's boat and thoughtlessly take an unknown boat out into unfamiliar waters with little knowledge of navigation and without making any of the essential checks on the safety equipment. It is always preferable to err on the side of caution and never to overestimate your ability to cope with a difficult situation. Never assume that you will be able to manage until you have proved to yourself in a supervized situation that you can. This applies to your entire knowledge of sailing, whether navigating on a coastal passage or carrying out a man overboard recovery routine.

As far as your crew's safety is concerned, you will need to know how far they can be relied upon to carry out various tasks. It demands a sensitivity to human psychology, but it may help if you organize a few seamanship tests at the beginning of any cruise to assess your crew's level of knowledge.

The sort of equipment you carry aboard the boat will depend on the type of boat, the size of the crew and the waters you are sailing in. In most countries the authorities responsible for

It is important that the crew wear safety harnesses and clip on their lifelines even in the cockpit if necessary, as they have done in this disabled boat.

sailing recommend basic safety equipment for pleasure boats. In the United States, the US Coast Guard lays down the regulations. The checklist on page 173 includes the basic items of safety equipment, and you should never carry less than this minimum but you may wish to add extra items. Remember that if you have children aboard you will have to carry the appropriate number of small lifejackets and safety harnesses.

It is not enough simply to buy the equipment and leave it on board, you must also know how to use it and how to keep it in good working order. Your flares (see pages 314–5) should be kept dry and easily accessible. Lifejackets will need inspection from time to time to make sure there are no flaws, and the carbon dioxide cylinder replaced regularly as these cease to function after a certain period of time. Make sure that all the crew know how their lifejacket is fitted and how to inflate it. When laying down safety procedures, such as the wearing of lifejackets, it is important that you, as the skipper, always observe the same rules. Always check that you have all the essential equipment aboard before you go afloat each time, and make sure that the boat and all its equipment is in sound working order.

Fighting fire

Fire is one of the most serious risks on board a boat and it is essential to take every precaution to prevent it. Proper maintenance of the engine, stove and electrical equipment is the best way of reducing accidents caused by fire (see Engines, pages 296—9, Electrical system, pages 300—1).

In the engine, fire can start as a result of fuel vapor being ignited by a spark from the starter motor, for example. Fuel pipes should be checked regularly for wear. Lining the engine compartment with a fire-retarding material, and fitting a fresh air blower and automatic fire extinguisher into the engine compartment, will also help, to make your boat safer. It is important to follow a proper refuelling procedure. Always stop the engine and turn off the fuel supply to the engine first. Turn off all electrical and gas appliances and keep the companionway closed. Before restarting the engine, check that the filler cap has been securely replaced and clean up any fuel which may have been spilled. If you carry extra fuel in separate containers, these must be specially designed for the purpose and stowed in outside lockers away from the engine and galley, where a spark might cause a fire.

In the galley, the greatest danger is from escaping gas, as it will collect in the bilges creating the threat of an explosion. A "gas sniffer" fitted in the boat will alert you to a dangerous build up of gas. The stove mountings and gas pipes should be examined for signs of deterioration from time to time. Make sure that your crew always observe the drill of turning the gas off at the bottle (to allow the remaining gas in the pipe to burn off) before turning the knob at the stove. Always remember to turn off the gas if you leave the cooker unattended and if you are going to leave the boat for any length of time, disconnect the bottle. In order to make sure that no gas or fuel vapor is allowed to accumulate in the bilges, it is a good idea to see that they are pumped out every day when the boat is in use.

One of the most frequent causes of fire on boats, as elsewhere, is careless smoking and it is therefore sensible to lay down some rules governing smoking on board. Never allow smoking when refuelling, when fitting a new gas cylinder, when working in the engine compartment or when lying in a bunk. Never leave a lighted cigarette unattended and, if possible, try to limit smoking to the above deck area.

If a fire does break out, it is important to be calm and try to identify the source of the fire and then use the appropriate fire extinguisher (below) to put it out. It is helpful if you can reduce draught around the area of the fire to deprive it of oxygen. Continue to use the fire extinguisher until sometime after the flames have gone out as there is always a risk of a fire restarting. If you are unable to control the spread of the fire, you should prepare lifejackets, flares and the liferaft in case you have to abandon ship (see pages 316—7).

Equipment

Your boat should carry a variety of fire extinguishers to deal with different sorts of fire. They must be of a type approved by the Coast Guard and you must be careful to have them checked periodically. Two different fire extinguishers are illustrated, right. The most common is the dry powder extinguisher. It is suitable for use on all types of fire. A foam fire extinguisher is particularly effective for fighting fires caused by fuel oil or cooking fat. However, this type should not be used on electrical fires and if carried, should be supplemented by the dry powder type or a third extinguisher of the carbon dioxide type. These are mainly used for tackling fire in engines and electrical systems. A fire blanket is an important fire fighting aid which should always be kept close to hand in the galley. Using the blanket, a fire in a pan on the stove can be quickly smothered. You must remember to leave the blanket over the pan until it is cool, otherwise the fire is likely to restart.

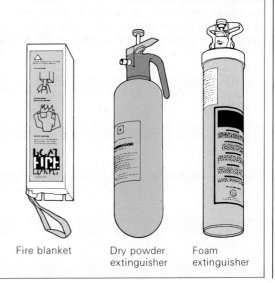

Fire blanket   Dry powder extinguisher   Foam extinguisher

Going aground

Although there may possibly be times when you wish to put your boat on the ground deliberately (see Drying out, pages 190–1) there will, unfortunately, be others when you go aground accidentally. You can at least take comfort in the fact that you won't be the first – there are very few boat owners who can honestly claim never to have been aground. You can also take comfort from the fact that the more times you go aground, the more practiced you will become at getting free. In theory, careful navigation and common sense should prevent it happening in the first place.

The boat above is firmly stranded and will have to wait for the next rise in tide to float off.

There are occasions when going aground can be dangerous because of the type of ground or the state of the sea. With a one-design the problem is not usually too serious, and with any luck you may be able to pole the boat off into deeper water, using an oar or a spinnaker pole, particularly if you can shift the weight around and heel the boat over to reduce its draft (see opposite).

With a cruising boat, which has a deeper, and usually fixed, keel, you may have more difficulty. Although going over the side and physically pushing the boat off the ground can

often free it, beware of leaping overboard into soft mud or unexpectedly deep water. Poke about first with a spinnaker pole or boat-hook to discover the nature and depth of the seabed.

If you have the misfortune to go aground on the top of a spring tide (known as being neaped) you may have to wait for a couple of weeks before you can get the boat floated off. In this case, before you leave the boat, lay out anchors to keep it from drifting off should the high tide recur earlier than you expected. In an emergency you could organize a working party to dig you a channel into deeper water.

Preparing the boat

Knowing how to deal with the situation once you are grounded is one of the most important factors. The first essential is not to panic. The next is to work out which method of freeing yourself is the most likely to be needed. If you happen to have gone aground with the boat heeling towards deeper water (right) you will have to try and heel it over in the opposite direction, to prevent it from flooding later or from lying down-hill and getting damaged. The best way is to move all the gear and crew weight over to the other side of the boat. If the boat has already settled, heeled in the wrong direction, you will have to try and pivot it around, until it lies facing the other way. Do this by poling from one end, or by laying out an anchor and using the rode to haul on. Your other main priority is to discover the nature of the seabed. If you have gone aground on jagged rocks, you will have to do something to try and protect the hull from further damage (and, of course, plug any

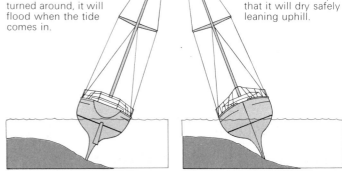

This boat is leaning downhill. Unless it is turned around, it will flood when the tide comes in.

This boat has been heeled deliberately so that it will dry safely leaning uphill.

hole that may have been torn in it in the process). The hull can be protected by sandwiching a folded sail or bunk cushions (or a partially deflated inflatable) between the hull and the rocks Fix some lines from the padding to the boat or you may lose the padding when the boat floats off. The other danger is that the boat may either be on top of one large isolated rock, from which it will

fall when the tide recedes further, in a gulley or on the edge of the bank. In the latter case, the danger is that the mast may snap when the boat heels as it dries. If possible, try and turn the boat so that it lies against the uphill bank, but if that fails, the only recourse is to pad the hull with anything available, to prevent the mast from hitting the ground and breaking.

Getting off

You first need to establish whether the tide is rising or falling. If the tide is rising, there is no real problem as you only have to wait for it to rise sufficiently to float the boat off. If there is any danger of the boat being pushed further into shallow water as the tide rises, for example if an onshore wind is blowing, then you will have to take steps to prevent this happening. The best solution in this case is usually to lay an anchor in deeper water so that you can haul on the anchor rode and pull the boat free.

If you have gone aground on a falling tide you will have to do your best to free the boat before the water leaves you high and dry. So the first step is to work out where the deeper water is and, if you were under sail, decide whether the sails are helping you or hindering you in your efforts to get free. If the latter, you need

to get them down and stowed as quickly as possible. If you have gone aground on the edge of a channel (it often happens when tacking up a narrow river) you need to turn the bow of the boat to point into deeper water. In smaller boats and dinghies this can usually be managed by poling from the bow using the spinnaker pole, or in shallow water with a firm seabed, by going over the side yourself and pushing. If you do go over the side, make sure you first attach a line from yourself to the boat so that you cannot be left in the water waving goodbye to your boat. Once you have managed to turn the boat in the direction in which you wish to leave, the next step is to try and reduce the draft so that it will float free. If the boat has a centerboard and you have not already raised it, you should do so.

Reducing draft

The draft of the boat can be reduced in a number of different ways. The wind in the sails, if it is coming from the right direction, will heel the boat; alternatively you can try putting as much weight as possible on one side of the boat. If you can, get the crew to sit on the boom, and then swing this over the side of the boat (having first made sure the topping lift is strong enough to take the weight!) or if they prove unwilling, attach an anchor to the end of the boom. Climbing the mast will also help to make the boat heel more easily. In some boats, moving the crew from bow to stern may sometimes help — if the boat is deeper aft than forward and all the crew congregate at the bow it may be enough to float it off.

Hanging a heavy weight from the boom end may heel the boat enough to float it free.

When the boat is deeper aft than forward, moving the weight to the bow can help to lift the keel free.

Bilge keels

Twin-keeled boats, conversely, will dig themselves deeper into the ground if they heel. So if you are in a bilge keeled boat which is heeled when you go aground, try to get it upright; you may be able to float it off.

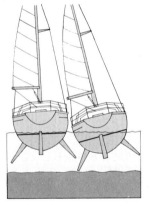

Using an anchor

If you have not succeeded with any other method, you may have to use an anchor to pull yourself clear. This will, of course, only work with cruising boats, and you need a dinghy from which to lay the anchor. Speed is important as water depth may be decreasing. Normally you use the kedge anchor and a rope rode (see page 198) and the anchor is laid as far as possible into deeper water, with the end taken back onto the most powerful winch on the boat. If necessary, use two winches. As the crew grind on the winches, any spare crew member should try to heel the boat or rock it — it helps break up the suction. If this fails, you are stuck fast until the next high water.

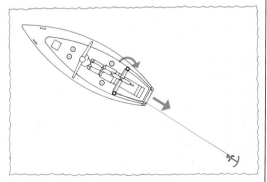

An anchor can be used to try and drag the boat off. Here the anchor line is led around both sheet winches for extra power.

311

Rescuing the boat

If your boat is so badly damaged that it can no longer proceed under its own power, you will have to summon help. The causes of disablement could be numerous, but the skipper will have to decide what to do about the effect. If the boat is so badly damaged that salvage is impossible, he will have to abandon ship (see page 316). But, if the boat can be salvaged, he must try and summon appropriate assistance, or else try and get the boat back to port himself, if possible.

Once the boat has been disabled the first job is to prevent further damage occurring and, if possible, to make sure the boat is in adequately seaworthy condition to be towed back to harbor (opposite). In some cases, if the accident occurred near to shore, the boat may be able to make the journey back to port under its own steam. However, if you have a VHF radio transmitter and there is any doubt at all, the Coast Guard should be alerted and the position of the boat, and the nature of the problem explained, so that if anything should go wrong, the situation is already known.

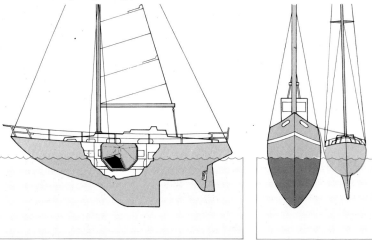

A racing boat disabled in the Fastnet race, 1979, being towed to safety by a lifeboat.

Salvaging

Depending on the cause of the damage to the boat, there are ways of getting it into a condition to be able to limp back to port. If the hull has been damaged and the skipper decides to head for home, it is best to do this as quickly as possible. Make for the chosen port, while the emergency repairs are under way, and use both sail and motor (if you have them) to make as fast a passage as possible. If the boat is taking on a lot of water, for example, you can often keep a diesel engine running in a waterlogged boat by attaching a pipe to the engine air intake to prevent this becoming waterlogged. Use the liferaft and the inflatable dinghy as additional internal buoyancy

to keep the boat afloat (below). This latter suggestion should only be followed if very close to port when the damage occurs. Your liferaft may otherwise be more necessary for the crew to escape.

Always try to aim for the part of the shoreline which has an accessible beach so that the boat can be dragged above the tideline by motor vehicles. Alternatively, try to tie up alongside a much larger boat, like a fishing trawler, which can support you with heavy ropes or wires until proper salvage help can be summoned. If you radio ahead to the port, the local fire brigade may send out a mobile pump to get rid of the water.

An inflatable dinghy or liferaft can be used (right) to provide buoyancy for a sinking boat. Care must be taken to prevent it pressing against any sharp objects which could burst it. Once in port, it may be possible to tie up alongside a larger vessel such as a trawler (far right). At least two heavy lines should be used and are taken right under the boat by dropping a large bight in the lines over the bow and stern and pulling them back a little towards the center. They are then secured firmly to the trawler.

Taking a tow

Once you realize that you can no longer cope with an emergency yourself and need outside help, you will first have to summon assistance and then deal with the organization of the rescue. One of the problems is in organizing a salvage operation in difficult conditions, but you must think of the financial considerations to some extent, because the law of the sea enables the salvaging vessel to claim a fee which is usually proportional to the value of the vessel being rescued. Negotiation for the fee should be done at sea before the rescue if possible. Another point to consider is the size of the vessel offering assistance; if it is very big indeed, and cannot

travel at less than five to six knots, more damage may well be created than will be saved because it will have to tow your boat at a higher speed than it was designed for. Once you have agreed the terms, you must, of course, make sure that the boat is towed as safely as possible. Use your own lines if you can and make sure that the line and the boat are both protected from chafe. The secret of successful towing is to have a long springy line or a heavy chain. A mixture of the two is often ideal because the chain and line together absorb any snatching, keep the tow tensioned at all times and the boat travels at an even speed.

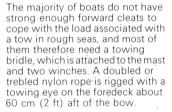

The majority of boats do not have strong enough forward cleats to cope with the load associated with a tow in rough seas, and most of them therefore need a towing bridle, which is attached to the mast and two winches. A doubled or trebled nylon rope is rigged with a towing eye on the foredeck about 60 cm (2 ft) aft of the bow.

When being towed, left, try to prevent the boat over-running the line. To slow the boat down it helps to trail a line with a heavy weight from the stern — this also helps prevent the boat from veering about.

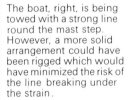

The boat, right, is being towed with a strong line round the mast step. However, a more solid arrangement could have been rigged which would have minimized the risk of the line breaking under the strain.

Distress signals

In an emergency you have to be able to attract the attention of any passing vessel or be able to summon the coastguard. There are several ways of summoning help, and appropriate equipment must be carried on board with which to do so. Some countries stipulate the number and type of distress signals which specific craft must carry while others prefer to leave the decision to the skipper of the boat. Most boats which travel regularly off shore will have a very high frequency (VHF) radio transmitter on board (with a licence and an operator qualified to use the VHF set), as well as distress flares and flags. The latter are useful if other signals let you down.

It is essential that all crew members know how to make distress calls, and each should be familiar with the equipment on board, knowing both where to find it and how to handle it. Which distress signals you use depends to some extent on the nature of the emergency. If you have one, a VHF set can be used for most emergencies but you may need to use flares as well to show your position clearly. In fog or at night, you will need white flares if a collision is imminent. These are not used for any other form of emergency.

Flares

Distress flares are used for two purposes: to raise the alarm and to show the position of the boat. You must be in real danger when you use one – if you call the Coast Guard out unnecessarily you may be fined. The number and range of flares you carry on board will depend on personal choice, unless the authorities stipulate which ones you should carry. It is important to make sure you have enough of them; remember that the first flares you send up may not be seen. The crew must be instructed as to which flares to use and how they work. The flares must be stowed carefully in a place known to all crew members, and which is accessible even in the dark. Some flares are designed for night use and others for the day. The different types of flare are shown, right, and the purpose for which they are used is also explained. White flares should be stowed where the helmsman can lay hands on them easily. If you have to fire a flare, follow the directions on the packet. The type you use depends on the distance and the nature of the emergency. Always point the flare downwind.

VHF Radio

The VHF radio transmitter has a range roughly confined to the line of sight between the transmitting and receiving aerial. When buying a VHF set, do not economize; when you need it urgently, you do not want to be hampered by poor transmission. Many coastal stations have their aerials positioned high up so that a small boat, coastal cruising, can still make contact within a range of 64 km (40 miles). Between two boats at sea, the range is likely to be reduced. Most boats use VHF sets with about 12 channels, one of which must be channel 16, and the rest all have specific uses such as calling from ship to shore or ship to ship. Distress calls, however, are made on channel 16, and are always preceded by a Mayday call. You then give the name of your boat, your position as a range and bearing from a known landmark and the nature of the emergency.

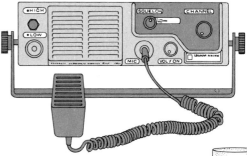

Hand-held white flare
Gives out a strong, bright white light. Use only to draw attention to yourself if collision is likely. The collision pack has four white flares and is not used for any other form of emergency.

Hand-held red flare
Burns with a bright red light for one minute. Use to show exact position. Range of visibility – 4·5 km (3 miles).

Hand-held orange smoke
Has the same use as a red hand-held flare but is used in bright daylight, when visibility is good and winds are light. It burns for about 40 seconds.

Red parachute rocket
Use this when a long way from help. The rocket projects a bright red flare up to 330 m (1000 ft) high which burns for 40 seconds.

Buoyant orange smoke
Burns for about three minutes. After ignition, drop it into the water to leeward of the boat. Useful for signalling position to an air search.

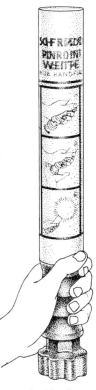

Hand-held white flare

There are two types of VHF set. The fixed set, left, has 12 channels, while the hand-held set above only has the distress channel, 16, although other channels may be installed. Although the hand-held set has a shorter range than the fixed one, it is useful in emergencies, as it can be used aboard a life raft or dinghy, or in the water.

Phonetic alphabet

A	Alpha	J	Juliet	S	Sierra
B	Bravo	K	Kilo	T	Tango
C	Charlie	L	Lima	U	Unicorn
D	Delta	M	Mike	V	Victor
E	Echo	N	November	W	Whisky
F	Foxtrot	O	Oscar	X	X-ray
G	Golf	P	Papa	Y	Yankee
H	Hotel	Q	Quebec	Z	Zulu
I	India	R	Romeo		

Other signals

Flags can also be used to make distress signals. They should be large enough to be identifiable at some distance. You need at least four principal flags – the V, W, N and C. The V flag signifies, "I require assistance". The W flag, "I require medical assistance", and the N flag flown over the C indicates, "I am in distress and require assistance". A black square flown with a black ball shape above or below it also indicates distress. A torch can be used to flash the Morse distress signal, right.

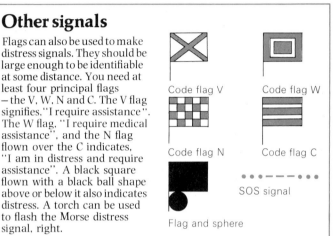

Code flag V

Code flag W

Code flag N

Code flag C

SOS signal

Flag and sphere

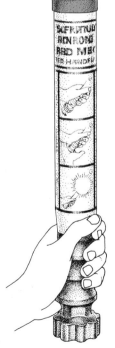

Hand-held red flare

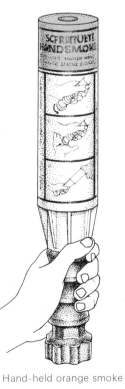

Hand-held orange smoke

Red parachute rocket

Buoyant orange smoke

315

Abandoning ship

In a desperate situation, you may have to abandon your boat and take to the life raft. The decision as to when to abandon ship will probably be quite easy, if and when the time ever comes. Before doing so, you need to think hard about whether you would be safer in your boat. Following the disaster which struck the Fastnet race in 1979, some people now consider that the life raft is not the only chance of salvation; many boats abandoned in the race were found, still floating comfortably, many hours later. Once you decide to take to the life raft, you must make sure that you have as many things with you as you are likely to need. One solution is to pack a panic bag which contains any items you may want, that are not already included in the life raft kit, and which are not used at any other time.

You may, of course, be rescued directly from your own boat or by another boat, or helicopter (see below). If you have time, protect your boat as much as possible by closing all the washboards, shutting all the seacocks, and lashing down the equipment. It may be possible to salvage the boat at some later time.

The last survivor on a competing boat in the Fastnet race, 1979, about to be winched aboard a naval helicopter.

Rescue at sea

If you abandon your boat with rescuers standing by, much will depend on the nature of the rescue. If the Coast Guard is alerted, it is likely you will be rescued by helicopter, particularly in foul weather. The helicopter cannot usually hover directly over a sailing boat, for fear of becoming entangled in the mast and rigging, so you will have to move away from the boat first. This means either getting into the dinghy, if you have one, or simply jumping overboard into the sea (when instructed by the rescuers) and waiting to be picked up. If you are being rescued by another boat, it may not be easy for it to come alongside. If you have a dinghy, use it, but attach a long line between the dinghy and the rescue boat to ensure that you do not lose touch. In most cases, a rescue boat crew will instruct you as to what to do. With a large rescue boat, when the boarding ladder is dropped over the side, wait for the top of a wave before jumping for the ladder, otherwise you may be crushed.

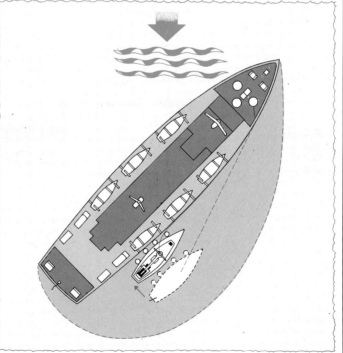

A very large rescue boat should lie at the angle to the wind illustrated above, to give maximum shelter to the rescue operation. Only one line, from bow to bow, should be attached.

Life rafts

The life raft is the last resort in an emergency. However, bear in mind that in many countries any manufacturer can put a raft on the market and sell it without a certificate approving its manufacture. So, make sure that the life raft you have on board has been approved by a national sailing body and is large enough to take all your crew comfortably. Once the decision has been made to take to the life raft, you must make sure that you have everything you need. See that the crew are dressed in as much warm clothing as possible. Once you have taken to the life raft, your survival will depend on being able to make distress signals, having adequate food and water and keeping warm. The basic essentials are included in the life raft but it should be emphasized that this is the minimum you will need.

The life raft, right, is for four people, and is fully inflated. It comes complete with the kit, below, and a boarding ladder.

The life raft pack contains all the equipment illustrated. Any extra you will have to pack yourself in a special bag to take with you.

First aid kit

Sea anchor

Paddles

Fishing line

Bailer

Water, can openers, cup, seasickness pills

Quoit and line

Bellows

Repair kit, flares, stopper, sponge, knife

Survival leaflets

Flashlight, batteries and bulb

Re-sealing lids

Plastic bag

Taking to the life raft

Cut or untie the life raft from its stowed position. Check that the painter is tied to a strong point on the boat. The painter is designed to break at a certain load so the life raft will not remain attached to a sinking boat. Normally, however, the last man aboard the life raft cuts the painter.

1 Pick the life raft up (it will be either in a cannister, above, or a bag) and throw it over the leeward side of the boat.

2 Inflation will take about 30 seconds from the moment it hits the water.

3 When it is fully inflated, the first person climbs into the life raft and any extra gear is passed down. The method of boarding is the same as that used on page 172. Once everyone is aboard the painter is cut.

Medical care and first aid

Ideally every crew member of a boat should be in perfect health before putting out to sea. If anyone suffering from an illness or disability does go sailing, they should make their condition known to the skipper beforehand. If he agrees to take them, they should make sure that they have all the medical supplies they need.

The medical care and general welfare of the crew is, of course, the skipper's responsibility. One of his first tasks is to make sure the boat has adequate first aid equipment. Clearly, before you decide exactly what kind of medical equipment you need on board you must first have established what kind of sailing you will be doing. If you are simply going on day excursions or port-hopping along the coast, you can put an ill or wounded member of the crew on shore fairly quickly and will need only basic first aid equipment. If you are going on longer trips — offshore for several days — you not only need more equipment but you also need to have a reasonably good knowledge of first aid, and you will have to be prepared to put it into practice when necessary. For any cruising boat, a good first aid manual is essential and, for dealing with serious injury, some grounding in first aid is a prerequisite.

On the whole, the kind of medical attention you will mostly have to carry out is simple — attending to minor injuries, such as bumps, cuts and abrasions. Now and again more serious accidents occur, and you should at least know how to control bleeding, what to look for in concussion, and how to resuscitate someone who has stopped breathing. Anyone cruising will also have to deal with the common minor complaints most people suffer from occasionally.

Before you go out and purchase equipment for a medical kit, think about the type of crew you are likely to have on board — old or young, healthy or not so healthy — and the climate and type of waters you will be sailing in. It is always a good idea to consult your own doctor first and if he sails himself, or knows a doctor who does, you will be able to get some useful advice.

Remember to keep your medical kit in a watertight container and divide it into at least two sections — one for general everyday care and one for emergencies. The list, above right, gives a broad suggestion of what it should contain but the final choice is up to you. Remember to make sure that the person to whom any medicine is given is not allergic to it for any reason. When confronted with an emergency, do not hesitate to contact the Coast Guard or a passing ship. If you are in any doubt at all, get the patient to hospital as soon as possible. Your first aid kits, divided into a general and an emergency section respectively, should contain the following:

First aid kit (general)
Painkillers (aspirin or equivalent and a stronger variety); calamine lotion; throat lozenges; sea-sickness tablets; salt tablets; antiseptic (liquid and cream); anti-insect bite cream; sun barrier cream; sodium bicarbonate; eye wash and ointment; thermometer; scissors; safety pins; butter-fly bandages; eye dressings; plasters; first aid tape; gauze dressings; bandages — narrow cotton and wide stretch crepe; absorbent cotton; non-adhesive dressing; Q-tips.

First aid kit (emergency)
Butterfly bandages; surgical scissors and gloves; safety razor; surgical tape; gauze pads; elastic bandages and gauze bandage roll; cotton bandages; safety pins; dressings — sterile and vaseline gauze; alcohol; local anesthetic ointment and spray; splints; space blanket.

Seasickness

Seasickness is such a common complaint when sailing that there are few sailors who can claim they have never suffered from it. At best, it can simply be mildly unpleasant and, at its worst, it can be so bad as to kill all enjoyment of sailing. There are certain things you can do before going afloat to help prevent seasickness — don't eat rich foods, and don't drink too heavily beforehand. When on board keep your liquid intake down and your dry food intake up. Sea-sickness is not a stomach disorder however — the problem is one of balance. It does help to keep busy and concentrating on a job. If you start to feel queasy, lie down as soon as possible. Moving about down below in a cruiser will only make you worse. There are a number of proprietary drugs to help control seasickness but in the end the individual user has to find out by experiment what suits him best. The small print on any seasickness remedy should be read first. It is worth bearing in mind that some drugs will make you drowsy. Don't forget that taking tablets once you are already seasick is unlikely to be successful as you won't keep the tablets down long enough for them to work. Take them at least a couple of hours before sailing (or when you are expecting bad weather to arrive).

First aid

One of the first things to look out for in the case of major injury is shock (see right). This is a serious condition and if left untreated can result in damage to the kidneys or brain and even death. As well as taking care of shock, the priority after any injury is firstly to restore breathing, secondly to attend to any major bleeding, thirdly to attend to the position of the casualty and keep him warm, and lastly to attend to any fracture. If any internal injury or spinal fracture is suspected, do not move him until professional help arrives.

Cuts and abrasions

With small cuts and grazes, you need to clean the wound out very thoroughly with plenty of fresh (not salt) water. Dry the area around the wound and apply a sterile dressing – either a plaster or a non-adhesive dressing and bandage. For deeper wounds your first job will probably be to stop the bleeding by applying pressure to the wound. In most cases, this will be enough to start the blood clotting and the flow should stop. If an artery has been severed, this will not be adequate and you will have to stop the bleeding by exerting pressure on the artery (bottom right) that feeds the area (bottom left) and by applying pressure on the wound at the same time. If the artery is severed, you need to get the patient to hospital as quickly as possible. Deeper cuts should be closed with butterfly bandages to keep the wound edges together (below right). Much larger wounds may need to be stitched. Offshore cruising sailors can buy ready-made suture kits complete with instructions – but do not use one unless you know how to.

Cover the wound with a clean gauze pad and apply pressure to it. Hold the limb up if possible – it helps to stop the bleeding.

Gaping wounds can be closed by using steri-strips. Hold the edges of the wound together and fasten the strips as shown.

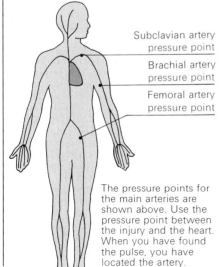

Subclavian artery pressure point

Brachial artery pressure point

Femoral artery pressure point

The pressure points for the main arteries are shown above. Use the pressure point between the injury and the heart. When you have found the pulse, you have located the artery.

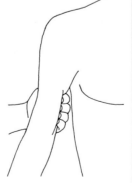

Squash the artery by pressing its overlying skin against the bone. Here the wound is in the arm and the brachial artery is squeezed.

Shock

Any serious injury can result in the person going into a state of shock. When this happens, the patient becomes grey and pale, cold and clammy, and starts to sweat. He will be confused. His condition is more serious than a patient simply being "shocked" – that is pale and faint. The first task is to put him into the recovery position with his feet elevated (see page 322) and to keep him as warm as you can so that the blood circulates as well as possible. Feel the person's pulse – one of the classic signs of shock, even if the others are missing, is a very weak but rapid pulse (and in someone very fit who suffers an injury, other symptoms are not always apparent). It should normally be around 60–90 beats a minute, and it should be strong. If there is no suspected internal injury, the person can also be given hot, sweet tea. Shock often occurs when there is some internal injury, so watch out for any signs of this – vomiting, pain in the abdomen and a swollen or hard abdomen, for example. Shock is a serious condition and should be treated as such. Do not let your concern (apart from artificial respiration and controlling severe bleeding) for another injury divert your attention from dealing with the shock. Get the patient to hospital without delay.

Blows

A blow to the head – a fairly common injury on board a boat – may not have any obvious results apart from a swelling on the surface of the skull but the person should be watched for any possible signs of concussion. These are nausea, vomiting, drowsiness and unequal or dilated pupils. It is a good idea not to let the person sleep for a while after a severe blow. Be very careful if the person was knocked out or has lost any part of their memory: keep the patient quiet and get them to a doctor without delay.

Burns

Most burns suffered on board a boat are caused by accidents in the galley or the engine area. Apart from immediate pain and discomfort, extensive burns cause shock and dehydration. One of the first things to establish when someone is burned is the severity of the burn. Burns can be classified as first, second or third degree (see below).

When treating a burn, the first priority is to cool the burned area. Apply cold fresh water to the burned skin and keep the area cooled by renewing

the applications for at least ten minutes. The next priority is to make sure the patient is given plenty of fluids – little and often. The burning dehydrates the patient considerably. If the patient has only suffered a first degree burn, it can simply be covered lightly with a non-adhesive dressing. Large second and third degree burns should be treated professionally. A bad burn will result in shock – so follow the treatment described on page 319 and give painkillers as necessary.

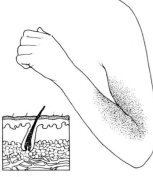 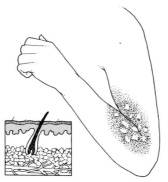 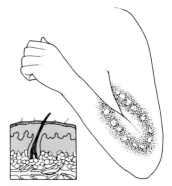

With most minor burns, known as first degree burns, there will be redness and slight swelling in the burned area. The skin does not blister but it will be painful.

A second degree burn will cause redness of the skin with white patches, and the skin will blister. The whole area looks shiny – pain may be intense.

With third degree burns, the skin is hard and white. Although the severity of the burn is greater, pain is less because the nerve endings have been burnt away.

Acid and alkali burns

An accident with cleaning fluid, or acid from a battery or detergents for example, can be serious. If acid of any sort gets on the skin, wash it off immediately. Remember not to use any substance which gives off noxious vapours inside the boat, where ventilation is limited. If the acid gets in the eyes, treat immediately or sight may be lost. The first step is to wash the eye thoroughly with plenty of fresh water and to continue to do so for

at least five minutes (see below left). Then rinse the eye with a solution of baking soda (sodium bicarbonate) and water (1 tsp baking soda to a quart of water). Cover the eye with clean gauze dressing and bandage. Get the patient to port and to medical treatment as soon as possible. If the burn is caused by a non-acid substance, follow the same procedure but *do not* rinse with the baking soda solution.

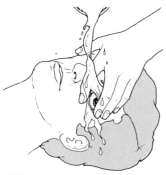 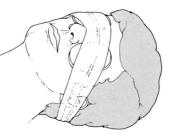

1 Turn patient's head to one side and tip water from inner to outer corner of eye for ten minutes.

2 When thoroughly rinsed, cover eyes with gauze pad and bandage to keep pads in place.

Sunburn and sunstroke

Although most people take some precautions against sunburn and sunstroke on land, they often forget about it when sailing. To prevent sunburn, a good sun barrier cream is needed and you should wear a wide brimmed hat to protect you. If you do get sunburned, drink plenty. Sunstroke or heat collapse are also the result of over exposure to the sun. Someone suffering from heatstroke will feel weak, nauseous, and may break out in a cold sweat. The condition is not serious and the patient simply needs to lie down and drink plenty until recovered. Sunstroke, however, can result in loss of life. The patient suddenly becomes unconscious with a great rise in body temperature. Keep him cool by wrapping him up in wet towels. Get him treated professionally as soon as possible.

Dislocations, sprains and fractures

One of the more common injuries on board a boat is a dislocation or sprain of a joint. If the joint becomes dislocated, it will look distorted and the patient will be in considerable pain. Administer painkillers and get him to hospital as soon as possible. If a joint is sprained it will be swollen and very painful but all movements are possible. Strap the injured limb with a crepe bandage and give painkillers as necessary. When a fracture occurs, the area becomes swollen, the joints will not move, and pain is localized in a particular area when the affected part is pressed. If a fracture is suspected, first immobilize the limb.

The best way of immobilizing a limb is to fasten it to a splint — taking care not to move the limb while doing so. A splint can be improvised from a deck broom handle for example or an adjoining limb makes an excellent splint. Pad the splint if possible and make sure it is long enough to immobilize the limb above and below the fracture.

If the fracture is so severe as to

have caused the bone to penetrate the flesh, there is considerable risk of infection. Before attaching the splint to the limb cover the wound with a dressing.

Fractures of the ribs are also fairly common. These are nearly always simple fractures in which case the only treatment is to give the patient painkillers. If, however, the ribs have punctured a lung (or some sharp object has done the same thing) the patient will be short of breath. If there is an open wound, cover it immediately with your hand and then plug the whole wound with a sterile dressing and get the patient to hospital straightaway. If he begins to turn blue, start artificial respiration (see below) and continue until professional treatment is at hand.

A spinal fracture on board boat is a grave problem, as the rocking movement of the boat prevents the patient from being kept still. Try to stabilize the patient as much as possible and immobilize him by strapping him to an oar or similar straight object.

Splint a finger by strapping it to the next finger using plaster or gauze bandage.

Padding is inserted between the fractured leg and the good one which are bandaged together above and below the fracture.

Resuscitation

The expired air method of ventilating the lungs in order to restore breathing has been proved the quickest and most efficient. It is an effective way of letting air into the lungs and of restoring breathing when it has stopped — for example, from cardiac arrest, near drowning or carbon monoxide poisoning. (If the latter occurs, you will need to continue the resuscitation for much longer.) Mouth-to-mouth resuscitation can be given in almost any position (even in water — although a life jacket

would have to be removed first as it floats the person's head too high). If his mouth is damaged, mouth-to-nose resuscitation can be given instead. The method is the same as below except that the nose is not pinched and the mouth is kept closed by lifting the jaw. In both cases, the mouth should be cleared first of any obstruction (broken teeth, dentures, vomit or blood, for example). Continue giving mouth-to-mouth resuscitation until the patient begins to breathe of his own accord.

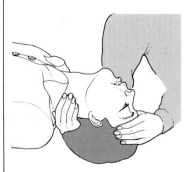

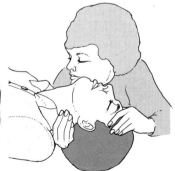

1 Lay the casualty flat on his back and kneel alongside him. Extend the head and neck by tilting the head backwards, and clear the mouth of debris.

2 Take a deep breath and pinch the patient's nose. Blow into his mouth after making sure you have obtained a good seal. The chest will then rise if you are successful.

3 Take another breath yourself. The patient's chest will fall. Repeat steps 2 and 3 until the patient gasps and begins to breathe of his own accord.

Heart attack

The symptoms of a heart attack are mainly dizziness, pains in the chest, shortness of breath, numbness in the left arm (spreading across to the right), and possibly pains in the neck. If these symptoms occur, get the patient to lie still, loosen any tight clothing and let him have plenty of air. If there is no carotid pulse, the pupils are widely dilated and skin turns blue-grey, the patient has suffered a cardiac arrest. Your task is then two-fold: to get breathing started and to start the

heart beating again. Mouth-to-mouth resuscitation is used to try and start breathing and external heart massage to get the heart beating again. If two people are available, one should carry out the mouth-to-mouth resuscitation and the other the heart massage. If on your own, give 15 strokes of external heart massage followed by three breaths into lungs and repeat the process until the patient recovers or for 30 minutes (or until you are exhausted and can no longer continue).

1 Lay patient flat on his back on a hard surface and kneel alongside. Pull patient's head back while your helper delivers a sharp blow to the center of his chest.

2 Give one breath into patient's mouth (see Resuscitation, page 321).

3 Helper places heel of one hand on top of lower part of patient's breast bone and other hand on top of first. Keeping arms straight, he presses down, then relaxes, and repeats three times. Alternate steps 2 and 3, 20 times a minute.

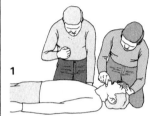

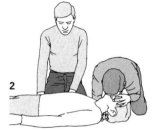

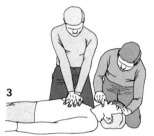

Hypothermia

One of the biggest dangers to sailors is the cold. Only if you wear the correct clothing will you maintain body temperature. If you become too cold, or if you are immersed in water colder than 20°C (68°F), your body will lose heat (see right) until you become unconscious and finally die. How long this process takes depends on a number of factors – physical condition, age and bodyweight. The remedy for hypothermia is to get the person out of any wet clothing, and wrap him in insulating layers of clothing and blankets. (A space blanket is ideal and will keep the heat in even if wet.) Give him a sweet warm drink.

Body temp (approx)	Symptoms of hypothermia
37°–33°C 99°–91°F	Intense shivering which becomes uncontrollable; difficulty in speaking
32°–30°C 90°–86°F	Shivering decreases; lack of coordination; thinking muddled
29°–27°C 85°–81°F	Unable to reason; muscles cease to function; pulse and respiration slowed
26°–25°C 80°–78°F	Unconscious; heartbeat erratic
Below 25°C Below 78°F	Brain cells not functioning; heart and lungs do not function – death

Drowning

If someone falls overboard and is picked up unconscious and not breathing, your first task is to start resuscitation (see page 321). As soon as breathing has started, get his wet clothes off and cover him up. Keep him in the recovery position to let water drain from his mouth. He will probably also be suffering from shock and from hypothermia. Take all possible steps (see left) to get the circulation working normally again after you have started respiration.

Recovery position

Put the patient on his front with his head to one side, as shown right. If possible raise the legs a little, as this helps the flow of blood to the brain. The recovery position is used primarily when the patient is in shock or is suffering from hypothermia.

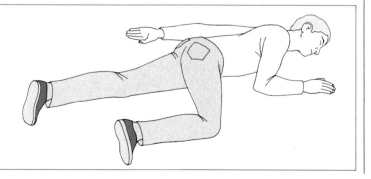

Appendix

Aerodynamics · Hydrodynamics · Ropework
Boat ownership · Glossary of terms · Index

Aero- and hydrodynamics

Once you have sailed a boat it soon becomes obvious that when the sails are set to catch the wind the boat moves forward. You will also begin to realize that some sailors know a great deal about the theory of how a boat sails while others know nothing, and that both groups can produce successful sailors. It is vital to accept that people who learn to sail by observation, trial and error can be as successful as those who have spent time studying the theory as well. However, some understanding of the principles of aerodynamics and hydrodynamics, could save time spent in sailing practice. In any event, it is interesting to know the underlying causes of something that you have discovered for yourself by observation. If you are interested in racing your boat, be it a one-design or a cruiser/racer, you will benefit from an understanding of the subject.

As the boat's performance depends on its environment, the nature and characteristics of both water and air are equally important. The successful sailor makes the best possible use of his boat, the water and the air. He can only do so if the boat designer has already understood what is required and has produced a boat with an appropriate shape, both in terms of the hull and the sails, to achieve the optimum performance. It is then the sailor's job to modify and utilize the capabilities of the boat to meet any alterations in the water and wind conditions which may occur.

Of the two, the theory of hydrodynamics is easier to grasp because water is both visible and tangible, but aerodynamics is possibly of greater interest to the sailor since the hull shape is more rigid than the sail area, and there is less he can do to modify its effect.

In its natural state the moving air which sailors harness is a mixture of warm and cold air which has been well mixed by weather systems and from contact with the earth's surface. If it could be taken in section, it would be very much like any fluid, with much the same propensities – it moves in a straight line if possible, and it will move around obstructions with great reluctance. Airstreams tend to create an aerofoil shape (a tapering oblong, with the wider part facing into the flow, shown on page 327) around any obstruction in an attempt to maintain a smooth flow. Parts of an airstream which slow down cause friction with the faster moving streams around them. According to its density and speed an airstream can be either heavier or lighter than average. The sail itself is in many ways similar to both the wing of an aircraft or a bird. The object of the sail is to obtain the maximum drive from an airstream.

Properties of air

Air possesses stored up energy and it moves in parallel streams that are not easily deflected. Air in areas of low pressure is less dense than air in high pressure areas. Low pressure will also occur when an airstream speeds up and high pressure occurs, therefore, when it slows down. All this was discovered by two scientists, Bernoulli and Venturi, in the 18th century. Venturi showed that when air was forced through a tube with a constriction in it, the air in the constricted part was at a lower pressure because it was travelling faster. A well designed sail, with the draft in the correct place, will succeed in creating an area of lower pressure on the convex side and one of higher pressure on the concave side. This situation permits the sail to have the maximum amount of lift (divided into forward drive and heeling force).

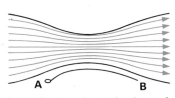

In the diagram, above, the shape of the sail, A–B, is placed below a constricted tube with air flowing through. The curved shape of the sail makes a similar shape to that of the tube, and will deflect the air in the same way.

The sail, A–B, is shown again in an airstream. The air is moving faster over the convex part of the sail, creating low pressure, and slower on the concave side which creates a high pressure area.

Terminology

Various technical terms are used in describing air flow around an aerofoil section and scientific values are given to the forces acting on the aerofoil. In a sail, the curve of the sail is known as the camber, and is given two values, the depth of the camber (taken from the point of maximum curve) and the draft ratio – measured from the luff as a percentage of the chord. The airflow divides at the point of separation.

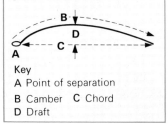

Key
A Point of separation
B Camber   C Chord
D Draft

Properties of sails

In its simplest form, any shape of sail can be used to harness the power of the wind to blow the boat in the same direction that the air is flowing. Moving air is best regarded as a collection of molecules moving like ping pong balls in an ordered fashion. When an obstruction is placed in the path of the flow, the molecules divide at the point of separation and flow around the obstruction squeezed by the adjacent streams which do not wish to be displaced. As can be seen from the diagram (above right) some of the air flows around the sail creating eddies known as turbulence, while further out from the sail the airstream, while bulging, maintains a continuous shape. It is the property of air to isolate obstructions by flowing around them, speeding up to do so, that helps explain the function of an aerofoil section. In simple terms an aerofoil section produces lift, the ability to convert the energy of the wind into forward motion, not necessarily in the same direction as the airstream. The reason for this is that the airstream over the convex surface has to travel further and faster to join up with the air flowing over the concave surface, divided at the point of separation, which has a shorter distance to travel. Contrary, therefore, to what is often assumed, the sail is sucked along by the airstream rather than being pushed by it.

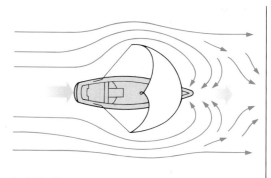

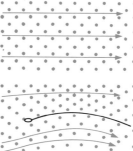

The diagram, above, shows how turbulence is created by an object in the path of an airstream. The diagram, left, shows the molecules in the airstream moving in an uninterrupted line, and below left, when forced out of line by an object, such as a sail.

Lift and flow

It may help to envisage how a sail works if you think of the way the wing of a bird, or of an airplane, functions. Both have a similar aerofoil shape and both obtain lift in the air when power is applied. The sail is the same shape but works on a vertical rather than a horizontal plane. The same force, therefore, that will give lift to an aeroplane or bird wing creates a force for movement in the sail. Because the aerofoil shape of the sail is lying vertically in the airstream, this movement is sideways rather than upwards. Were it not for the fact that the sail is attached to the hull of the boat, the power would be a sideways drive rather than the forward drive it experiences as a result of the hull's resistance to sideways movement.

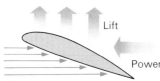

A simplified diagram showing how an aerofoil shape will start to lift upwards when power is applied.

Drive

The approximate relative strength of the energy forces acting on the sail, that is to say the pull on the sail produced by the low pressure on the convex side and the push introduced by the high pressure on the concave side, produces the effect seen in the diagram on the right. The shape of the sail will determine how much of this force is converted into forward movement and how much into a backward drag. Once the airstream is moving past the maximum point of the curve of the sail it is no longer producing the forward driving motion and the sail is causing more resistance than drive. The forces produced by the sail also include a heeling force which detracts from the forward movement to some extent. The total forward movement of the boat, the drive, is therefore a balance between the various forces operating on the boat, the forward drive of the sail against the backward drag, and the heeling force. However, the heeling force can be counteracted by the crew or the keel balancing the boat.

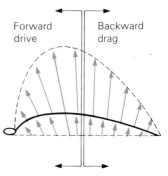

The forces produced, acting at right angles to the sail surface, produce both drive and drag.

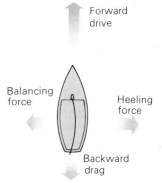

From all the forces acting on both the sails and hull, a surplus of forward drive results.

325

Airflow

It is not difficult to understand that air flowing over a sail produces a force which moves the boat forward but as soon as this happens an interesting phenomenon occurs – the direction of the airstream appears to come from further forward of the boat. This apparent wind is caused by the difference between the true wind and the wind created by the boat's own movement through the air. To understand what occurs, hold a candle flame in front of you and walk forward; you will find that the flame ceases to become vertical and starts to blow back towards you, away from the direction in which you are moving. All moving objects create their own airflow, and a sailing boat has to be designed so that the sails can be adjusted to match the apparent wind rather than the true wind. In order to check the direction of the wind, it helps if you either have a wind indicator, in the form of a burgee, or windex, or tell-tales attached to the sails.

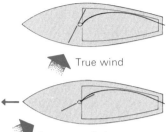

True wind

Apparent wind

In the diagram top, the true wind can be seen blowing over a static boat, but it then moves further forward (the apparent wind) when the boat starts to move (above).

Setting sails

A key factor in getting a sail to perform well is the angle at which it is set to the wind. The angle must be such that an air flow is maintained over both sides of the sail so that the difference in pressure is at a maximum. Most sailors find that the best method of checking that the air is flowing correctly over both sides of the sail is by attaching tell-tales to both sides of the sail, which then have to stream out parallel if the sail is accurately set. They are extremely accurate guides and if the air-flow on either side of the sail no longer flows smoothly along the sail, the tell-tale on that side of the sail will immediately flutter away from the surface of the sail.

Interaction of sails

For a number of reasons early sailors found it easier to split the sail area into more manageable units by using several smaller sails. By chance, they created a system where the maximum amount of drive was produced particularly when sailing to windward, which had previously been impossible. The air treats the two sails as one large aerofoil with the added benefit that the air travelling between the two sails speeds up and improves the flow of air over the rear sail. Much of the skill in racing is gauging the inter-relationship between the sails to obtain maximum airflow.

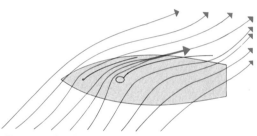

The wind flowing through the slot between the two sails is speeded up, increasing the efficiency of both of the sails.

Boat shapes

Boat shape evolved through the use of different types of building material available in various parts of the world, such as wood, reeds and so on. The simple dug-out log was remarkably stream-lined and its rounded sections offered an ideal shape for the best flow of water. Shape at and below the waterline is vital. Almost every boat is designed to have a waterline shape which is aerofoil-shaped with the widest part just forward of the centre. This particular waterline shape is known as a laminar profile. Because water is more viscous than air, it does not tolerate disturbance well so all hull designs have to present as little resistance as possible to the flow of water, which otherwise breaks up and slows the boat down. This turbulence can also be created by any indentations or imperfections in the surface of the underwater section, but by far the greatest amount of drag is caused at the waterline where friction is produced by the air, water and hull meeting one another.

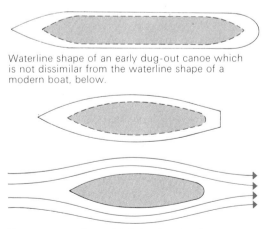

Waterline shape of an early dug-out canoe which is not dissimilar from the waterline shape of a modern boat, below.

The water can flow with little disturbance around a suitably designed aerofoil shape, which is the typical shape of most up-to-date sailing boats.

Hull speed

When a boat which does not plane moves, it creates two waves which become further apart the faster the boat moves. At a certain speed, the distance between the wavecrests is close to the waterline length of the boat and the two crests are situated near the ends of the waterline shape of the boat. Effectively, the boat is trapped between its own bow and stern waves. It cannot move any faster, since the waves cannot move further apart. A boat such as the Contessa 32, for example, has a theoretical maximum hull speed of just over 7 knots. Only boats which can plane, or which have very narrow hulls, can travel faster than this theoretical maximum speed.

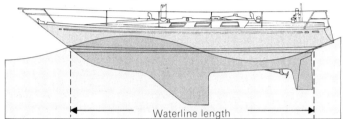

The boat, above, is travelling at its maximum hull speed – the crests of the waves are at either end of the waterline length.

Waterline length

Foil shape

The centerboard and rudder of a sailing boat are designed to create as much lift as possible and to present the least resistance to forward movement. The point of maximum thickness is usually nearly half way back from the well-rounded leading edge and the rest tapers off gradually to a thin angular trailing edge. The profile shape of centerboard or rudder is often dictated by class rules but the ideal shape is usually deemed to be similar to the well rounded wing of an aircraft.

The foil shape above is the one normally used for a centerboard or rudder. The shape is similar to the curve of a sail.

Function of keel

By acting as a preventer of sideways drift, the keel or centerboard of a boat enables it to sail to windward. It acts in water in a similar way to the sail in the air – the water flow produces areas of high and low pressure resulting in lift. The angle of attack (or incidence) of the keel to the water is produced by the sideways drift of the boat (or leeway) and the flow of water is generated by the forward movement of the boat induced by the sails. The same pushing and pulling forces are generated and these result in a considerable sideways force. If you place the two, the force of air and the force of water, together on one diagram you can see their relationship to each other more clearly. A successfully designed and sailed boat is one which balances these forces in such a way as to produce a surplus of forward movement.

In the diagram, right, the forces are shown which work on both the hull and the sails; they produce a surplus of forward movement.

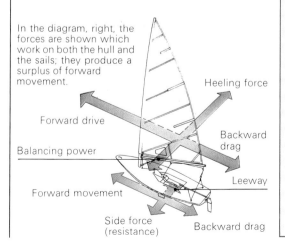

Forward drive

Balancing power

Forward movement

Heeling force

Backward drag

Leeway

Side force (resistance)

Backward drag

Keel shapes

Where the ballast is suspended below the boat in the form of a keel, designers are faced with numerous problems of how to produce the most efficient shape. Early boats had keels which extended from bow to stern, with a rudder attached to the back. Such boats are seaworthy but generally slow because of the large amount of the hull in contact with the water, which produces a lot of drag. Modern racing boats have well rounded canoe-shaped hulls which have slim keels attached to them and independently hung rudders (which tend to get damaged easily). Boat designers will no doubt continue to experiment with boat shapes, but some designs are classic, and will probably always be popular.

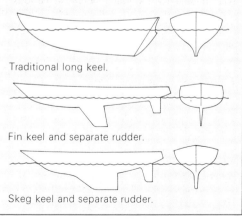

Traditional long keel.

Fin keel and separate rudder.

Skeg keel and separate rudder.

Ropes and basic knots

Learning how to handle lines and how to look after them is one of the first priorities for any sailor. Rope forms a vital part of the boat's equipment and is expensive to replace. Whenever possible, try and make sure that lines do not chafe against sharp or abrasive objects.

If a line unravels or breaks it is useful to know how to repair it. The ends can be joined together by twisting the strands (known as splicing) or bound with twine to prevent them unravelling (known as whipping). The instructions are given on page 335.

Knowing how to tie knots that both hold securely and can be undone quickly and easily is very important: you must be able to trust the knots that you tie. Some knots are more suitable for particular purposes than others: the following pages give a selection of the most commonly used ones in sailing and the purpose they best serve. Naturally, there are many others – ropework has been a respected skill which sailors have developed over the centuries. However, the ones shown in this section will suffice for most general purposes.

All rope when not in use should be coiled neatly and stowed away – never leave it in a tangle on the deck.

Types of rope

Rope is used mainly for the running rigging on the boat, and for mooring lines. The type and thickness of the rope used depends on the job it has to do. Formerly rope was always made of natural fiber, such as cotton, hemp or manilla, but these days synthetics are usually used instead. Synthetic rope is very hard wearing but traditional knots can come undone because the texture is more slippery than natural fiber. Special knots have been developed to cope with the problem (see page 334). All rope is constructed from long filaments which are spun into yarn, which is then twisted into strands. The strands can be combined together in different ways and thicknesses, to form the various types of rope: the most common construction is either braided or laid. Braided rope is very durable and can be used for sheets, for example, which receive a lot of hard wear. Laid rope is three-stranded and is often used for mooring lines. Polypropylene ropes are useful for mooring lines too as they float in the water, and nylon braided or plaited rope can be used instead of anchor chain as it absorbs shock loads well.

Parts of the knot

It is important when learning to tie knots that you understand the terminology used. The bend you make in the rope is known as the bight, the part the bend is made over is known as the standing part, and the end of the rope as the bitter end.

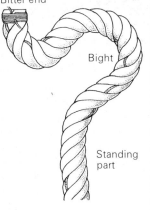

Bitter end

Bight

Standing part

Polypropylene three strand

Polyester three strand

Nylon octoplait

Nylon braidline

Nylon eight plait

Manilla three strand

Figure eight

The figure eight knot is very quick and easy to tie. It is commonly used as a stopper knot in the end of a line or sheet. One of its advantages is that it is easy to untie, even when wet.

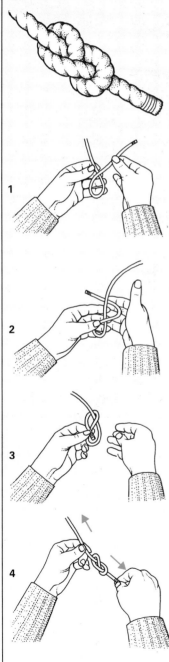

1

2

3

4

Double overhand

Although some people say that an overhand knot is an unseamanlike stopper knot, when tied as shown below it forms a quick and firm stopper on the end of a jib sheet, for example. The knot can be untied by simply pulling the two twists apart to loosen it.

1

2

3

4

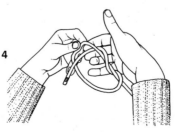

5

6

Undoing the knot

Hold the knot in both hands and pull the two twists apart with your thumbs. It will then be loose enough to undo quite easily

Square knot

This knot is formed with a half-hitch in one direction followed by another in the opposite direction. When both hitches run in the same direction, the knot is known as a granny knot, and will not hold firm. Care should be taken, therefore, to tie the knot as shown below.

Sheet bend

This knot is usually used to attach a thinner line to a thicker one. It is tied so that the ends finish on the same side of the knot. To loosen the knot, bend it and then push the bight down on the half-hitch.

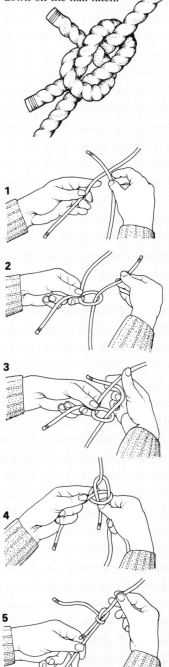

1

2

3

4

5

Undoing a square knot

A square knot can be quickly and easily untied by grasping one free end of the knot in one hand and the standing part in the other, and then pulling the knot apart. Push the knot along the standing part of the rope until it slips off.

1

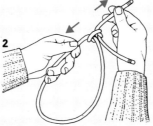

2

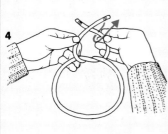

3

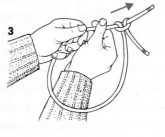

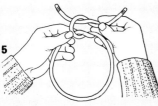

Bowline

This knot forms a standing eye on the end of a line and has a variety of uses. An easy way of tying it is shown below in which the loop in the standing part of the line is formed by twisting the hands as shown in step 1. Once the loop is formed, the other steps are simple.

Bowline on a bight

The bowline on a bight is used if a double eye is needed at the end of a line —for a bosun's chair, for example. The first two steps are the same as for tying a bowline but in the final stages the double loop is inserted through the single one to finish off.

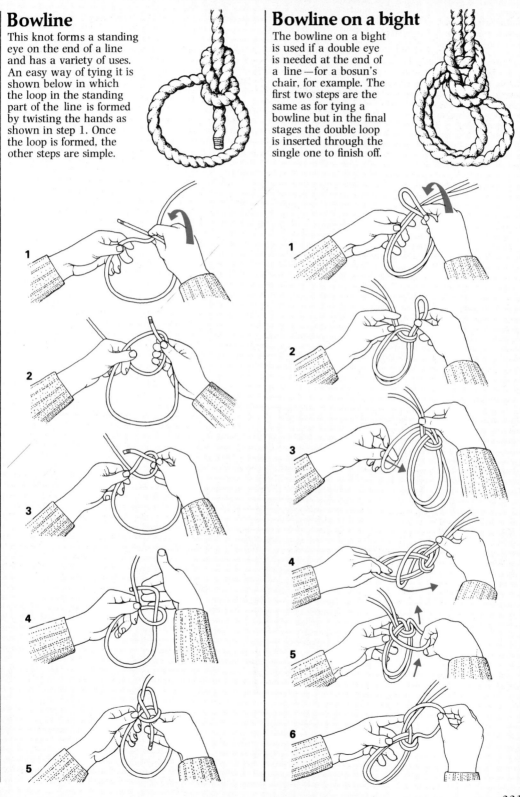

Single becket hitch

The single becket hitch is used to secure a line to an eye or hook. It is quick to tie and is very strong and reliable, even under great pressure. It has the advantage of being easy to undo, even when wet.

1

2

3

Double becket hitch

A double becket hitch performs the same function as a single becket but it is stronger and can take extra strain. It should be tied in the same way as the single becket but two twists, instead of one, are made in the final step.

Rolling hitch

A rolling hitch is particularly useful when tying a line to a vertical object such as a mast, as the knot will not slip downwards under strain. The more downward pressure applied, the tighter the knot becomes.

1

2

3

4

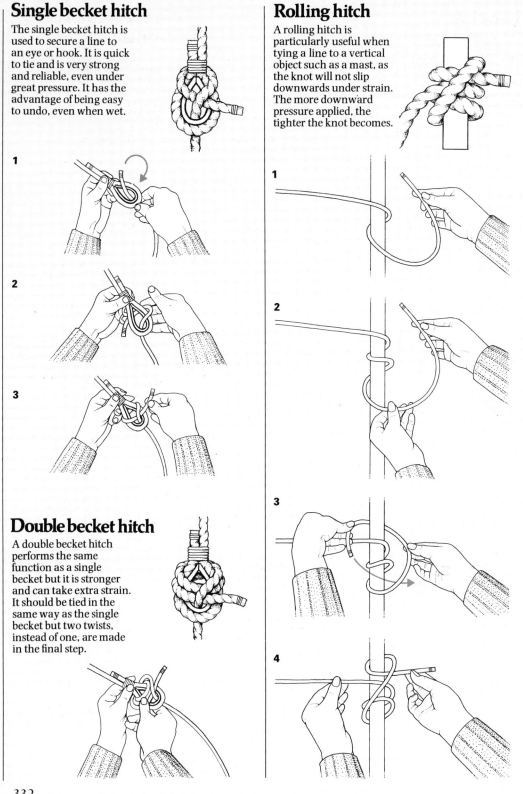

Clove hitch

The clove hitch is used as a short stay mooring knot. It is quick and easy to tie but holds well only when the strain on the knot is at right angles to the fixing. The knot can easily come undone under sideways tension.

Round turn and two half hitches

This is the most commonly used knot when tying a line (without a great deal of strain on it) to any standing object such as a spar, rail or shroud. It can be tied quickly and easily and is equally easily untied. Two hitches are normally enough to secure it.

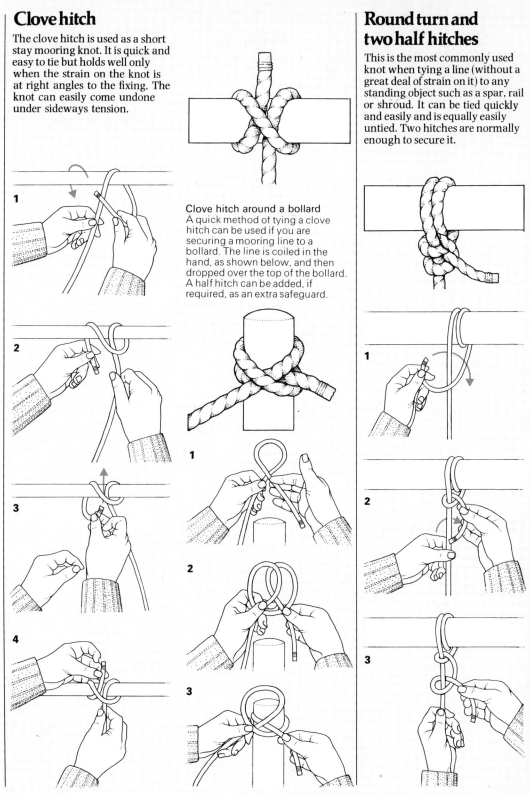

Clove hitch around a bollard
A quick method of tying a clove hitch can be used if you are securing a mooring line to a bollard. The line is coiled in the hand, as shown below, and then dropped over the top of the bollard. A half hitch can be added, if required, as an extra safeguard.

Hunter's bend

The hunter's bend is a comparatively new knot specially designed for slippery synthetic rope. It is used for joining two ropes of any thickness together and can be used as an alternative to the sheet bend (see page 330).

Truck driver's hitch

This is the best knot for securing boat onto a car. After stage 3 below, the bitter end is passed around the bumper or another part of the chassis, and through the eye of the knot, giving a purchase for tightening the rope. The end is then secured with a round turn and two half hitches (see page 333).

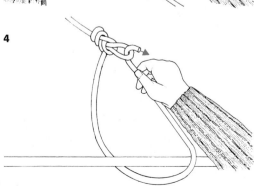

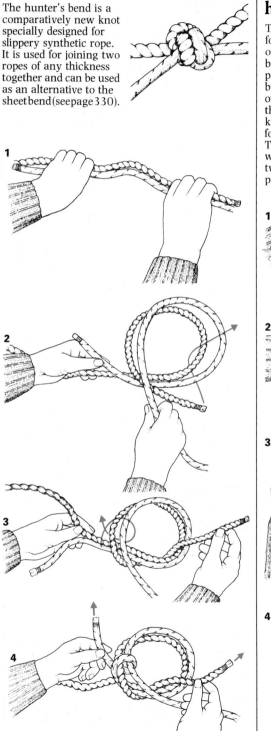

Jury rig knot

If your boat is dismasted, a spare spar can be rigged as a temporary mast by using a jury rig knot. It provides three loops (a fourth one can be formed by tying the two loose ends with a bowline) to which you can attach warps to act as stays.

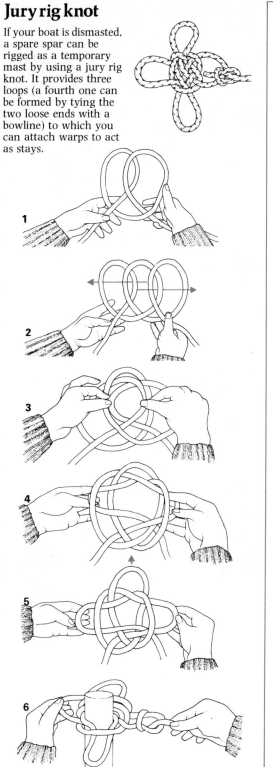

Whipping

To prevent ropes unravelling, they should be finished by whipping the ends with twine. There are many different types of whipping, an easy method is shown below. You must be careful to wind the twine in the opposite direction to the lay of the rope.

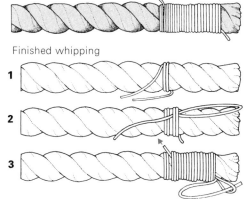

Finished whipping

1

2

3

Splicing

Splicing is a way of joining two ropes by weaving the ends together. One of the many methods of splicing is shown below. You will need a marline spike (or another pointed instrument) to separate the strands, and whipping twine to bind the ends while you work.

Finished splice

1 Bind each rope 15 cm (6 in) away from the end and unravel them to this point. Place the two ends together as shown.

2 Bind the loose strands of one rope to the other and remove the twine from the first rope. Start to weave in the loose strands in turn as shown above, turning the rope as you work. Continue until each strand has been threaded through at least three times. Repeat the process with the other rope and trim the ends.

Buying a boat

Cruising boats represent a considerable investment, often running a close second to home ownership. Unlike a home, a boat is only used for a part of the year and the rest of the time it swings from a mooring or languishes in a marina berth, quietly deteriorating. Owning a boat can be a complex matter, often influenced by laws relating to luxury taxes, but if an owner decides to buy a boat for recreation rather than as an investment or for tax avoidance purposes, it no longer remains a purely financial transaction but rather it is an investment in the anticipated recreation a boat provides: in its ownership, upkeep and sailing.

Although a boat does not actually appreciate in value, it tends to hold its value in times of inflation, enabling the owner to realize a good second-hand price which could well double that paid a few years previously. This means that the owner can trade it in for a larger boat from time to time without a great loss of original capital.

Marine finance

There is a long history of the financing of ships by merchant banks and, to some extent, the same enterprising spirit prevails in the world of marine finance for smaller boats. There are many ways of financing the purchase of a boat and it is up to the prospective purchaser to secure the best deal.

Personal bank loans

Borrowing from your own savings or commercial bank is usually the cheapest way, especially if you offer collateral of some kind. Banks tend to restrict the amount which can be borrowed and have short repayment periods. Much depends on the level of inflation and the fact that the bank rate fluctuates, so you could end up paying a higher or lower rate than at the time of the loan.

Bank service companies

These represent local or regional banks and originate loan applications for the banks.

Finance companies

Some specialize in granting boat loans or have boat departments that have access to large sums of money. They have longer repayment periods.

Secondary mortgage

Inflation has resulted in a steady increase in house prices, so that house owners with a mortgage can borrow by obtaining a second mortgage on the difference between the amount of the first mortgage on their house and the valuer's assessment of the present value. This can often give an adequate amount with which to buy a boat, provided of course that you are deemed capable of keeping up the payments on both mortgages. Second mortgage rates vary (usually 10 per cent higher than first mortgage interest), but repayment periods extend up to ten years in most countries.

Marine mortgages

There are a number of options with this form of finance. Normally, the purchaser is required to pay a deposit, usually 20-25 per cent of the total price, and then to pay the balance, plus interest, over a period of five to ten years. The interest is normally computed on a formula, "the sum of the digits". This formula takes into consideration the fact that you pay more interest in the beginning of a loan when you have the use of more of the money, and you pay less interest as the debt is reduced. Because each payment is the same size, the part going to pay back the amount borrowed increases as the part representing interest decreases. When you decide to pay off a loan early the lender uses the "sum of the digits" rule to determine your "rebate" – that portion of the total interest charge you won't have to pay.

Some lenders use a method called simple interest, or actuarial rate, comparable to the payment schedule you get with a home mortgage. In both "the sum of the digits" and this method, you pay more interest in the early years of the loan. Be cautious, as in some cases you may be required to pay one or two years' interest as a penalty should you choose to pre-pay the loan.

Another method is the fixed rate agreement in which the repayments and interest remain fixed, no matter what happens to the base rate. One disadvantage of this method is that unless an early resettlement clause is negotiated on signing, the borrower may have to pay the full-term interest even when paying off the loan before its full-term has expired. With this scheme, merchant banks and other financiers set their own rate of interest. They lend money to borrowers on the basis that the interest throughout the repayment term will be calculated on the loan outstanding. This means that the payments reduce as the loan is repaid. Interest is usually fixed on the basis of that of the financial house concerned, plus 5 per cent payable quarterly in arrears and calculated on the daily rate throughout each quarter.

Another method is where borrowers repay the loan on an agreed equal monthly instalment, throughout the period of the loan. Any additional interest is paid for during an extension of the repayment period, or by reducing the term of the loan if the interest rate drops.

Shared finance

By tradition, the ownership of a boat is divided up into 64 shares, indeed many commercial vessels, including fishing boats, operate on the principle of share holding so that if a boat makes a large catch everyone – crew, owners, financiers alike – share in the profit. Many boats are owned on a shared basis which enables the participants to enjoy the use of a larger boat. Others are purchased by syndicates and chartered out, usually through agencies to non boat owners.

Law and insurance

Marine insurance is, once again, an old-established market. Underwriters agree to insure vessels, their contents and cargoes on the instructions of a marine broker. In the event of a total loss, underwriters pay up the amount insured on the receipt of a satisfactory report from a claims surveyor. All boat owners should insure their vessels for their market value as well as against claims by third parties. As with house purchase. the sum insured has to be raised periodically to allow for inflation. As with all other insurance, it pays to shop around the brokers and inspect the quotations to determine what each is offering.

Maritime law

The law relating to the sea is international and affects the skipper of a cruising boat as much as the captain of a large tanker. The law requires that each is a competent master of his own vessel and understands the laws governing collision and buoyage. Nowhere is maritime law clearer than in the matter of salvage. If you accept a tow, especially if you use the salvor's lines, you could be liable to a claim against your vessel for salvage. A verbal agreement, made at the time is binding, so check, even in the most innocent situation, especially when commercial or fishing craft are involved, what the terms are.

Buying a second-hand boat

The only sound advice to the person who is buying for the first time is that they should engage the services of a marine surveyor and be guided by his advice. Old boats usually come with a multitude of ailments, many of which need drastic surgery. Boats are often placed on the market because their owners have given up the unequal struggle against rot, decay and corrosion, hoping that an unsuspecting enthusiast will pay a good price to take the burden off their back. No boat should ever be bought in the water; it must be slipped and inspected for damage and decay.

Wooden boats usually present the largest problems because they are constructed of so many individual wooden components held together with metal fastenings. Principal trouble spots are at the junction of the keel and the bottom planking (known as garboards) and the stern and sternpost – again where the planks join the stern and sternposts.

Nail sickness is a term given to the decay of the fastenings which hold the boat together. It can be caused by a chemical reaction between the fastening and the chemicals in the wood or by the gradual ingress of water around the metal fastenings. The result is the same, the wood decays and the planking detaches itself from the frames. On a freshly painted boat, it can be detected by orderly rows of blisters coinciding with each nail head. If the blister is broken, a stained, watery liquid seeps out. Dry rot is a common defect especially in nooks and crannies. The wood softens under fungal attack, causing a breakdown in the cellular structure. Boats can also suffer from a number of ailments, either stemming from defects in their manufacture or from damage caused through accidental collision or stress. One particularly dangerous defect, known as osmosis, occurs when a breakdown in the resin content of the molding permits water to come through the outside coat. Again, with such a large investment of capital the best course is to use the services of a surveyor and to use his written report, which will include estimates for the cost of rectifying faults, as the basis for negotiating the price with the vendor. It cannot be stressed too strongly that, except in the case of small boats, a surveyor should always be engaged once you have found a boat you wish to purchase. Many boats are advertised on the basis of being equipped with the latest modern equipment. However, the prospective purchaser of a second-hand boat should not be lured away from considering the more expensive basic equipment first – such as the sails or the engine, which will both cost a great deal to replace if not in good working order.

Legality of ownership

When buying a second-hand boat, it is essential to establish that either the vendor, or his agent, is the legal owner. Those boats which are registered by their national maritime service are given an official name and an official registered number. Each change of ownership must be registered with the registrar of shipping as must a change of name. Unregistered boats often have production or class numbers by which they can be identified for insurance purposes.

Berths and maintenance

The majority of owners prefer to keep their boats in sheltered harbors where it is possible to step aboard from a float or staging. Marinas have proved to be ideal answers to the age-old problems of where to keep a boat once it has been purchased. Marinas offer a wide range of services including water-and shore-based power points on the floats and chandlery, ship-wrighting, laundry and restaurant services ashore. Where marinas do not exist, one of the traditional methods is normally chosen. The simplest of these is the swinging mooring where a heavy sinker, to which a heavy mooring chain is attach ed, is set in the seabed . The boat is secured to the mooring buoy. Alternatively, a ground chain is laid to which are attached numerous chains and buoys. Many harbors have been spoiled because they have been filled with swinging moorings. Instead of swinging around single buoys, boats must be moored fore and aft between two buoys especially when room is limited.

Operating schedules

Owning a boat can be very demanding on leisure time unless tasks are scheduled. There is a special section on maintenance but we are talking about the many day-to-day operating tasks which must be expected, such as the checking of the engine, electrics, steering and sailing equipment, and the up-dating of charts and publications.

Joint ownership

If you want to go sailing but don't have a great deal of spare time, or enough money, you may well decide to form a syndicate with others and to-gether buy a suitable boat. Whatever the reasons, it is essential that the transaction is very carefully thought out beforehand and that the agree-ment is drawn up on a legal basis, spelling out very carefully the specific commitments and benefits accruing to each member. The main factor to be taken into consideration before buying a boat is its intended uses related to the experience of the syndicate members. The options include: cruising with some racing; cruising; racing and racing with some cruising. The final choice of boat is deter-mined by whether the boat is to be used locally or will be expected to sail offshore. Decisions must also be made as to whether the boat is to be used solely by syndicate members and their immediate families, or whether friends can be invited along, or can borrow the boat. Even if the boat is to be used exclusively by members it must be determined, for example, whether they alone shall make up the crew when racing, when the boat shall be available to each member and how the sailing season shall be allocated for weekends, weeks and longer holiday periods.

The management of the syndicate is of paramount importance. It may be run on a committee basis or on an *ad hoc* arrange-ment. Financial responsibilities may be delegated to a treasurer who collects dues and pays bills – or the group pays into a boat fund account by banker's draft at regular intervals making up any shortfall at the end of the season. A boat keeper is usually elected to see to the day-to-day running of the boat and the payment of bills; this person usually makes decisions con-cerning minor expenditure but the major financial decisions – berthing, slipping, storage, insurance, maintenance, re-placement and new equipment – are made by the whole syndicate. Some syndicates charter the boat to offset costs, but as this represents taxable income in most countries, proper arrange-ments have to be made.

One of the advantages of a syndicate is that one person does not have to do all the maintenance work, or pay the yard bills. This often results in better maintained boats. The only decisions to be made are whether the members or the yard do the work.

Insurance companies have policies for syndicated boats – the premium is often determined by the experience of the members, so it pays to ensure that every-one is or eventually becomes a competent skipper.

Each member should be sent a copy of the insurance policy, especially if the boat has limitations as to use, particularly concerning cruising use during the winter months.

One of the fastest growing types of syndicate is that formed to purchase a vessel for world voyaging. If it's successful, it's the obvious way of enjoying a boat larger than you could otherwise afford, but it can be a total disaster if it fails. If you are interested in forming a syndicate, try to find others who have different working hours. That way someone is always free to use the boat, and holiday periods are staggered. If only one member of the syndicate is an experienced sailor, it will be unfair to expect him to teach the others without due recom-pense. This can be in the form of a reduced syndicate member-ship – more exclusive use, or some other agreed basis such as a reduced commitment to maintenance.

Leaving a syndicate

Leaving a syndicate is often much more difficult than buying one's way in. The main problems are associated with the value of one's share in the syndicate. The most sensible answer is for the syndicate to determine whether they wish to buy the member's share at the original price or allow a new member into the syndicate at a new fee based on the second-hand value of the craft. The retiring member is then paid accordingly.

Going abroad

It is possible that, in time, once you have gained expertise in boat-handling, seamanship, navigation and so on, and have cruised in your home waters, you will want to venture further afield and possibly go abroad. In addition to all the necessary preparation for cruising in home waters, going abroad raises a number of points worth considering. Firstly, you, your crew and your boat have to be ready, in every respect, for going to sea. This has already been covered but there are some other considerations. There are many guides for cruising in foreign waters available.

General guidelines
Each country has its own rules and regulations which govern pleasure craft, native and foreign. When planning to cruise abroad, it is vital to acquaint yourself with the law which applies in any country you are going to visit. The following points should all be included in your pre-planning. A few countries still require an entry visa. If you are going to one, make sure your visa is in order before you leave. Check out currency and import and export restrictions in any countries to be visited. Some countries require vaccination certificates. Find out what the requirements are from your national authority, or relevant embassy or consulate. If your boat is officially registered in its country of origin, these registration papers will be accepted internationally. If your boat is not registered, then you should apply to your national authority for an international certificate for pleasure navigation. It is advisable to possess a certificate of competence, as some countries, where by law, yachtsmen have to hold a current certificate of competence, require it. It is wise to carry such a document, as inability to produce it can have serious consequences, like the impounding of your boat. In countries where certification is not compulsory (the UK is one of them) most national authorities run voluntary certification schemes through which it is possible to obtain an inter-nationally acceptable certificate of competence. Each country or authority has its own criteria with which you will have to comply in order to get your certificate or "card".

Insurance
Check your insurance policy very carefully. Make sure that you have the necessary cover to sail to any chosen country. Never assume that you are automatically covered. Check that your insurance covers: the area you intend to sail in; the total period of intended cruising abroad (allow for delays); damage to your boat and damage caused by your boat, including collision; your own personal cover; the contents of your boat; third party claims against you by, for example, a member of your crew and, lastly, possible salvage claims.

If you trail your boat in a foreign country make sure that your insurance covers not only the boat while it is being trailed but also when it is put into the water. A car policy alone does not cover you; you need marine insurance.

Inland waterways
If your foreign cruise is going to take you to the inland water-ways of another country, check to see if there are special entry permits you will require and that the locks will be open (in operation). For anyone who sails without an engine, or whose engine is out of commission, remember that in some canals it is not possible to tack, so auxiliary power is a must.

Flags
When arriving at another country by sea it is customary to fly your own ensign (your national maritime flag). The usual place to fly this ensign is from the stern, though it can vary. The maritime flag of the country you are entering should be flown from the cross-trees on the starboard side. This is referred to as the "courtesy ensign" and should be more or less the same size as any other signal flags you carry. Continue to fly the courtesy ensign while you are in that country's waters.

Many countries have named ports of entry. When entering a foreign port it is necessary to fly the Q flag indicating a healthy crew and to contact the customs/immigration officials. You must wait to be boarded by a customs/immigration officer who will check you and your papers and those of crew and ship. In some areas it will be necessary for one person, usually the skipper, to go along to the shore customs/harbor office and take with him all the necessary documentation. No one else should go ashore until this has been done.

It takes time and effort to plan for cruising in foreign waters but in the long run it will avoid delays, embarrassment and expense. As an additional check, see that you have: correct charts for the area in which you intend to sail; tide tables; tidal stream atlasses; list of lights for area in which you cruise; list of radio signals; list of met services; pilots; sailing instructions; phrase book, passport, insurance papers and money.

Glossary

A

Aback Said of a sail when, with its *clew* to *windward*, it is pressed back against the mast. It may occur due to a sudden change of wind or be done on purpose as when hove-to (see *Heave-to*).

Abaft Behind or towards the *stern* of a boat.

Abeam At right angles to the *centerline* of the boat.

Adrift A free floating object which is unable to move under its own power.

Aft Towards, near or at the *stern*. It may also be behind the stern.

Afterpart The part of the boat behind the *beam*.

Ahull A boat is ahull when it is *hove-to* with all its sails *furled*.

A-lee The side away from the direction of the wind.

All hands The entire crew.

Aloft Overhead.

Amidships The middle of the boat, either *fore*, *aft* or *athwartships*.

Anchor A heavy metal implement used to secure a vessel to the seabed.

Anchorage The ground in which the anchor is laid. It usually denotes a sheltered area in which it is safe to anchor because of the good holding ground, the shelter from the wind and the lack of strong tides or a combination of all three.

Anchor light see *Riding light*

Anemometer An instrument for measuring wind speed. It can be fitted to the masthead of a boat and the information read from an instrument panel in the cockpit or it can be a self-contained, hand-held unit.

Apparent wind The wind that flows over a moving boat. The sum of the true and the created wind.

Aspect ratio The ratio between the *foot* length and the *luff* length of a sail. A high aspect ratio refers to a tall, narrow sail while a low aspect ratio refers to a low, broad sail.

Astern Behind the boat.

Athwartship At right angles to the *fore-and-aft* line of a vessel.

Auto-pilot Electro-mechanical steering device, incorporating a compass which when set and coupled to the boat's steering system maintains the boat on a constant course.

Aweigh Describes an anchor raised from the seabed.

B

Backing a sail To push a sail out so that the wind fills it from the opposite side. Used to slow a boat down.

Backstay A *stay*, fitted as *standing rigging* to halt any forward movement in the mast.

Bail To bail or bail out is to remove water from an open boat.

Ballast Weight, usually metal, placed low in the boat or externally on the *keel* to provide stability.

Barber hauler A line or *tackle* attached to a *sheet* between the *clew* and the *fairlead*, used to adjust the sheeting angle.

Bare poles, to sail under To sail without any sails set.

Batten Light wooden or plastic strip inserted into a pocket in a sail to support the *roach*.

Batten down To secure and, if necessary, tie down fittings, such as hatches, in preparation for heavy weather.

Beam The width of the boat at its widest point.

Bear away (or **Bear off**) To alter course away from the wind.

Bear down To approach something from upwind.

Bearing The direction of one object from another. It can be measured in degrees true or degrees magnetic.

Beating To sail to *windward*, *close-hauled*, tacking as you go, to reach an objective to windward.

Becket A loop or a small eye in the end of a rope or a *block*.

Belay To make fast a line around a *cleat* usually with a figure eight knot.

Bend To attach a sail to its *spar*; (2) to attach two ropes together by means of a knot.

Bermudan rig see *Marconi rig*.

Bight The bend or loop in a rope.

Bilge The lower, rounded part of a vessel.

Bilge keels Shallow *keels*, usually used in conjunction with or in place of a center keel. Attached to the bilge of the boat, they provide lateral resistance and stability.

Bitts Small posts fixed through the foredeck of a vessel to which the *bowsprit* is attached or to which mooring lines are made fast.

Block The nautical term for a pulley. It can haul one or more *sheaves*.

Bobstay A *stay* from the *bow* of the boat to the end of the *bowsprit* to counteract the upward pull of the *forestay*.

Bolt rope A reinforcing rope along the edge of a sail.

Boom A *spar* which is used to extend the *foot* of a sail.

Boom preventer see *Preventer*.

Boom vang A *tackle* secured to the boom to prevent it lifting.

Bosun's chair Usually a canvas bucket seat on which a person can sit and be hoisted up the mast.

Bottlescrew see *Turnbuckle*

Bow The forward end of a vessel.

Bowsprit A *spar* which projects from the *bow* of some boats, and extends the sail plan by allowing *headsails* to be secured further forward.

Breast rope Any line used for tying up to a jetty which is led approximately at right angles to the side of the boat.

Brightwork Term which covers all varnished woodwork and polished fittings.

Bring about To reverse direction.

Broach The action of a boat when, *running* before a sea, it slews round inadvertently, broadside on to the waves.

Bulkhead A partition across the boat which strengthens and divides the hull.

Bulwarks A parapet around the deck of a vessel which prevents things from falling overboard and protects the decks themselves from the sea.

Burgee Small triangular flag, flown from the top of the mast identifying the owner or the yacht club to which the boat belongs.

By-the-lee Sailing on a *run* but with the wind blowing from the *lee* side of the boat. This is likely to lead to an accidental jibe.

C

Cable A nautical measurement; a cable equals one tenth of a *nautical* mile; (2) the anchor cable or rode is the line or chain attached to the anchor.

Camber The curve of the deck from one side of the boat to the other; (2) the curve of a sail.

Cast off To let go any lines tying the boat to another object.

Caulking Fiber and compound placed between planking to make it watertight.

Centerboard A pivoting plate, of wood or steel let down below the *keel* of a sailing boat, and intended to lessen *leeway*.

Centerline The center of the boat, on a *fore-and-aft* line.

Chain plates Metal fittings on the side of boats to which the *shrouds* are attached.

Chart datum The level to which *soundings* are reduced on a chart and below which the tide is unlikely to fall. It is usually taken as being the level of the lowest astronomical tide (LAT).

Chine The angle of a junction between two flat sides of a hull.

Chord An imaginary line between the *luff* and the *leech* of a sail, parallel to the *foot*.

Chute An opening in the deck near the *bow* from which the *spinnaker* is hoisted.

Class General category into which boats of the same or similar design are grouped.

Claw ring A C-shaped fitting which can be slipped over the boom, for example, when the sail has been roller *reefed*, to allow the *boom vang* to be re-attached.

Cleat A wooden or metal fastening with two arms around which ropes can be made fast.

Clew The lower *aft* corner of a *fore-and-aft* sail.

Close-hauled Said of a boat which, with its *sheets* pulled in, is sailing as close to the wind as possible.

Cocked hat Term used in navigation when three position lines are plotted on a chart and do not pass through a common point but form a triangle when crossing.

Cockpit The after-well in a sailing boat, where the helmsman puts his feet.

Coffee grinder A large and powerful *sheet winch*, mounted on a separate pedestal. It has two handles which rotate about a horizontal spindle.

Come about To bring the boat from one tack to the other when sailing into the wind.

Committee boat The boat from which race officers direct a race.

Companionway A ladder leading from the deck to the cabin, or saloon.

Compass An instrument used to indicate direction relative to the earth's magnetic field.

Cradle A frame (wooden or metal) in which a boat can stand when ashore or when being launched.

Cringle A ring sewn into a sail through which a line can be passed.

Cross-trees Metal or wooden struts attached to the mast on either side to increase the spread, and thus the holding power, of the main *shrouds*.

Cunningham hole An eye in the *luff* of a sail above the *tack* which allows the tension of the luff to be adjusted.

Cutter A single masted *fore-and-aft* sailing boat having an inner *staysail* and outer *jib*. It could be *gaff rigged* or *Marconi-rigged*.

D

Dagger board A board in the center of a boat, which can be raised or lowered. When lowered it performs as a *keel* does.

Day mark A shape, usually painted white, which is used to identify a shore feature during hours of daylight.

Day sailor An open boat used for day sailing.

Dead reckoning A method of navigation where a position is plotted based on speed, elapsed time, and a course steered from a known position.

Deck Covering of the interior of a ship, either carried completely over it or over only a portion.

Dew-point Temperature at which moist air becomes saturated and releases the water as droplets. The temperature varies with the amount of water vapor in the air.

Displacement The weight of water displaced by a floating boat (the weight is the same as that of the boat itself).

Dodger Screen of cloth or other material fitted up to protect the crew from wind and spray.

Dolphin A mooring buoy or spar.

Double-ender Any boat designed with a pointed *bow* and *stern*.

Downhaul *Tackle* used for pulling down the *tack* and tensioning the *luff* of a sail.

Draft Vertical distance measured from the waterline to the lowest point of the hull.

Draw A sail is said to be drawing when it is filled by the wind.

Drogue Object towed over boat's *stern* in order to reduce speed.

Drying features Areas (shown on a chart) which are covered over at high water but which are exposed as the tide drops.

E

Ease To let out a *sheet* or line gradually.

Ebb A falling tide (going out).

Electrolysis The chemical reaction between two dissimilar metals immersed in sea water.

Ensign A nautical version of the national flag of a boat's country of registration. It is flown at the *stern*.

F

Fairlead Any ring, bolt, eye or loop which guides a rope in the direction required.

Fairway Main channel down which boats should proceed in restricted waters.

Fall The part of a *tackle* which is hauled upon.

Fathom A measurement used for depth. One fathom equals six feet.

Fender A cushion of durable material inserted between a boat and some other object in order to prevent direct contact.

Fetch To sail *close-hauled* without having to *tack*.

Fiberglass Glass reinforced polyester. A material used for boat construction.

Fin keel Single ballasted *keel* centrally attached to the bottom of the hull.

Fix To find a boat's position by celestial or land observation.

Flood A rising tide (coming in).

Flotsam Any of the contents or equipment of a boat which have been washed overboard.

Fluke The points of an anchor that dig in.

Following sea A sea which is travelling in the same direction as the boat.

Foot The lower edge of a sail.

Fore Towards, near, or at the *bow*.

Fore-and-aft In line from *bow* to *stern*; on, or parallel to, the *centerline*. Also, a sailboat's sailing rig.

Forepeak A space in the bows of a vessel right forward.

Foresail Triangular-shaped sail set fore of the mast.

Forestay A *stay* leading from the *masthead* to the bow to stop the mast falling backwards.

Foul To entangle or obstruct.

Freeboard The portion of a vessel's hull which is free of the water; that is which is not submerged.

Freer A wind shift further aft relative to the boat.

Furl To roll a sail and secure it to its *spar* or *boom*.

G

Gaff A spar which extends the head of a four-sided *fore-and-aft* mainsail.

Gaskets Small cords by which a sail is *furled*. They are also called ties and furling lines.

Genoa A large *foresail* which extends aft behind the mast.

Geographical range The range of a light, assuming it is powerful enough, governed only by the height of object and the curvature of the earth.

Geostrophic see *Gradient wind*

Gimbals A system by which an object is suspended so that it remains horizontal.

Gnomonic projection A form of map or chart projection which produces straight lines of longitude radiating from the nearest pole and curved lines of latitude.

Go about To turn the boat *head-to-wind* so as to go about on the other *tack*.

Gooseneck The universal joint fitting on a mast, by which the *boom* is attached to a mast.

Goosewing To sail before the wind

341

with the mainsail set on one side and the *foresail* out on the opposite side.

Grabrail A pillar or handhold on a boat.

Gradient wind The wind (usually at 20,000 ft) which is unaffected by friction with the earth's surface.

Grid The parallel lines on a chart to which direction can be related.

Grommet A ring of rope or a metal ring fastened in a sail.

Ground tackle Generic term for anchoring equipment.

GRP Glass reinforced polyester. A material used for boat construction,it comprises fiber glass cloth impregnated with polyester resins.

Guardrail Safety rails which are fitted around open decks.

Gudgeon A fitting into which the *rudder pintle* is inserted. It enables the rudder to pivot.

Gunter rig A rig whereby a *gaff* slides up a mast to form an extension to the mast.

Gunwale The upper edge of the side of the hull.

H

Halyard A line used to hoist sails.

Hanks Rings or piston hooks by which sails are attached to *stays*.

Hard-a-lee Command to come about.

Harden up To sail a boat closer to the wind.

Hard eye A reinforced wire loop.

Header A wind shift further forward relative to the boat.

Heading The direction in which a boat is pointing.

Headsail A sail set forward of the main mast.

Head sea A sea which is travelling in the opposite direction to that of the boat.

Head-to-wind With the *bow* facing into the wind.

Heave-to To stop the boat by backing the *foresail* or *jib* and lashing the tiller; (2) to slow the boat by letting the sails flap on a beam *reach* (used for short periods only).

Heel A boat is said to heel when it lies over at an angle when sailing; (2) the bottom end of the mast.

Helm The steering apparatus

Helmsman One who steers.

Hiking strap Either of two fore-and-aft straps attached to the floorboards or centerboard trunk so a crew member can support himself by hooking his feet under one when he is hiking out in a race.

Holding ground That part of the seabed where the anchor digs in

Hove-to see *Heave-to*

Hull speed The maximum speed a hull can achieve without planing.

I

In irons A boat is said to be in irons when it has stopped or is moving backwards because it is pointing directly into the wind.

Isobars Lines drawn on a weather map to link areas of equal barometric pressure.

J

Jackstay Rigged line to which safety harness may be clipped.

Jackyard A yard or pole extending the head or foot of the topsail beyond the topmast or the *gaff* of a gaff-rigged boat.

Jam cleat A *cleat* designed to allow a line to be made fast quickly by jamming it.

Jetsam Anything thrown overboard.

Jib The foremost sail. It is a *fore-and-aft* sail and is triangular in shape.

Jibe The swinging over of a *fore-and-aft* sail when *running* before the wind. It may be a controlled maneuver when a boat is changing its course, or can happen accidentally.

Jibstay Forward stay (forestay or headstay) on which the jib is hoisted.

Jury rig A temporary replacement of any part of the boat's rigging, set up after damage or breakage, which enables the boat to be sailed.

K

Kedge A small auxiliary anchor; to kedge is to move a vessel by laying out the kedge and pulling on it.

Keel The fixed underwater part of a sailing boat used to prevent sideways drift and provide stability.

Ketch A two-masted, *fore-and-aft* rigged boat. The forward mast is the mainmast—the *mizzen* mast, stepped *aft*, is always forward of the *rudder post*.

King post A vertical post usually employed as a support.

Knot A nautical mile covered in one hour; (2) a means of tying a rope or line.

L

Lacing A length of line or thin rope.

Landfall Arrival at land.

Lanyard A short line or rope used to attach one thing to another.

Lapper A large *foresail* which extends aft behind the mast.

Lashing A rope used for securing any movable object in place.

Latitude The distance north or south of the Equator, measured in degrees north or south.

Lay up To store a yacht during the winter, or just take a boat out of commission.

Lazy guy A guy which is not in use, i.e. is taking no strain.

Lazyjacks Ropes extending from the *boom* to the mast which help in gathering in a sail when lowering it.

Lead A lead weight which is attached to the end of a line and used to ascertain the depth of water beneath a boat and the nature of the bottom; (2) the path taken by a rope, usually between a sail and a *fairlead* or *winch*.

Lee The area to leeward (down-wind); to be in the lee of an object is to be sheltered by it.

Leeboards Boards fixed vertically to the outside of the hull to prevent *leeway*; (2) boards fitted to the outboard of a bunk to prevent the occupant falling out.

Leech The aftermost edge of a *fore-and-aft* sail. Both side edges of a square sail.

Leeway The distance between the course steered by a vessel and that actually run.

Lie To remain without motion. More precisely, it means to keep a ship as steady as possible in a gale.

Lifeline Safety line fitted around an open deck.

Lightship A stationary vessel carrying a light as an aid to navigation.

Limber holes Gaps at the lower end of frames, above the *keel*, to allow water to drain to the lowest point of the *bilges*.

Line A rope chosen for a specific function.

Liquid-filled compass A compass filled with a mixture of 50% alcohol and 50% water in order that the movement of the card is dampened.

Lock The part of a canal or waterway included between two floodgates, by means of which a vessel is transferred from a higher to a lower level or vice versa.

Log The instrument used to measure the vessel's speed through the water; (2) to record in the ship's journal (or logbook) the principal events which have happened while on board, normally distances covered, course sailed, and weather conditions.

Longitude The distance east or west of the Greenwich meridian

342

measured 180° east or west. The 180° meridian is the International Date Line.

Loose To loose a rope is to let it go while to loose a sail is to unfurl or *set* it; (2) a loose-footed sail is one which is not laced to a *boom*.

Loran A system of long-range radio navigation.

Low water The lowest level reached by each tide.

Luff The forward edge of a sail; (2) to luff is to bring the vessel's head closer to the wind; (3) to luff up is to turn the vessel's head right into the wind.

Lug (or lugsail) A four-sided sail, *bent* onto a yard, and slung to the mast in a *fore-and-aft* position. There are three kinds: the standing or working lug, the dipping lug and the balanced lug.

Lugger A boat, usually a fishing boat, rigged with *lugsails*.

M

Magnetic north The point to which the north-seeking pole of a magnetic compass is drawn.

Magnetic variation The difference (angle) between true and magnetic north.

Main In all rigs of vessels the word main applies to the principal object of several similar ones. Hence mainmast, maindeck and so on.

Make fast To secure a line.

Marconi An alternative name for *Bermudan*.

Mark An object which is a guide while navigating.

Marline spike A pointed tapering iron or wooden spike used for opening the strands of rope when *splicing*.

Mast A pole or system of attached poles, placed vertically on a vessel, for spreading sails.

Mast gate The position where the mast passes through the foredeck of a boat.

Masthead The top of a mast.

Masthead sloop A *sloop* whose *forestay*, on which the *foresail* is set, reaches to the masthead.

Mast step A recess in a vessel's *keel* into which the base of the mast is positioned.

Measured mile A measured *nautical mile* is usually shown by sets of *ranges* set up on land adjacent to deep sheltered water.

Mercator projection A form of map or chart projection which produces straight lines of latitude and longitude which cross at right angles. (See also *Gnomonic*).

Meridian An imaginary circle which passes through the north and south poles and cuts the Equator at right angles and has as its center the center of the earth. Lines of *longitude* are all meridians.

Meter class A form of rating for a boat based on a certain measurement formula.

Midships (or Amidships) In the middle portion of a vessel; (2) the midship spoke is the upper spoke of the wheel when the rudder is lined up *fore-and-aft*.

Millibar A unit of barometric pressure.

Miss stays A sailing vessel is said to miss stays when, in *tacking*, it fails to *go about* and remains on the same *tack* as before.

Mizzen The aftermost mast of various rigs; (2) the *fore-and-aft* sail hoisted on the mizzen mast.

Moor To fasten a vessel to a *mooring*.

Mooring Any arrangement of anchors and rodes which are permanently laid.

N

Narrows Small passage or channels between lands.

Nautical almanac An annual book containing astronomical and tidal information for the use of sailors and navigators.

Nautical mile One 60th of a degree of latitude (a minute); slightly longer than a standard mile.

Navigation lights Lights with different-colored sectors required to be shown on vessels at night, to enable identification to be made.

Neap tides Those tides with a smaller range than *spring tides* which occur about two days after the first and last quarters of the moon.

No go zone Area into which a boat cannot sail without tacking.

Nominal range The range of a light, in 10 miles visibility. It is governed solely by the power of the light and does not take into account the height of the light or the observer, or the curvature of the earth.

O

Observed position A vessel's position which is plotted on a chart through the observation of landmarks and so on, as distinct from *dead reckoning*.

Offshore Away from the shore.

Offwind Any point of sailing away from the wind.

One-design Any boat built to conform to rules so that it is identical to all others in the same *class*.

Onshore Towards the shore.

Outhaul A rope which hauls out something, as the *mainsail* outhaul does the *clew* of the mainsail.

Outpoint To sail closer to the wind than another boat.

Overfall A wave that breaks sharply over a shoal or where currents meet.

P

Paddle A small oar; it is used to propel a boat, over the side or *stern* without *rowlocks*.

Painter A rope attached to the *bow* of a small boat, by which it may be *made fast*.

Palm A sailmaker's version of a thimble; it is strapped to the palm of the hand when pushing the needle through the cloth.

Peak The upper corner of a four-sided sail, usually applied to a *gaff* sail; (2) the upper end of a *gaff*.

Pennant A long triangular flag.

Pier A structure built out into the water to serve as a landing place.

Pilot A person licensed to navigate vessels through channels and in and out of port; (2) USCG.

Pinch To sail too close to the wind.

Pintle Metal pin on *stern* fitting on which the *rudder* hangs by its *gudgeons*.

Pitch The residue of boiled tar used for *caulking*; (2) the downward motion of the bow of a boat plunging into the trough of a wave.

Pitch-pole Said of a boat which somersaults *stern*-over-*bow*, usually up-ended by a wave.

Plane To gain hydrodynamic lift causing the boat to lift up on its bow wave.

Planking The covering of the ribs of a hull with planks.

Plot To mark courses, bearings and directions on a chart.

Point Division of a compass which has 32 points; (2) in geography a projection from a coastline.

Point high To sail very close to the wind.

Points of sailing The different angles from the wind on which a boat may sail.

Poop A raised deck on the *after-part* of a ship. When a wave comes over the stern of a vessel it is said to be pooped.

Port The left-hand side of a vessel when looking forwards. A boat is on a port tack when the wind is blowing over its port side.

Position line A position line is a line along which the boat's position must lie. It can be obtained by various means and may be straight or curved.

Preventer Additional stay line or *tackle* set up to prevent movement in a mast or boom. A boom preventer is a line or tackle or boom vang set up to prevent an accidental jibe.

Prop walk The sideways effect the propeller has on the *stern* of a boat, particularly at slow speeds.

Protest signal A signal which is hoisted during a sailing race when a boat believes it has been fouled by another competitor.

Prow The *bow* and *fore* part of a vessel.

Psychrometer An instrument used to find the relative humidity of air.

Pulpit An elevated guard rail set up at either the *bow* or the *stern* or both. The one at the stern is sometimes called a stern rail.

Punt Flat-bottomed boat, square at either end, and usually propelled by a pole. Only suitable for shallow inland waterways.

Purchase Any *tackle* or manner of leverage used to raise or move some object.

Pushpit see *Pulpit*

Q

Quarter That portion of the ship midway between the *beam* and the *stern*. On the quarter applies to a bearing 45° *abaft* the *beam*.

Quarter berth A bunk which runs under the side of the *cockpit*.

Quartering With the wind or waves on the quarter.

R

Race A strong confused tide or current.

Range The length of rope or chain required for any particular purpose. The range of rode is the length of chain drawn out on deck in preparation for letting go the anchor; (2) the difference in the depth of the water between high and low tides.

Rating A method of measuring certain dimensions of yachts of different sizes and forms so that they can race on a handicap basis.

Ratlines Small lines tied across the *shrouds* to form steps.

Reach To sail with the wind approximately *abeam*; (2) in a river a reach is the distance between two bends.

"Ready about" An order to stand by in preparation for coming about onto the other *tack*.

Reef To reduce the sail area by folding or rolling. Reef bands are horizontal strengthening bands of canvas running across a sail and perforated with holes or eyes, to hold reef points.

Reef cringles The eyes or loops on the *leech* of the sail through which the reef lines are passed.

These latter are for securing the *cringle* of a reefed sail to a boom.

Reef points These are short pieces of rope hung, one on each side of the sail, from the eyes in the reef band, for tying up the reefed portion of the sail.

Reeve To pass something through a hole. To reeve a *tackle* is to pass a rope through the *blocks*.

Restricted class A class of boats all of a particular set of fixed dimensions but with others which may vary.

Ribs The timbers which form the frame or skeleton of a boat, to which the planking is secured.

Ride To lie at anchor; (2) to ride out a gale is to wait for a gale to pass when at sea.

Riding light An all-round white light, usually hoisted on the forestay when at anchor.

Rig The form or manner in which a vessel's mast, *spars* and sails are arranged.

Rigging The system of all the wires and ropes employed to keep the mast in place and work the sails. See *running rigging* and *standing rigging*.

Rise The rise of a tide is the height difference between low water and the sea surface at any time.

Roach The curved *leech* of a sail.

Rode An anchor line.

Rowlock A space in the gunwale which supports an oar and acts as the fulcrum when rowing.

Rubbing strake Wood beading running around the outside of a boat just beneath the *gunwale* to protect it against damage when touching piers or other boats.

Rudder Movable underwater part of a vessel used for steering.

Rudder post The aftermost timber of a boat.

Run To sail with the wind aft, or very nearly so.

Running backstay A movable *backstay*. There is usually one on each side and when sailing only the windward one is set up tight.

Running rigging The generic term for *sheets* and *halyards*. The ropes which hoist and sheet sails.

S

Safety harness A harness with a line. Used to attach crew to a boat in bad weather.

Sampson post A strong vertical timber or iron post onto which lines or rodes can be secured.

Schooner A boat with two or more masts where the mainmast is the aftermost mast.

Scope Ratio of anchor rode let out to depth of water beneath the keel.

Scull To propel a dinghy forwards using one oar over the stern in a figure eight movement.

Scuppers Openings in the *bulwarks* of a ship to drain off deck water.

Sea anchor A *drogue*, or drag device, employed as a floating anchor to help a boat ride out a gale.

Sea breeze An onshore breeze caused by warm air rising off the land.

Seacock A valve fitted to an underwater inlet on a vessel.

Sea mile see *Nautical mile*

Self-steering Usually refers to a mechanical wind vane steering system which when set maintains a yacht on a constant course, relative to the wind.

Set To set sail is to haul up the sails preparatory to starting; (2) set flying refers to a sail set with no stay, gaff or yard; (3) the set of the tide is the direction of a tidal current.

Sextant A navigational instrument used for measuring the altitudes of the celestial bodies, and thereby determining the position of a vessel.

Shackle A U-shaped link with a bolt. Used to connect links and eyes.

Shackle key A 'key' (metal) for unscrewing shackle pins.

Shake To cast off or loosen as in to "shake out a *reef*" meaning to let it out.

Shank The main shaft or leg of an anchor. A shank painter is a line which holds the anchor to the vessel's deck.

Sheave The pulley wheel in a *block*, and sometimes in a *spar*.

Sheer The straight or curved line which the deck line of a vessel makes when viewed from the side.

Sheet The rope attached to the *clew* of a sail so that it may be trimmed. When the sheets are brought in and made fast they are said to be sheeted home.

Shell The metal casing of a *block* which holds the pin.

Shock cord A form of strong elasticated rope.

Shrouds Wires which support the mast on either side. Also referred to as the *standing rigging*.

Side lights Red and green navigation lights. Red is to *port* and green to *starboard*.

Single up To cast off all lines except one at each position.

Skeg Projecting part of the underwater surface of a boat on which is hung the rudder.

Slack tide A short period at the turn of the tide when there is no tidal flow either way.

Slip To let go, purposely, as to slip

the anchor. A slip line is a doubled line with both ends made fast on board. (2) A berth or location at a dock where a boat may be made fast.

Sloop A single masted boat with only one headsail. It can be *gaff* or *Marconi-rigged*.

Snatch block A *block* into which a line can be placed from the side without having to be threaded.

Soundings Assessment of depth of water.

Spar A generic term for masts, booms, gaffs or bowsprits.

Spill To spill wind is to allow a sail to shake thus spilling the wind out of it.

Spinnaker A lightweight, three-cornered sail *set flying* from a spinnaker pole and controlled with sheets from each *clew*.

Spit A small projection of land, or a sand bank projecting into the water at low tide.

Splicing A way of joining ropes by unlaying the strands and inter-weaving them — there are different methods for different purposes.

Spreaders see *Cross-trees*.

Spring A mooring line led from the *stern* of a boat forwards (the bow spring) or from the *bow* of a boat *aft* (the aft spring). It is used to prevent the boat ranging back-wards and forwards.

Spring tides These are tides which bring the highest high tides and the lowest low tides (opposite of *neap*). They occur at or near full and new moon.

Sprit A *spar* that extends from the mast near the *tack* of a four-cornered sail to the peak.

Square rig The method of setting sails so that they hang *athwart* the ship. Hung on yards, the sails are four-sided.

Stanchion An upright post used to support the *guardrails* and *lifelines*.

Standing rigging The *shrouds* and *stays* which support the mast.

Starboard The right-hand side of the vessel looking forward. A boat is on the starboard tack when the wind is blowing from the star-board side.

Stays The parts of the *standing rigging* which support the mast in a *fore-and-aft* direction.

Staysail A triangular *headsail* hanked to a *forestay*.

Steerage way Sufficient movement through the water to enable a boat to be steered.

Step A recess into which the heel of the mast is placed. It is either a wooden block or a metal frame.

Stern The *afterpart* of a vessel.

Stern rail Elevated guard rail set up at the stern of the boat.

Stock The upper part of a *rudder*

to which the *tiller* is attached.

Sweat To haul up tight.

T

Tack The forward lower corner of a *fore-and-aft* sail; (2) to turn the *bow* of a boat through the wind so that it then blows across the opposite side. A boat is said to be on *port* or *starboard* tack.

Tackle A purchase system using ropes and *blocks*. Used to gain a mechanical advantage.

Tang A metal fitting by which *stays* are attached to the mast.

Tell-tales Small lengths of wool sewn through a sail near the *luff* and *leech* to allow the air flow over the sail to be checked.

Tender A small boat used to ferry people and stores to a larger vessel.

Thimble A metal loop around which a rope is applied or seized to form a *hard eye*.

Thwart A seat running across a dinghy.

Tidal current The horizontal movement of water caused by variations in tide height.

Tide Vertical rise and fall of water caused by gravitational attraction, principally of the moon.

Tide-rode A boat is said to be tide-rode when it is facing into the tidal stream, for example when moored to a buoy or anchored.

Tideway Part of a channel where current is strongest.

Tiller An attachment to the *rudder*, of wood or metal, by which the *rudder* is controlled.

Topping lift A *tackle* or rope used for supporting the *boom*.

Track Prospective course to be followed by the boat.

Transit Two objects are said to be in transit when they are in line. Transits are often used as leading marks to help navigation into a harbor.

Transom The *afterpart* of the boat square to the *centerline*.

Trapeze A support used by the crew of a racing dinghy to enable him to place his weight outside the boat.

Traveller A slide which travels on a track and is used for altering *sheet* angles.

Trolling Fishing with light, baited lines.

True wind The speed and direction of the wind felt by a stationary object.

Trysail A triangular loose-footed sail fitted *aft* of the mast and used to replace the mainsail in heavy weather.

Turnbuckle A device used to maintain correct tension on standing rigging.

V

Vang A line used to prevent a *gaff* or *sprit* from sagging to *leeward*.

W

Wake course That actually travelled by the boat.

Warp To warp is to move a vessel by lines (warps).

Washboards Boards used to close of the *companionway*.

Weather The area to *windward* (upwind).

Weigh anchor To raise the anchor from the bottom.

Whipping Method of binding the ends of a rope to prevent fraying.

Whisker pole A pole used to boom out of the *jib* when *goosewinged*.

Winch Deck-mounted fitting which provides extra purchasing power for handling *sheets* and *halyards*.

Wind-rode Said of a boat when it faces into the wind at a mooring or anchorage.

Windward Towards the wind.

Y

Yard The spar from which a square sail is suspended.

Yawl Two masted fore-and-aft rigged vessel with the *mizzen* mast stepped just behind the rudder post.

Index

Acknowledgments

Photographic sources
(B = Bottom, C = Center, T = Top, I = Inset,
L = Left, R = Right)
All photographs by Steven Wooster except the
following:
Avon Inflatables Ltd 317
W. E. Banks 10,IC
R. R. Baxter 280B, 281T
Beken 12/13 (Main and IR), 19, 22/23
Alastair Black 2/3, 6/7, 10/11 (except IC), 12/13, IL,
    14/15, 17, 20/21, 24/25, 28/29, 30/31, 32, 69,
    100, 106, 108, 116T, 118T, 119, 124T, 127, 128,
    131, 132, 133, 138, 139 (except TL), 143, 144,
    145, 146, 151BR, 210R, 211, 219T, 221, 223, 227
J. Blackman 76
Bob Bond 139TL
Magda Bond 97, 291, 292BR
Andrew de Lory 33
Jonathan Eastland 151BL
Dick Everitt 292L, 293, 295
Ambrose Greenway (Popper) 308, 312
Sarah King 263
Chris Meehan 40, 61, 168BL
National Sailing Centre 85, 149
Kevin O'Keefe 281B
R. Palmer 280T
RAF Culdrose 316
Sue Rawkins 80, 306
RNLI 313
Stephen Sleight 151T, 136, 137, 142, 167TL,
    172T, 234
George Taylor 224
University of Dundee 270
John Watney 26/27, 220, 307
Alan Watts 264, 265, 268, 269
P. J. Weaver 280C, 281C
Rodger Witt 310
Yachting World 5TL, 99, 117TR

Special thanks to the National Ocean Survey
for permission to reproduce details of their
original charts.

Dorling Kindersley
would like to thank the
following for their help:
Magda Bond for the text
    on maintenance and
    safety, as well as
    general research
Steve Sleight for the
    text on navigation
Alan Watts for the text
    on meteorology
Chris Meehan and
    Patrick Nugent for
    initial work on the
    design of the book.
The Director and staff of
    the National Sailing
    Centre, Cowes, for the
    use of their boats and
    for their general help
    and advice.

Robert Ashby
Bruce Banks Sails Ltd
Nigel Brown
Denny Desoutter, Editor,
    Practical Boat Owner
M. G. Duff and Partners
Peter Dunford
Dr. Helen Dziemidko
Dick Everitt
Ken Hone
Island Cruising Club
Debbie Lee
Rodney March
Dick Middleton
Model Shipwrights of
    London
Niall Morrow
National Sailing Centre,
    Cowes
Mark Neal
Oxford and District
    Schools Sailing
    Association
Dr Jim Phillips
Heather Pinniger
Stuart Quarrie
Jeremy Rogers Ltd
RAF Culdrose
Royal National Lifeboat
    Institution
Gina Smart
Capt. O. M. Watts Ltd
Marilyn Wise
Nigel Vick
Volvo

Main illustrations by:
David Ashby
Dave Etchell
Andy Farmer
John Ridyard
Les Smith
Venner Artists

Other illustrations by:
Roger Full
Nick Hall
Shian Hartshorn
Hayward and Martin
Gary Marsh
Nigel Osborne
Ros Pickless
Mark Richards

Typesetting: Vantage
    (Southampton) Ltd

Headline setting: Tom
    Blake

Reproduction: Photo-
    print Plates Ltd

Artwork services:
    Frederick Ford and
    Mike Pilley of Radius
    Negs Photographic
    Services Ltd
    N. J. Paulo (Colour Lab)